THE OUTER COAST

ALSO BY RICHARD BATMAN

American Ecclesiastes, an epic journey through the early American West

The Outer Coast

RICHARD BATMAN

CASTLE BOOKS

This edition published in 2001 by

CASTLE BOOKS
114 Northfield Avenue
Edison, New Jersey 08837

Library of Congress Cataloging in Publication Data

Batman, Richard

The outer coast.

Bibliography: p.

Includes index.

1. California—History—To 1846. 2. California—Description and travel—To 1848. 3. Explorer—California—History. 4. Pioneers—California—History.

I. Title

F864.B26 1985 979.4 85-7613

ISBN: 0-7858-1346-2

Design by Amy Hill
Maps by Anita Karl and Jim Kemp
Printed in the United States of America

To My Father
Victor H. Batman
1908–1984

Contents

Maps and Illustrations

MAPS

ILLUSTRATIONS (inserts)

Foreword

Midway through the nineteenth century Spanish-speaking California was suddenly and dramatically invaded by the rest of the world. Yet long before California became part of the United States, long before gold was discovered, foreigners were already a familiar sight. The first foreigner, a Frenchman, arrived well before the end of the eighteenth century, as did the first Englishman and the first American. By the early years of the nineteenth century several more English and American ship captains had also entered the various ports of California. It was part of the Spanish Empire then, and it was illegal for foreigners to visit, but they came anyway.

Those who came to California in these early years were unusual men. They were sailors—ship captains, officers, and common deck hands—who were first lured into the Pacific after members of Captain Cook's third voyage brought back tales of the great market for fur in China. And they were completely undismayed by the then all but unknown nature of California—what I have chosen to call the Outer Coast after an early Spanish term, La Costa Exterior. In the late eighteenth and early nineteenth centuries they came for sea-otter furs, later many switched to cattle hides, but whatever they were looking for they thought little of voyages that stretched into two, three, or even four years. Some of them, as often happens with sailors, eventually decided there was nothing at home to compare with the delights of California and so they stayed. Even before Spain lost control of California several deserting sailors had already been quietly, and illegally, absorbed into California society. Then when Mexico—and California—broke away from Spain and allowed foreigners to enter, many traders and ship captains who had long been working as smugglers along the coast came ashore and took up residence as respectable merchants.

About the same time other foreigners were approaching Mexican California from a different direction. They were fur trappers who in their search for beaver had pushed into and finally across the Great American Desert. And they found that the rumor that it was an empty, dry, dangerous land inhabited only by hostile Indians was true. They also found that it was crossable, and that on the other side, in California, there was an almost untouched supply of beaver. So they too came in increasing numbers, and many of them also discovered that the easy life of California was preferable to fighting Indians or plunging into freezing mountain streams to set beaver traps. Many dropped out of the fur brigades as they passed through California, and when the business itself came to an end because the beaver were all gone, the number of trappers coming to California seeking a new livelihood reached floodlike proportions.

As these foreigners settled down to stay, they had a major impact on Spanish-speaking California. The Californians had developed a culture that in the beginning, at least, differed little from that of most other frontier areas of Latin America. But the arrival of large numbers of foreigners soon changed all that. Eventually, under Mexico these foreigners became naturalized citizens, obtained land, established businesses, married into prominent California families. They also dabbled in politics, occasionally becoming involved in revolutions, sometimes on one side, sometimes on the other, and sometimes, seemingly, on both sides at once. Clearly, these foreigners, mostly Englishmen and Americans, seriously undermined the old way of life, and long before California became part of the United States they had already changed it into something different from other parts of Spanish-speaking America.

The story of these foreigners and their impact on California has concerned me in the *Outer Coast.* In telling it, however, I have not felt it necessary to recount everyone's story, nor to mention by name every foreigner who ever visited California. Many have been passed by in silence although they had compelling stories, some of which are themselves worthy of an entire book. But either the story was little more than a minor variation on a way of life already seen through someone else's eyes, or it was only peripheral to the subject at hand, and therefore I chose not to tell it. Instead, I have concentrated on those people who I felt were typical of various aspects of life on the Outer Coast and those who were atypical to the extent that they were dissatisfied with that life and tried to change it. Often, of course, those who began as typical became atypical; those who were atypical later settled into a typical routine life. It is the way of history.

I have also attempted to convey a sense of how it felt to be directly involved in these events, how it felt to live on the Outer Coast which, at that time, was on the very edge of the world. Consequently, whenever possible, I have concentrated on men for whom there was some kind of firsthand account that allowed me to see events from their point of view. I have not, however, automatically accepted a story without checking it against other firsthand accounts, against the vast amount of secondary material available, and also against what I hope is a commonsense assessment of what the world was like at the time. Still, I am aware that one man's point of view, however much others may differ, is his own personal truth—the truth that causes him to act as he does—and I have weighed it accordingly.

Those who would like to form their own independent judgments, or those who would like to pursue the subject further, are invited to turn to the end of the book where I have provided brief, informal notes and a bibliography. I hope they will be led to the vast amount of written material available about various aspects of the Outer Coast. A book of this kind could not have been written without the contributions of these historians, past and present, who have minutely studied the large number of subjects involved and through their writings pointed the way for me.

I would also like to thank several people who have made important contributions to this book. Carole Hicke read the entire manuscript and made penetrating comments. My agent Fred Hill, my editor Don Knox, and his assistant Naomi Grady were there with professional help and advice whenever I needed it. My wife, Ann, as always, provided constant support, reading the manuscript, listening as I read it aloud, and accompanying me on long, strenuous trips to most parts of the Outer Coast as well as to such related areas as the beaches of Kauai, the Islands of Tahiti, and Bora Bora. It's tough to be a historian's wife.

San Rafael, California

R.B.

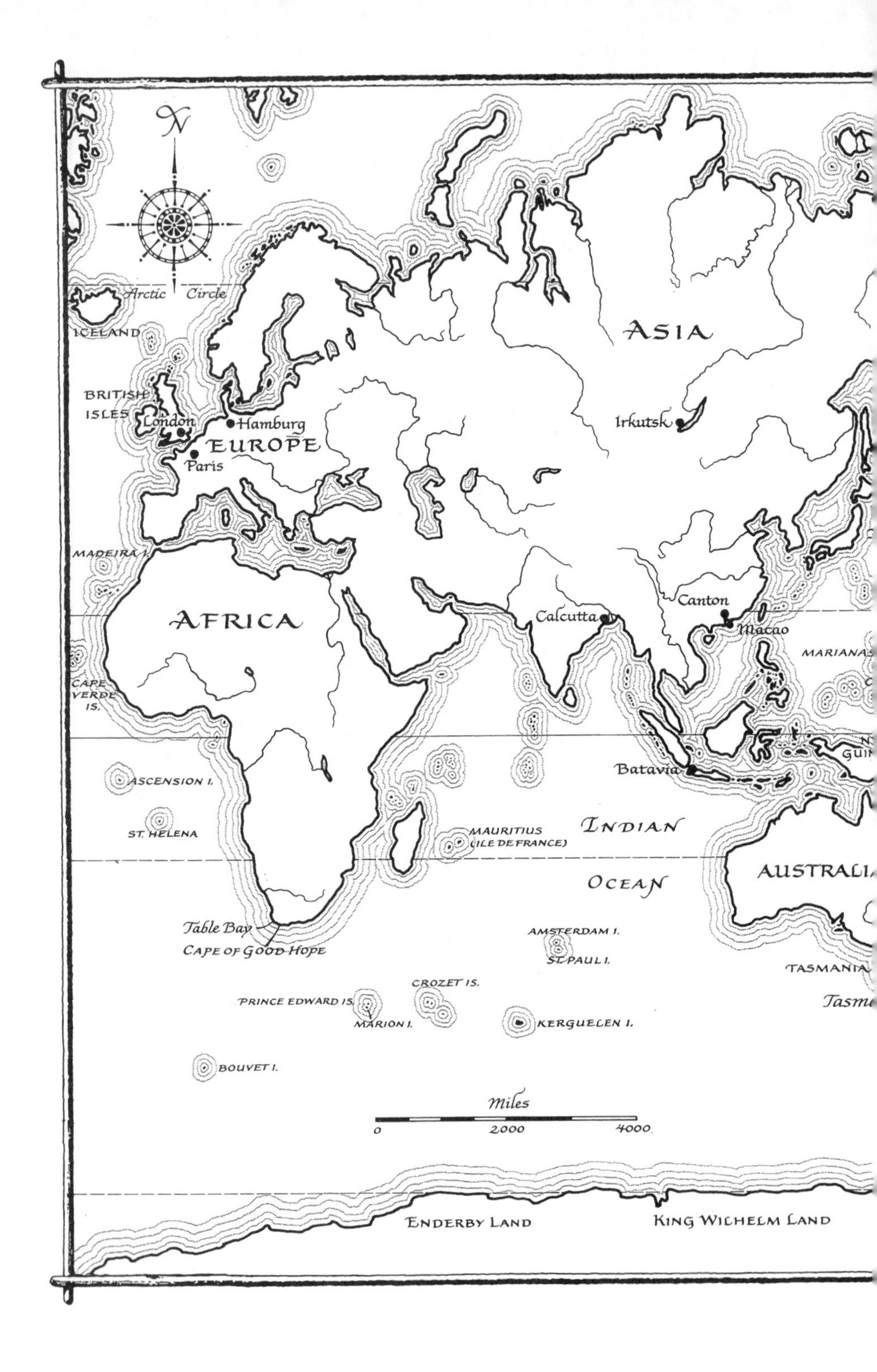
N
Arctic Circle
ICELAND
BRITISH ISLES
London
Hamburg
EUROPE
Paris
ASIA
Irkutsk
MADEIRA I.
AFRICA
Calcutta
Canton
Macao
MARIANAS
CAPE VERDE IS.
Batavia
ASCENSION I.
ST. HELENA
MAURITIUS (ILE DE FRANCE)
INDIAN
OCEAN
Table Bay
CAPE OF GOOD HOPE
AMSTERDAM I.
ST. PAUL I.
TASMANIA
CROZET IS.
PRINCE EDWARD IS.
MARION I.
KERGUELEN I.
BOUVET I.
Miles
0
2000
4000
ENDERBY LAND
KING WILHELM LAND

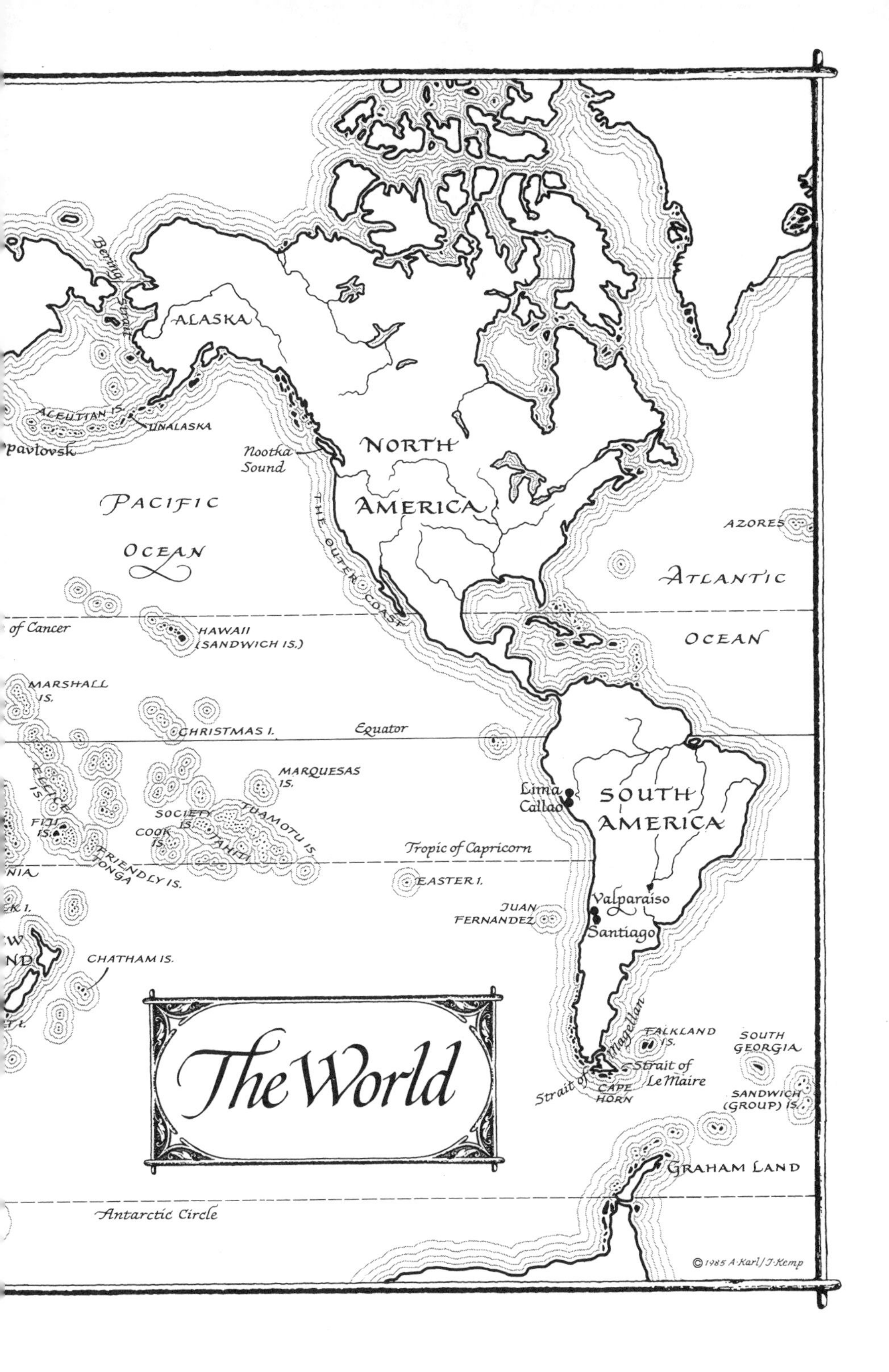
The World
ALASKA
Bering Strait
ALEUTIAN IS.
UNALASKA
Pavlovsk
Nootka Sound
NORTH AMERICA
PACIFIC OCEAN
THE OUTER COAST
ATLANTIC OCEAN
AZORES
of Cancer
HAWAII (SANDWICH IS.)
MARSHALL IS.
CHRISTMAS I.
Equator
MARQUESAS IS.
ELLICE IS.
FIJI IS.
SOCIETY IS.
TUAMOTU IS.
TAHITI
COOK IS.
FRIENDLY IS.
TONGA
Tropic of Capricorn
EASTER I.
JUAN FERNANDEZ
Lima
Callao
SOUTH AMERICA
Valparaíso
Santiago
CHATHAM IS.
FALKLAND IS.
SOUTH GEORGIA
Strait of Magellan
Strait of Le Maire
CAPE HORN
SANDWICH (GROUP) IS.
GRAHAM LAND
Antarctic Circle
© 1985 A. Karl / J. Kemp

MAY 14, 1769

SAN DIEGO

In 1769 spring arrived in California much as it always had. Officially winter ended and spring began in late March, but in much of California the changing of the calendar made little visible difference. The high mountain country still lay covered with snow, for spring would not reach there until May and in many spots not until June or July. In the interior valleys and deserts the weather was still relatively cool, and another two months or more would pass before the coming of the great heat marking the true change in season. Only along the coast was the change noticeable as the winter storms blowing in from the Pacific began to diminish in intensity and frequency. Even there rain could fall well into the spring, and just such a late season storm struck the California coast in mid-May of 1769.

Because of that storm a group of Spaniards, camped some fifteen miles below San Diego, awakened wet and miserable on the morning of May 14. It had rained most of the night until shortly before daylight when the downpour stopped momentarily. Then, at dawn, the sky darkened and a hard rain began falling again. After an hour and a half, the sky started to clear. Although it was Sunday, the first Sunday of Pentecost, the military commander of the group, Captain Fernando de Rivera y Moncada, and the missionary, Father Juan Crespi, agreed to forgo saying Mass. Not only was everyone thoroughly wet, but the expedition was in a hurry to move on.

The day before, after almost two months of traveling through the desert, the Spaniards had reached a height of land where, off to the north, they saw the ocean extending far inland. And in that bay they could see, just barely because of the distance, the masts of two ships, the *San Carlos* and the *San Antonio.* They knew they were within sight of their destination, San Diego Bay, and they decided to attempt to reach it even if it meant an unusually long day.

Late in the afternoon the expedition arrived on the shores of San Diego Bay. As soon as they came within sight of the ships, the soldiers in the group began firing their guns in greeting, and those on board the ships answered them with musket and cannon fire. The ensuing celebration soon turned into an exchange of tales between those who had come by ship and those who had arrived overland.

The story of Juan Perez, captain of the *San Antonio,* was simple. He had left Baja California on February 15 and after 54 days had reached San Diego Bay. His main problem on the trip north was not the sea but scurvy, and by the time he arrived in San Diego half his crew was ill, two were already dead, and only a few were capable of any work. Yet his experience could have been worse, Perez realized, after he heard about the fate of the other ship, the *San Carlos.*

That ship had left Baja California five weeks before the *San Antonio,* and thus Perez had been surprised to reach San Diego and find the *San Carlos* not yet there. Three weeks later it entered the harbor and dropped anchor. Since no crew members made any move to come ashore, those from the *San Antonio* boarded it and found so many of the *San Carlos* crew members down with scurvy that there were not enough men to lower its launch. Even most of the soldiers it was carrying—volunteers from the Spanish province of Catalonia, commanded by Lieutenent Pedro Fages—were ill and unable to help.

The voyage of the *San Carlos* had been difficult from the beginning. As it rounded the tip of Baja California it encountered opposing winds from the north, and when it broke away from them a storm drove it several hundred miles off course. Errors in latitude reported by earlier expeditions caused the *San Carlos* to wander as far north as the Santa Barbara Channel before turning back and finding San Diego Bay after 110 days at sea. By then almost everyone on board was ill with scurvy.

Eventually the crews from both ships were moved ashore where the ill greatly outnumbered the well. Even after the land expedition arrived late on the afternoon of May 14, its members could do little more than nurse the sick.

VELICATA, BAJA CALIFORNIA

The same day the land expedition was reaching San Diego Bay a second and larger expedition was moving north through the interior of Baja California. Three days earlier it had left the last outpost of civilization, the former Jesuit mission of Santa Maria de Los Angeles. This expedition was also bound for San Diego, but its first stop was to be Velicata, a desert valley forty miles north of Santa Maria, where the missionary, Father Junipero Serra, planned to found the first Franciscan mission in California. By Saturday, May 13, however, it was clear that the expedition's slow-moving mule train would not make it to Velicata until late Sunday evening. Serra, approaching Captain Gaspar de Portola, the expedition commander, asked permission to take a light escort and push ahead of the main column. Thus, on the morning of Sunday, May 14, Serra was at Velicata ready to found his first mission.

Religious ceremonies at this new mission, christened San Fernando de Velicata, took place in a small, crude hut. Several months before, members of the first, smaller land expedition had used the valley to hold their cattle until they were ready to leave for the north. They had built some huts at Velicata, and on the morning of May 14 Serra ordered a group of soldiers and servants to clean one of them so it could be used as a chapel.

A large cross was erected, bells were rung, and Serra, vested in surplice and stole, blessed the holy water and sprinkled it on the chapel, the yard, and the cross. Surrounded by soldiers who had donned their best uniforms, complete with leather jackets and shields, Serra said Mass and preached on the subjects of the coming of the Holy Spirit and the founding of the mission. After Mass he sang "Veni Creator," but in the absence of an organ, the soldiers accompanied him by firing their weapons. And not only did the sound of musket fire take the place of musical accompaniment, but the heavy smell of gunpowder also substituted for burning incense, which was lacking. "The congregation," Serra said, "was made up of ourselves, the soldiers and the Indian neophytes who came with us, while no gentile dared come near, frightened perhaps by so much shooting."

TAHITI

That same Sunday, four thousand miles west of Velicata at Point Venus on the island of Tahiti, another group of Europeans were also attending church services far from home. The previous summer this band of Englishmen had sailed from Plymouth Harbor on HMS *Endeavor,* Lieutenant James Cook commanding. On April 11, 1769, they sighted the island of Tahiti, and two days later dropped anchor in Matavai Bay.

Unlike the Spaniards at Velicata, the Englishmen at Point Venus had few natives among the congregation. At first it appeared there would be none, for by the time church services were held, most of them had gone home to eat. But the scientist, Joseph Banks, crossed the river and brought back two friendly natives, Tubourai and Tamio. Leading them into the tent which was to serve as a church, he seated them and placed himself between them. During the services they imitated Banks—standing, sitting, and kneeling at the proper time. They also appeared to understand that this was serious business, for during the services they yelled at the natives outside to be quiet. But when the services were over they asked no questions and showed no interest in the explanation that Banks tried to give. Banks was somewhat confused and ended his journal entry for May 14 with the comment, "We have not yet seen the least traces of religion among these people, maybe they are entirely without it."

That same night the Englishmen witnessed a Tahitian custom that Cook described, in his casual understated way, as "an odd scene. A young fellow above 6 feet high lay with a little Girl about 10 or 12 years of age publickly before several of our people and a number of the Natives." Among the natives were several women including Queen Obarea, "a fat, bouncing, good-looking dame," who considered it their duty to instruct the girl on how to perform her role. Apparently some instruction was necessary, for Cook thought the girl "young as she was, did not seem to want it."

Cook viewed the scene rather broad-mindedly and guessed that it was done "more from Custom than from Lewdness." Other witnesses were not so charitable and accused Obarea of forcing the couple into the situation. They pointed out that both the girl and the man were so terrified they could not perform successfully. Later, Queen Obarea was severely criticized by many of her own people for instigating the performance.

THE BLUE RIDGE MOUNTAINS

Two thousand miles east of the California coast, and on the other side of the world from the island of Tahiti, another band of explorers was also moving through the wilderness. This expedition was not sponsored by a government that demanded carefully kept records, and there were no educated sea captains, scientists, or missionaries to keep journals. The group was made up of six North Carolina hunters—Joseph Holden, William Cooley, James Mooney, John Findley, John Stewart, and Daniel Boone.

Daniel Boone, of course, became famous enough to be encouraged to tell his own story. And of this expedition he later said, in words provided by his ghost writer, John Filson, "It was on the first of May, in the year 1769, that I resigned my domestic happiness for a time, and left my family and peaceable habitation on the Yadkin River, in North Carolina, to wander through the Wilderness of America, in quest of the country of Kentucke."

From Boone's house on the Yadkin River in the westernmost part of North Carolina, the six hunters scaled the Blue Ridge Mountains at a place called the Stairs, then went over Iron Mountain and into Holston Valley. They continued west across the valley, passed through Clinch Mountain by way of Moccasin Gap, crossed Clinch River, Powell's Mountain, Wallen's Ridge, and finally entered Powell's Valley. By now they were well on their way to Cumberland Gap, the main entrance to Kentucky, although given the time and distances involved, they surely had not penetrated that far into the wilderness by May 14.

Wherever they were on the fourteenth, their routine was undoubtedly much the same as on any other day. Findley, Stewart, and Boone were hunters and had brought Cooley, Mooney, and Holden, all of them Yadkin Valley farmers, to take care of routine camp duties. These three were responsible for making camp each night, unloading the pack horses and reloading them the next morning with camp kettles, extra rifles, traps, blankets, and supplies. By the fourteenth they had been on the trail two weeks, and the days had probably begun to blur together. Unlike the Spaniards in California or the Englishmen on Tahiti, they had no church services that day. After two weeks in the wilderness they may even have forgotten it was Sunday.

On May 14 Junipero Serra, James Cook, and Daniel Boone were all beginning their historic lives. None of them was a particularly young man. Serra, the eldest, was already fifty-five, Cook was forty, and even Boone, the youngest at the age of thirty-four, was on the brink of middle age. None had lived an entirely futile life. Serra had already made important contributions to the Franciscan missions of Mexico. Cook had been responsible for drawing detailed naval charts of the waters around Newfoundland. Even Boone had a local reputation as a wilderness hunter and could point to the time during the French and Indian War when he had been part of Braddock's expedition, although only as a wagon driver. Had any of their lives ended before the spring of 1769, they would have warranted, at most, a brief footnote in history. Until recently, too, each man's life had been marked by a routine that made any move in a radically new direction seem entirely unlikely.

By the late 1760s Junipero Serra was living a quiet, settled life at the Franciscan's College of San Fernando in Mexico City. After arriving from his native Majorca in 1750 he had spent several years as a missionary among the Indians in the Sierra Gordo region north of Mexico City. But in 1758 he was recalled, and during the next decade served as choir director, master of novices, college counselor, and home missionary at San Fernando.

The life of James Cook had also reached a point of predictable routine. He first went to sea aboard coal ships sailing out of the North Sea port of Whitby, then joined the Royal Navy and worked his way up from common sailor to sailing master aboard a ship that was part of the fleet sent to capture Quebec during the Seven Years' War. It was while serving in Canada that Cook first learned surveying. He soon became so adept that when the war ended and Canada became part of Great Britain, he was assigned the task of surveying the waters around Newfoundland. By the late 1760s his life was a set routine each summer in Canada surveying, each winter back in England drawing charts at the Naval Base at Deptford.

In the back country along the Yadkin River of North Carolina, Daniel Boone's life had also taken on a certain pattern, although not one that brought him much success or contentment. Since returning from his wartime service as a wagon driver with Braddock's ill-fated expedition against the French, Boone had married and tried to settle down, doing some subsistence farming and earning a little extra as a blacksmith. But, as always, he preferred life in the woods and spent more and more of his time hunting and trapping. Occasionally he did well, more often he did not, and throughout the 1760s he was continually plagued by debts. He was also getting older and at least once convinced himself that a group of younger hunters had refused to take him along because, at the age of thirty-four, he was too old.

Each man, seemingly, had reached a point in his life where, for better or, in Boone's case, for worse, nothing startlingly new was likely to happen. Then widely separated historical forces lifted each from obscurity and placed him at the center of events that changed not only his own life but the world in which he lived.

The first to experience such a change was Junipero Serra. One of his duties at the College of San Fernando was to make mission tours in the country surrounding Mexico City. In the summer of 1767 as he visited the village of Ixmiquilpan, he received a message ordering him to return to the college immediately, no reason given. Back in Mexico City he found out why he had been recalled.

Spanish reformers had long been suspicious of Jesuit power and in February 1767, Carlos III, King of Spain, had signed a decree expelling all members of the Society of Jesus from Spain and its colonies. This secret order was opened in Mexico City on June 24 by the Viceroy, the Marquis de Croix, who learned he had been made responsible for expelling the Jesuits from Mexico. The missions of Baja California would thus be without missionaries, and the viceroy recommended they be assigned to the Franciscans of the College of San Fernando. Father Jose Garcia, guardian of the college, selected a group of Franciscans for the task, and appointed Junipero Serra to lead them as president of the missions.

It was well that Serra led a simple life, for he had almost no time to prepare for the move to another part of the world. He returned to the college and heard of his new assignment on July 12. Two days later he was on the road again, this time bound for Baja California with his band of Franciscans. After a month of hard travel they reached the city of Tepic, filled with soldiers and missionaries bound for the

Jesuit's abandoned missions, scattered over much of western New Spain. Serra and his group took up temporary residence in the city's Convento de Santa Cruz de Zacate, where they were soon joined by several other Franciscans who had come directly from missions in the Sierra Gorda region.

The Franciscans' rapid move from Mexico City to Tepic was supposed to continue without delay to San Blas, the port from which they were to sail for California. But suddenly and for no apparent reason the plan was changed and those from San Fernando found they were to go instead to Pima Country in the far northwestern part of the mainland. They were incensed because they had volunteered not as general missionaries but specifically for duty in Baja California. Serra sent an emissary back to Mexico City to voice these objections, and as a result the viceroy reversed his decision and agreed to allow the fathers from San Fernando to go to Baja California. The delay meant that Serra and his missionaries did not sail from San Blas until the following spring.

On April 1, 1768, the ship *Concepcion* entered the roadstead at Loreto, and Serra and his fellow Franciscans landed the next day, ready to assume their new responsibilities. Within a week Serra, as president, had taken up residence at Loreto, the former Jesuit headquarters, and assigned the rest of the Franciscans to the fifteen missions spread from San Jose del Cabo at the tip of the peninsula to Santa Maria on the far northern frontier.

If Serra thought he would now have time to organize and consolidate the new mission field he was mistaken, for the rapid changes in his life were not over. He was no sooner established in his new headquarters at Loreto than he was visited by Jose de Galvez, whom Carlos III had recently appointed Visitor General of New Spain and sent to the new world, in the hope of bringing about badly needed reforms.

A Visitor General in the Spanish Empire was a powerful figure, for in carrying out his investigations and bringing about the necessary changes, his orders were equal to and sometimes superior to those of the viceroy. In this specific case the King, faced with heavy expenses of the Seven Years' War, which had just ended, gave Galvez the task of finding new sources of revenue in New Spain. In pursuit of this goal, Galvez proposed that the far northwestern frontier—Sinaloa, Sonora, Chihuahua, and the Californias—be reorganized into a new governmental agency called a commandancy-general. As part of this plan, Spain would send settlers to California, hoping that crops from its fertile land would help offset the barrenness of the Baja California missions, which had been a constant drain on the Spanish economy. Also, if the rumors of foreigners in the Pacific turned out to be true, these new settlements would provide the necessary buffer to protect Spanish interests.

Galvez had come to Loreto in 1768 to make plans for this move north. When they were completed, the plans called for both land and sea expeditions. Two ships, the *San Carlos* and the *San Antonio,* would sail to California at the same time that two land parties would proceed north. Captain Rivera, the long-time commander of the garrison at Loreto, would lead the first and smaller band. Its priest would be Juan Crespi, who was now relieved of his assignment of Purisima Concepcion. Don Gaspar de Portola, the recently appointed governor of both Californias, would command the second, larger contingent. Junipero Serra, who was to become president of the newly founded missions in the north, would accompany Portola, leaving Francisco Palou behind as president of the Baja California missions.

James Cook's routine of spending each summer in Canada surveying and each winter in England drawing charts ended suddenly in the spring of 1768. He was in the midst of preparing for his annual trip to Newfoundland when he was relieved of his command of the surveying ship, *Grenville,* and placed in command of the *Endeavor,* bound for the Pacific Ocean.

The *Endeavor* was being sent to the Pacific because of the demands of eighteenth-century science. In 1639 Jeremiah Horrocks had first observed the transit of Venus across the face of the sun, and since then astronomers had come to realize this observation was an important element in determining the distance between the earth and the sun. Unfortunately the transit occurred only rarely, and after Horrocks' discovery it did not happen again until 1761. By then, many scientists around the world were prepared to observe it, but cloudy skies, the complications of a world at war, and various other problems had hampered them. Another transit was to occur in 1769, but if successful observations were not made then, there would not be another chance until 1879. Consequently the Royal Society was making careful plans to observe the 1769 transit from various parts of the world, including some point in the South Pacific Ocean.

His Majesty George III had also agreed to support the expedition by giving the Royal Society £4,000 and furnishing a ship and crew. In March 1768 the Admiralty Board purchased the *Earl of Pembroke,* an east-coast coal cat built in the shipyard at Whitby. A few weeks later James Cook was relieved of command of the *Grenville* and placed in command of the coal cat, now renamed the *Endeavor.* The events leading up to Cook's appointment are not well-documented, and the reasons for appointing a lowly master to such an important position are none too clear. Still, he had considerable experience in surveying. A few years earlier he had attracted the attention of the Royal Society with a report on an eclipse, and he had spent his first years at sea as a sailor, then an officer, on Whitby coal cats.

Events moved rapidly during the spring and summer following Cook's appointment. The ship was taken to the docks at Deptford to be converted from a coal cat to an exploratory vessel. A crew was found, as were scientists including Sir Joseph Banks, Fellow of the Royal Society. A specific destination was chosen, for in May, Captain Samuel Wallis returned to England after circumnavigating the globe in the ship *Dolphin* and reported the discovery of King George's Island, soon to be known as Tahiti. It was decided to use that island as the point from which to observe the transit of Venus. On July 30, 1868 Cook was handed his orders. He was to sail to Tahiti and establish an observatory in time for the transit of Venus on June 3 of the following year. That accomplished, he could open the rest of his orders, which were to remain sealed until then.

Cook sailed from Plymouth, England, and through the summer, fall, and early winter worked his way south down the Atlantic. In late September the ship was at Teneriffe, a month later it crossed the equator, and by mid-November reached Rio de Janerio where it anchored for the next three and a half weeks. In early December it sailed from Rio and seven weeks later, in January 1769, the *Endeavor* rounded Cape Horn and Captain James Cook entered the Pacific for the first time.

Some time in the fall of 1768, as Cook sailed the *Endeavor* through the South Atlantic, fate also knocked on the door of Daniel Boone's cabin in the Yadkin River settlements of North Carolina. It came in the person of John Findley who, years before, when they were both wagon drivers for Braddock, had impressed Boone with his stories of Kentucky. Now Findley was down on his luck, working as an itinerant trader, leading three old horses loaded with packs containing needles, thread, ribbons, cloth, and various odds and ends that might appeal to a frontier housewife.

The two men had apparently not seen each other since both had fled from the Pennsylvania battlefield where General Edward Braddock's army had almost been destroyed thirteen years before. During those years Boone had built a reputation as a wilderness traveler, and he was exactly what Findley needed. Although he told Boone he just happened to be in the neighborhood, Findley probably had come all the way to North Carolina to find him, for he badly wanted to see Kentucky again and Boone was the ideal man to go with him.

Findley's arrival was the turning point in Boone's life. Although his small farm provided him with a living of sorts, Boone had never been satisfied with that. He was restless, he was in debt, he was looking for something better, and as a first step toward finding it, he asked Findley to spend the winter. In the months that followed, Findley occupied his days as a trader moving from cabin to cabin selling his wares and his nights telling stories of Kentucky to Daniel Boone, Boone's brother Squire Boone, and their brother-in-law, John Stewart. And during that winter, the talk slowly evolved from entrancing tales of what Findley had once seen into concrete plans for what they would do when spring arrived.

A major problem, however, was lack of money. Not only did they need financing for the trip, but Boone himself was so far in debt he had been summoned to appear in court during the March session. They turned to Richard Henderson, a North Carolina lawyer and speculator who had recently formed a land company. Boone promised to explore Kentucky and find land for Henderson's company to claim. In exchange, Henderson would finance an expedition and also use his skills as a lawyer to get a continuation of the suits against Boone. They reached an agreement, Henderson providing the money and also successfully obtaining a continuance, and thus on May 1, 1769, Boone,

Findley, Stewart, and three men they had hired as camp tenders were on their way into the wilderness bound for Kentucky.

By Sunday, May 14, 1769, Junipero Serra in Baja California, James Cook on the Island of Tahiti, and Daniel Boone in the Blue Ridge Mountains had begun a series of events that would change their own lives and point their worlds in entirely new directions. By the time these events had developed, clashed, mingled, and eventually worked themselves out, that part of the west coast of America known as California would be changed forever.

THE SPANISH MAIN

N
Bering Strait
Cook Inlet
SANAK I.
KODIAK
Prince William Sound
New Archangel (Sitka)
QUEEN CHARLOTTE IS.
THE OUTER COAST
Nootka Sound
VANCOUVER I.
Columbia R.
Ft. Vancouver
Missouri R.
Umpqua R.
South Pass
Platte R.
Green R.
San Francisco
Monterey
Colorado R.
Arkansas R.
Santa Barbara
Canadian R.
Santa Fe
San Diego
Gila R.
San Quintin Bay
Velicata
Rio Grande
Loreto
PACIFIC OCEAN
San Blas
Mexico City
NEWFOUNDLAND
St. Lawrence R.
Salem
Boston
New York
Philadelphia
St. Louis
Yadkin River Settlement
BLUE RIDGE MTS.
ATLANTIC OCEAN
North America
Miles
0
400
800
© 1965 A. Karl/J. Kem

I

It was spring 1770 and a full year had passed since that day in May when Junipero Serra founded the mission of Velicata in the Baja California desert. The year had not been a particularly good one for Serra who, by now, was almost sixty years old. Instead of continuing his former quiet life at the Franciscan College in Mexico City, he had been appointed president of the California missions and had spent the year, plagued by one problem after another, on the very edge of the civilized world.

The first trouble came soon after leaving Velicata. Although the expedition moved smoothly along the road to California, Serra himself found traveling difficult because of severe leg pains. He had had frequent trouble with his leg since arriving in America, particularly in times of stress. When he was assigned to the California missions, the problem flared up again. Now as the expedition actually set out for the north, his leg swelled and eventually became so painful that he could not walk or even stand on it long enough to say Mass. Captain Portola, commander of the expedition, wanted to send him back, but Serra refused. Instead he asked one of the mule drivers to do for him whatever he would do for a mule with a sore leg. The packer picked some herbs, mixed them with tallow, and made a poultice to apply to Serra's leg. The next morning the leg was enough improved that Serra, with effort, was able to travel. Each succeeding day was better, and although the pain lingered, Serra was able to keep up with the expedition until it arrived in San Diego.

But there he faced new difficulties. Originally, the expedition, which had come north in four parts, two by land and two by sea, was to have regrouped at Monterey where a mission and a presidio were to be established on the shores of the great bay discovered by Sebastian Viscaino in 1602. But the ships, having arrived in San Diego with crews so ravaged by scurvy it was impossible to continue, waited for the arrival of the ones who came by land. By the time Serra reached

San Diego with the main land party in early July, conditions among those waiting there were truly dreadful. According to Serra, eight sailors from the *San Antonio* were dead and the entire *San Carlos* crew, except for the cook and one sailor, had died.

Regardless of these conditions, Captain Portola insisted he must carry out his orders to settle at Monterey. From the crews of the two ships he found enough sailors to man—barely—the *San Antonio* and he sent it back to Mexico for more men and supplies. Then, taking all the men well enough to travel, he set out toward Monterey, leaving those who were ill, including Serra with his sore leg, in San Diego.

On Sunday, July 16, 1769, two days after Portola left for the north, Serra officially founded the mission of San Diego de Alcala. Whatever satisfaction he received was brief, for the Indians were hostile and resisted all attempts at conversion. In August a fight broke out between Indians and soldiers and three Indians and a Spanish mule packer were killed. A wall then had to be built around the mission, and Serra, instead of running a mission open to all comers, found himself barricaded behind a stockade. When Portola returned from the north several months later, Serra had not converted a single Indian.

Portola had discovered a great new bay—San Francisco—but he had been unable to identify with any assurance the bay of Sebastian Viscaino because of the vagueness of the explorer's reports. It was very discouraging, and as supplies began to run out, he seriously considered abandoning the whole project.

In the spring of 1770 everything changed dramatically when, on March 19, the *San Antonio* returned from Mexico to enter San Diego Bay, with food, supplies, and men, allowing Portola to make another attempt to settle at Monterey Bay. The *San Antonio,* with Serra aboard, was sent north while Portola and his soldiers again went by land. The ship arrived at Monterey on the last day of May, guided into the bay by fires lit by the soldiers of Portola, who was now convinced Monterey was the bay Viscaino had discovered.

On June 3, 1770, the first Sunday after his arrival, Serra officially founded a mission at Monterey. All the men who had come north gathered on the beach where a makeshift brush arbor had been constructed to contain the altar. Serra appeared in his alb and stole, and as the assembled crowd knelt before the altar, he chanted the "Venite

Creator Spiritus." A cross was then installed and blessed, and Serra sprinkled the beach and fields with holy water, "putting to rout all infernal foes."

One of those present at the ceremony was Gaspar de Portola, military commander and governor of both Californias, whose performance that day thoroughly impressed Serra and his fellow Franciscans. Ordinarily the act of possession by the King's representative—in this case the governor—would have come first, but Portola, by reversing the order, subtly recognized the dominance of the missionaries in California. Later he re-emphasized that dominance by saying the primary purpose of coming to California was to extend the faith and therefore the cross should precede the flag. Portola had acted generously but then he would not have to live with the implications of having recognized publicly that the church was more important than the state. Shortly afterward, Portola, his task of organizing the move north complete, sailed for Mexico on the *San Antonio.* Before he left, he turned the governing of California over to his second-in-command, Lieutenant Pedro Fages.

It was now up to Fages to establish working relations with Father Serra, and he soon found it would not be easy. Fages, forty years old, had served in the Spanish Army since the Seven Years' War, but he had been in America for only a few years and had little experience as a commander under frontier conditions. Besides, as he took over in California, he was still a lieutenant, officially only military commander and not the governor—a title belonging to an official stationed in Baja California and too far away to exercise any authority in the north. But the fact remained that Fages was not governor. He had also been second in command to Portola, and those who had served with him during that first year in California were accustomed to viewing him as an underling. Moreover Serra, almost twenty years older than Fages, was the officially appointed Father-President of the missions and in complete and absolute charge of all who served under him.

Fages was not a particularly tactful man, and when faced with someone as formidable as Serra, he overreacted in attempting to demonstrate his authority. Soon Serra found himself bombarded by a series of incredibly detailed orders and complaints concerning the church, the location of its doors, the church cemetery, even the placing of the cross in the cemetery. Once, Serra said, he received a complaint from the commandante "because I buried a dead man a little farther away than he liked."

Yet if Fages was overzealous in his attention to detail, Serra also found reason to complain about even the most selfless acts of Fages. In May 1772 supply ships were late in reaching San Diego, and because of storms could not continue on to Monterey. The northern missions were almost out of food and Fages, whatever his shortcomings in dealing with people, was always able to handle crises. He quickly organized a party of soldiers to go to Los Osos Valley near San Luis Obispo to obtain a supply of bear meat. Serra, hearing of this venture, asked that a missionary be allowed to go along as there were plans to establish a mission at San Luis Obispo and this seemed an excellent opportunity to become acquainted with the natives. Fages refused, saying the soldiers were in a hurry to start, they would be moving rapidly, and they would not be staying in any one place for long.

Under the circumstances Fages' refusal was understandable, but it infuriated Serra, who considered it an attempt by the military commandante to prevent the missionaries from doing something that might bring them credit. The hunt went well, large amounts of bear meat were sent back, and many people gave Fages credit for staving off famine. Serra, however, dismissed the whole thing with the comment, "The officer came back here before the end of a month's absence with a few loads of bear meat."

In late August 1772, not long after the bear hunt, Serra and Fages, with an escort of soldiers, left Monterey together for an inspection tour that took them all the way to San Diego. They visited the new mission at San Antonio de Padua, which Serra thought was progressing slowly because Fages had removed several soldiers who had been helping with the construction. Farther south, they stopped long enough for Serra to found a mission at San Luis Obispo, then continued on to San Buenaventura where they looked over the site for another one. They also visited the mission at San Gabriel where Serra vigorously protested to Fages when he learned that a much-liked corporal had been reassigned to Monterey. Fages gave in and ordered the man returned to San Gabriel.

Serra and Fages finally reached San Diego on September 17. They had been traveling together for nearly a month and supposedly had had plenty of time to express their opinions and talk out their differences. Apparently not, however, for a few days after they arrived Serra wrote a formal letter to Fages—who was also in San Diego—telling him how he thought California should be run.

Specifically, the letter concerned the founding of the new mission at San Buenaventura, but in the guise of making requests, Serra virtually told Fages how to conduct his business. He told him how many soldiers would be needed for the new mission, how many mules would be needed, how the courier service should work, that the sailors and mule drivers should be responsible to the missionaries rather than to the military, how the rations should be divided. Certainly Serra knew more about founding missions than Fages, and although many of the requests made sense, the letter itself was both tactless and presumptuous.

Fages noted in his reply that some of the requests could not be granted simply because "it is not possible to give what one does not have." He was well aware that the true problem was not these specifics but the broader question of authority. He pointed out that he had never questioned that the missions were under the complete control of Father Serra, and in return he hoped that Serra would recognize that all political and military authority belonged to him. Serra, however, missed the point entirely, for in his response he talked about specifics and ignored the question of who ruled what in California.

A few days later, Fages sent Serra some excerpts from a letter written by His Excellency Don Antonio Maria Bucareli y Ursua, the recently appointed viceroy of New Spain. The letter had been addressed to Fages, who was instructed to see that the Father-President and all other missionaries "stimulate all by example and persuasion to obey and comply with your orders." In sending the excerpts to Serra, Fages said only that he hoped the missionaries might "take note of it for due compliance with such an important object."

At last Serra understood what Fages was driving at, and in his reply he seemed shocked by the implications. He said he had always insisted that everyone in California obey Fages's orders, and he cited several examples of his support for the acting governor. As far as the missionaries were concerned, he was unaware that any of them had ever done anything contrary to Fages's orders. Yet for all the humble protestations of support, Serra was preparing an offensive, for at the end of the letter he asked if he could see the original communication from the viceroy. Not, he said, because he doubted the accuracy of the quotations but because he wanted to understand from the context why the letter had been sent. "If—as I rather suspect—it is the work of an enemy, I may be able to defend the honor of our holy habit by laying bare the truth."

Serra apparently decided not to wait for a reply. He called a meeting of the other missionaries in San Diego, and after discussion they all agreed that Serra should go to Mexico City and lay the entire problem before the new viceroy. Four days later, on October 17, 1772, he sailed on the *San Carlos,* bound for Mexico.

Serra reached Mexico City in February 1773 at just the right time to have the viceroy's almost undivided attention to matters concerning California. Bucareli, when he took office in 1771, had found himself faced with the vast complexities of governing New Spain, of which California was only one small part. He was an experienced colonial administrator, having spent the past five years as governor and captain-general of Cuba, and he well knew the wisdom of becoming fully informed before making drastic moves. Thus, during his first two years as viceroy he had done little that influenced California one way or another.

In early 1773, however, Bucareli received orders concerning the new organization of frontier provinces. In them the King indicated he felt California merited special attention. Bucareli also began to receive copies of letters written by the Spanish ambassador in St. Petersburg containing somewhat exaggerated reports of Russian activities on the Pacific Coast of North America. Then, to cap it all, Serra arrived demanding that significant changes be made in the way California was run.

Bucareli needed information, so he asked the Father-President for a full report on California and its missions. Serra retired to his old home at the College of San Fernando and spent the next month writing a long statement filled with suggestions and recommendations. When he submitted it to the viceroy, it contained thirty-two points, and, as usual, Serra expressed an opinion on almost everything. The document discussed establishing forges in California, assigning carpenters to specific missions, and even included a suggestion on how to regulate the measuring scales at the port of San Blas.

It was point six, however, that Serra considered crucial. It said "A measure that seems to me of special importance is the removal, or recall, of the Officer Don Pedro Fages from command of the presidio at Monterey, and the appointment of another in his place."

Serra had to justify this request, not a simple task since most of the arguments between himself and Fages had been over small items which, when isolated in the cold print of an official government report, sounded ludicrously petty. At the same time, Serra could not say, even had he been aware of it, that the real reason he wanted Fages removed was because he would not recognize the absolute supremacy of the Father-President. Serra took advantage of some very real problems that faced the acting governor to frame the charges so as to indicate Fages's lack of ability as military commander.

Fages was constantly plagued by complaining and deserting soldiers. Yet given the working conditions, it is not surprising that maintaining rigid military discipline proved difficult. In these early years California was not a particularly attractive assignment, and often the worst troops were assigned there. They were discontented when they arrived and they faced long stays with little hope of returning home. Most of the troops were scattered over the various missions where usually only a corporal and a handful of soldiers were stationed. Not only were they free of the rigid supervision of the military commander, who remained in Monterey, but they often became quite friendly with the local missionaries. It was easy for a soldier to take his troubles to the fathers who, after they had their own troubles with Fages, were willing to listen sympathetically. And the soldiers—discontented, far from home, and out from under the control of their commanding officer—poured out their unhappiness.

Thus the fathers saw only one side of the trouble between the soldiers and their commander, and Serra justified the demand for Fages' removal by saying, "Otherwise there will be no stopping the desertions of soldiers . . . Their grievance is not only because of long hours of work and a lack of food—as I have on numerous occasions heard them declare—but because of the harsh treatment, and unbearable manners of the said officer."

Although Bucareli, who had long served as an army officer himself, was not particularly impressed by these charges, he did recognize that Junipero Serra and Pedro Fages could not get along. And since Serra could not easily be replaced, he had no real choice but to recall Fages and appoint a replacement. Serra had suggested the post be given to Jose Ortega, a sergeant stationed in California, but Bucareli felt he did not have sufficient rank to contend with the problems he would have to face. He appointed Captain Fernando Rivera y Moncada, who, after his service in an early exploration, had returned to Baja California to brood over the fact that he had not been appointed governor in the first place.

Bucareli also made another decision concerning California. Since the coast above San Francisco Bay was virtually unknown, he outfitted a ship, the *Santiago,* commanded by Juan Perez, and sent it into the North Pacific to explore. On its way north, it would also stop at Monterey to deliver supplies, thus providing Serra, who had accomplished his purpose in Mexico, return passage to California.

II

The *Santiago* sailed from San Blas in late January 1774, bound directly for Monterey. Somewhere off the coast of Baja California it sprang a leak and put in to San Diego Bay for repairs. Serra, who by then had had his fill of the sea, went ashore to continue the trip by land. He left San Diego on April 6 and for the next month traveled north, arriving in Monterey on May 11. By then the *Santiago,* its leak repaired, had already reached Monterey, and Serra was denied the pleasure of telling Fages that the viceroy had ordered him back to Mexico. A few days later Captain Rivera and his troops arrived after a long march north from Loreto. Rivera, an old Creole soldier who, having been outraged earlier when he was passed over as governor, was now triumphant, and could not resist the temptation to gloat and show his contempt for Fages. Peremptorily, with little courtesy, he ordered Fages to get ready to sail and to take all his Catalan Volunteers with him. Fages, never one to give up without a fight, demanded the right to depart from San Diego rather than from Monterey, claiming he needed to obtain receipts from various missionaries and soldiers stationed there. After luring Rivera into refusing, he produced a permit from the viceroy allowing him to stop at San Diego. Rivera was forced to yield, and having achieved that much triumph, Fages and his Catalan Volunteers left California.

Serra, back in California after a two-year absence and free of his old nemesis, could now set about the long-term development of the missions. First, however, he had to make an immediate decision about the missionaries to assign to the *Santiago* which was in Monterey making final preparations for the trip north. Such voyages required priests, and Serra finally decided to send two men. One was Juan Crespi, who had come to California with the first overland expedition and who, on several occasions, had shown himself thoroughly able to adjust to the rough conditions encountered by explorers. The other was Tomas de la Pena, who had only recently arrived in California and had not yet been given a specific mission assignment.

On June 6 Fathers Crespi and de la Pena, accompanied by Father Serra, went down to the beach where they received the Father-President's blessing and boarded the *Santiago.* That night the sailors began raising the anchor, but the delays that plagued the ship were not ended. Since sailing from San Blas in January, it had spent several weeks in San Diego repairing a leak, then a month in Monterey unloading supplies for the northern missions. Now, with final preparations made and the anchor raised, winds began blowing hard out of the northwest, keeping the ship in port. When the winds stopped, a dead calm descended on the bay and again it was impossible to sail. Not until June 14, eight days after first raising the anchor, was the *Santiago* able to put to sea and set its course for the northwest.

Captain Juan Perez' orders concerning the voyage had been written by Viceroy Bucareli the previous December, but they had been sealed and Perez was forbidden to open them until he was out of sight of Monterey. Now, six months later, he could finally break the seal and read his instructions. As was usual under such circumstances, they were extremely detailed and attempted to cover all possibilities. He was given permission to sail as far north as he wished provided he reached at least 60° latitude and provided that when he turned south again, he sailed as close to the coast as possible, trying never to lose sight of it. He was not to attempt any settlement himself but was to identify likely places for the future. When he found them, he was to take possession by erecting a large wooden cross and also by building a stone cairn in which he was to hide a glass bottle, stoppered with pitch, which would contain a copy of the act of possession.

Perez, after clearing Monterey Bay, set a northwest course until he reached 50° where he began to steer due north. By then, almost a full month had been passed at sea, the *Santiago* was in the fog and mist of the northwest, and those on board were constantly on edge for fear they might suddenly strike the rocks of some unknown coast. The ship was also beginning to run short of water, and on July 15 Perez called a meeting of his fellow officers. They decided to ease their way in toward the coast and find a place where they could take on water. Since it might also be a suitable place for a settlement, the carpenters were put to work making a large cross, inscribed with the letters INRI—*Jesus Nazerunus Rex Jucadrun*—and containing the words *Carolus III Hispaniarum rex, año de 1774.*

Not until July 18, after three more days in the fog, did the men aboard the *Santiago* catch their first glimpse of the northwest coast—snow-covered mountains at least twenty leagues away. The next day they reached the Queen Charlotte Islands where three canoes approached the boat, paddled by Indians stroking in cadence to a chant. They stopped well short of the ship. A brave, standing in the largest of the canoes, began spreading feathers on the water and making signs that Perez interpreted to mean welcome. At first the Indians refused to come closer, but eventually were lured up to the ship by presents and soon became vigorously involved in trading seal and sea-otter skins for knives, bits of metal, and old clothes. So accustomed did they seem to such activities that Perez thought, mistakenly, that they had experience in trading with white men.

As Perez spent the next several days exploring what seemed to be an opening just north of the Queen Charlotte Islands, he was almost always within sight of canoes with Indians who came out to look and to trade. Eventually he sighted land on the other side of the strait—Cape Muzon at the southern end of the Alaskan panhandle. He was still well short of 60°, but the fog, the strong current, and the adverse winds kept him from entering the strait and also made it almost impossible to continue north. Finally, he decided to turn back.

Two weeks later, while sailing along what Perez and his crew thought was the mainland but was actually the outer coast of Vancouver Island, they sighted what seemed to be an opening into the interior. They worked the ship in toward the coast, and on the evening of August 8, 1774, dropped anchor just outside Nootka Sound, their only stop on the entire voyage.

Early the next morning, which for once dawned bright and clear, Captain Perez ordered the launch over the side to take the officers into the Sound to look for a better anchorage and also to perform the necessary ceremonies for taking possession. Father de la Pena and Father Crespi, with the large cross hammered together by the ship's carpenters, were also going ashore to take part in the ceremonies. Watching these activities were at least a hundred Indians who had arrived in a fleet of canoes and had virtually surrounded the *Santiago* as soon as it dropped anchor the night before.

The launch was barely in the water when the wind suddenly freshened, then began blowing hard. Suddenly, the *Santiago* began to drag its anchor and sweep toward the beach. Perez, realizing the peril, cut the anchor, ordered the sails unfurled, and attempted to get away from the coast. He also recalled the launch, and its passengers, after some dangerous moments, were able to return to the ship. They had not landed, they had not planted the cross, and they had not performed any act of possession.

The Indians, who until now had been content to watch from their canoes, realized the ship was leaving and came alongside indicating they wanted to trade. Despite the wind, the men aboard the *Santiago* were willing, and soon a brisk business developed with the Indians, who were offering sea-otter furs in exchange for the abalone shells the Spaniards could provide. It was during the course of this trade that the young second pilot, Esteban Martinez, threw a large shell into one of the canoes and accidentally hit an Indian boy on the head. Nothing came of it, but if Martinez later laughed over his inaccuracy, he soon found something to grumble about as well—during the trading some warriors had been allowed aboard the *Santiago* and one of them stole two silver spoons belonging to Martinez.

Captain Perez, when he left Nootka Sound, had not only failed in his mission, he had also failed to take on any water. He hoped he would find a better place to obtain it farther south, but during the next several days there was no opportunity to land. Scurvy broke out, and rain squalls, high winds, heavy seas, and thick fog made it impossible to approach the coast. Finally he decided there was no other choice but to return to California and he ran for it. On August 26, lookouts spotted the Farallon Islands, and the following day the ship entered Monterey Bay where at four in the afternoon it dropped anchor. Captain Perez spent the next month there, then sailed for San Blas to report on his not very successful expedition to explore and take possession of the northwest coast of America.

III

While all this was happening in the North Pacific, Pedro Fages, having been removed as acting governor of California, had made his way back to Mexico, where he was placed in command of the Second Company of Catalan Volunteers stationed in Guadalajara. And during those quiet years in garrison in the settled regions of Mexico, certain things became clear about Pedro Fages.

Viceroy Bucareli, at the time he agreed to Serra's demand that Fages be removed, had never met him personally. When Fages reached Mexico City, the viceroy was much impressed with him and with his long report on California that gave an accurate and intelligent account of the country.

It soon became evident, also, that Serra could not get along with Rivera, who replaced Fages, or with Felipe de Neve, who replaced Rivera. Eventually Bucareli came to the conclusion that much of the trouble had been caused by Serra and that it had been a mistake to remove Fages from command in California.

At some time during these interim years in garrison, Fages married Dona Eulalia Callis, the daughter of the man who had once been Fages' commanding officer. Possibly it was his marriage to the daughter of a high-ranking officer or the new-found respect of the viceroy that won him new attention. Possibly, too, someone remembered that in the early days of California he had been a tough, capable soldier.

Whatever the cause, in 1778 Fages was promoted to the rank of lieutenant colonel and with his Catalan Volunteers returned to the frontier where he was placed in command of the presidio at El Pitic.

There, in August 1781, word arrived that a band of Spaniards had been killed at the Yuma villages in the north. At first there were few details—only the vague confused story that arrived via the Indian grapevine. The Pimas, who lived just east of the Yumas, had picked it up and passed it on to the soldiers at Tucson, who sent it south. Then one of those taken prisoner by the Yumas escaped and reached the presidio at Altar with a firsthand account of the disaster. Several Spanish missionaries, settlers, and soldiers had been killed by Indians.

Teodoro de Croix, Commandante-General of Internal Provinces, called a council of war at his headquarters in Arizpe. After reviewing the reports from the north, it was decided that the Yumas had risen without provocation and thus were in open rebellion against the Crown. Soldiers in sufficient force must be sent to the villages to investigate, to ransom captives, and to punish the leaders of the rebellion with instant execution. Chosen to command this punitive force was Lieutenant Colonel Pedro Fages, commandante of the presidio of El Pitic.

On September 16, 1781, Fages led his troops north toward the Yuma country. When they arrived at the villages on the east side of the Colorado, most of the Indians had already fled across the river, sending messages indicating they did not want to fight. Fages, seeing several hundred armed warriors on the other side of the river, did not entirely believe them, but knowing they still held Spanish prisoners, he opened negotiations and by offering blankets, beads, and cigarettes was able to ransom most of the captives.

There were still some captives among the Yumas, and Fages would have liked to continue negotiations until they were all free, but he could not control his Indian allies, the Pimas and Cocomaricopas, who had joined him for the express purpose of attacking the Yumas. They became impatient with all the talk and bluntly told Fages they were going to attack the next morning. Since there were at least six hundred of them, Fages had no choice but to agree, and when several Yumas were killed in the attack all negotiations had to be abandoned. It seemed unlikely that the few captives still left among the Yumas could be ransomed, so Fages left the river and retreated to the Papago village at Sonoyta, 120 miles to the east, where he remained for several weeks. Then receiving new orders, he returned to the Yuma villages, crossed the river, found the bodies of the four missionaries who had been killed and brought them back to Mexico for burial.

Beyond that Fages accomplished little. He fought a few inconsequential battles with the Indians, but he was unable to subdue the Yumas or to capture and punish the ringleaders of the rebellion. Upon his return to Arizpe in January 1782 another council of war was held, and it was decided that Fages would once more lead a campaign against the Yumas, but this time he would go first to California where he would be joined by additional troops under Governor Felipe de Neve. In August 1782 after months of delay, the combined forces left San Gabriel bound east toward the Yuma villages on the Colorado.

The troops were still several days short of the river when a messenger caught up with them, carrying dispatches containing new assignments for the two leaders. De Neve now became Inspector General of Internal Provinces while Fages was promoted to De Neve's position as governor. On September 10, 1782, at the small desert camp of Saucedo, the office of Governor of California was formally turned over to Pedro Fages. The next day, instead of continuing with the military expedition, he turned west again and rode back to California to take up his new post.

IV

Fages arrived in Monterey in the fall of 1782. There is no account of his first meeting with Serra, but it cannot have been entirely comfortable. The two men had spent five years between 1769 and 1774 at odds, and Serra had used all his influence to have Fages removed. Now Fages was back, and he returned with more power and more prestige. Previously he had been merely a captain and a military commander acting as governor. Now, in 1782, he was a Lieutenant Colonel and the full, official Governor of California.

There are things that never change. Soon Serra and Fages were at odds again, this time over the franking of mail. Since the early days in California, missionaries had enjoyed the right of free mail, but in

1783 Serra received a packet of letters bearing a mark of eleven reales. He wrote to the governor, saying that he considered himself an official of the Crown and entitled to free mail. Fages replied that the eleven reales was marked on the packet, not as a charge but only as a means of keeping things straight in the post office account books. Serra accepted the explanation, and when he received a packet marked twenty reales, he signed for it, assuming it was again only a matter of internal accounting. Later, when he received a bill for postage, he wrote to Mexico asking that the matter be brought before the postmaster general. Eventually the matter was decided in favor of the missionaries.

Fages, on his part, complained that the missionaries had stopped conducting Mass for the soldiers at the presidios. Serra explained that since their arrival in California the missionaries had, without obligation and without pay, provided religious services. Fages had come to expect it although the missionaries claimed conducting such services was not their responsibility.

Not only did Serra resent being taken for granted in general, but at Monterey, he said, "the provocation was even greater." The lieutenant there often made fun of the missionaries and also, Serra said, "although they had wine to drink—and good wine too—they never wanted us to sample any of it, not even for Mass." Consequently, the fathers had to supply their own wine. By constant hammering at Fages, the missionaries finally got him to provide wine. A few days after promising it, Fages left Monterey, saying he would leave a cruet of wine for Mass. But the next Sunday the lieutenant at the presidio notified the missionaries to bring wine, as the soldiers had none. Serra was never sure if the governor had broken his promise or if the soldiers had drunk all the wine as soon as he left.

Once again Serra and Fages were arguing, seemingly over minor points, but actually over who would dominate California. Serra had won the first round by having Fages removed. Now he had little hope of being able to repeat his victory. Fages had returned with increased rank and power, and Serra's inability to get along with Fages' successors had eroded much of his credibility. Besides, Serra was no longer the vigorous man he had been a decade before. Now he was old and tired.

In the fall of 1783 Serra went south to visit the missions. By the time he reached San Gabriel he had a chest ailment so severe that those at the mission thought he was going to die. Even the Indians noticed and told the missionaries "the old father wants to die." They were not far wrong, for while Serra was at San Gabriel he wrote, "Though I do not know when I am to die, I yet am convinced that I am not far distant from it. Above all I know that from here onwards I am quite useless for making the rounds of the missions."

Yet Serra recovered enough to return to Carmel, and the following spring made another trip, this time to the mission at San Francisco to see his old friend Francisco Palou. On his way back Palou accompanied him as far as Santa Clara where Serra stopped to dedicate a new church building. He lingered for a time at the mission and insisted that Palou do the same, saying it was possible they would never see each other again and he wanted to prepare for death. Serra made a general confession to Palou, "shedding many tears." Palou also wept, fearing this would be their last meeting. On May 24, Serra, now prepared for death, set out for Carmel where he arrived two days later.

It was another false alarm. Serra lived on through the summer, and in August, Palou, in response to a letter, came to Carmel. He found Serra, although weak and suffering from chest pains and swollen legs, was up and able to sing Mass in his normal, clear voice. Palou—with a considerable amount of wishful thinking—said to a soldier that Serra did not seem very sick. The soldier, who had known Serra since they had come to California together in 1769, said, "Father, there is no basis for hope. He *is* ill. This saintly priest is always well when it comes to praying and singing, but he is nearly finished."

Serra spent the next several days holding conferences with Palou to discuss mission business. The pain persisted and on August 22, the surgeon of a Spanish ship in the harbor came to the mission. He found Serra in such bad condition that he suggested cauterizing his chest to help rid him of some of the phlegm. Serra told him to go ahead with whatever remedy he thought necessary. The doctor's treatment only increased the pain, but Serra continued to go about his duties at the mission.

On August 26 he arose so exhausted after a bad night that he told Palou he wished to prepare himself for whatever God had in store. He spent the entire day in seclusion allowing "not a single distraction," and in the evening repeated his General Confession to Father Palou. Then, after a brief meditation, he had a cup of broth and lay down, saying he did not want anyone in the room with him.

At dawn the next day Father Palou looked in on Serra and found him with his breviary in his hands as he always said Matins before daybreak. He said he felt all right, but asked Palou to consecrate an extra Host and reserve it so that he could receive the Viaticum that morning. After Mass Palou said he had done so and Serra announced he would go to the church to receive the Viaticum in preparation for his death. Palou was startled and told Serra it was not necessary, for the Blessed Sacrament could be brought to his room. Serra, however, replied, "No, I want to receive Him in church, for if I can walk thither, there is no need for the Lord to come to me." Palou was forced to agree and let Serra walk the hundred yards to the church by himself.

Afterward Serra returned to his small room where he spent the rest of the day in meditation. No one was allowed to disturb him, not even the presidio carpenter who, at Serra's request, had come for detailed instructions on the coffin he was to make. Instead, Palou sent him away, telling him to make the coffin like the one he had made earlier when Father Crespi died.

That night Serra asked for the sacrament of extreme unction, and Palou quickly complied. Serra spent the rest of the night on his knees with his chest pressed against the bed. Once Palou suggested he lie down and rest, but Serra said he was more comfortable as he was. By dawn he was somewhat better, and later in the morning when some officers from the ship in the harbor came to visit him, he received them as if nothing were wrong. He knew them from earlier years and listened as they told about their most recent voyage. At noon he asked Palou to sprinkle some oil around the room. Then suddenly he said, "Great fear has come over me. Read for me the Commendation for a Departing Soul and say it aloud so that I can hear it." Palou read the ritual and when it was over, Serra said, "Thanks be to God, I have no more fear." He then had a cup of broth and lay down on his plank bed to rest for the first time in thirty hours. His visitors and Father Palou left to have lunch.

But Palou felt ill at ease and returned to Serra's room to see if he was asleep. "I found him just as we had left him a little before, but now asleep in the Lord, without any sign or trace of agony, his body showing no other sign of death than the cessation of breathing; he seemed to be sleeping."

At Palou's bidding the Indians began tolling the bell, and as the double tolling announced Serra's death, grieving people, Indian and Spaniard alike, arrived at the mission to view the remains. Eventually the crowd became so great it was necessary to close the door and place Serra's body in the redwood coffin he had ordered the day before.

While the door was closed, Father Palou, with the help of another missionary, made the final, simple preparations. They removed Serra's sandals but left him in the habit in which he died. They placed the body in the coffin, lighted six candles, and then opened the door to his cell. Throughout the rest of the day a long line of Indians and Spaniards filed through, praying for his soul. The same crowd followed the body in the evening as it was removed to the church and placed on a table where, again, six candles were lighted.

The funeral took place on Sunday morning, August 29, with Father Palou officiating. Throughout the day the double tolling of bells continued, while each half-hour the ship in the harbor fired its cannon and was answered by a cannon fired from the presidio on shore. The mournful bells and the solemn booming of the cannon, according to Palou, "melted the hearts of all." Then, at four in the afternoon, Serra's body was lowered into a grave in the sanctuary floor, on the gospel side, near that of his old friend and follower Juan Crespi.

V

When Junipero Serra died in late August 1784, slightly more than fifteen years had passed since the first Spaniards settled in California. In that time, they established nine missions ranging from San Diego to San Francisco, and built four presidios at San Diego, San Francisco, Santa Barbara, and at the capital in Monterey.

Despite these events, California was still isolated. Few ships ever called there, and knowledge of the rest of the world was limited to who was King in Spain and who was Pope in Rome. The American Revolution, just entering its final phase as Fages took office, was unheard of. An associated event, however—the war between Spain and England—sometimes indirectly affected California in the form of orders from Spain that precautions be taken against the encroachment of foreigners. These orders were sent first to Mexico, then forwarded to California where they were read publicly with great formality but without creating the least amount of interest or concern. Those in California knew just how unlikely it was they would be encroached upon. By the fall of 1786, seventeen years had passed since the Spanish had arrived and in all those years no one had seen so much as a strange sail.

Then, on September 14, 1786, two foreign ships appeared through the light afternoon fog doubling Point Pinos and making for Monterey. As they came closer, they were recognized as the French ships, *Boussole* and *Astrolabe,* which did not entirely surprise the Spaniards in Monterey, for Governor Fages had been warned of their arrival in recent dispatches from Spain. Two Spanish ships were in the harbor, and the captain of *La Princesa,* Esteban Martinez, once second pilot aboard the *Santiago* and now commander of his own ship, began firing his cannon every fifteen minutes to guide the Frenchmen through the fog. With his help, the ships anchored two leagues offshore, and by ten that night, boats from the Spanish ships had arrived with pilots offering to conduct them into port. The next morning they entered the harbor and anchored just off the presidio where a seven-gun salute was fired in honor of the French fleet commander, Jean François Galaup de la Perouse.

La Perouse was forty-four years old and a thoroughly experienced sailor. Thirty years before, when little more than a child, he had gone to sea as a midshipman and soon found himself in the midst of the Seven Years' War. He was on board the French ship *Formidable* when it attacked the British fleet, was wounded during the battle, and when the *Formidable* surrendered he was taken prisoner. He was released at the end of the war, and served for the next fifteen years in the peacetime navy. In 1777 France again went to war with England, this time as part of the American Revolution. La Perouse was promoted to the rank of first lieutenant and given command of a ship operating in Canadian waters. That war over, he returned to France and three years later was chosen to lead a French expedition into the Pacific.

This expedition had been organized at the express command of Louis XVI and was intended to obtain scientific data on the Pacific. The ship had a full complement of scientists, including a geologist, a botanist, and an ornithologist. Yet France had a practical purpose in mind, for La Perouse was also ordered to look into the possibilities of opening the fur trade along the northwest coast of America. This, however, was likely to cause some conflict with the Spanish who had already settled on that coast at least as far north as Monterey. La Perouse was to investigate the state of these settlements, see if there were any new ones, and determine whether there was any unoccupied area the French might develop. Since France and Spain were allies, he was not to sneak along the coast, but boldly enter the port of Monterey to obtain supplies. To facilitate this action, he carried an open letter of introduction from the Spanish minister in France. At the same time La Perouse obtained his letter, orders were sent to California instructing the governor to extend every hospitality to the Frenchmen.

Governor Fages quickly showed he meant to do more than pay lip service to these orders. Monterey in 1786 consisted of little more than the governor's home where Fages lived with his family and the presidio which housed a force of about fifty soldiers. The Fages home and servants were put at La Perouse's disposal, and soldiers at the presidio were ordered to help the French sailors take on wood and water. Whatever foodstuffs were available—garden produce, beef, mutton, milk—were also sent aboard the ship in abundance. The hospitality threatened to disrupt military etiquette as Governor Fages and Captain Martinez, commander of *La Princesa,* began vying with each other for the right to supply the Frenchmen. The Spanish even refused to take payment, and after La Perouse insisted, the charges were so low they embarrassed him.

The missionaries arriving from San Carlos Borromeo at Carmel soon after the ships anchored also demanded the right to be involved in welcoming the visitors. They invited the Frenchmen to dine at the mission, and La Perouse, wanting to see as much of California as possible, accepted. Governor Fages provided the horses, and also rode with the French officers across the wide plain, filled with cattle, that separated Monterey and Carmel. When they arrived at the mission, La Perouse said, "We were received like the lords of manors when they first take possession of their estates." The Indians were lined up on the square in front of the church, and awaiting the party at the church door was Father Fermin de Lasuen, President of the California mission. Lasuen, his holy-water sprinkler in his hand, greeted the visitors, then conducted them to the high altar where he chanted the "Te Deum" to give thanks for a successful voyage.

La Perouse wanted to repay the Spaniards with gifts for all their hospitality. To each of the soldiers at the presidio he presented a piece of blue cloth. The mission received seeds, as well as implements and tools including a corn grinder which La Perouse claimed would allow four women to do the work of a hundred. Not to be outdone, Governor Fages and the missionaries stripped themselves of their poultry and sent it to fill the hencoops on La Perouse's ships.

By the evening of September 22 the French were ready to sail. Adverse winds held them up the next day, but on the 24th the *Boussole* and *Astrolabe* weighed anchor and sailed out of Monterey Bay. The first foreign visit to California was over.

At the time it seemed to mean little, for after only ten days the French, having taken on fresh supplies, sailed away. Neither did their visit break down California's isolation—for it would be six more years before another foreign sail was sighted in Monterey. Yet in many ways, Spanish California's future experiences with foreigners had been characterized by La Perouse's visit.

First, there was the overwhelming expression of Spanish hospitality. It was lonely living on the edge of the world, particularly for men like Pedro Fages and most of the missionaries who originally came from Europe. Surely, the welcome the Spanish gave La Perouse came not so much from government instructions as from true happiness at seeing visitors from the outside world. This time it was all very proper because a warm welcome had been ordered by the government in Spain. In the future, government orders concerning foreigners would be just the opposite, but people in California always had difficulty overcoming their joy at seeing someone new.

The significance of La Perouse's gifts was not lost on the missionaries. The supply lines between Mexico and California were still tenuous, and tools, implements, and particularly something such as a corn grinder was virtually impossible to obtain. The Frenchmen were not on a trading voyage and had only a few items they could leave as presents. In the future, however, foreign ships would purposely include such items in their cargoes, providing a temptation that many Spaniards, particularly the missionaries, found very difficult to resist.

But a lure was needed to attract foreign ships to the California coast, and even as early as 1786 La Perouse and the Spanish both knew exactly what it was. While he was at Monterey, La Perouse met Vicente Vassadre y Vega, who had come to California specifically to open the sea-otter trade. His plan was simple. The supply ships from Mexico, instead of returning from California empty, would bring back fur which would then be sent to China and traded for quicksilver, always in short supply in the Mexican mines.

La Perouse became interested in the fur trade, and in discussions with Vassadre and Governor Fages learned that the sea otter was abundant in California. In fact, Fages, possibly more to impress than to inform his visitor, said he knew the country well and was sure fifty thousand furs could be collected in California each year. La Perouse also compared sea-otter furs taken in Monterey Bay with some he had obtained earlier in Alaska. He thought the California furs inferior, but the differences were so slight that there would be no effect on the prices the furs would bring in China. What did surprise La Perouse was how long the Spanish had taken to discover the possibilities of the fur trade.

He knew why the Spanish had finally awakened. "It is to Captain Cook and the publication of his work," La Perouse wrote, "that they are indebted for the dawn of this information." But even after awakening, the Spanish could do little. Vassadre put his plan into operation, but the jealousy of Spanish officials in Manila, where the furs were shipped on their way to China, was frustrating and he finally abandoned the whole project.

There were others, however, able to make much fuller use of the information Captain James Cook brought back from the Pacific.

CAPTAIN COOK'S AMERICA

I

In July 1776 Captain James Cook sailed from England, for the third time, once again bound for the Pacific Ocean. Seven years had passed since his first visit to Tahiti where, on a day of glorious sunshine, the Transit of Venus had been successfully observed. Cook had then opened sealed orders and found he was now required to sail south and west to search for a great, undiscovered continent in the South Pacific. He left Tahiti, sailed as far as forty degrees south and, not finding any sign of land, turned west until he reached New Zealand. When he returned home he reported categorically that no such continent existed.

Cook's statement enraged a Scotsman named Alexander Dalrymple, one-time hydrographer for the East India Company. Dalrymple, after years of collecting and reading accounts of Pacific exploration, was convinced of the existence of a great southern continent in the Pacific. Hearing of the plans for Cook's voyage, he thought it an excellent opportunity to prove his theory, and using his considerable influence in the admiralty, was responsible for the orders to search for the continent. Cook had done so and found nothing, but Dalrymple refused to accept that. Claiming Cook had not looked hard enough, he demanded another voyage be sent into the Pacific.

Cook did not believe such a continent existed, but he knew there were large gaps in the exploration of the Pacific and had already suggested a second voyage, a circumnavigation in the high southern latitudes to explore not only the South Pacific but the South Atlantic and South Indian Oceans as well. The expedition was approved and in the summer of 1772 Cook set sail from England aboard the *Resolution*. For the next three years he was at sea, spending summers exploring the ice fields of Antarctica, the winters sailing from island to island in the South Pacific. Again he found no great continent and in July 1775 returned to England.

This time Cook's reception was very different from the one following the first voyage when Joseph Banks had been a member of the expedition and much of the attention had centered on him. Banks had been presented to the King at St. James Palace, and the newspapers were filled with stories of Mr. Banks, of his voyage, of his discoveries, and of his experiences in the South Seas. The naval lieutenant who had commanded the ship received little attention. He was so obscure that when the *Evening News* first noted the return of the *Endeavor* it had referred to him as Captain "Cooke." The Navy, too, had been cautious in rewarding him, for he was promoted not to the rank of captain, but only to commander which, in the British Navy of the time, was usually a dead end for a career officer.

Banks, after a disagreement with the admiralty, refused to go on the second voyage, so this time all the glory went to James Cook. Immediately upon his return he was promoted from commander to post-captain which moved him from a dead-end rank to one that placed him squarely on the path to an admiralty. The scientific community in England elected him a Fellow of the Royal Society, thus recognizing him as a full and equal member.

Cook was a prominent man and a popular prize at London dinner parties. One man he met during his now frequent excursions into London society was James Boswell. Once they had tea together in the gardens at Mile End; another time they had a long talk during dinner at the Mitre and later continued their talk over coffee at Brown's Coffee House. The conversation so inspired Boswell that he confided to his diary that he would be tempted to accompany Cook if, of course, he were "encouraged by Government by having a handsome pension for life." At another dinner Boswell saw Captain Cook and his wife, Elizabeth, and thought that together they made a rather strange appearance. He said, "It was curious to see Cook, a grave steady man, and his wife, a decent plump Englishwoman, and think that he is preparing to sail round the world." By then it was known that Cook was planning another voyage to the Pacific.

Leading a third expedition was a difficult decision for Cook. The captain's berth he had been given in 1775 was not aboard ship but at Greenwich Hospital, a sinecure with a good income, no pressing duties, and an office with a fine view of ships riding at anchor in the river. Therefore the admiralty assumed Cook would not be available and the new expedition would be commanded by Charles Clerke, his second lieutenant on the *Resolution* and a veteran of three earlier voyages into the Pacific. But the admiralty soon realized it was senseless not to use the talents of Captain James Cook, the most qualified man in the world to lead such an expedition. Cook apparently decided, too, that a sinecure such as he held was not for him—at least not at the age of forty-seven—and in February 1776 he volunteered to lead the expedition. Once again he would command the *Resolution,* while Charles Clerke would command the second ship, the *Discovery.*

The purpose of this new expedition was to solve a major geographical problem. Cook, on his second voyage, had conclusively destroyed the myth of a great habitable southern continent. Now he was being sent to prove, or disprove, the existence of another great unknown of eighteenth-century geography, the Northwest Passage. Since the discovery of America and the realization that it blocked the way to the Orient, the major European powers had been searching for a passage through the continent. After centuries of exploration, wishful thinking, misunderstanding, and outright lying, by now it was clear that such a passage, if it existed, must enter the Pacific somewhere on the northwest coast of America. Thus, Cook was to explore that coast and find, or not find, the legendary Northwest Passage.

As word of this mission circulated through the British Navy, several members of previous Cook expeditions stepped forward to volunteer, among them George Vancouver, who had served during the second voyage as a midshipman on the *Resolution.* He had first come aboard at the age of fourteen as a "young gentleman" and had to serve as such for two years before becoming eligible for the official rank of midshipman. He turned fifteen the day the ship sailed, and for the next three years he would spend each succeeding birthday at sea. On his sixteenth he was in the South Pacific several hundred miles from the nearest land, on his seventeenth he was at anchor off Niue Island, and on his eighteenth somewhere in the mid-Atlantic on his way home to England. By the time his nineteenth birthday arrived in 1776, he had volunteered for another voyage and was within a few weeks of sailing for the Pacific again. This time he would not be on Cook's flagship but on the *Discovery* where he would be a midshipman.

The sailing of the *Discovery,* however, was to be delayed, for in the summer of 1776, with both ships ready to leave, trouble developed in a totally unexpected quarter. Charles Clerke was thrown into debtor's prison not for money he owed but for having stood security for loans made his brother, Sir John Clerke, a captain in the Royal Navy. Sir John had escaped repaying the loans by taking a long voyage to the East Indies, but when his creditors discovered his brother was also about to sail for the Pacific, they had him brought before the King's Bench and imprisoned until the debts were paid. Not even pressure brought by influential friends, including Lord Sandwich, could change the Justices' order. Clerke was still confined in mid-July when Cook sailed from Plymouth after asking him to follow to the Cape of Good Hope as soon as he was free. A few weeks later Clerke, having somehow obtained his release, raced to Plymouth, went aboard the *Discovery,* and sailed for the Cape. By then, though, he was already suffering the first symptoms of tuberculosis, contracted during the weeks he had spent in the cold, damp, unhealthy King's Bench prison.

II

The *Resolution* and the *Discovery,* after being reunited at the Cape of Good Hope, remained there until the end of November, then sailed east across the Indian Ocean, dipped beneath Australia, and in late January 1777 touched at Tasmania. The following week they continued east and on February 12 dropped anchor in one of Cook's favorite sites, Queen Charlotte Sound on the northeastern tip of New Zealand's South Island. They spent two weeks there and in late February sailed into the South Pacific.

During the next several months Cook explored the Friendly Islands, stopping at Nomuka, Lifuka, Nomuka again, and finally to Tonga, the main island in the chain. Then the ships turned east toward the Society Islands, another of Cook's favorite calling places in the Pacific. They reached Tahiti in mid-August, stayed six weeks, moved over to Moorea for two weeks, then to Huahine for two more weeks, and finally in early November arrived at the island of Raiatea. Even before the ships were well into the bay, they were surrounded by a circle of canoes filled with natives, live hogs, and great piles of fruit. Soon, according to the surgeon's mate, "great Numbers of fine Girls came on board." Like Tahiti, Moorea, and Huahine, Raiatea was a tropical paradise with everything a man could want. But beyond it, the Pacific was unexplored; no one knew what might be found as the ship sailed north.

And so the desertions began. On the night of November 12 John Harrison, a marine detailed to guard the observatory on Raiatea, deserted and took his weapon with him. After several unsuccessful attempts to have him returned, Cook himself led a party to the other side of the island where Harrison was supposed to be hiding. He was there in a native house, in native dress, sitting between two women, with his musket lying in front of him. The two women pleaded for him, but Cook ordered them out and they burst into tears and left. Harrison had nothing to say for himself except that the women had lured him away. Cook apparently believed him, for he said, "the punishment I inflected upon him was not great." It wasn't, given the time and the place, although it seems brutal now. Harrison was given a dozen lashes on the 21st of November, another dozen on the 22nd.

There were no more desertions on board the *Resolution,* but a few days later two men were reported missing from Captain Clerke's *Discovery.* Clerke, ill with tuberculosis, went ashore with two armed boats and a party of marines but was unable to find the deserters, mainly, he thought, because the natives kept giving him false information about the direction of their flight. Cook ordered the seizure of three members of a chief's family to be held captive until the natives themselves returned the two men. Eventually, both were captured on the nearby island of Bora Bora and brought back to the *Discovery,* where they were kept in irons until it sailed.

The two ships left Raiatea on December 7, and seventeen days later they saw a small island lying to the north. The next day was Christmas and Cook, after anchoring, "dedicated this day to feasting and mirth." He also named the new discovery Christmas Island. Beyond the name and the festivities there was little that was happy about this barren island made of coral, sand, bird dung, brush, and four diseased coconut trees. But if the plant life was sparse, the island abounded in wildlife. There were huge numbers of birds—frigate birds, tropic birds, terns, curlews, and two different kinds of boobies. The ocean, too, was filled with fish, and boats from both ships were sent to catch them. It was not hard to obtain large amounts of red fish, although the lines were often carried away by the sharks that surrounded the boat and struck at the bait.

Cook and his company remained anchored off the island until just after the New Year when they again sailed north into the unexplored reaches of the Pacific. They continued to see large numbers of birds as well as sea turtles, taking this as a sign they were near land. They saw nothing until daybreak on the morning of January 18, 1778, when land was sighted to the northwest. It was the island of Oahu, but adverse winds kept them from approaching it. Soon the island of Kauai came into sight and they made for it instead. As they did so, canoes began pushing off from shore bringing sweet potatoes, fruit, and live hogs to the ship. Much to the delight of the crew they found that the inhabitants of these newly discovered islands were the same kind of people they had left behind in the Society Islands.

III

Cook's main task was to search for the Northwest Passage, and on February 2 he sailed from Hawaii bound for the coast of America. Five weeks later he caught sight of a point of land in such bad weather that he called it Cape Foulweather, a name it bears to this day. After a brief loop to the south he turned north to begin serious exploration. The weather was still so fierce that he was forced to push far out to sea, missing both the mouth of the Columbia River and the entrance to Juan de Fuca Strait. In late March he again put in toward the coast and on the 29th dropped anchor at Nootka Sound on Vancouver Island.

This was a far different world from the South Sea Islands, but once again canoes filled with natives wanting to trade surrounded the ships. Instead of sweet potatoes, hogs, and fruit, these people wanted to trade furs from what one of the Englishmen called a "sea beaver." The sailors, knowing they were headed into the far north, wanted the furs to keep them warm, but they had been so lavish in giving nails, hatchets, and other trade goods to the natives in the South Pacific they had little left. After some dickering they discovered the Indians of the northwest coast had little idea of the value either of the furs or of the things being offered by the white men. A piece of iron hoop was worth as much as a hatchet in Tahiti, an inch-long nail would buy as much as a foot-long nail there. Since the natives were also willing to take buttons in trade, the sailors stripped their clothes of them, and when they discovered the Indians wanted pieces of brass and copper, they began to knock apart their pans and teakettles.

During this trading Lieutenant James Burney noticed one of the Indians in a canoe alongside the *Discovery* offering two old-fashioned silver table spoons he had been wearing around his neck as an ornament. They were exchanged for a pewter wash basin and brought to Cook, who examined them and speculated on earlier explorations along this coast. According to the Indians, the spoons had come from Spaniards, but Cook was not sure, for in his journal he said, "there was no mark upon them and the shape was such as I had never seen any like them before."

The brief stay at Nootka Sound made a profound impression on John Ledyard, a young marine corporal on board the *Resolution*. Ledyard was an American, a native of Groton, Connecticut, who had spent much of his early life drifting from place to place and from occupation to occupation. He had worked for a short time in his uncle's law office but decided he "was adverse to that dull pursuit." He enrolled in the new Dartmouth College but soon dropped out, studied briefly for the ministry, gave that up and, like many another New Englander caught without a future, went to sea. In early 1775, however, life on board his ship was so bad that when it reached Falmouth, England, he jumped ship and went to Bristol, hoping to find something better. There he was arrested, thrown in jail, and given the choice of going aboard a ship bound for the coast of Guinea or entering the British Army. He chose the army as the lesser of two evils, and later was able to transfer to the marines with the rank of corporal. In that role, in July 1776 he was assigned to the marine complement sent to serve aboard the *Resolution*.

Thus far he had performed his duties well, although he had ambitions of being something more than a marine corporal. He suggested he be made expedition historian, although there was no such position, and had there been, virtually every literate man would have been his rival for the appointment. So rampant were literary ambitions among those on the expedition that both ships put out weekly newspapers which, when weather permitted, they exchanged. It was in the columns of the *Resolution*'s paper that Ledyard attempted to demonstrate his literary qualifications by writing a description of the manners of the Society Islanders. His effort has not survived, although James Burney later remembered it well enough to say that "his ideas were . . . too sentimental, and his language too florid."

Ledyard also kept a journal, which has survived, and his entry on Nootka Sound easily bears out Burney's criticism. He wrote, "It was the first time too that I had been so near the shores of that continent which gave me birth from the time I had first left it; and though more that two thousand miles distant from the nearest part of New-England I felt myself plainly affected: All the affectionate passions incident to natural attachments and early prejudices played round my heart, and indulged them because they were prejudices. It was harmonized by it. It soothed a home-sick heart, and rendered me very tolerably happy." Sentimental and flowery though he was, he could also be intelligent and enterprising, as he would soon prove to Captain Cook.

From Nootka Sound, Cook sailed north, turned west along the coast of Alaska, then north again through the Bering Strait and into the Arctic Ocean. The company entered the ice in bad weather, crossed the Arctic Circle, reached and passed 70° north latitude. Finally, on August 18, off Icy Cape, they had come as far as they could and Cook ordered the ships brought about. The two ships crossed over to the coast of Siberia and sailed south, passing through the Bering Strait again and anchoring off Unalaska Island in the Aleutians. Here an Indian came aboard the *Resolution* bringing a salmon baked in rye flour and a note in a language no one could read but which appeared to be Russian. Cook, hoping to obtain information, decided to have one of his men accompany the Indians to the Russian settlement, taking with him some rum and some wine to insure a proper welcome. The man he chose was Corporal John Ledyard, who had been among those volunteering for the mission.

Ledyard went with the Indians, walking the first day about fifteen miles and just before dark reached a village of some thirty huts where the people all crowded around him. Dinner was simple, consisting of dried fish supplied by the Indians, bread and liquor provided by Ledyard. At daylight they were off again, walking until mid-afternoon when they came to a large bay. The guide took all the baggage and pushed off in a canoe into the bay, abruptly leaving Ledyard to follow on foot around the edge. He feared he had been abandoned, but two Indians came along in a kayak to take him across the bay. The kayak had only two apertures for passengers and the only place for Ledyard was the space between them where he lay on his back, unable to see where he was going and incapable of extracting himself in an emergency. After an hour or so, he felt the kayak strike the beach and soon three or four men drew him out by the shoulders.

It was dark by now, but Ledyard could make out the huts of a village. This time there were white men—the Russians he had come to find. He had been on the way for two days and he was tired, wet, and cold. The Russians took him to a hut where they gave him fresh clothes, a blue silk shirt, drawers, boots, a gun, and a fur hat. Once he was warm and comfortable he brought out his presents and told them, as well as he could, that they were from "Commodore Cook, who was an Englishman." The Russians, in turn, somehow conveyed to him that they were subjects of the Empress Catherine. With the formalities out of the way, they brought out the food—boiled whale, broiled salmon, halibut fried in oil, and rye bread. While Ledyard ate, the Russians devoted most of their attention to the gift of rum "which they drank without any mixture or measure."

After dinner he crawled into a bed made of furs, both under and over him, and stayed awake long enough to watch the Russians lead the Indians in Greek Orthodox services. Then he slept until late the next morning when he was put through a most formidable test. First he was taken to a special hut for a steam bath and then he was conducted to breakfast. He was hungry, but somehow could not face the sea-lion, whale, or bear meat, all of which "produced a composition of smells very offensive at nine or ten o'clock in the morning." Unwilling to offend his hosts, he claimed the hot bath had made him ill, and asked for just a bit of dried salmon to eat with his own biscuits. He also managed to sneak a little of the brandy he had brought with him.

The following day Ledyard returned to the *Resolution* accompanied by three Russians. Cook described them as "well behaved intelligent men, and very ready to give me all the information I could desire." Communication was severely hampered by the language barrier, although Cook was able to obtain at least some vague geographical information. It did him little immediate good, however, for the northern winter was closing in and, a few weeks after this meeting, Cook sailed for Hawaii where he planned to spend the winter, then return to the north the following summer.

By late November, the two ships were within sight of both Maui and Hawaii, but they spent the next five weeks standing out to sea because of adverse winds. Finally, on January 17, 1779, both the *Resolution* and the *Discovery* dropped anchor in Kealakakua Bay on the island of Hawaii.

IV

Cook, as he went ashore on the island of Hawaii, seemed to cause an unusual stir among the natives. He had visited many Polynesian Islands before and had even landed at Kauai the previous year without attracting quite the same kind of attention he did on Hawaii. Now, whenever he went ashore, a priest rode in the bow of his pinnace waving a long wand and shouting a warning that Erono was coming, all of which caused the natives in the canoes to squat down and those on the beach to prostrate themselves. When Cook visited a house he was always put in what was clearly the place of honor, dressed in red cloth, and after a sacrificial pig was killed, ritually fed pork. And constantly there was the recurring chant of "Erono" whenever he approached.

Erono, or Rono—or more usually Lono—was a Hawaiian god. Unlike the terrible Ku, god of war and human sacrifice, Lono was the god of light, of peace, of abundance, and of the tilling of the earth. It had been prophesied that he would return bearing gifts, and the *Resolution* and the *Discovery* had arrived in such a way as to fulfill that prophecy. Thus Cook had become Lono. And although he was somewhat embarrassed by the adulation, he felt it necessary to honor the customs and for a few weeks to cooperate in the ceremonies.

Besides, it made for a pleasant stay. The carpenters, when they went on a timber-cutting expedition, were accompanied by natives who carried the heavy loads. Men interested in seeing the countryside were welcome everywhere, were fed, entertained, and allowed to watch anything from demonstrations of surfing to exhibitions of boxing and wrestling.

All this placed a severe strain on the natives, particularly since they were responsible for feeding the entire crews of both ships. Thus, in early February 1779 when the *Resolution* and the *Discovery* put to sea bound for the coast of America and another summer of exploration, the Hawaiians were happy to see them go. Then, a week later the ships returned. The *Resolution* had sprung a mast in a gale and there was nothing to do but to anchor somewhere and repair it. Cook was aware he had worn out his welcome at Kealakakua Bay and would have preferred to go elsewhere. Yet he did not want to take the time to search for a new anchorage and the only other place he knew in the Hawaiian Islands, Waimea Bay on Kauai, was too exposed. Reluctantly he returned to the former anchorage and immediately put the crews to work repairing the mast.

But it was not fast enough to avoid trouble. The natives were sullen, and although theft had always been somewhat of a problem, Captain Clerke thought it much worse than before. His ship, the *Discovery,* was especially plagued with pilferage, possibly because Cook—Lono—was aboard the *Resolution,* or possibly because Clerke, who was being steadily weakened by tuberculosis, ran a much looser ship. Most likely the reason was that the *Discovery* was anchored closer to shore. Whatever the cause, Clerke had continual trouble. Not long after the ship anchored in Kealakakua Bay, a native stole the armorer's tongs and when he was identified, seized up in the rigging, given forty lashes and left hanging there until the tongs were returned. They were brought back within half an hour.

Those tongs seemed to have a fatal attraction for the natives. On the afternoon of February 13 Captain Clerke was entertaining Parea, a friendly Hawaiian chief, in his cabin, while most of the crew under the direction of sailing master Thomas Edgar was on deck working on the ship's masts and rigging. Despite the crowd, which included Midshipman Vancouver, a native suddenly ran to the forge, grabbed the tongs and a chisel and, before anyone could react, dove overboard. Immediately the canoe that had brought Chief Parea picked him up and headed for shore. Captain Clerke, hearing the commotion, rushed on deck and ordered muskets fired at the departing canoe, but it was already well out of range. He ordered Edgar to take Vancouver and two sailors and pursue the thief in the ship's cutter. In the rush to take up the chase they did not stop to obtain firearms. The canoe with the thief on board moved so rapidly that before the cutter carrying Edgar and Vancouver could reach shore it met another canoe bringing back not only the stolen tongs and chisel but also the lid from a water cask which no one had even missed.

The incident should have ended there, but the pursuit had set off a chain reaction that could not be brought to an immediate halt. When the chase began, the *Resolution*'s pinnace was also in the water, just off the beach waiting for Captain Cook who had previously gone ashore. Seeing the cutter in pursuit of a canoe, those in the pinnace also took up the chase, and Edgar, made bold by their support, decided that recovering the stolen goods was not enough. Instead, as punishment, he would confiscate the thief's canoe. He and Vancouver jumped ashore and began dragging it into the water.

The canoe actually belonged to the chief Parea, who had come ashore in another boat after promising Clerke he would see that all the stolen items were returned. That had been accomplished, and he objected to having his canoe taken. He grabbed Edgar and began struggling with him, at which time one of the pinnace's crew members hit him over the head with an oar. By now a large crowd of Hawaiians gathered on the beach and began to throw stones at the white men. The crew members of the pinnace, which had been beached, quickly swam out to the cutter lying offshore out of range of the stone-throwers.

Edgar was unable to leave because he could not swim. Standing on a rock, up to his knees in water, he saw a native coming at him with a broken oar clearly intending to knock him into the water. Suddenly Midshipman Vancouver, who had stayed with him, jumped in front of Edgar and took the blow, was hit in the side and knocked down. The crowd swarmed forward and began beating both men. Their lives were saved only by the intervention of Parea who managed to get control of his people. He told the two white men to get in the pinnace and leave the beach as quickly as possible. But all the oars had been stolen, and Parea went to find them. As soon as he was gone, the mob began throwing rocks again. Edgar, still fearing the sea, decided to go ashore to look for Captain Cook even though it meant fighting his way through a hostile mob. This time Vancouver refused to accompany him, and was left alone with the beached pinnace.

As soon as Edgar left, the Hawaiians attacked Vancouver, pushing him aside, knocking him down to get at the boat, which they began to ransack. They were in the process of pulling the ring bolts out of the bow and stern when Edgar returned. Being unable to find Cook, he had found Parea who had recovered the oars and Edgar and Vancouver were able to get the pinnace off the beach and rejoin the cutter. Some time later a canoe bearing Parea caught up with them and returned Midshipman Vancouver's cap which had been knocked off during the struggle.

While Edgar and Vancouver were being jostled by the mob, Cook was also having trouble. He had been ashore when he heard the muskets being fired from the *Discovery* and saw the canoe racing for shore. With Lieutenant King and a marine he had run down to the beach to intercept it but he was too late. Ignorant of exactly what had happened, and misled by the natives, Cook tried to follow the thief but was taken on a wild-goose chase which finally ended with the marine threatening to shoot into a crowd of jeering natives—hardly the respect due Lono—and Cook was forced to beat an embarrassing retreat to the ships. All this occurred on February 13, 1779. The next morning, at daybreak, when Lieutenant Burney took over as officer of the watch, he discovered that the *Discovery*'s cutter had been stolen. Since the cutter was absolutely essential for exploring the coast of America, Cook sent a squad of marines ashore to take a native chief hostage and hold him until the cutter was returned.

Although the official records say nothing, both John Ledyard and James Burney later claimed that originally Clerke was to have led this party, but was too ill to do so. Whatever the reason, Cook decided personally to lead the detachment of marines consisting of Lieutenant Molesworth Phillips, Sergeant Samuel Gibson, Corporal James Thomas, and seven privates. The *Resolution*'s other marine corporal, John Ledyard, was stationed ashore with another band of marines that morning and saw nothing of the day's events. George Vancouver, undoubtedly still aching from the previous day's adventures, remained aboard the *Discovery,* as did James Burney for he was officer of the watch and commander of the ship whenever Captain Clerke left to consult with those on board the *Resolution.*

Since none of these men went ashore, their knowledge of what happened was based mainly on what they heard from eye-witnesses, particularly Lieutenant Phillips. Later, Phillips would tell how they arrived peacefully enough at the chief's hut; how he readily agreed to accompany them to the *Resolution;* how his two sons raced ahead and leaped aboard the pinnace in anticipation of the visit; and how when they reached the water his wife and two men began arguing with him. It was then, Phillips said, that the chief suddenly "appeared dejected and frightened," as if he had been told he would be killed. By now another mob had formed, and Phillips heard Cook say, "we can never think of compelling him to go aboard the ship without killing a number of these People." At this point Phillips thought Cook was about to order a return to the ship when a native threatened him with a dagger and he fired a barrel of small shot which hit but did not damage the woven mat a warrior was using as a shield. With that, everything broke loose and Phillips remembered little beyond his own danger. A native tried to stab him, and as Phillips hit him with the butt end of his musket, the stones began to fly. In the confusion he saw Cook fire at a native who went down and heard him order the marines to open fire. Then, just as Cook yelled, "Take to the boats," Phillips was knocked down and he saw no more of his commander.

On the deck of the *Discovery,* Lieutenant Burney was watching through the telescope, and he saw Cook receive a blow from a club and fall into the water. With that, the marines, who had never been very well disciplined, began fleeing toward the boats to save their lives. Their commander, Lieutenant Phillips, "scrambled as well as I could into the water and made for the Pinnace . . ." He made it, but Captain Cook and four of Phillips' marines—Corporal Thomas and Privates Theophilus Hinks, John Allen, and Thomas Fatchett—did not. All were killed on the beach at Kealakakua Bay. Later, official reports would laud Phillips for his bravery that day, but his precipitous retreat and that of his men would win him the undying contempt of sailing master William Bligh of the *Resolution.*

Like the rest of those who remained aboard the *Discovery,* George Vancouver had seen all of this only at a distance. Late that afternoon, however, he again became directly involved when he accompanied Lieutenant James King of the *Resolution* ashore to recover the bodies. A few stones were thrown as they approached the shore, but most of the natives honored their flag of truce. One of the chiefs, a man who had spent much time abroad the *Discovery,* recognized Vancouver and began to talk. He said that Cook's body had been taken a long way across the hills and that it could not be brought back until the next day. Faced with this impasse and unsure of how to proceed, King sent Vancouver to Captain Clerke, now in command of the expedition. Soon Vancouver was back with orders for King to return to the ship, but only after telling the Hawaiians that if the body was not brought the next morning their town and all the people in it would be destroyed. Apparently not every Hawaiian was impressed by the threat, for as King's boat rowed away one man turned his backside to them in a sign of contempt. It made King angry, and he raised his musket to fire but stopped when another crew member pointed out it would be ill-advised to set off another riot because of one man's actions.

The Hawaiians did not immediately make good their promise to return the body, but on the afternoon of February 19 a procession came down the hill toward the beach. The people in it were beating drums, uttering loud cries, carrying flags, and bearing gifts—hogs, fruit, and other food. In the lead was a chief with a package "decently wrap'd up" and covered with a black and white feather cloak. When it was opened in the cabin of the *Resolution* it was found to contain the skull, the leg bones, thigh bones, and arm bones of Captain Cook. In accordance with Hawaiian custom, all had been stripped of their flesh except the hands which had been cut and the gashes filled with salt to preserve them. Cook's body had been returned, and two days later, on the evening of February 22, it was "committed to the deep with all the attention and honour we could possibly give it in this part of the World." The next day, the *Discovery* and the *Resolution,* its mast now repaired, sailed out of Kealakakua Bay.

V

On January 10, 1780, letters left by Captain Clerke with the Russians at Petropavlask on the Pacific Coast of Siberia reached London. They were opened by the Earl of Sandwich, First Lord of the Admiralty, who immediately forwarded them to King George III. The most important news—the only thing Lord Sandwich mentioned in his cover letter to the King—was that Captain Cook had been "massacred by the Natives of a new discovered island." The same day, in a less formal, more personal note, he also notified Sir Joseph Banks that "poor Captain Cook is no more."

The news soon appeared in London papers, and on January 15, James Boswell noted in his diary, "Was much affected with reading tonight in the *London Chronicle* that the celebrated Captain Cook was killed." Another person who heard the news was the novelist Fanny Burney, who wrote to a friend to say, "How hard, after so many dangers, so much toil—to die in so shocking a manner—in an island he had himself discovered."

A few months later another piece of news arrived. This time Miss Burney wrote, "Poor Captain Clerke is dead! I was willing to doubt it as long as possible, but it has been confirmed to my father by Lord Sandwich." Lord Sandwich also informed her father that Cook's journal had arrived and was in the hands of the King. Hearing this, Fanny, like everyone else in England, was "very impatient to know something of its contents."

Fanny Burney had more than a passing interest in all this, for the deaths, shocking as they were, brought advancement to her brother James. One rumor reaching the family was that he had taken command of the *Discovery*. It turned out to be false, for upon Cook's death, Clerke had moved to the *Resolution* and its first lieutenant, John Gore, had taken command of the *Discovery*. Then when Charles Clerke succumbed to tuberculosis on the cold Siberian coast, Gore had gone back to the *Resolution* as captain and commander of the entire expedition while James King took command of the *Discovery*. That move also made James Burney first lieutenant aboard the *Resolution* and third-ranking officer of the expedition.

By then it was time to go home. Cook had been sent out to discover the Northwest Passage and, it was hoped, to use it to return to England. If he failed to find it, he was to use his own judgment, and Gore, who had inherited these orders, decided to sail southward, investigate the Kurile Islands and the coast of Japan, then call at Canton, China, for supplies before sailing home. Bad weather kept the company from catching more than a few glimpses of either the Kuriles or Japan, but in early December Canton was finally reached. The *Resolution* stayed for six weeks while the rigging and caulking were overhauled. At least one crew member thought the whole stay was both "tedious and unnecessary."

There was one advantage. The sea-otter furs obtained on the coast of America were sold, and the Chinese, very anxious to obtain furs, "gave us from 50 to 70 dollars a skin . . . for what we bought for only a hatchet or a Saw." A little later two sailors from the *Resolution* stole the ship's cutter and deserted, presumably hoping to make a fortune in the fur trade. Although no one else deserted, these two were not alone in their dreams of striking it rich as fur merchants. Lieutenant King said, "The rage with which our seamen were possessed to return to Cook's River and buy another cargo of skins, to make their fortunes, at one time, was not far short of mutiny."

The officers kept control, however, and in mid-January the two ships sailed for home. By April they had rounded the Cape of Good Hope and entered the Atlantic where, almost immediately, they encountered gale winds that drove them far off course. Thus it was not until August that the *Resolution* and the *Discovery* approached the English Channel. Then the wind shifted against them and they were forced to stand to the north along the west coast of Ireland. At first Captain Gore intended to put in at Galway, but the wind was such that he had to give up. The two companies continued north until August 21 when they sighted the Orkney Islands north of Scotland where, the next day, they put into the harbor at Stromness. Here they were delayed a full month.

After four years at sea this was a frustrating experience, particularly for the young officers. War had broken out and while "a constant foul wind" kept them confined at Stromness, other young officers were making wartime reputations that would bring rapid promotion. But "the wind at last came fair," and on September 20 both ships sailed from Stromness. Since Lieutenant King, captain of the *Discovery*, had been sent ahead to London, James Burney, at long last, was placed in command of the ship for the final leg of the voyage home. It was for the briefest of times, however, for two weeks later, on October 6, 1780, the Friday edition of *New Lloyd's List* of shipping activities took notice of their homecoming. Midway down the list of ships arriving at Gravesend from the West Indies, Hamburg, Archangel, and Aberdeen, were the *Resolution*, commanded by Gore, and the *Discovery*, commanded by Burney, arriving from "round the world." It was a prosaic ending to Captain Cook's last voyage.

VI

Officially, the news Cook's third expedition brought back was slow in spreading through England. The task of editing the official journals was given to Dr. John Douglas, Canon of Windsor and St. Paul's. It was not new to him, for he had also edited the journals of Cook's earlier voyages. Still, the third voyage had been particularly long and involved and the editing would take almost as long as the voyage itself. It was not until 1784 that the official publication appeared.

Unofficially, however, the news spread rapidly. As soon as the two ships anchored in the Thames, the *Resolution* at Deptford, the *Discovery* at Woolwich, people began swarming aboard. Collectors came looking for birdskins, dried plants, and other curiosities, while booksellers came searching for any kind of publishable journal or diary. Eager sightseers and friends of the men came for a tour of the ships that had spent the last four years in distant lands.

Officers and sailors were paid off and went their separate ways to spread tales and legends of the South Seas, of Hawaii, of the northwest coast of America, of the Arctic, of Kamchatka, and of China. Wherever they went—to the drawing rooms of London society or to the sailors' bars on the waterfront—they took with them the same stories. Much in demand was the story of Captain Cook's death. Few of those on either ship had actually been on the beach when he was killed, but they were close, and undoubtedly by the time they reached

England the fine line between seeing and almost seeing had disappeared. Beyond that, like men everywhere, they would have forgotten the bad times and remembered mostly the exotic islands, the clear beautiful weather, and the brown, willing women. Some, too, undoubtedly remembered the sea-otter furs that had been purchased so cheaply in America and sold at enormous profits in Canton.

It was the news of these profits that caused the biggest stir in the London business world, particularly in the offices of Richard Cadmon Etches of 38 Fenchurch Street. It was appropriate that the excitement start here, for the company sat in the midst of what had been, almost since time immemorial, the center of the London trading world. Off to the south along the Thames was the site of the Steelyard where in medieval times traders from Northern Europe had congregated. Their power had long since declined, and they had been replaced by southern Europeans whose homeland had given its name to Lombard Street, the western extension of Fenchurch. On Lombard Street, at the corner of Abschurch, Edward Lloyd had opened a coffee house that quickly became a favorite gathering place for merchants and shipowners. The marine insurance company that first began in Lloyd's coffee house had, by now, moved to offices a few blocks away on Fenchurch. But Lloyd's shipping list was still published here and could be picked up each Tuesday and Friday at James Phillips's print shop on Lombard Street.

Etches' offices in London's historic trading center were in the heart of the contemporary financial world of the 1780's. The district was filled with small banking houses dominated by the huge Bank of England building on Threadneedle Street. Just as prominent were the large number of trading firms that looked to all parts of the world for their livelihood. Dominating them in a small way was the South Sea Company, which did business from offices at the end of Threadneedle Street where it entered Bishopgate. A much more powerful force in the world of London traders was the East India Company whose trading house on Leadenhall Street virtually backed up to the offices of Richard Cadmon Etches.

In May 1785, in his offices on Fenchurch Street, Etches gathered several London traders to form the King George's Sound Company for the purpose of trading on the northwest coast of America. There was more to it than simply forming a company and raising money to send ships to the Pacific Northwest. At the time, the South Sea Company had a monopoly over trade in the Pacific and although it did no business there itself, it could prevent anyone else from doing so. Still, the company was willing to issue a license for a fee, and Etches was able to obtain one with little trouble.

But there were more difficulties, for the major market for furs obtained in America was China, where the monopoly was held by the East India Company, a powerful organization actively involved in trading. And although it was willing to grant a license, more than payment of a fee was required. It demanded conformity to stringent rules, laid down to protect the monopoly, which spelled out the routes the Etches ships could follow, the ports they could visit, the goods they could trade, and even insisted that all furs obtained in America be sold to the East India Company at "a fair price." To make certain the rules were obeyed, Etches and the King George's Sound Company were required to post a £20,000 bond at the time the license was granted.

Having formed a company, raised the money, and obtained the necessary licenses, Etches and his colleagues began planning the expedition itself. Since the whole plan was based on the report of Cook's third voyage, they purchased two ships of the size Cook had recommended as the best for sailing along the little-known coasts of the Pacific. They also hired two veterans of Cook's third voyage to captain the ships. Nathaniel Portlock, who had been master's mate aboard the *Discovery,* would be captain of the larger 320-ton ship *King George* as well as commander of the entire expedition. George Dixon, onetime armorer on the *Discovery,* would command the smaller 200-ton *Queen Charlotte.*

In late August 1785 the two ships sailed, first for Spithead, where they took on more stores, then to the Isle of Guernsey for another brief stop. On Monday morning, September 26, they cleared Guernsey Road and sailed south toward Cape Horn and the Pacific.

VII

For a man like Richard Cadmon Etches there are certain advantages in having an office at 38 Fenchurch Street in the heart of London's financial district. Sometimes, however, it can be a disadvantage to be in the midst of the established world, for while there, one tends to follow the crowd, to obey all the rules. Certainly Etches had done so by carefully forming a company, inviting prominent London merchants to invest in it, and obtaining the necessary licenses from the proper companies. All these preparations took time, and while he was making them, some men in China, far removed from the formal rules of London business, had already opened trade with the northwest coast of America.

They were led by John Henry Cox, who had arrived in Canton in 1781. Originally he was from London where his father ran an export business that specialized in "singsongs," a pidgin term for clocks, watches, and fantastically shaped mechanical toys, such as a jeweled bird that sang when the lid of its cage was opened. Most of these musical toys, highly popular in China, were manufactured in Birmingham and sent to the Orient by London suppliers, one of whom was John Cox of Shoe Lane. Upon his death his son obtained permission from the East India Company to go to Canton to sell the remainder of his father's stock.

At first there was no problem, for Cox and his singsongs were not in direct competition with the Company. But many of his Chinese customers were insolvent, and instead of paying cash they gave him trade goods. That put him in competition with the Company, and dispatches came from London ordering his expulsion. Cox asked that he be allowed to remain one more year, and East India officials in China agreed, "as he has always conducted himself with great propriety."

There was another reason why company officials in Canton were willing to allow Cox to stay. The monopoly applied not only to outsiders but also to East India Company employees who were expected to devote themselves solely to Company business and not to trade on their own. Cox, however, formed a company through which East India personnel could trade for their own benefit, and with their backing he purchased two ships for the import of cotton and opium from India. Cox also heard, while in China, how the crew members of Cook's ships had sold their sea-otter furs in Canton at a substanial profit. In 1785, again with the backing of several friends connected with the Company, he purchased a 60-ton ship, the *Harmon,* and sent it to the coast of America to gather sea-otter furs. Unlike Etches he did not bother with the formality of obtaining a license.

The man Cox hired to command the ship was James Hanna, of whom nothing is known before he appeared in early 1785 in Macao, the Portuguese colony and longtime smugglers' paradise on the coast of China. Whoever he was, wherever he came from, being chosen captain indicates some experience as a sailor in the China Sea. He also had a reputation as a man who could handle the unexpected, for he was being trusted to take a small ship, barely the size of an Indian canoe, with just twenty men, to cross an unknown ocean and to trade with savages on an unexplored coast.

The *Harmon* sailed from Macao in April 1785 at a time of year when the northeast monsoon, blowing against ships bound from China into the Pacific, was beginning to die. This year it apparently lingered, for progress was very slow at first. By late May the ship was no farther along than the coast of China near Amoy where Hanna put into a small bay to obtain supplies. He was able to purchase water and some fresh fish and fowl, but at great expense, for the inhabitants, he said, were "exorbitant and thievish." The seasons had changed, the southwest monsoon was pushing the ship, and by June it was off the coast of Japan where its crew watched an active volcano which rumbled like a distant cannonade and spewed repeated clouds of black smoke that left the ship covered with a layer of ash that looked like lampblack.

The ship turned northwest and began its slow crossing of the Pacific and by the end of July was approaching the coast of America. The weather was warm, the sea was calm, and the winds were moderate, but for several weeks it had been so foggy that they had not seen, day or night, a sky clear enough to make observations. On August 3 Captain Hanna himself saw tree trunks floating in the water and assumed that land was near. Not until five days later, however, did they see the land which, Hanna said, appeared to be filled with bays or rivers. They were on the northwest coast of America and the next day the *Harmon* dropped anchor off Nootka Sound. Captain Hanna took time to write in his journal, "At nine o'clock in the evening three canoes approached; as the night was dark, the arms were got up. And they hallowed at a distance 'Maakook'—this was asking to trade. We soon got them alongside."

Here Hanna's journal ends abruptly, quite likely because after this he had little time to reflect or write. There is no firsthand version of what followed, although later visitors among the Nootka Indians heard enough stories that they could piece together an account of this first trading venture and of the fight that occurred.

Hanna and his crew on the *Harmon* were not the first white men these Indians had ever seen. The Spanish had been there in 1774, and Cook and his two ships had anchored in the same bay four years later. Both of those expeditions had come in relatively large ships manned by sizable crews, there had been no clashes, and no one had felt it necessary to fire a gun. Thus the Indians knew nothing of the white man's firearms. Now, however, Hanna arrived with only twenty men in a ship scarcely longer than one of their own canoes, and the Indians tried to force their way aboard in broad daylight. Hanna and his crews opened fire and repulsed the Indians with "considerable slaughter." That victory, plus the fact that once the battle was over Hanna treated the wounded as best he could, won him new respect and for the rest of his stay the Indians traded peaceably.

One Indian, however, was left with lingering scars, both physical and psychological. His name was Maquinna, and like the rest of the Nootkas, this was not the first time he had seen white men. He had been just a boy back in 1774 when the Spanish first came, but he remembered well enough to confirm several stories told by the Spaniards. He remembered being given shells by the pilot of the ship, Esteban Martinez, and he remembered how one Indian had stolen two silver spoons from the ship. Certainly he also remembered how Martinez had thrown a shell into a canoe and hit an Indian on the head, for the victim was Maquinna's own brother. Later he had been among those who had gone aboard Cook's ships to trade while they were anchored at Nootka Sound.

Now, seven years later, Maquinna was a chief and in that capacity he was invited to come aboard the *Harmon* and receive the salute reserved for someone as honored and important as he. He was seated in a chair under which a sailor placed a pile of what Maquinna thought was black sand. The sailor also laid down a thin train of the sand which, again, Maquinna assumed had something to do with the honor he was to receive. When the sailor touched a match to the train, it exploded into flames which raced to the pile of gunpowder under the chair and Maquinna, as he would later complain to a visitor, "was thrown into the air with his bottom burned." As proof he would lift up his robes and show the scars still visible years later. Faced with the white man's firearms, and gunpowder, there was little chance of successful retaliation, and trading went on without incident.

When the weather turned bad in September, Hanna sailed for China. By December he was back in Macao where he and the man who had financed him, John Henry Cox, were able to sell the furs he had obtained for $20,000. The trip had been enormously successful and he and Cox immediately began to plan another voyage.

VIII

In early 1786, when James Hanna had already been to America, returned, sold his furs, and was planning another trip, the two ships sent out from London had not even reached the Pacific. Just after New Years's the *King George* and the *Queen Charlotte* arrived at the Falkland Islands in the South Atlantic where they remained until late January, when they finally sailed, rounded the cape, and set their course for Hawaii.

Reaching Kealakakua Bay in late May, they were the first Europeans to arrive since Cook's ships had left seven years before. Both Captain Portlock and Captain Dixon were veterans of that earlier voyage, and remembering the events that led to Cook's death, they were tense as they entered the bay. So, too, were the natives who showed signs they thought this expedition had come for revenge. Still, they were willing to trade, and Portlock allowed them to come aboard the ships. Since there were still many signs of tension, he refused to allow his men to go ashore, and within a few weeks both ships sailed for the coast of America.

In mid-July the men on the *King George* and *Queen Charlotte,* sailing through thick, foggy weather, noticed a change in the color of the ocean. They began sounding, and early on the morning of the 16th struck bottom in seventy fathoms of water. By evening the fog had dispersed and there before them, extending from north by east to west by north, lay the coast of America. Three days later, just off the entrance to Cook Inlet in Alaska, they were startled by the boom of a large gun on shore. It was too foggy to see where the sound came from, but they fired their own gun and heard an answering report. Clearly, some other European power had beaten them to this point, and soon a boat came rowing out to meet them. When the occupants came on board the *King George,* Portlock saw they were Russians.

No one on either of the English ships spoke Russian. Communication was difficult although Portlock was able to establish that his visitors had left their ship on Kodiak Island and crossed to the mainland in canoes. The two parties cooperated in finding a safe anchorage, after which the Russian commander presented Portlock with enough salmon to supply both ships for a day. Portlock gave them some yams, some beef and pork, and a few bottles of brandy. They were happy to receive the gifts, although Portlock noticed that, "contrary to Russian custom," they did not get drunk on the brandy. The reason, he thought, was not a dislike of liquor but a fear that while drunk they might be attacked by Indians. They were in a dangerous business, and one of Portlock's mates who visited their camp said that they were constantly on the alert and that each Russian slept with his rifle under his arm and his knife and cutlass by his side.

For the Englishmen it was a pleasant visit, except that they had come to trade and, unfortunately, the Russians had already stripped the area of fur. Portlock decided to move elsewhere, although bad weather kept his ships anchored in Cook Inlet for several more days. They were unable to sail until mid-August, and two weeks later, when they reached Prince William Sound, the weather was again so bad they could not enter. Faced with this obstacle Portlock gave up the attempt to trade on the Alaskan Coast, at least for the season, and sailed south where he hoped he might find better weather. It was a false hope, for the weather continued bad throughout the next month as they worked their way down the coast as far as Nootka Sound. At the end of September Portlock decided their efforts were hopeless and ordered both ships to sail for Hawaii where they would spend the winter.

Five weeks later they reached the island of Hawaii, but adverse winds and the memory of earlier times kept them from entering Kealakakua Bay. Instead, both ships continued on past Molokai and Maui, and on the last day of November dropped anchor in Maunalua Bay on the south coast of Oahu, just under Koko Head. Here they stayed for three weeks, then moved west, where they spent the rest of the winter refitting, sometimes at Waimea Bay on Kauai, at other times at Yam Bay on Niihau.

The crews spent much of their time repairing the ship, butchering hogs, curing pork, and stowing away as much of the island produce as possible. Each man also had a native woman who in the evening would come aboard calling out the name of her man. She would spend the night, then return ashore the next day. Almost everyone on board had a woman, but it was the ship's gunner who outdid the rest. He chose what one man described as "the fattest woman I ever saw in my life. . . . We were forced to hoist her on board; her thighs were as thick as my waist; no hammock in the ship would hold her." As might be expected, the gunner and the fat lady were the butt of many a joke.

There was other entertainment as well. Once, several of the crew from the *King George* took their allowance of brandy ashore and spent a delightful afternoon. Hawaiian women danced while the men demonstrated their spear-throwing ability. Behind each man stood a woman who handed him spears, allowing him to keep up a continual barrage. The natives were so agile they assumed that the slowness and clumsiness of the white men was caused by some ailment like rheumatism. The Hawaiians also demonstrated their wrestling skills and occasionally a sailor tried to join in, but "the stoutest man in our ship could not stand a single throw with the least chance of success."

All in all, as sailor life went in the eighteenth century, it was not bad duty, but the long, easy winter ended in March 1787 when the two ships again sailed for America. By late April they had reached the coast of Alaska where they entered Prince William Sound and dropped anchor. They began trading with the Indians who, much to their confusion, kept saying the word *Nootka* and pointing up the Sound. Investigating, Captain Dixon found a small ship, the *Nootka,* still frozen fast in the ice at the edge of Prince William Sound. When he went aboard he found it was commanded by John Meares, a former British naval officer.

IX

When John Meares sailed in the *Nootka* from the Bengal Coast of India in February 1786, he was another of those not quite legitimate traders looking to America. By then John Henry Cox, having made large profits from the voyage of the *Harmon,* had sent Hanna back across the Pacific for another cargo of fur. He had also used his influence among East India Company officials in India to organize the Bengal Fur Company, which would finance the expedition of the *Nootka* from Calcutta to the northwest coast. To command the ship, he hired John Meares who, like so many other naval officers, had become a commander of merchant ships after the war ended in 1783. As such he had come to India where he was hired as captain of the *Nootka.*

Meares, after the long voyage from the Orient, reached the coast of Alaska in August 1786 and anchored in Cook Inlet. He had little success trading, however, for the Russians, as well as Portlock and Dixon who had been there a few weeks before, had taken all the fur. He continued on to Prince William Sound where again he had little success. By now it was late September, the weather was bad and it promised to get worse, for the near-arctic winter was rapidly approaching. Momentarily, Meares thought of wintering in Hawaii, but his sailors were already discontented, and he was afraid that if he left he could never force them to go back to America. Therefore, he decided to spend the winter in Alaska.

In early October he brought the ship well up into Prince William Sound, unrigged it, and sent the crew ashore to build a house. Indians began to arrive in such large numbers they frightened the sailors, but Meares was able to keep control by firing a shot from the ship's cannon to impress the natives with his power. Other problems were not so easily solved. The temperature dropped below freezing and snow fell almost constantly, becoming so deep it was difficult to get around. The Sound had also begun to freeze, making it possible for the Indians to walk out to the ship. Adding to the bitter cold and the fear was the almost constant darkness, for by December there was only a "very faint and glimmering light" even at noon.

Scurvy appeared, and by the end of January four men had died, another twenty-three were confined to their beds, including the extremely ill ship's surgeon. The first mate, however, after realizing he had a mild case of scurvy, got rid of it by continually chewing on young pine branches and swallowing the juice. Unfortunately it tasted so bad that few of the others were willing to follow suit.

The cold remained through the months of March and April and crew members continued to die of scurvy. Among them was the surgeon and once he was gone there was no medical aid. The only ones capable of functioning were Meares, his first mate, still persisting in his pine-tree remedy, and a sailor who had not been affected. They tried to care for those who were ill and they also had to bury the dead. Later Meares said, "Too often did I find myself called to assist in performing the dreadful office, of dragging the dead bodies across the ice, to a shallow sepulchre which our own hands had hewn out on the shore. The sledge on which we fetched the wood was their hearse, the chasms in the ice their grave."

It was in this distressing condition that Captain Dixon of the *Queen Charlotte* found Meares and his men in the spring of 1787. Soon rumors began to circulate that it was not just scurvy that caused the trouble. Aboard the *King George* one man heard that "they had caused their own distress, by their inordinate use of spirits on Christmas eve. They could not bury their own dead; they were only dragged a short distance from the ship and left upon the ice." Others, too, would charge that most of the difficulty came from overindulgence in liquor, although Meares bitterly denied it, claiming that he allowed his crew only "a half a pint a day per man . . . half in its raw state and the other half in water."

The immediate problem was not what caused it but that Meares and his crew were in a disastrous condition and badly needed help. Portlock provided them with flour, sugar, molasses, brandy, and whatever else he could spare from the *King George*. He also assigned two members of his crew to help sail the *Nootka* to Hawaii. Yet Meares was outraged and later complained bitterly that Portlock had demanded, as the price of his assistance, that Meares leave the northwest coast immediately. Portlock felt he was entirely within his rights, for he was the representative of a company that had obtained all the proper licenses to trade in the area. To him Meares, who was flying the British flag but had no license from either the South Sea Company or the East India Company, was nothing but a poacher. Therefore he demanded that Meares sign a £500 bond which would be forfeited if he continued to trade on the coast. Meares concurred and soon afterward left the coast of America to the *King George* and *Queen Charlotte*.

X

Already those who read Captain Cook's *Journals* and dreamed of finding the easy road to great wealth were becoming disillusioned. No matter which way they turned they found difficulties. John Meares, when discovered on the coast of America without a license, had been forced to leave under bond not to return. Etches, on the other hand, had obtained a license only to find its provisions so restrictive that he could make little profit. Even John Henry Cox, although he had made considerable money from Hanna's voyages, was beginning to run into trouble because of the disguises he used for illicit business purposes.

East India Company officials had tired of Cox's private trading and forced him to leave Canton. But his business continued to flourish under his partner Daniel Beale, who was allowed to remain for, although he was an Englishman, technically he was not a British subject. On his way out to China, he had stopped in Prussia where, for a price, he had obtained documents naming him the Prussian consul in Canton. As such he was able to operate free of the restrictions of the East India Company.

This was only one of the disguises used by Cox and Beale. They also obtained an English ship, the *Loudon,* hired Charles Barkley, a veteran East India Company sea captain, and sent him across the English Channel to Ostend, then a part of the Austrian Empire. There, re-named the *Imperial Eagle* and re-registered under the Austrian flag, the ship became the official vessel of the Austrian East India Company, consisting of Cox and Beale as well as several East India Company employees who were privately backing them.

Barkley, flying the Austrian flag, had sailed to the coast of America where he had done quite well. Upon his return he sold furs in

Macao, took on a cargo for Mauritius, then returned to Calcutta where he expected to be enthusiastically welcomed by those who had sent him out. Instead, he found them thoroughly frightened. East India Company officials were irritated at the frequent practice of dodging regulations by flying fake flags, particularly of countries such as Austria and Prussia, which had no possessions in the Pacific. They had begun to crack down, and to avoid trouble those who had invested in the *Imperial Eagle* sold it out from under Barkley. Everything was taken, including his nautical instruments and the charts he had made of the northwest coast which soon found their way into the hands of John Meares.

To Meares also came Barkley's former associates Cox, Beale, and the East India Company employees who in their panic had abandoned him. Under the direction of Meares they organized a new company, the Merchant Associates, and raised enough money to purchase and outfit two ships to send to America. Joining them was Richard Cadmon Etches, who apparently was tired of obeying the rules and applying for licenses that seriously cut into his profits.

This time, hoping to do a better job of disguising the nationality, they registered the ships in Macao under a dummy Portuguese owner and even hired nominal Portuguese captains and provided them with instructions written in Portuguese. All this was for show, however, for John Meares himself was the captain of one ship while another Englishman, William Douglas, was captain of the other. And they were carrying secret orders, written in English, that outlined the true purpose of the voyage—to trade on the northwest coast of America.

XI

Seemingly, on the morning of July 2, 1789, Esteban Jose Martinez, captain of the Spanish warship *Princesa* at anchor in Nootka Sound, could breathe a sigh of relief. Just after daylight the English ship *Princess Royal* had been towed out of the Sound to catch the wind that would take it out to sea and away from the coast of America. Finally, after months of constant harassment, Martinez was free of the English ships that, he believed, were poaching in Spanish territory.

When he sailed from Mexico the previous February, he was carrying orders to explore the northwest coast and to occupy Nootka Sound to keep what was considered the only decent bay north of San Francisco from falling into the hands of foreigners. The Spanish felt they had a legitimate claim to the Sound, for Juan Perez in the *Santiago* had discovered it in 1774, four years before Cook. His second in command at the time had been young Lieutenant Martinez who now, fourteen years later, was back, this time in command of his own ship, the *Princesa*.

Upon reaching Nootka Sound, Martinez found a British ship commanded by Captain Douglas who, along with Meares, had arrived in the northwest the previous year. Now he had been left behind to continue trading while Meares went to Macao to sell the furs they had obtained.

Martinez immediately ordered Douglas's arrest for being in Spanish territory without a license, but then began to have second thoughts. He had been instructed to explain Spanish claims to any foreigners he encountered but to avoid any actions that might lead to a clash. By ordering the arrest of Douglas he had pushed those instructions well beyond their limit. Besides, Douglas was now insisting that he had no idea the Spanish had a claim to Nootka Sound, that he was not there to trade but only because his ship was in distress, and despite its poor condition, if Martinez would allow, he would depart immediately. Faced with this explanation, Martinez changed his mind and released the ship. Soon afterward it left Nootka Sound bound for its home port of Macao. At least that was the destination given to Martinez, although as soon as it was clear of the Sound, Douglas ordered a change of course toward the trading areas in the north. He had no intention, he said, "of running for Macao with only between 60 and 70 sea-otter skins which I had on board."

Not long after Douglas left, another ship, the *Princess Royal,* also on a trading voyage from China, arrived at the Sound. Its captain, Thomas Hudson, quickly realizing that the presence of the Spanish Navy precluded any trading, claimed he was there only because his ship was in poor shape. Martinez accepted the story and allowed the ship to remain long enough to make repairs and take on wood and water. As Hudson prepared to sail, Martinez told him that upon leaving Nootka Sound he was not to approach the coast again until he was beyond the entrance to Prince William Sound, for up to that point everything belonged to Spain. Although Hudson intended to resume trading as soon as he was out of sight of the Spanish Navy, he not only agreed to avoid the coast but indicated to Martinez that he had given up his trading plans and was going directly to the Orient. When he sailed on the morning of July 2, Martinez was rid of all the intruders.

At eight that same evening, however, a Spanish lookout shouted that he had sighted another ship entering the Sound. At first Martinez thought it was a Spanish supply ship he had been expecting. He soon discovered, however, that it was the *Argonaut,* still another of those British ships from the Orient.

XII

Like so many others in the early fur trade, James Colnett, captain of the *Argonaut,* was a former British naval officer. As a midshipman he had served under Captain Cook on his second voyage into the Pacific, then upon his return had joined a fighting ship. He had worked his way up through the ranks to first lieutenant aboard a warship, but by then the American Revolution was over and there were few opportunities in the peacetime navy. Colnett had taken command of a trading vessel bound for America and spent two seasons trading along the Pacific Coast. In early 1789 he was given command of the *Argonaut,* owned and outfitted by John Meares and his associates Cox, Beale, and Etches. It sailed from China and in early July was on the coast of America where it entered Nootka Sound and dropped anchor.

Once again Martinez came aboard to request an explanation of the ship's presence in Spanish territory. Undoubtedly he hoped that the captain would say he needed a brief time to refit before going back to sea. He had already accepted that story twice and there was no reason why, if it was tactfully presented, he would not accept it again.

Colnett declined to take this approach and told Martinez that he had come to take possession of Nootka Sound for the King of England, to fortify it, and to establish a fur-trading post to deal in otter skins. Martinez explained that this would be impossible since the area was clearly owned by Spain, but Colnett insisted that the entire northwest belonged to England because of the discoveries of his old commander, Captain Cook.

Martinez could counter that argument with the testimony of the Nootka Chief Maquinna who lived in a nearby village. In an earlier discussion with Martinez and Captain Douglas, Maquinna remembered the coming of the Spanish ship and even showed them the shells Martinez had personally given him in 1774. He also remembered his brother being hit on the head by a shell and the two silver spoons being stolen by an Indian who was now dead. Martinez pointed out that the silver spoons had been mentioned in Captain Cook's journal. Clearly, he said, it established that Spain had a prior claim to Nootka Sound and it also established that the British knew—or from Cook's journal should know—that this was Spanish territory.

Momentarily, Colnett was convinced, or so Martinez thought, for he bowed to Spanish authority enough to ask permission to construct a strong building to protect him and his men from Indian attack. Martinez refused, saying it was contrary to orders from the viceroy.

No hostility was aroused, apparently, for Martinez remained aboard the *Argonaut* where the two captains spent much of the night drinking and conversing through an interpreter.

Whatever friendly feelings developed between them ended the next day, however, when Colnett went aboard the *Princesa* to show Martinez his passport and other papers. Both men later agreed that a violent scene took place, but each had an entirely different version of how it came about. Colnett claimed that upon going to Martinez' cabin he found the commandante distantly polite. After considerable hemming and hawing, Martinez announced that as an officer in the Spanish Navy he was authorized by the King to capture any English vessel he found on the coast of America. In reply, Colnett said, he calmly told the Spaniard his papers would show that he too was a naval officer deserving of respect and demonstrate that he had his Britannic Majesty's permission to be in these waters.

Martinez contemptuously—or so the Englishman thought—said the papers were forgeries and that Colnett was nothing but a pirate. At that Colnett, by his own testimony, lost his temper and launched a personal attack. He said Martinez had earlier promised that if he entered the Sound he would be allowed to leave whenever he wanted. Now the Spanish commandante had changed his mind which, Colnett implied, was an act totally devoid of the honor that might be expected from an officer of the King. Then Colnett, again by his own testimony, berated Martinez for his unofficerlike appearance when he had come aboard the *Argonaut* the previous day. Having delivered his personal insults, Colnett announced his plan to sail despite Martinez' objections.

At this, Colnett reported, Martinez flew out of the cabin while three or four sailors armed with muskets rushed in. One of them pointed a cocked gun at Colnett, another snatched his sword, and a third grabbed him and tore his shirt and coat. After that, Colnett said, "I was confined a close prisoner in the Cabin and Deny'd the privelege of any of my Officers speaking to me."

Martinez also left an account of the incident, but he saw everything through an entirely different lens. Colnett came aboard the *Princesa,* he said, and produced his passport but refused to show his instructions on the grounds they were directed to him alone. Martinez demanded to see them, at which time Colnett admitted he had no instructions other than his passport. He also insisted that he be allowed to sail at once, but Martinez refused permission until he was allowed to examine the *Argonaut*'s papers. Colnett then became arrogant, Martinez said, "showing slight regard for the flag of his Catholic Majesty and for me, who on this occasion, as a commander of his, represented his royal person." Not only that, but he was also personally abusive, speaking in a loud voice and placing his hand on his sword as if to threaten him. And although Martinez knew little English he did recognize, and understand, the meaning of the phrase "God-Damned Spaniard." Yet despite all this provocation, Martinez said, he kept trying to calm Colnett, but when that failed he ordered him arrested.

Thus we finally have it, the story of two innocent men, each trying to remain calm and reasonable only to be outraged by the arrogant and unreasonable behavior of the other. And there is little outside testimony to clarify it. It has been suggested that the quarrel arose because the two men were drinking heavily, but there is no evidence to prove it. Colnett does say that they had spent much of the previous night drinking, but says nothing about the next day. Possibly they were tense and irritable because they were both fighting hangovers.

Actually, the main source of the trouble was in the personalities of the two men. Colnett was an overbearing man and once the argument began he was unable to confine himself to the fine points of maritime law and began to question Martinez' honor and insult him for his unofficerlike appearance. Nothing could have enraged Martinez more. He, too, was a difficult man, and his entire career had been hurt by his inability to get along with others. Yet he had been given major responsibilities without increase in rank or in pay. He took himself, his position, and his task seriously, and Colnett's condescension was more than he could bear. Later, a Spaniard who investigated the incident summed it up by saying, "It is likely that the churlish nature of each one precipitated things up to this point, since those who sailed with both complain of them equally and condemned their uncultivated boorishness."

Whatever its cause the emotional confrontation between these two abrasive men resulted in Colnett's arrest. And having gone that far, Martinez was emboldened to take the step he had long been threatening and seized the *Argonaut.* A week later Captain Hudson in the *Princess Royal,* which was supposed to be well on its way to China, returned to Nootka Sound and that ship too was seized. Spanish crews were placed on board both vessels and they were sent off to Mexico as prizes, victims of their violation of Spanish territory.

INTERNATIONAL WATERS

I

On New Year's Day 1790 the British Admiralty officially commissioned a new ship for use in exploring the northwest coast of America. The 340-ton vessel, capable of being rigged for close-in surveying work, was already near completion in a Thames River shipyard when it was purchased by the Admiralty. When it was finished it was launched, given the name *Discovery,* and commissioned a sloop of war under the command of Captain Henry Roberts, a veteran of Cook's second and third voyages. The ship was moved to the naval yards at Deptford to be outfitted for its voyage to the Pacific. That work would be supervised not by the captain but by the ship's newly appointed first lieutenant, George Vancouver.

When Vancouver, at the age of thirty-two, reported aboard his new ship it had been almost a decade since he had arrived home from the Pacific aboard another ship, the *Discovery,* which had also anchored at Deptford. At the time he had been a midshipman, but soon after his return he was commissioned a lieutenant and assigned to the sloop-of-war *Martin.* In the years to follow, he served aboard several ships in both Europe and the West Indies. When the Admiralty ordered the making of accurate charts of the Carribbean, Vancouver, who had considerable knowledge of surveying from his two voyages with Cook, was one of the officers chosen to survey Kingston Harbor and the waters around Jamaica. He performed the work well, and when the Board of Admiralty began planning a surveying expedition to the Pacific, he was given the berth of first lieutenant on the new *Discovery.*

Vancouver reported aboard ship in early January 1790 to supervise final preparations for putting to sea. Each day he watched as dockyard workers set the masts, tested them, and added the spars, the rigging, and the sails. He was also responsible for receiving and supervising the storing of the vast amount of supplies being brought aboard for the long voyage. There were five anchors, three weighing more than a ton each, as well as large rolls of canvas and coils of rope and cable.

There were also barrel after barrel of salt beef, salt pork, and other supplies including the necessary antiscorbutics to fight scurvy.

Vancouver worked steadily throughout the spring until the afternoon of May 4 when Naval Captain Sir Hyde Parker suddenly came aboard the *Discovery* with a party of officers and men. Parker announced his intention of using the ship as a staging area for his press gangs and he soon gathered a pool of boats for all the other ships in the river. That night the boats were sent ashore and within a few hours were back aboard the *Discovery* where beer and grog were served to both the press gangs and those who had been pressed. The following morning a London man noted excitedly in his diary that "during the last night all the sailors on the Thames were pressed, and that war was on the point of being declared against Spain."

England and Spain stood on the brink of an actual shooting war mainly because of the bitter argument on the isolated coast of America between those two difficult men, Esteban Martinez and James Colnett. Martinez had lost his temper and seized Colnett's ship, the *Argonaut,* then, having gone that far, also seized the *Princess Royal.* Both ships belonged to the Associated Merchants trading to the northwest coast of America—John Meares and Associates and Richard Cadmon Etches and Associates.

The ships themselves had been seized and sent to Mexico in July 1789, but it took a long time for the word to travel all the way to Europe. It was not until early 1790 that an incomplete and garbled account reached London. A few weeks later, the Spanish government lodged an official protest against the British activities at Nootka Sound, citing, as always, those silver spoons as evidence of Spain's prior rights. In response they received, not an apology or an explanation, but a harsh reply from Prime Minister William Pitt, saying that the seizure of the two British ships by Martinez was not only a violation of the law of nations but an insult to His Britannic Majesty as well. Furthermore, it was also illegal, for the British had every right to visit, land, and even settle in unoccupied places on the coast of America.

From the beginning Pitt took the view that the silver spoons proved nothing. It was not enough, he said, simply to discover an area. Instead, a country must settle and effectively control the land in order to have a valid claim. He knew that if he could force Spain to acknowledge this, much of the northwest coast would be opened to Great Britain. Spain, of course, knew the same thing and for a time refused to admit it. Pitt persisted, for he was finding considerable support in England for his strong stand.

Then in April 1790 John Meares himself arrived in London with his version of how the Spaniards had seized his ships. In the past, Meares had been a minor and somewhat disreputable trader who registered his ships under the Portuguese flag to avoid British trade regulations. But now his association with prominent businessmen like Richard Cadmon Etches gave him access to powerful government figures including the prime minister. And whatever Pitt thought of Meares personally, he was willing to use him, and at his request Meares submitted to the cabinet a written memorial of the seizure. It was a highly indignant account of the insults and cruelties committed by the Spanish commandante against a British citizen. Filled as it was with half-truths and less, it had the necessary effect. Four days later, the press gangs swept through the London waterfront bursting into pubs, brothels, and rooming houses. The next day Pitt dispatched a stiff note to the Spanish ambassador notifying him of England's intention to protect the unquestionable rights of its citizens to hunt, fish, trade, or settle in unoccupied parts of the northwest. Clearly, war with Spain was imminent.

Pitt also mounted a propaganda campaign to build support for a war with Spain. One of the main ingredients was John Meares' memorial which, after being made public, was the lead story in the June issue of *Gentleman's Magazine,* and was also circulated in pamphlet form throughout London. Its inflammatory charges caused outrage all over England and gave Pitt the necessary support to maintain his stand.

Spain realized that its major ally, France, now into the second year of revolution and virtually incapacitated by it, would be unable to help. Spain gave in to British demands and on October 18, 1790, the Conde de Floridablanca signed the Nootka Sound Convention. In it Spain agreed to make reparations for the seizure of the British ships, and, more important, agreed not to obstruct British subjects from navigating, fishing, trading with the natives, or settling in places that were not already occupied.

II

The threat of war with Spain brought about the immediate cancellation of the *Discovery*'s voyage, and its first lieutenant, George Vancouver, was reassigned to another ship of the line. With the threat removed, interest in such a voyage revived, particularly because of a provision in the Nootka Sound Convention. Spain promised "that the buildings and tracts of land situated on the Northwest Coast of the continent of North America, or on islands adjacent to that continent, of which the subjects of His Britannic Majesty were dispossessed about the month of April, 1789, by a Spanish officer, shall be restored to the said British subjects." To those who knew the transient nature of British fur trading in the northwest it surely came as a surprise that anybody had been dispossessed of buildings, tracts of land, or anything else.

The original claim leading to this agreement came from John Meares who had interpreted various facts as loosely as possible. In 1788, while building the small schooner *Northwest America* at Nootka Sound, he had obtained permission from Maquinna to build a house for the carpenters working ashore. It was little more than a hut, it was torn down when he left, and at the time Meares was flying the Portuguese, not the British, flag. Later Meares would claim that Maquinna had granted him a large tract of land on which he had built a house, surrounded it with a breastwork, fortified it with a cannon, and raised the British flag over it. However careless Meares was with his facts, the story sounded plausible at least to William Pitt who was willing to use it in his negotiations with Spain. And the Spanish, unsure of the exact facts and fearing war with Great Britain, agreed to return whatever it was they had seized at Nootka Sound.

The agreement having been made, Great Britain decided to send an expedition to the Pacific both to take possession of the lands and buildings at Nootka Sound and to explore the northwest coast more thoroughly. One ship would be the *Chatham*, commanded by Lieutenant William Broughton, the other the *Discovery*, which had been all but ready to sail for the Pacific when the war scare came. Since its original captain, Henry Roberts, had resigned and was now in command of a warship in the Carribbean, command of the *Discovery* and of the entire expedition was given to Lieutenant George Vancouver.

On April 1, 1791, the two ships sailed for the northwest coast of America. During the next year, Vancouver revisited all the places he had seen as a boy with Captain Cook—the Cape of Good Hope, Australia, New Zealand, Tahiti, Hawaii. On April 17, 1792, a month after leaving Hawaii, the *Discovery* and the *Chatham* were sailing through thick, rainy weather somewhere in the Pacific. About noon they began to encounter driftwood, grass, and seaweed which, added to the increasing number of birds and the changing color of the water, indicated that land was near. Visibility was limited to just a few miles and Vancouver, anxious to sight land before nightfall, stood to the east with as much sail as the ships could carry. By four in the afternoon they reached soundings at fifty-three fathoms and shortly afterward saw in the distance land on which the surf was breaking with great violence. They had reached America and by sunset the next day were within sight of Cape Mendocino on the California coast.

Vancouver immediately began to survey the coast, working the ship in close to shore during the day, standing off each night, then running in close again the next day to continue the survey. For several weeks the ships worked their way north until reaching Cape Foulweather where, fourteen years before, Vancouver, with Cook, had first seen the coast of America. Soon after passing that point he noticed that the sea had changed from its natural to river-colored water, which he attributed to streams flowing into the ocean somewhere to the north. Seeing nothing else worth a closer look, he said, "I continued our pursuit to the N.W. being desirous to embrace the advantages of the now prevailing breeze and pleasant weather."

Vancouver continued north and two days later spotted another sail. Upon being sighted, the ship hoisted an American flag, fired a gun in recognition, and coming within hailing distance of the *Discovery,* announced itself as the *Columbia,* out of Boston, Mr. Gray commanding.

The announcement rather surprised Vancouver, for while the name *Columbia* meant nothing to him, he had certainly heard of Captain Gray. While Vancouver was still in England, John Meares had published his *Voyages Made in the Years 1788 and 1789 from China to the Northwest Coast of America,* in which he claimed that Nootka Sound was not, as Cook had assumed, on the mainland of North America but on a large island. To prove it he cited the story of a certain Captin Gray, commander of the *Lady Washington,* who, he said, had entered Juan de Fuca Strait and sailed entirely around the island. Meares even included a map on which he wrote in the space between the mainland and the island, "Sketch of the Track of the American Sloop Washington in the Autumn of 1789."

Meares's claim that Nootka Sound was on an island had caused a geographical controversy in England and one of Vancouver's specific instructions was to explore Juan de Fuca Strait. Now, on the coast of America, just a few miles below the entrance to that strait, Vancouver had hailed a ship commanded by a Captain Gray. Presumably it was the same Captain Gray, and Vancouver sent Lieutenant Peter Puget and the surgeon Archibald Menzies to the *Columbia* to find out.

The two men boarding the ship found that this was indeed the same Captain Gray, somewhat startled to discover that he was famous. He had long been out of touch with the civilized world and knew nothing of the publication of Meares's book except for what he now learned from Puget and Menzies. And like most men who came into contact with Meares, he was astonished by some of his statements. Admittedly, during earlier days on the coast when he was captain of the *Lady Washington* he had entered Juan de Fuca Strait. But instead of sailing entirely around an island, he said, he had penetrated the strait for only about fifty miles, and finding that trade was disappointing, returned to the ocean by the same route he came. The passage, he added, was about five leagues wide, and the Indians had told him it extended far to the north. Other than that he could supply no information on the subject.

He did pass on a bit of geographical knowledge he had picked up during an earlier cruise along the same coast. In the latitude of 46°10′—not far south of the place where the two ships were now—Gray said he had apparently been off the mouth of a great river, for the current from water pouring into the ocean had been so strong as to keep him from approaching the coast. He was describing the same area where Vancouver, a few days before, had seen river-colored water but had not investigated. Having this additional information, Vancouver could, even now, turn back and explore more fully, but he was more excited about the possibilities of Juan de Fuca Strait and after Puget and Menzies returned to the *Discovery,* Vancouver sailed north. Gray continued south and less than two weeks later discovered and entered the great river which he named after his ship the *Columbia.*

By then Vancouver had entered Juan de Fuca Strait and found a secure anchorage where he established an observatory to determine latitude and longitude, overhauled both ships, and used the boats to investigate surrounding waters. Throughout the rest of May he explored Puget Sound, and in June began to work his way north into the Strait of Georgia. At Point Grey on June 22 he encountered two Spanish ships, the *Sutil,* commanded by Dionesio Galiano, and the *Mexicana,* commanded by Cayetano Valdes. Like Vancouver, they had been sent to survey the inland sea.

Vancouver had been ordered to cooperate with any Spanish ships engaged in exploration and survey work. He and the Spanish commanders agreed to continue the survey together. The four ships sailed north, anchored at the entrance to the Strait of Georgia and sent out surveying crews.

One of these crews, led by James Johnstone, master of the *Chatham,* was sent out on July 3 with enough provisions to last seven days. When they returned on July 12, two days late, Johnstone announced that he had found a channel leading to the ocean. He had proved what others had only guessed—that Nootka Sound was not on the mainland of America but on a large island. Vancouver, in passing the information on to the two Spanish captains, told them he planned to attempt the passage as soon as possible. They declined to accompany him on the grounds that their ships were in no condition to keep up with his. On July 13 the *Discovery* and the *Chatham* weighed anchor and sailed, hoping to reach the Pacific Ocean. They worked their way through Johnstone's Strait, and in rainy, foggy weather entered Queen Charlotte Strait. As they passed through, both ships, first the *Discovery* then the *Chatham,* ran aground. Luck was with Vancouver, however, for with the next high tide both floated off, no serious damage done. Eventually, the two ships reached Queen Charlotte Sound and anchored at Safety Cove on Calvert Island.

While the *Discovery* and the *Chatham* were at Calvert Island, another ship, also flying the English flag, appeared off the entrance to the cove. It rather surprised Vancouver, for it seemed to be a trading ship, yet he had no idea why its captain would want to visit such a desolate and inhospitable region. One of Vancouver's lieutenants was sent aboard, and he returned with information that the ship was called the *Venus,* it was out of Bengal, and its captain, Henry Shepherd, had found the price of sea otters so exorbitant on the coast that he had taken to the inside passage looking for cheaper fur. More important, at least to Vancouver, was news from Nootka Sound that Don Juan de la Bodega y Quadra, the Spanish commissioner empowered to turn over land at Nootka, was there impatiently awaiting Vancouver's arrival. Although Vancouver had planned to spend another month surveying the coast, he changed his course and headed south. On August 28, 1792, the *Discovery* and the *Chatham* entered the Sound and anchored at Friendly Cove.

III

At Nootka Sound, George Vancouver, as official representative of His Britannic Majesty, immediately set about establishing proper relations with his Spanish counterpart Don Juan de la Bodega y Quadra. Lieutenant Peter Puget was sent aboard Bodega's ship to announce that the British would salute the Spanish flag if the Spanish would answer with the same number of guns. Bodega agreed and the two commanders, as the official representatives of Spain and Great Britain, exchanged thirteen-gun salutes.

Although Vancouver and Bodega could not communicate directly, for neither spoke the other's language, they got along well, possibly because they had so much in common. Bodega, the son of a prominent Spanish official in Peru, was the elder by fourteen years, but like Vancouver he had spent most of his life in the Navy. He had entered the Marine Guard at the age of nineteen, was promoted to ensign a few years later, and in 1774 was sent to San Blas in Mexico as a lieutenant. He was one of a group of young officers sent to join Juan Perez and Esteban Martinez in exploring and surveying the west coast of America. Bodega, in command of the ship *Sonora,* had sailed far enough north to sight a high mountain towering over what is now Sitka, Alaska. But, faced with a diminishing crew because of the ever-present scurvy, the survey party had turned back to California.

Now, almost twenty years later, Bodega was the naval commandante of San Blas and the man chosen to finish the Nootka Sound negotiations with the British commissioner, George Vancouver. When Vancouver came aboard his ship, he greeted him with utmost politeness and in turn was invited on board the *Discovery* for breakfast the next morning. When he arrived, and again when he left, he was given a thirteen-gun salute, and for the rest of the day there was a round of ceremonies. Bodega returned the hospitality that evening by inviting Vancouver and his officers to an elaborate five-course dinner served with great elegance. A royal salute was fired during the drinking of toasts to the sovereigns of both England and Spain, and another salute to the success of Vancouver's and Bodega's missions.

Despite the warm personal relations Bodega and Vancouver could not agree officially. Vancouver claimed that the convention of 1790 and a letter written by Count Floridablanca said Spain was to surrender "the buildings and districts, or parcels of land which were occupied by the subjects of His Britannic Majesty in April, 1789 . . ." To Vancouver that meant all of Nootka Sound. To Bodega, who had been doing some investigation as to who owned what at the Sound, it meant he had to surrender only what Meares had actually occupied in 1789—namely, a hut on a narrow piece of ground. He was willing, he said, to remove his forces from the area and to turn the settlement over to Vancouver until their governments could reach an understanding. But he would do so only if Vancouver agreed that this did not prejudice Spain's claim to the area. Vancouver refused on the grounds that the two governments had already decided the question of who owned what on the Pacific Coast, and he did not consider himself authorized to reopen the subject.

Besides the technical question of exactly what should be turned over to the British, there was substantial disagreement on who had a valid claim to the northwest. Although Bodega was willing to turn over specific areas, even Nootka Sound itself, he refused to surrender Spain's general claim to the coast north of California. Vancouver, who always insisted on calling all this land "New Albion," refused to agree to anything that recognized so general a claim for fear of violating, if not the letter, the spirit of the Nootka Sound Convention. They had reached a deadlock and decided to refer the matter to their home governments and await further instructions.

Winter was approaching and Vancouver decided to leave the northwest until the following year. On October 12 the *Discovery* and the *Chatham* sailed from Nootka bound for California. On the way south Vancouver planned to explore the Columbia River, but the *Discovery* was too large to enter its mouth and the *Chatham* was left behind to investigate while the *Discovery* sailed on to California.

IV

Shortly after noon on November 14 the *Discovery* was just off the outer entrance to San Francisco Bay. A rapid outgoing tide kept it out of the bay until late afternoon when it began to make slow headway against it. Through the rest of the afternoon and into the evening the ship moved along the southern shore, taking soundings all the way. Those on board could see several men on horseback riding along the shore, and they could hear the firing of welcoming guns. When it got dark someone built a fire on the beach and guns were still being fired but Vancouver, not knowing what the signals meant, kept moving into the bay, hoping to see the lights of a Spanish town. By eight o'clock, however, nothing had appeared on shore and finding himself in a snug, landlocked cove he dropped anchor.

The next morning Vancouver found he was in Yerba Buena Cove, "A most excellent small bay." In spite of rainy weather, he could see herds of cattle on shore and flocks of sheep grazing on the surrounding hills, "a sight we had long been strangers to." As the day dawned, the Englishmen hoisted the ship's colors and fired a gun, bringing several people on horseback down to the beach where they stood waving their hats. In response one of the ship's boats was sent ashore. Soon it returned bringing a priest wearing the habit of a missionary, a sergeant, and two soldiers.

Once aboard, the missionary expressed his great pleasure at meeting the English captain, while the sergeant announced that in the absence of his commander he was instructed to render whatever assistance he could. Vancouver gave them breakfast, then accompanied them ashore, where they demonstrated their sincerity by providing him with an ox, a sheep, and some excellent vegetables. The friar also pointed out the best place to obtain wood and water, and Vancouver soon had his watering crews ashore while he and the other officers went quail-hunting in the hills above the cove.

Back aboard ship they enjoyed their dinner of quail, shot by the officers, and beef, mutton, and vegetables, provided by the Spanish. During dinner, they had an official visit from Hermenegildo Sal, acting commandante at the San Francisco presidio. Vancouver was somewhat concerned about how he would be received in Spanish California, but it was soon clear that he had little to worry about, for Commandante Sal greeted him "with the honest frankness of an old Castilian." He promised Vancouver whatever he needed, and even offered to provide horses and guides to take him wherever he wanted to go. Not only was he personally happy to welcome him, Sal said, but he had also recently been in Monterey where the naval commander, Bodega y Quadra, had requested that Vancouver, if he touched in at San Francisco, be supplied with whatever the settlement could offer.

Vancouver also learned from Sal that the shots he had heard and the fire he had seen on the beach the previous night were attempts by the Spanish to indicate the proper place to anchor. He had passed by that point, however, and now at low tide he discovered that a large mud bank cut him off from shore until the tide returned. The next morning, in a drizzling rain, he hoisted anchor and moved the ship back to the usual Spanish anchorage just off the presidio.

Vancouver spent the next ten days anchored in San Francisco Bay, giving him and his officers an opportunity to visit Commandante Sal and his family at home. They lived at the presidio, which was still unfinished, and the Englishmen saw no guns except a broken one lying at the entrance to the fort. The commandante's home was small, with a dirt floor and only a few rough pieces of the most ordinary furniture. It hardly fit in with "the ideas we had conceived of the sumptuous manner in which the Spaniards lived on this side of the globe."

Vancouver also visited the mission at San Francisco; there was another mission at Santa Clara some fifty miles to the south. To visit it, he and several of his officers and men set out on horseback on the morning of November 10, riding south along the bay. Commandante Sal could not accompany them but he sent Spanish soldiers to serve as guides, and they kept the party at a full gallop for almost twenty miles. When they stopped along a stream in a beautiful valley surrounded by tree-covered hills, the English sailors, tired and sore from the unaccustomed riding, could rest and have lunch. All too soon, the soldiers caught and saddled fresh horses and they were off again at a gallop. The Englishmen would have liked to have rested longer, but the soldiers said they were less than halfway to Santa Clara and there was no stop in between. They galloped on through the afternoon until four o'clock, when they reached low ground turned into a swamp by the recent rains. They had to walk their horses slowly, at first a welcome change, but soon the sailors began to stiffen up from the cold dampness. Finally, a little after sunset, they arrived at the mission where they were greeted with the utmost hospitality, this time by Father Tomas de la Pena. The welcoming activities, however, were lost on two of Vancouver's officers who were so tired and ill from the long ride that they went immediately to bed.

The rest were given a dinner of fish, fruit, and sweetmeats during which Father Tomas constantly tried to anticipate their every want. He was an old man, quite fat, "yet he trudg'd about in the most lively manner to administer every comfort to his guests." Beyond that, with most of the Englishmen dead tired from the long ride, he also carried the burden of enlivening the dinner conversation.

De la Pena could tell almost endless stories of the early days at Santa Clara, for he had been a missionary there since its founding fifteen years before. Possibly of more interest to Vancouver were the stories he told of the earliest days on the northwest coast. De la Pena had been aboard the *Santiago* when Nootka Sound was discovered. He too could talk of exploration in the north, of encounters with northwest Indians, of the naval officers Juan Perez and Esteban Martinez, and of those two famous silver spoons which, by now, Vancouver was surely getting tired of hearing about.

After spending a full day visiting the mission, the contingent returned to San Francisco where they found the *Chatham,* left behind to explore the Columbia River, in the bay. By now the *Discovery* was almost ready to sail and Vancouver, planning to move south to Monterey, began taking on supplies. The Spanish were more than generous, giving him cows, sheep, chickens, 190 pumpkins, 400 eggs, and a cartload of vegetables. When Vancouver tried to pay, Commandante Sal refused. Bodega had expressly forbidden his taking anything, saying that he would settle all accounts.

In appreciation for all the supplies and all the kindness, Vancouver presented their friends in San Francisco culinary and table utensils, some bar iron, a few ornaments for the church, and best of all, a hogshead of wine and another of rum. All this he left with Commandante Sal, asking him to see that it was equally divided between the presidio and the missions at San Francisco and Santa Clara. On November 25 the two ships sailed from San Francisco and arrived in Monterey the next day.

Vancouver and his men were received just as warmly there as they had been in San Francisco. Not long before their arrival, Governor Jose Romeu had died, and since his replacement had not yet arrived the commandante of the Monterey presidio, Jose Dario Arguello, was acting governor of California. However elevated his position, in rank he was only an army lieutenant and he deferred to Naval Commandante Bodega who was in Monterey to see that Vancouver received a proper welcome.

Again the thirteen-gun salutes were exchanged, again there was a series of social affairs both on shore and on board the British flagship. Occasionally there were problems, as when a dinner on board the *Discovery* for Spanish officers and their wives had to be abruptly terminated when several of the ladies became seasick. At another dinner party several Spanish ladies danced, and in response to Vancouver's request two Hawaiian girls sang and performed native dances. Unfortunately several Spanish women left in a huff, apparently believing the Hawaiians were mocking their own fandango.

Beyond the social life, Vancouver spent much of his time in Monterey putting the final touches on his first year in the field and preparing for the next year. He was conducting a scientific expedition and with Bodega's permission established an observatory on shore as he had at each place he visited in the Pacific. There, after his abortive attempt to give a dinner aboard ship, he entertained his Spanish guests on solid ground.

Other details needed attention. Vancouver was still not sure how to deal with Bodega on the Nootka Sound question, particularly in light of a new development. Bodega had recently received orders to arrest all non-Spanish ships trading on the west coast except for those of England. This led both men to think their governments had reached a final agreement concerning possessions on the west coast of America. Vancouver badly needed instructions from his government and he also wanted to make a full report of his past year's activities. He decided to send Lieutenant William Broughton, commander of the *Chatham,* back to England. Broughton was an ideal choice, for he had been involved in all the negotiations with Bodega and was qualified to be placed in command of a larger vessel that could rejoin Vancouver in the Pacific. As usual Naval Commander Bodega eased the way by offering to take Broughton when he sailed to San Blas and to help him cross Mexico and find a ship bound for Europe.

With all the arrangements made, Vancouver set about finishing the reports and charts he planned to send to England with Broughton. The crews began to caulk the ships' hulls, repair the rigging, and load supplies, including more cattle, sheep, and fresh fruit provided by the Spanish. Again Bodega refused to allow anyone to take payment, and again Vancouver left some presents for those at the presidio and the mission. By early January, the *Discovery* and the *Chatham* were ready to sail for Hawaii where they would spend the winter. They were delayed at the last moment when two men, the ship's armorer James Etchison and marine James London, suddenly turned up missing.

Neither man seemed the type to desert. Etchison had a reputation as an industrious worker and London was considered one of the *Chatham*'s best marines, but both were now gone. Vancouver was not completely surprised because several sailors had deserted earlier. One had been caught and brought back in chains, but three others were not to be found. Neither were Etchison or London, even though a reward of twenty-five dollars was offered for their return. Finally, when Bodega offered the local Monterey blacksmith as a replacement for the armorer, Vancouver decided to leave without them. On January

15, 1793, the *Discovery* and the *Chatham* sailed and soon disappeared beyond Point Pinos. Once again Monterey was left in lonely isolation, but this time five foreigners, all of them deserters from an English ship, were left behind in California.

V

Vancouver, after leaving California, went to Hawaii, spent a few months there, then returned to the northwest coast of America, establishing a pattern that he would follow for the rest of the voyage—winter in Hawaii, spring and summer surveying on the northwest coast, a fall visit to California, and another winter in Hawaii. It was an effective way to accommodate to the variation in climate, although at least one problem developed when Vancouver made his second visit to California in the fall of 1793.

Unlike his first visit to Monterey Vancouver was coldly received by a new acting governor, Jose de Arrillaga. He was so insulted that he sailed away after only a few days. Some time later, Arrillaga was removed as governor—Vancouver understood he had been sent to "some inferior establishment"—and Vancouver was willing to risk a third visit to California in the fall of 1794. It worked out well, for when he reached Monterey, Jose Arguello, who had treated him so kindly in 1792, was again in temporary command. A few days later, the new, officially appointed governor of California, Don Diego Borica, arrived in Monterey from Mexico.

By now, in the fall of 1794, a little more than twenty-five years had passed since that rainy Sunday in 1769 when the first Spaniards had arrived overland in San Diego. At that time, there had been no settlements in all of upper California. In fact, the entire west coast of America was virtually untouched by white men and all but unknown to Europeans. Now, less than three decades later, there were almost a thousand Spanish-speaking whites living along the five-hundred-mile stretch of coast from San Diego to San Francisco. Other Europeans had found their way to California—La Perouse in 1786, Vancouver six years later. And Vancouver by his presence, by his explorations, and by his continual visits to Monterey, was a reminder that Spain, in the Nootka Sound Convention, had given up its exclusive claims to the west coast of America.

California was now an important area, not only in its own right but as a buffer against all the increasing foreign activities in the north. Consequently when the Conde de Revilla Gigedo, Viceroy of New Spain, found it necessary to appoint a new governor, he purposely sought someone with "talent, military skill and experience, robust health, . . . , and a true zeal for the service." And the man in whom he found all these attributes, or at least enough to warrant appointing him governor, was Don Diego de Borica, a fifty-two-year-old Basque who had spent the past thirty years as a soldier in the Americas.

In November 1794 the newly appointed governor of California arrived in Monterey and found the two English ships, the *Chatham* and the *Discovery,* riding at anchor in the harbor. The next morning Vancouver and his officers came ashore to congratulate Borica on his new position and to explain why the English ships were in a California port. Much to Vancouver's relief, Borica said they were welcome, and crew members could camp on shore while obtaining wood, water, and supplies. He also allowed them to establish an observatory, as they had done in 1792, but which Arrillaga had pointedly forbidden the following year.

Another piece of serious business needed to be settled with Captain Vancouver. During his first visit in 1792 he had left without being able to find several deserters. Eventually they were captured by the Spanish and ordered expelled from California. When Vancouver returned for his brief second visit in the fall of 1793, the deserters were all in Mexico. The viceroy changed his mind and ordered them sent back to California for delivery to Vancouver. Thus, when the British expedition reached Monterey for the third time, there were six men whom the Spanish claimed had deserted from one or another of the English ships. It is not entirely clear who they were for no names were given and after some investigation, Vancouver found that only three were British subjects. Those he took aboard, rejecting the others, two Portuguese and a Dane, who were shipped back to Mexico on a Spanish vessel. Borica also presented Vancouver with a bill for $325 the Spanish government had spent on the deserters. Vancouver, lacking instructions on how to handle such a situation, refused to pay in cash, but said he would place the whole thing before the British Admiralty. Borica, friendly and accommodating, accepted the offer without objection.

Vancouver had now been away from England for more than three years and had finished one of his major tasks, that of surveying the northwest coast of America. He had still received no further instructions from his government on how to proceed in taking possession of Nootka Sound. His counterpart, Jose Manuel de Ayala, who had replaced Bodega, had heard from Spain that a new convention had been signed, and that the British would be sending a new commissioner to take possession. Vancouver assumed his task was now over, and in early December, the ships having been careened and the bottoms cleaned, the yards and mast replaced, the rigging put into seagoing condition, and the holds filled with wood, water, and provisions, he set sail from Monterey for England and home. Once again all of California was free of foreigners.

VI

Governor Don Diego de Borica could not have taken much comfort that all the foreigners were gone, for like other Spanish officials he clearly understood the implications of the agreement giving up exclusive rights to the northwest coast. Upon being appointed governor he had also received orders to prevent foreigners from entering California, although with the constant shifting in European relations, he was now told to treat English vessels more hospitably than others. Still, no foreigners were to be allowed to stay long or be permitted to inspect the interior of the country in any way.

To comply with these orders Borica began strengthening California's meager fortifications, asking the viceroy to send armorers, guns, and ammunition for the newly revived presidios. The viceroy agreed, and after receiving word that Spain and France had gone to war, also sent seventy-two Catalan Volunteers armed with the best weapons available. Borica never had a chance to see how his new defense would work, for the war remained on the other side of the world, and the French offered no threat to California. Instead, the invasion began obliquely with the appearance of an English ship just off Santa Barbara on a summer day in 1795.

The ship was the *Phoenix,* a private trading vessel commanded by Captain Hugh Moore, working out of its home port of Calcutta. It was first sighted on the northwest coast back in 1792 when it put into Prince William Sound in Alaska to repair a mast damaged during a storm. Later that same year there were several reports of it being anchored far to the south in Nootka Sound, but then it disappeared from the coast for two years, undoubtedly having gone to China to sell its cargo of furs. By summer 1794 it was back, and in early August, when Vancouver again visited Nootka Sound, the *Phoenix* was riding at anchor in Friendly Cove.

By then the men on Vancouver's ships had already been to California twice and apparently described it in such glowing terms that Captain Moore decided to see for himself. A year later, after a not very successful season of trading, Moore left the northwest. Instead of following the established fur-trader's routine of going first to Hawaii, then on to the Orient, he sailed south, staying close to the coast. On August 28, 1795, he dropped anchor just off Santa Barbara.

Unlike the earlier foreign visitors, La Perouse and Vancouver, Moore was not part of an official expedition and he arrived without warning, not at the capital but in the small, provincial town of Santa Barbara. And since there was no rapid means of communication with the governor in Monterey, the responsibility for handling the situation fell on Felipe de Goycoechea, commandante of the presidio at Santa Barbara. Goycoechea was an able man, and like all other commandantes, had been given very precise orders concerning foreigners. If they were clearly in distress he was to treat them hospitably and give them whatever aid was needed. But they were not to stay long and they were not to be allowed to inspect the country.

Goycoechea followed his instructions to the letter. He interviewed the captain who said he had put into port because of bad weather, and Goycoechea admitted the ship did look waterlogged. Captain Moore also said he needed wood, water, a few provisions, and a chance for some crew members who had been ill to recuperate. The commandante allowed the *Phoenix* to stay briefly and donated provisions, a few sheep, some chickens, and some bunches of onions. He also invited the captain and the mate to a dinner, followed by a bit of music played by Indians from the missions. After spending only a week in port, the *Phoenix* raised anchor and set sail. All had gone almost as the orders had anticipated, except that when the *Phoenix* sailed, it left one of its crew members behind.

On the evening of September 5, while the *Phoenix* could still be seen working its way out of port, Goycoechea wrote to Governor Borica informing him that Captain Moore had left a man whose name he did not know behind, describing him simply as a "lad" who was asking permission to remain in California. Such a request clearly violated Spanish law, but Goycoechea was not particularly disturbed for, as he pointed out to Borica, the man was an experienced sailor and a good carpenter, both skills badly needed in California.

Goycoechea wrote again with more information. The man's name was Joseph O'Cain, he had been born in Ireland and had emigrated to America with his parents who now lived in Boston. Beyond that there was no clue as to how this young man from Boston had ended up on the deck of an English ship from Calcutta. Probably he had reached there like so many others, for the sea had always been a means of escape for New England boys seeking their fortunes. And with the opening of worldwide trade after the Revolution, American sailors who had been left, willingly or not, in some strange port often ended up on British merchant ships.

The letter also offered no clue as to how Joe O'Cain came to be left behind. Possibly Moore forgot that one of his men was still ashore; possibly O'Cain had angered the captain who retaliated by abandoning him. Neither explanation seems likely for although the Spanish commandante called him a lad, O'Cain was a ship's officer who had to be replaced before the necessary orders could be given to sail. Besides, neither reason explains why the *Phoenix* had come to California in the first place. Although Moore claimed it was because he needed assistance, the ship had been provisioned before leaving Nootka Sound and also had to wander far off the normal fur-trader's route to be even near Santa Barbara. It all seemed part of a plan in which Moore sailed to California intentionally, entered the harbor at Santa Barbara, away from the watchful eye of the governor, then left behind one of his men to ingratiate himself with the Spanish in order to open future trading. However it came about, in the approaching darkness on the evening of September 5, 1795, as the *Phoenix* slowly worked its way out to sea, Joe O'Cain was still in Santa Barbara, the lone foreigner in all of California.

THE COAST OF BOSTON

I

One of the first things George Vancouver saw when he arrived on the northwest coast in 1792 was a ship flying the American flag. It was the *Columbia,* out of Boston, and unknown to either Vancouver or its own captain, Robert Gray, it was a harbinger of things to come.

Vancouver had been sent to the Pacific because of an international incident arising from the complaints of John Meares, one of the British traders who, until now, had dominated trade on the west coast. A few traders had made fortunes, but most of them had been severely hampered by having to arrange complicated and expensive disguises to evade the East India Company's monopoly. The Americans faced no such restrictions, and even as Vancouver and Bodega debated minute questions of territoriality, ship captains from Boston were working out an efficient trade system with which they would soon dominate the northwest.

The first of these Americans had entered the Pacific after hearing the stories of another member of Captain Cook's third voyage, John Ledyard. Ledyard was the marine corporal who, on the Island of Unalaska, had been sent out alone with a band of Aluet Indians to search for Russians. He had found them, brought them back to Cook, then rejoined his ship, the *Resolution,* on which he served for the rest of the voyage. Upon his return to England, he was promoted to sergeant but soon found himself in a difficult position, being an American and unwilling to serve against his fellow countrymen. When he tried to leave the service his resignation was refused, but he was allowed to remain in England. After Cornwallis surrendered, Ledyard volunteered to serve on a British man-of-war being sent to America. When it anchored in Long Island Sound, not far from his mother's home, he obtained a week's leave to visit her and never returned, going instead to his uncle's home in Hartford, Connecticut, where for the next several months he wrote an account of his years with Cook. In mid-1783 *A Journal of Captain Cook's Last Voyage to the Pacific Ocean and in Quest of the Northwest Passage* was published.

In it Ledyard, remembering the days at Nootka Sound, told how "skins which did not cost the purchaser sixpence sterling sold in China for 100 dollars." This was a sure way for a man to make his fortune and Ledyard, having recently deserted and being without an occupation, set off to find someone to finance a fur-trading expedition to the northwest coast.

He presented his plan to several men in New York who dismissed it as wild and visionary. He called at three different firms in Philadelphia, none of which showed the slightest interest. He also visited the docks and saw, dramatically, the depressed state of the shipping industry at the close of the Revolution. Most of the ships had come from foreign countries, there was almost no home shipping, and sailors were leaving Philadelphia for other ports in the hope of finding a berth. Not only were there no investors but Ledyard doubted he could even find a job as a common sailor.

Staying at the Crooked Billet, the same inn that had housed Ben Franklin when he first came to Philadelphia, Ledyard counted his money, "turned it over and looked at it; shook it in my hand, recounted it." There wasn't much and eventually he went to see Andrew Hodge, his step-uncle by marriage, with whom he was not particularly close but, Ledyard said, "necessity has overcome my delicacy. I have unbosomed myself to H. and laid my poverty open to him. He has relieved me for the present."

More hopeful was his contact with Robert Morris, Philadelphia financier, who not only listened but told him to present a detailed plan. After seeing it Morris agreed to finance the project and Ledyard returned to Boston to find a suitable ship for the expedition. The war had also left Massachusetts shipping in bad shape, with many of the better ships captured by the British and the rest too rotten for Ledyard's purpose. Before he could find a ship, Morris changed his mind and the agreement was canceled.

The next approach was to a ship captain in New London, Connecticut, whom Ledyard tried to convince of the fortune they could both make in the fur trade. Ledyard made it sound good—in fact he made it sound too good to be true and the captain balked. Years later, after seeing the fortunes made in the Northwest fur trade, that same captain would admit Ledyard had been right and he should have listened to him. The admission did Ledyard no good now, in 1783, and until early 1784 he continued to haunt the various seaports hoping to find some kind of backing. He had no luck and in June 1784, after one more failure, he wrote to his mother, "You have no doubt heard of my very great disappointment at New York. For a moment all the fortitude that ten years' misfortune had taught me could hardly support me. . . . This will probably be the last letter I shall write you from this country. I shall sail within twelve days for Spain, whence I expect to go to France, and there again to renew the business I was so unfortunate in at New York."

By early February 1785 Ledyard was in the French port of L'Orient where he wrote his brother, "I have a fine ship of four hundred tons, and in August next I expect to sail on another voyage round the world." Either it was an idle boast or it fell through, for nothing more was heard of it and Ledyard moved on to Paris where he approached John Paul Jones, now at loose ends after his heroic career during the Revolution. Jones was excited by the plan—excited enough to support Ledyard in Paris for the next five months—but then this plan too began to go sour. Jones suspected that the cost of the expedition would be much higher than Ledyard estimated, and he also heard that two Englishmen, Portlock and Dixon, had sailed for the northwest and would thus cut into the trade. The blow that destroyed the plan, however, came when Spain let it be known that it was officially opposed to any such expedition into the Pacific. Since Jones planned to use a French ship and to obtain backing from the King of France, that ended it, for Louis XVI would never allow himself to become involved in a plan that violated Spanish law.

It was about this time that Ledyard met Thomas Jefferson, who was in Paris as the United States Ambassador to France. Until now Ledyard's proposal, to all outward appearances at least, had been a straightforward business deal aimed at making a fortune in the northwest fur trade. When he met Jefferson the whole thing began to move in a different direction.

Jefferson had long been interested in the trans-Mississippi West, and he seized upon Ledyard and his plan as an opportunity to obtain some firsthand information. Later he would write, "while I resided in Paris, John Ledyard of Connecticut arrived there . . . His immediate object . . . was to engage a mercantile company in the fur trade of the western coast of America in which, however, he failed. I then proposed to him to go by land to Kamchatka, cross in some of the Russian vessels to Nootka Sound, fall down into the latitude of the Missouri, and penetrate to and through that to the United States." Later, when Jefferson wrote his autobiography, he corrected some factual errors about Ledyard but he let the basic interpretation stand and said, "I suggested to him the enterprise of exploring the Western part of our continent."

In later years John Ledyard, for better or for worse, would be portrayed as the creator of the fantasy of walking through Russia and Siberia, taking a ship to the northwest coast, then walking across the entire North American continent to the east coast. Yet Jefferson claims the original idea was his and all the evidence agrees, for Ledyard had shown no sign of being interested in anything more than a business proposition. Now the scheme had become much more wildly imaginative, with most of the imagination provided by Jefferson. Ledyard only listened to him, then "eagerly seized the idea." In light of this, it is ironic that in later years Jefferson would say of Ledyard, "unfortunately he had too much imagination."

Given his situation at the time, Ledyard could do little else but accept. His plans to form a company had failed, he had no job, he had no prospects, and he "felt himself as he really was, a wanderer without employment or motive." He was broke, so broke according to an early biographer that "he was compelled, however reluctantly, to be a pensioner of the bounty of his friends." Cutting through the polite, old-fashioned language, it is clear Ledyard was sponging off anyone he could. Thus he jumped at the suggestion, and Jefferson set about obtaining the necessary permission for Ledyard to cross Russia and Siberia to the North Pacific where, hopefully, he would find a Russian ship to take him to the northwest of America.

While he was waiting for the details to be worked out, Ledyard lived just outside Paris in the small village of St. Germaine, on the edge of the royal forest through which he ran four miles every day to keep in shape. He was often in Paris, visiting Jefferson, Lafayette,

John Paul Jones, and—just before he returned to America—the grand old man, Benjamin Franklin. Once, too, he saw the King of France, Louis XVI, shooting partridges in the field. "He was dressed in common musqueto trowsers, a short linen frock, and an old laced hat without a cockade. He had an easy, gentlemanly appearance; and had it not been for his few attendants, I should have taken him for the captain of a merchant ship, amusing himself in the field."

Beyond that, there was little to do but wait for permission to cross Russia. Yet if Ledyard was now committed to the plan of exploring North America, he was not particularly interested in traveling through Siberia if he could find another way to reach the northwest. In the summer of 1786, when he heard of an English ship bound for the west coast of America, he gave up the Russian project and went to England instead. From London he wrote Jefferson telling him that in three days a ship would sail for Nootka and that he had passage on it. He added, "I bought two great Dogs, an Indian pipe and a hatchet. My want of time as well as more money will prevent my going otherwise than indiferrently equipped for such an enterprise." The ship sailed but it was barely out of sight of land when a government cutter intercepted it and ordered it back. Customs officials seized it and impounded everything on board including, Ledyard wrote, "all my little Baggage—shield, Buckler, Lance, Dogs, squire, and all gone."

Ledyard returned to Paris where he learned that Catherine II of Russia had also declined to permit his expedition because "she thinks it chimaerical." He had now become so desperate that he ignored this and went to St. Petersburg in the spring of 1787. In June he headed east, crossing first Russia, then Siberia, and by mid-September had reached Yakutsk, only a few hundred miles from the Pacific. There he met Joseph Billings, another veteran of Cook's third voyage, now working for the Russians. Ledyard accompanied him back to Irkutsk to spend the winter and while there was arrested and taken first to Moscow, then to the Polish border where he was thrown out of Russia.

He worked his way back to Paris, then on to London, where Joseph Banks, President of the Royal Society, was planning an expedition to explore the interior of Africa and wondered if Ledyard would be interested. Ledyard replied that he had always intended, after exploring the interior of America, to do the same in Africa. He decided to do it the other way around and in late June, less than two months after returning from his shattering experiences in Russia, he set out for Egypt. He stopped briefly in Paris to promise Jefferson that once the African venture was over he would return to the United States and go to Kentucky and from there attempt to penetrate westward as far as the Pacific.

He would not have the chance for he never returned from Africa. In August 1788 he wrote to Jefferson from Alexandria, and in September and again in November he wrote long letters from Cairo. Then there were no more letters and Jefferson began to hear rumors that Ledyard was dead. He made several unsuccessful attempts to find out if it was true, but it was not until the summer of 1789 that he received a letter from Thomas Paine who was in London. Enclosed with Paine's letter was a communication to Joseph Banks containing an account of Ledyard's death. Dated January 27, 1789, it said that "Seventeen days ago poor Mr. Ledyard went to his eternal rest. He suffered himself to be transported with anger against the persons who had engaged to conduct him to Sennar because of the delay setting out on their voyage for want (as they said) of a fair wind. He was seized with a pain in his stomach occasioned by Bile and undertook to cure himself. Excessive vomiting ensued, in consequence of which he broke a blood vessel and died in six days."

II

The great irony is that John Ledyard should have stayed at home in New England. Instead of being lured to impractical schemes that became progressively wilder until he ended up dying alone in Egypt, he should have kept to his original idea of finding backing for a simple money-making expedition to trade for furs. For even before he died—in fact while he sat alone and frustrated in Siberia waiting for something that would never happen—his idea had taken hold and two American ships were on their way from New England to the northwest coast.

Joseph Barrell, a Boston merchant, after reading the account of Cook's third voyage, used his influence to raise enough money to finance a trading expedition to the Pacific. Besides Barrell five other men were involved—Samuel Brown, a Boston merchant; Charles Bulfinch, an architect; Crowell Hatch, a Cambridge ship captain; John Pintard, a New York merchant; and John Derby, a ship captain and member of a well-known seafaring family from Salem. The enterprise was privately financed by selling fourteen shares at $3,500 each. They purchased and outfitted two ships, the *Columbia,* slightly over eighty feet long, and the *Lady Washington,* somewhat smaller. John Kendrick, a forty-seven-year-old veteran of the coastal trade, was hired as captain of the *Columbia,* and Robert Gray, a veteran of Revolutionary War naval service, was given command of the *Lady Washington.*

Those who organized the expedition were also interested in anyone who had been to the Pacific, and they were able to find another veteran of Cook's third voyage, Simeon Woodruff, a New Englander who had served as gunner's mate on the *Discovery.* He was hired as first officer on the *Columbia.* Quite likely, if John Ledyard had been at home in New England he too would have found a place on board.

By Sunday, September 30, 1787, the *Columbia,* fully loaded with stores and provisions for the voyage, was riding at anchor at Castle Roads in Boston Harbor. About noon Captain Kendrick came aboard bringing with him the furrier, the surgeon, and the astronomer. He also brought a large crowd of well-wishers, the sponsoring merchants as well as many others from Boston who came to see them off. The visitors were given a small taste of life at sea when the ship was moved a short distance down to Nanataskit Roads where it again anchored, this time in company with its consort, the *Lady Washington.* Then those on board began to celebrate the impending departure. It was, according to one crew member, "the last evening we spent on that side of the continent, and it was celebrated accordingly." There was much "murth and glee," as well as "jovial songs and animating sentiments," and it was not until late at night that the crowd began to dwindle. Early the next morning, Monday, October 1, 1787, the two ships weighed anchor, and by the time the sun rose they were already out of Boston Harbor.

The ships were barely at sea, however, when trouble developed between Captain Kendrick and his first mate, the Cook veteran Simeon Woodruff. Eventually the discord became so intense that Kendrick removed Woodruff as first officer and he left the ship when they reached the Cape Verde Islands. So did the surgeon, who went so far as to complain to the governor of the island of the inhuman treatment he had received at the hands of Captain Kendrick. While the ships lay at anchor in Cape Verde for the next six weeks, Kendrick was also criticized by his fellow captain Robert Gray of the *Lady Washington* who felt the long delay was entirely unnecessary.

The ships finally sailed for the Pacific, but while rounding Cape Horn they were separated in a violent gale. Captain Gray, instead of being upset, congratulated himself on his good luck in losing sight of his cautious, slow-moving commander and estimated he saved six weeks by sailing alone. At 10 a.m. on Saturday morning, August 2, 1788, ten months after clearing Boston Harbor, those aboard the *Lady Washington* "to our inexpressable joy saw the coast of America."

They were off the coast of Oregon, and from the time they arrived they could see native Indians watching from the shore. After a good deal of persuasion, a small canoe came alongside and received presents. That enticed several others to come out, each bringing large amounts of berries and cooked crabs that were offered not for trade but as presents. Having established such amicable relations, trading began for sea-otter skins and continued in a friendly fashion on through the evening.

The next day several crew members went ashore, some to cut grass, others to visit the native village. One of the grass-cutting party, however, left his cutlass stuck in the ground and when an Indian grabbed it and ran, he foolishly chased him right into the midst of the village. When he grabbed the thief, he was attacked and killed by the mob that had gathered and in the riot that followed several other seamen were wounded as they fought their way back to the ship's boats and pushed off. They were pursued by canoes but reached the ship and were able to drive off the Indians by firing the swivel gun. All night long, they could hear Indians whooping and shouting and see them dancing on the bench silhouetted against their fires. It was two more days before the *Lady Washington* could get out of the newly named Murderer's Harbor, and even then it dangerously struck the bar across the mouth of the bay.

Once clear of Murderer's Harbor, the *Lady Washington* worked its way north up the coast until mid-September when it reached Nootka Sound. Less than a week later Captain Kendrick brought the *Columbia* into the Sound. And thus, a full year after leaving Boston Harbor, the *Columbia* and the *Lady Washington* were reunited on the northwest coast of America.

III

Three years later, on a bright sunny afternoon in early August 1790, the citizens of Boston heard cannon fire coming from down-harbor. It was the ship *Columbia* celebrating its return home after almost three years by firing a thirteen-gun salute in recognition of the United States flag flying over the castle. Working its way into the harbor, it dropped anchor and fired another thirteen-gun salute. By now large crowds had gathered on all the wharves, and they greeted the salute with loud cheering. A rumor began to sweep through the crowd that a native Hawaiian was on board. Soon it was found to be true as the ship's captain came ashore with a young native of Kauai wearing a feathered helmet and cloak of scarlet and gold feathers that glittered in the sunlight. A procession was formed and the two men, arm in arm, led it up State Street to call on Governor John Hancock.

It was an exciting, even spectacular, end to the first American attempt to penetrate the northwest fur trade, but Captain John Kendrick, who had been in command of the *Columbia* when it left Boston, was not there to enjoy it. Instead he had switched commands with Captain Robert Gray, who sailed first to China, then on to Boston, while Kendrick in the *Lady Washington* stayed behind in the northwest to continue trading.

Possibly Kendrick preferred to remain on the northwest coast rather than face the ship's owners, for financially the voyage had not been very successful. The delays caused by Kendrick's ineptness, lack of knowledge of trading conditions, damage to part of the cargo of tea, and the fact that another ship had recently arrived with China goods had all cut into the profits. Two of the investors, John Pintard of New York and John Derby of Salem, sold their shares in the enterprise. The other partners were encouraged, if not by specific results, at least by future promise, and within six weeks the *Columbia* was ready to sail again.

It was not fast enough, however, for a week earlier the owners of the Boston firm of Magee and Perkins had watched as their own small brigantine *Hope* cleared Boston harbor for the Pacific. Its captain was Joseph Ingraham who, much to the irritation of his former employers, had been lured away from his berth as first mate on board the *Columbia.* Also on board, as supercargo, was Ebenezer Dorr, Jr., the eldest son of a Boston mercantile family which had also sensed the possibilities of the northwest trade.

The family's patriarch was the elder Ebenezer Dorr, a native of Roxbury, who in his early years had been a tanner and leather dresser like his father and grandfather before him. After marrying in 1761 he had moved to Boston where he continued in the leather business and also began investing in small trading ventures up and down the New England coast. He had done well and by 1790, when the *Columbia* returned from the northwest, he was now a merchant with a store at No. 27 Long Wharf and a house out on Boston Neck. He was also the father of a large family, seven sons and three daughters, the eldest of whom he sent aboard the *Hope* to gain experience in the fur trade.

The voyage went smoothly although Ebenezer Dorr soon developed an intense dislike for Captain Ingraham who, he claimed, was a fool, a coward, and a drunkard. At the Falkland Islands, before the ship was even out of the Atlantic, he noted in his diary that Ingraham "well stocked with rum" went off to search for a place to anchor but soon returned because he was too drunk to find anything. Dorr seems to have restricted all such comments to his diary, for Captain Ingraham, who was keeping his own journal, did not hint at trouble with the supercargo. Dorr, however, rarely let pass an opportunity to criticize, and a few days later, while still at the Falkland Islands, he wrote, "during the evening and night we found enough to do to quiet the captain whose fears were worked up to such a pitch that he behaved more like a madman than a man of sense." Ingraham's comment for the same day was, "nothing worthy of note took place."

Possibly Dorr's contempt came not so much from Ingraham's behavior as from the fact that he was Dorr's superior aboard the *Hope.*

Certainly the criticism of Ingraham was exaggerated, for although he undoubtedly drank, possibly even to excess on occasion, he can hardly have been the raging, alcoholic madman that Dorr portrays in his diary. Not only had he served well as first mate aboard the *Columbia* but he also took the *Hope* to the northwest, quickly obtained a cargo, and sailed for China. In Canton he sold the furs for enough money to refit the *Hope* for another trip to the northwest and to buy a shipload of tea which he sent back to Boston aboard the British ship *Fairy*. Ebenezer Dorr went aboard the *Fairy* and sailed for home, taking with him his diary to show those in Boston both the evils of Captain Ingraham and also the possibilities of the northwest fur trade.

IV

Boston investors had sent the *Lady Washington,* the *Columbia,* and later the *Hope* to the northwest, but in the years immediately after the Revolution, trade was reviving in ports all along the Massachusetts coast. It was at this time that a young man named Richard Cleveland went to work at a counting house in his native Salem. Later, he remembered, "in the ordinary course of a commercial education in New England, boys are transferred from school to the merchant's desk at the age of fourteen or fifteen. When I had reached my fourteenth year, it was my good fortune to be received into the counting house of Elias Hasket Derby, Esq., of Salem."

When Cleveland first joined the countinghouse its owner E. H. Derby was, at the age of forty-eight, well on his way to becoming one of America's wealthiest men. He was a member of a large seafaring family, although unlike his father and all his brothers, he had never been to sea and had never visited a foreign land. Instead, he entered the family mercantile business at an early age and had risen until, about the time the Revolution began, he took control. During the war he outfitted several ships as privateers that successfully preyed on British shipping. As soon as the war was over he began sending ships to open trade with the Baltic, the Mediterranean, the Cape of Good Hope, the Ile de France, and finally China itself.

Richard Cleveland, as he came to work for Derby, found himself at the very center of Salem's maritime activities. Just outside the countinghouse door in one direction was Derby Street, the landward side of which was lined with the mansions of prominent merchants, the seaward side with shipyards filled with spars, rigging, and furled sails waiting to be placed aboard ships tied up at the docks. In the other direction lay the wharf where ships owned by E. H. Derby arrived from all parts of the world.

In many ways the world inside the countinghouse was even more exciting, and Cleveland later remembered how he spent much of his time listening to talk about exotic ports newly opened to American ships. He also began to invest in a small way in foreign trade, for at the time ship captains and supercargos were willing to handle even the smallest "adventure." One captain, upon leaving Salem, was carrying a letter of instructions from Mrs. Harriet Elkins which said, "Please to purchase if at Calcutta two net bead with draperies; if at Batavia or any spice market, nutmegs, and mace, or if at Canton, Two Canton Crape shawls of the enclosed Colors at $5 per shawl. Enclosed is $10." He also had five dollars to use to buy Mrs. Mary Townsend one soup tureen, "14 by 10 inches, China."

Soon after he began working for Derby, Richard Cleveland started saving his pennies and using them to invest in small adventures. And when a ship came back with stores of great profit, Cleveland not only heard about them but saw them manifested in a small way in his own private investments. Finally, after four years in the countinghouse, he could stand it no longer. He said, "I became impatient to begin that nautical career on which I had determined, as presenting the most sure and direct means of arriving at independence."

Thus it was that Richard Cleveland sailed for the West Indies on board E. H. Derby's brig, *Rose.* He was just eighteen years old, as was the ship's captain, Nathaniel Silsbee. The two had been friends and schoolmates and at the age of fourteen, when Cleveland went into the countinghouse, Silsbee had gone to work for Derby as a clerk on one of Derby's ships bound for China. Now, at eighteen and with four years' experience at sea, Silsbee had been given command of one of Derby's small West Indian trading vessels.

At the same time Richard Cleveland, until now landlocked in the countinghouse on Derby wharf, was sent along to gain a new kind of experience. He served as captain's clerk, working as an ordinary sailor while at sea, but helping Silsbee when they were in port, and living not with the crew but with the captain in his cabin. It was, Cleveland thought, the best possible way to give a young man practical knowledge of the sea "free from the vulgarity of the forecastle." It also taught him the ways of doing business which would some day make him an accomplished supercargo.

After a long, hot, forty-day summer passage down the Atlantic into the Caribbean, the *Rose* reached Cap Haitien where Cleveland got his first glimpse of a foreign port. Even for a boy brought up in Salem, it was a marvelous spectacle, the likes of which he had never seen. He said, "The throng of boats by which we were instantly surrounded, to sell us the variety of strange fruits with which they were laden;—the number of large ships in port, some loading, others unloading; the daily arrival and departure of vessels of all nations;—the French slavers continually coming in from Africa, with a crowd of blacks on their decks;—the fine ships of war in beautiful order; and the multitude of boats passing to and fro, across the bay; form altogether, a scene surpassingly animated and brilliant."

It was Richard Cleveland's introduction to the world of foreign commerce and of foreign travel, and he was enthralled by it. Yet for all the excitement, his career at sea almost did not survive the trip. In September, the *Rose* arrived back in Salem to Cleveland's great joy and relief. He had completed his first voyage, something worth celebrating, but when he put his feet on the solidness of Derby wharf he was finally free from "the nausea, occasioned by the wearisome rolling and the bad odor of the vessel, which is probably not unusual, and will be duly appreciated by those who make their first passage at sea." Seasickness is a common problem for those going to sea for the first time, but in Cleveland's case it was somewhat more serious. For, he said, "the distress from seasickness, and its consequent prostrations of spirits, were such as to make it desirable to seek some other road to fortune." Unfortunately he had few other choices. He did not want to be a common sailor but a merchant like E. H. Derby. Yet he had no capital, and as he knew, "a merchant without capital was as incapable of making head-way, as a mechanic without tools." If he stayed ashore in Salem with no capital, all he could hope for would be to live out his life as a clerk or a bookkeeper "with no chance of ever being any thing else." If he wanted to avoid that, his only hope was to persevere in the profession he had chosen. And so he made his choice. And either he conquered his seasickness or he suffered, for he would spend the next eight years almost constantly at sea.

V

In late summer 1795 Captain Ebenezer Dorr, Jr., in his new ship the *Otter,* left Boston bound for the Indian Ocean, Australia, and eventually the Pacific Coast of America. By then it had been five years since he had returned to Boston aboard the ship *Fairy* commanded by William Rogers. Dorr, despite his unhappy experiences with Captain Ingraham on the *Hope,* apparently had told his father of the great possibilities in the northwest fur trade. He was no sooner home than the elder Ebenezer Dorr sent him back to the northwest as supercargo on the *Fairy,* still commanded by Rogers. This time Dorr made what he hoped would be a profitable addition by sending the ship via the South Indian Ocean where at barren, windswept Amsterdam and St. Paul Islands—midway between Africa and Australia and more than two thousand miles from either—it would drop off a crew to obtain sealskins. But when it touched at Amsterdam Island, it found a crew of Frenchmen under Pierre Peron already at work killing seals. The *Fairy* moved over to nearby St. Paul Island, left the seal hunters, and sailed on to the northwest. It spent the summer trading along the coast, then went back to Macao with its furs, and by July 1795 was back in Boston.

Ebenezer Dorr again had little time at home, for within a month he was once more on his way to the Pacific. By now the elder Dorr apparently felt his son, who had twice been to the northwest with others, was experienced enough to command his own ship, the *Otter.* In August 1795 his father handed him instructions to "embrace the first good wind and weather" to depart Boston.

Once at sea Dorr, in compliance with his father's instructions, set his course for St. Paul Island in the South Indian Ocean to retrieve the seal hunters left by the *Fairy* two years before. After taking them aboard, Dorr went to Amsterdam Island, where on his previous visit he had found Pierre Peron and his crew hunting seals. Now, in January 1796 the Frenchmen were gone, but lying on the beach was a large pile of cured sealskins ready for shipment. Since the island was apparently deserted, Dorr had the sealskins loaded aboard the *Otter,* then sailed for Australia.

This unexpected windfall for Dorr did not last long, for the *Otter* had barely dropped anchor in Sydney Cove when it was visited by the owner of the sealskins, Pierre Peron. He told Dorr that back in December another ship had put in at Amsterdam Island. By then he and his crew had been there for three years and for the last eighteen months had eaten nothing but seal meat. When the ship captain offered to take them off the island they accepted, but because of heavy weather, the captain refused to take the sealskins aboard. Thus three years' worth of work had been abandoned. Now Peron had learned that the American had picked up the sealskins and he came aboard the *Otter* to claim them.

Although Dorr recognized Peron's ownership, he was not willing to surrender the skins. Until such time as they could be sold he would keep them safely in the hold of his ship. He offered Peron the position of first mate aboard the *Otter* on its voyage to the northwest, China, and eventually back to Boston. There was little Peron could do but accept, for he was penniless and stranded in a remote penal colony. He was given an opportunity to stay near his sealskins which Dorr had under his control in the hold of the ship.

Although Dorr's original instructions were to touch at Botony Bay "for refreshments," a visit to the British penal colony had other advantages as well. Like all ship captains bound for the coast of America, Dorr knew he needed only a small crew to sail the ship but a much larger number of men to provide security while trading among the Indians in the northwest. If all these men were brought from Boston they would have to be paid, but in Australia there was an almost endless number of convicts willing to serve on a departing ship without being overly concerned with how much money they would get. When the *Otter* sailed from Sydney, it had on board seventeen convicts, including a woman named Jane who was smuggled aboard by the ship's carpenter, Andrew Lambert.

Not all the convicts reached America. A few weeks after leaving Australia, the ship was cruising through the islands and reefs of Tonga looking for a way to the open ocean. Native canoes pushed off from the islands, and soon the ship's deck was filled with the food they brought—five or six kinds of bananas, watermelons, yams, pineapples, coconuts, breadfruit, and sugar cane. One crew member said, "the women . . . did not appear to possess the slightest degree of modesty and gave themselves to the first person to pass by." It was too much for some who had just escaped from Australia, and they soon began to slip into native canoes and disappear onto one of the islands. Eventually six men deserted, becoming the first beachcombers in Tonga and among the first in the entire South Pacific. The rest of the convicts stayed with the *Otter* as it broke clear of Tonga and sailed to the coast of America, and by the spring of 1796 was trading with the Indians in the northwest.

VI

In September 1795 Joe O'Cain, the young Irishman from Boston, had been left in California, and despite orders to the contrary, was allowed to remain for the rest of the year and well into 1796. He lived in Santa Barbara which by then consisted of the presidio commanded by Felipe de Goycoechea and the mission presided over by Fathers Jose de Miguel and Esteban Tapis. The presidio buildings had been finished five years before, but at the mission there was still continual construction. In 1791 a guardhouse had been added, in 1792 two large corrals, in 1793 an adobe church—135 feet long, all of it tiled and plastered—and in 1794 a granary, a spinnery resting on a stone foundation, a wall around the cemetery, and a sheep corral. In 1795, the year O'Cain arrived, workers at the mission were building a passageway with a tile roof on the side of the square adjoining the presidio, as well as another spinnery and four new rooms for the friars. At the same time, most of the old building beams made of alder and poplar were being replaced with pine.

Clearly, the growing town presented possibilities for a man like O'Cain. His abilities as a sailor were undoubtedly of little use, but the fact that he was also a carpenter had not gone unnoticed. There had always been a shortage of artisans in California, and during the years just before O'Cain arrived, the government had made a concentrated effort to do something about it. Between 1792 and 1795, several craftsmen—carpenters, masons, stonecutters, tailors, blacksmiths, tanners, shoemakers, saddlers, weavers, even a ribbon maker—were sent to California. They signed contracts for four or five years, and some of them were paid surprisingly well, with a few "maestros" receiving as much as $1,000 a year. They were expected to teach their crafts at the various missions, one carpenter being told he was to teach his trade to at least twelve Indians during his four-year tour of duty.

Soon after O'Cain's arrival, the first wave of artisans began to go back to Mexico after having had mixed success. They had traveled throughout California teaching their trades, and within a few years most of the missions had carpenters, blacksmiths, weavers, and leather workers with at least limited training. Yet there had also been some complaints. Although the missionaries were happy enough to obtain skilled teachers for their Indians, they were outraged when they found they were expected to pay for them. They were also unhappy when they discovered that most of the artisans refused to see themselves as mission servants responsible for doing whatever the missionaries wanted done. The skilled workers considered themselves responsible to the governor, but that too caused some problems. Between Romeu's death in 1792 and Borica's arrival in 1794, the gubernatorial situation had been unsettled and the artisans had taken advantage of it by being, according to Borica, "loose and corrupt." Others who watched them at work objected to the fact that they behaved as if they were officers rather than teachers. Clearly the project had uneven results, but just as clearly it demonstrated the need in California for skilled craftsmen capable of passing on knowledge of their trades. And Joe O'Cain was a carpenter, a fact that Goycoechea, in his letter, immediately brought to the attention of the governor.

Thus, despite orders that foreigners who came to California were to be immediately expelled, O'Cain was not placed aboard any of the several supply ships sailing for Mexico. Almost a full year after his arrival he was still in California and he might have been allowed to stay even longer had it not been for events that began in the fall of 1796.

VII

In October 1796 a foreign ship sighted off San Francisco made no attempt to enter the bay but continued on south. A few days later it was seen by residents of Santa Cruz as it cruised offshore for several days. On October 27, a soldier arrived at the presidio in Monterey with news that a ship's boat carrying five "Ingles" had landed at Carmel near the mission. Sergeant Macario Castro immediately notified Governor Borica, then rushed off to the mission where he encountered Captain Ebenezer Dorr who presented a passport signed not only by the Spanish consul in Charleston, South Carolina, but by the famous General Washington.

Castro had brought horses for the foreigners to ride from the mission to the presidio, but Dorr, his first mate Pierre Peron, and the rest, being sailors, preferred to walk. At Monterey they were taken to a guardroom where, while they waited to see the governor, they were given a cup of chocolate, which Peron found excellent and said, "this delicate attention was very well received by us, as for men accustomed to salt fish and biscuit it was a great treat."

After the sergeant announced that the governor was ready to receive them, they were escorted across the plaza to his office which Peron found, like the rest of the presidio, rather small and insignificant. The governor was friendly, listening courteously as the American captain told what was already becoming a familiar tale in Spanish California.

The *Otter,* Dorr said, was almost totally devoid of provisions, and without them, and without water, it would be unable to continue its voyage. He asked to be allowed to anchor at Monterey long enough to obtain supplies and to take on water. Permission was granted and Dorr returned to the ship which was standing off Carmel. Throughout the next day the *Otter* slowly worked its way into port, guided by the firing of a gun from one of the presidio's batteries. By nightfall it had not reached the anchorage, and the Spanish kept a signal fire burning through the night. The next morning the *Otter* was able to drop anchor at Monterey, firing a seven-gun salute which was promptly answered by the firing of seven guns from the fort.

As always the Spanish treated the visitors well, and in the days that followed the *Otter* was loaded with flour, beans, meat, lard, vegetables, and fruit. When they found they needed several hundred more pounds of flour, Borica ordered an increase in the number of Indians milling flour in order to speed up the process. Peron, hearing the order given, expressed his surprise and said that in Europe the smallest mill could produce a hundred pounds in no more than an hour. In response, Borica led Peron to a workroom where fifteen or twenty Indians were sitting on their heels grinding the grain by hand on a metate, the common method used in this country although, Peron said, "for the capital of a government as extended as that of California I could not understand why a mill was not established like the ones in Europe." According to Borica, the Frenchman, La Perouse, had said the same thing ten years before and had even left a model for such a mill. Unfortunately, thus far no one had been found in California who was willing to build one.

Borica also had several long talks with Captain Dorr who explained that he had gathered a thousand otter skins in the north and now planned to sail to China to sell the furs. Having finished trading with the Indians, he no longer needed all the convicts he had on the *Otter,* and he asked Borica if he could leave them in California. Borica refused and that, seemingly, closed the subject.

Dorr, however, was determined to get rid of the convicts so he would not have to pay them their share of the ship's profits. The night after the *Otter* sailed, five men were found on shore, and the following night five more men and a woman were discovered on the beach near Carmel. They claimed the captain had forced them off the ship and into a small boat at pistol point. Thus California found itself burdened with Captain Dorr's unwanted crew members. Given the kindness that had been extended, Borica felt it was a dishonorable act on the part of the American captain, and even Pierre Peron, who had left with the *Otter,* later admitted, "the governor had a great deal to complain about M. Dorr."

Of those left behind, Andrew Lambert, John Rich, and James Smith were original crew members who had been on board since the ship left Boston. Another man, Thomas Moody, from England, had been picked up at Nootka Sound where he had been left by another ship. The other six men, Peter Pritchard, John Jones, John Turner, John

Gibson, Nicholas Phillips, and Joseph Hongate, a half-wit, were all convicts from Australia.

So, too, was Jane Lambert, the lone woman left behind. She gave Borica several versions of how she came to be aboard the *Otter,* including one in which she claimed that she was from Massachusetts, that she was legitimately married to the ship's carpenter, Andrew Lambert, and that they had a daughter living in Boston. The records show that she too was a convict from Australia and by the time the ship had reached California she had come to some kind of agreement with Lambert, for she was using his last name as her own.

Not long after these eleven foreigners were left in California, Borica received a letter from Spanish officials ordering him to send the American O'Cain to Spain. He replied that he would do so, and at the same time would send all those left behind by Dorr. But he delayed as long as possible. He was the governor of a growing area which lacked people with many basic skills, and he had put these foreigners to work as carpenters and blacksmiths. They were so industrious and well-behaved that he would have liked to keep them, but eventually, in obedience to royal orders, he was forced to send them to Mexico, and in October 1797, a full year after they arrived, they were loaded aboard the *Concepcion* before it sailed for San Blas. Apparently the young American carpenter Joe O'Cain went with them, for there is no further record of his living in California.

VIII

Early in the year 1798 Ebenezer Dorr, Jr., brought the ship *Otter* home to Boston. By then it had been almost eight years since he had first boarded the *Hope* as supercargo under Captain Joseph Ingraham. During all the following years he had been almost constantly at sea, on the *Hope,* then the *Fairy,* and finally as captain of the *Otter.* During those years, too, he had seen much of what was then strange and exotic—the Marquesas, the northwest coast of America, Hawaii, Macao, Canton, the convict colony at Botony Bay, the barren, windswept Amsterdam and St. Paul Islands in the South Indian Ocean, even the provincial capital of the Spanish California at

Monterey. Now, at the age of thirty-five having returned home after another highly successful voyage, he could afford to give up shipboard life and settle down ashore.

He was far from finished with the northwest fur trade, however, for his voyage had not only made money but had given him an idea of how to profit in the future. It was, of course, the very reason his father, the old leather-tanner Ebenezer, Sr., had sent him to the northwest in the first place. And now that he was back, the Dorr family—Ebenezer, Sr., and his seven sons—entered the trade with a vengeance. By August 1798 two more of their ships, the *Dispatch* and the *Hancock,* had cleared for the northwest.

As usual, the two ships were to go to the northwest coast to obtain furs which would be traded in China for Oriental goods to be brought back to Boston. In the past either the captain or a supercargo assigned to the ship tried to work out the best deal he could in Canton. Now, however, the Dorr family, undoubtedly on the recommendation of Ebenezer who had traded there, decided to provide an agent to help the ship captains through the complex maze of the China trade. The man they chose was Sullivan Dorr, the youngest of the seven sons, who at the age of twenty was sent to Canton to serve as agent for the family's ships.

Ebenezer Dorr was also aware of another possibility in the Pacific. During his stay in California he had seen many opportunities for trade, but having left eleven unwanted convicts and crew members in Monterey, he knew he would not be remembered kindly. Any indication that a ship belonged to someone named Dorr could have trouble, and the family's ships stayed well away from California.

Yet Boston traders were a close-knit group, and undoubtedly Dorr passed his information about California on to Thomas Perkins who, with no need to fear Spanish retaliation, decided to experiment in the California trade. When he sent the ship *Eliza* to trade in the northwest, he added instructions, "you will leave the Coast by say July and arrive by 1 August at Mont Rea." There the crew was to remain until early November, hoping to trade for Spanish dollars.

In August 1798 the *Eliza,* commanded by Captain James Rowan, left Boston bound first for the northwest coast, then California. By February of the following year, the ship had reached the coast of

America at Norfolk Sound, later to be known as Sitka. In the months to follow, the *Eliza,* using Norfolk Sound as its base, traded up and down the coast. It was not the only ship in the northwest that year, as was learned on April 9 when it returned to the Sound after a trading voyage and found another ship lying at anchor. Much to Captain Rowan's surprise it was the small cutter *Dragon,* out of Canton, on which he had once served as mate. Now renamed the *Caroline,* it had a new owner and captain, the old seasick sailor from Salem, Richard Cleveland.

IX

Almost seven years had passed since Cleveland, at the age of eighteen, had arrived home in Salem from that long miserable voyage to the West Indies on which he had suffered so much seasickness. Given his connections and his financial condition, and knowing that his only hope of avoiding a lifetime as a clerk or a bookkeeper was to go back to sea, he continued to work on vessels owned by E. H. Derby until a captain bound for India offered him the post of first mate and he accepted. But before the ship sailed, Mr. Derby decided the first mate's berth should go to his nephew, although he did offer Cleveland the opportunity to remain aboard as second mate. Cleveland declined, even though he knew that it ended any chance of advancement with E. H. Derby.

His decision paid off in the long run, for he soon found a first mate's berth on another vessel, and within a few years was promoted to the command of his own ship in the coastal trade. He left Salem in 1797 as captain of a ship bound for the Indian Ocean by way of Europe, but in France he received a message from the owner ordering the ship back to Salem. Cleveland was unwilling to give up the voyage, and sent the vessel home under the command of the first mate while he looked around for another opportunity.

He bought, on credit, a ship called the *Caroline* that had recently been a channel packet between Calais and Dover. He used what cash he had to buy a cargo, then in spite of the ship's tiny size—hardly bigger that an amateur pleasure craft—he headed for the Cape of Good

Hope. A storm virtually destroyed the *Caroline* before it had gone far, and Cleveland was forced to return to Le Havre where his crew deserted. Still he persisted. He repaired the ship and, after some difficulty, found more men who, "for aught I knew were robbers and pirates," and again put to sea. This time he made it to the Cape where the arrival of such a small vessel was so startling it aroused the suspicions of officials. After a personal appeal to the governor that prevented the seizure of his cargo, Cleveland was allowed to sell both it and the ship. Then he booked passage on a vessel bound for Batavia, hoping to find new fields of investment in the Orient.

Since trade was slow on the island of Java, Cleveland went on to Canton. Here, too, business was slow, and he was reluctantly preparing to go to Calcutta when the *Dragon* was offered for sale. It opened a way for him to reach the fur-trading areas of the northwest. With the backing of two American merchants in Canton, he bought the ship. Since all his papers were made out for the destroyed *Caroline,* he simply changed the name of the ship rather than go through all the complications of obtaining new papers. He purchased some left-over trade goods from a ship on its way home, scrounged through the shops of Canton for the rest of his cargo, then sailed for America.

The new *Caroline,* like the old one, was hardly bigger than a private yacht, but as always in the northwest trade, it was necessary to have a large crew—five in the cabin, and sixteen before the mast. In a port like Canton it was difficult to get good men, and Cleveland was forced to take whatever he could find among the beachcombers. Most of his sailors were deserters from East Indiamen, "the worst of a bad crew," and two were convicts recently escaped from Botany Bay. The crowded conditions, plus the constant exposure to wind and sea on board the tiny vessel, soon caused unrest, and even before Cleveland was clear of the China Coast he was faced with a mutiny. While the ship was anchored off Amoy, several crew members rebelled. With the help of a few loyal men, Cleveland put down the mutiny and forced the ringleaders, including the two convicts, ashore and left them on the island of Quemoy.

Cleveland's next problem was fighting his way clear of the China Coast and into the Pacific. In order to be among the first to reach America, he had left Canton in January, although experienced sailors in the China Sea had told him it was impossible to make it into the Pacific during the winter monsoons. Nonetheless the *Caroline* fought its way north, almost inch by inch, directly into the teeth of the northwest monsoon winds. Finally, on February 11, "after thirty-one days of great toil, exposure and anxiety," Cleveland saw "the north end of Formosa bearing south distant ten leagues." Fifty-one days later the *Caroline* dropped anchor at Norfolk Sound on the northwest coast of America.

When the Boston-based *Eliza* arrived soon after, Cleveland discovered that all his struggles with the winter monsoon in the South China Sea had still not made him the first trader on the coast. Captain Rowan came aboard the *Caroline,* and Cleveland learned that the *Eliza* had been there for two months and had been so successful that Rowan was ready to leave the northwest and head south to carry out his instructions to open trade with the Spanish in California. After that he would sail for China. Rowan also told Cleveland that at least ten ships from Boston would be arriving on the coast to trade that season. It was an exaggeration, but Cleveland had no way of knowing that, and as soon as he parted company with Rowan he began hurrying along the coast trying to obtain as many furs as possible before the horde of American ships arrived.

Soon after Cleveland left Norfolk Sound Captain Rowan, in the *Eliza,* headed south toward California, and on May 24, 1799, entered San Francisco Bay where he anchored off the presidio. Although Rowan's specific purpose was to trade with the Spanish, he told the officers who came aboard his ship the old, familiar lament of desperately needing to take on wood, water, and fresh supplies. Rowan even went a step further by saying he needed a safe place to spend the stormy season and asked if he could winter at Monterey. Surely his request surprised the Spanish for since it was only May it was a strange time to be worrying about winter storms. Possibly Rowan, running several months ahead of schedule, forgot he had not arrived in the fall as he had originally planned.

Governor Borica was not taken in by the claim which he had heard before. He also remembered that three years earlier he had treated another Boston captain with politeness only to have his guest dump eleven unwanted convicts and crew members on him. The governor issued orders that the *Eliza* might purchase a few supplies provided it left immediately and did not touch again on the California coast. Rowan agreed, and a few days later sailed out of San Francisco Bay.

X

While all the American ship captains were trading along the Pacific coast, Sullivan Dorr, the youngest of Ebenezer Dorr's seven sons, had been making his way to China. He had left Boston in early 1799 and after 178 days at sea arrived in Canton in late August to take up his position as the family's representative in China. Not long afterward trading ships began to arrive from the northwest coast of America.

The first to reach Canton was the *Caroline.* On September 17 Dorr wrote, "Two days since Cap. Cleveland in a country built cutter arrived here from the Coast . . . with a collection of 2300 skins." Dorr, however, was most interested in word of his own family's ships, the *Hancock* and the *Dispatch,* and obtained what information he could from Cleveland. The news was not good. He heard that both ships had arrived late, had collected only a few hundred furs each, and had little hope of getting more. He also heard that there had been trouble on the *Hancock,* although the captain had managed to maintain control of the ship. Still, Dorr was a little shocked by the way the uprising had been handled, for the captain "put 8 of the villains ashore at Norfolk Sound where the poor Devils will perish if not taken off. I am sorry he should do so, perhaps it was the only alternative."

At the same time Dorr, who had only recently arrived in China and was trying to get a feel for business there, watched Cleveland carefully and listened to rumors circulating through the trading community. He soon heard that Cleveland's furs had brought $25 each although "it being a secret Bargain am not able to say certain." Later he heard he had received more than $50,000 for them. Then, Cleveland left China bound "nobody knows where under English colours." There was considerable speculation about his destination, and at first Dorr suspected that the English flag was a deception and that Cleveland was bound for the "Spanish Main." Later he heard still another rumor that "Cleveland has really gone to Bengal for opium. It has risen in 6 months one hundred per Cent."

Speculation on Cleveland's destination was soon lost in the excitement caused by the arrival in Canton of the *Eliza,* and according to what Dorr heard, its voyage had been even more profitable than that of the *Caroline.* Supposedly it had on board 3,000 furs which Dorr estimated would bring $25 each, or a total of $75,000. Not only that but the *Eliza,* although unable to trade in California, had been more successful when it later touched at San Blas in Mexico. Dorr heard that the ship also carried $23,000 in cash "procured for goods upon the spanish main." In all, it meant almost $100,000 to invest in a homeward cargo of tea, nankeens, silk, and sugar.

A few weeks later the first of the Dorr family ships, the *Dispatch,* arrived in China with ominous news. Its captain, William Breck, was supposed to meet the family's other ship, the *Hancock,* at a certain point on the northwest coast where both crews would repair a leak in the *Hancock* before it sailed for China. The *Dispatch* had arrived a day early and waited for a week, but the *Hancock* never appeared, and Captain Breck had been forced to leave. The news worried Dorr but it turned out to be a false alarm, for a few days later the *Hancock* also reached port. And despite their late arrival and despite all their troubles, the two ships had not done badly. The *Hancock* had 1,600 furs, the *Dispatch* had 1,200, and although this was well below the take of the *Eliza* or even the *Caroline,* it still provided something with which to purchase a cargo to send to Boston.

One other thing bothered Sullivan Dorr, young and not very experienced in the ways of the world. It was the character and conduct of the men who commanded his family's ships. First there was the story told by Captain Breck of how they had kept warm aboard the *Dispatch* while in northern waters. Whenever they got cold, the captain said, each man, from the highest to the lowest, "from captain to cook," grabbed a cat-o-nine-tails, and they went racing through the ship having a running fight with the cats until everyone warmed up. The story shocked Dorr, and when he dutifully reported it in his letters home he added, "pretty business for a Captain." He was equally shocked by the story that John Crocker, captain of the *Hancock,* had abandoned part of his crew to almost certain death at Norfolk Sound.

Dorr also heard tales about the methods the two men used to obtain furs, which he summed up as "to get skins by all means, if not one way they must another, but skins they must have by all means." He complained to Crocker that the methods were both dishonest and dishonorable, but the captain dismissed his complaints and said that if necessary he would obtain furs even if he had to force the Indians to trade. Dorr concluded, "Crocker and Breck are such they should not have charge of a Ship of mine." He also said that while the two were staying with him in Canton, "the Vulgarity of their behavior precluded from inviting Gentlemen to my table, not chooseing to insult them by so doing."

Sullivan Dorr was not soon rid of those unwanted guests, for it was not until January that they sailed for Boston. Since both ships were poor sailors, it was decided they should sail together, but before they could leave, the *Hancock,* which Dorr described as an "old crazy leaking ship," had to be pulled out of the water and repaired. The operation took two weeks, after which both ships were loaded with the cargo bound for Boston. The major part consisted of tea, silk, and nankeens, but as always there were small adventures that private citizens had entrusted to Sullivan Dorr. To Mrs. B. Shaw he wrote, "Madam, Agreeable to your request at my departure from America have procured two pieces fine Canton flannel. There being a surplus of one Dollar, have purchased two laquered green silk mounted fans . . . Cap. Breck will deliver the above articles." To Mary Pope went another letter saying, that he had "procured one Tea and Coffee sett of China ware containing 84 pieces also 1 pair of pitchers and two pair mugs . . . My brother Henry will deliver the box."

Another purchase, stored in the hold of the *Hancock,* was on its way to Sullivan's older brother Ebenezer. A few years earlier, as master of the *Otter,* Ebenezer had visited China and should have had some idea of the kind of things available there, but his order was so vague that Sullivan was forced to rely on his own taste in making the purchases. He chose a considerable amount of china, including an 84-piece coffee set, an 84-piece tea set, and five "flour pots." He also chose several paintings which he purchased at three dollars each. Apparently they were intended for Ebenezer's Boston home to remind him of the time when he was a ship captain roaming the world. Three of the pictures were of sea battles, another a scenic view of Macao, another a view of Whampoa, and a third a panorama of the city of Canton. In all, these purchases had cost $120, and Dorr sent them home "in hopes they will please."

Finally, in January 1800 the *Dispatch* and the *Hancock* sailed from China loaded with Oriental goods bound for the United States.

XI

Richard Cleveland, upon reaching Canton in September 1799, was faced with a major decision. His voyage to the northwest had been highly successful, he had sold his furs for more than $50,000, and there was no reason why he could not repeat the process the following year. By now, however, he knew firsthand what it was to be crowded into a small ship for months with sullen sailors drawn from the dregs of the Canton waterfront. "Besides this," he said, "my inclination for such uncommon exposure and fatigues was diminished in proportion to the recent increase in my fortune." Rather than return to the coast of America he went to India instead.

Sullivan Dorr had heard a rumor that he had gone to Calcutta to obtain opium, but if so, Cleveland said nothing about it and there is no record of his bringing opium back to China. Instead he attempted to buy Indian goods to send back to the United States but discovered several American ships in port were bidding for such goods. They had so inflated prices that he began to look for another enterprise.

Talking to various people in Calcutta, he heard of an intriguing possibility. Supposedly, French privateers were capturing English merchant ships and taking them as prizes to the Ile de France in the Indian Ocean. Since all of Europe was at war and the island was virtually surrounded by privateers, it was almost impossible for them to leave. Both captured ships and cargoes were selling at almost unbelievably low prices.

It sounded good and Cleveland purchased a small ship, "so diminutive as to elude observation." Then, since Denmark was one of the few neutral countries, he took his ship to Serampore, the Danish settlement near Calcutta, and registered it under the Danish flag. And

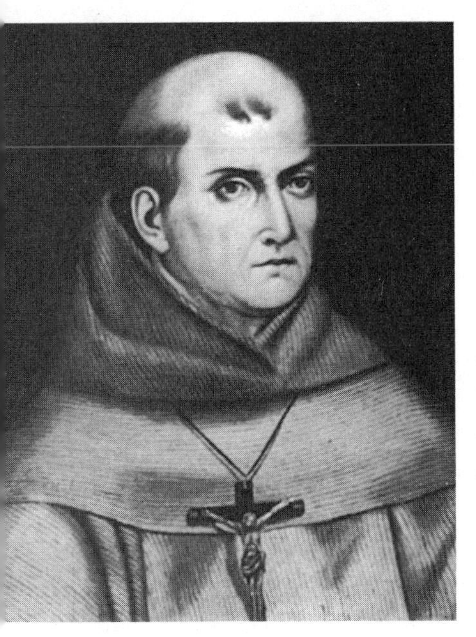

Fray Junipero Serra

Daniel Boone

Captain James Cook

Jean François de Galaup
Compte de la Perouse

Antonio Maria Bucareli y Ursúa

La Perouse at San Carlos Borromeo, 1786

George Vancouver

Don Juan Francisco de la Bodega y Quadra

Drawing of Monterey by a member of the Vancouver expedition, 1792

Esteban José Martinez

John Meares

A fanciful 1791 engraving of the seizure of James Colnett

The Columbia's *winter quarters at Adventure Cove in Nootka Sound*

Nootka woman

Nootka man

Salem, Massachusetts, 1792

Richard J. Cleveland

The Hongs of Old Canton

Aleut Indians in Baidarka

Alexander Baranov

Kodiak Island, 1798

Richard Henry Dana

Captain Francis A. Thompson

The Brig Pilgrim

with a small cargo of oil and wax, just enough weight to act as ballast, he sailed for the Ile de France.

As usual things did not quite work out the way they were supposed to. The rumors had a definite basis, but by the time Cleveland arrived the best ships had either already been sent to India under the Danish flag, or they had been purchased by speculators who were asking outrageous prices. Cleveland was able to sell his cargo of oil and wax, as well as his small ship, and he stayed on looking for any other possibility. While he was there he met another American, William Shaler.

The two men were almost destined to be friends. They were exactly the same age, and like Cleveland, Shaler was a New Englander and the son of a sea captain. His mother had died when he was eight, his father when he was thirteen, and by 1799 he too was a trader searching the world for his fortune. He had done some trading in Montevideo and Buenos Aires, then had come to the Ile de France looking for new opportunities.

With both Cleveland and Shaler seeking to invest money made in earlier trading ventures, they decided to pool their resources. Nothing on the Ile de France looked particularly good until late in 1800 when a privateer brought the ship *Kent* into port as a prize. It was sold to a Dane who promptly raised the neutral Danish flag and offered to lease it to anyone who wanted to take a cargo to Europe. Shaler and Cleveland contracted for exclusive use of the ship, purchased a cargo of coffee, and went aboard as passengers when the *Kent* sailed for Denmark.

They were just off the coast of Norway when, to their horror, they heard that England and Denmark were now at war. The British fleet, which had recently bombarded Copenhagen, was still in the vicinity, and if the *Kent* proceeded any farther it was almost certain to be seized. Their luck held, however, for the short war ended soon afterward and the *Kent* reached Copenhagen just in time to take advantage of a brisk demand for coffee which had become scarce during the British blockade. Cleveland also received a message that goods he had shipped from Canton had arrived safely in Salem. That, plus the profits from the coffee, "rendered me, as to pecuniary affairs, very independent."

He might have been expected to stop right there, for his ambition, always, was not to travel, not to see the world, but to make his fortune and use it to settle down to a comfortable life ashore in Salem, Massachusetts. But luck was running his way, and having found a congenial companion and fellow investor in William Shaler, he decided to try once more.

On the passage from Ile de France to Europe he and Shaler had talked about purchasing a ship and sailing it from Europe to the west coast of America. Now, with the profits from their latest voyage in hand, they began looking for a suitable vessel. They could find nothing they liked in Copenhagen and went to Hamburg, Germany, where they found an American ship, the *Lelia Byrd* from Portsmouth, Virginia, they could purchase at a reasonable price.

They now had a ship, but they also had a problem. Their investment was equal, both men were qualified masters, and it was not easy to determine who should be captain. Finally they left it to chance, drawing lots. Shaler became the captain, Cleveland the supercargo. The understanding according to Cleveland was that "these designations were only for form's sake; and that the duties of each station were to be reciprocally performed by each."

The two men began enlisting sailors and obtained a cargo, and as they did so they made a major decision. Ordinarily, the purpose of a voyage to the Pacific Coast of America was to trade with the Indians, and that required certain kinds of trade goods. Yet in recent years a few ship captains had attempted to trade, illegally, with the Spanish settlements and that required an entirely different kind of trade goods. It was possible to carry both kinds, but they were not interchangeable, and to gain maximum advantage decisions on the destination had to be made before the ship was loaded. Although Shaler and Cleveland, whenever they entered a Spanish port, always claimed they were bound for the northwest, the *Lelia Byrd* never went near that coast. Instead, after entering the Pacific in early 1802, it went into Valparaiso harbor in an attempt to trade. When that failed, the two Americans sailed on to San Blas, Mexico, where they encountered a friendly local official who agreed to trade. False hopes were raised, however, for soon the Mexican governor himself countermanded the orders.

Shaler and Cleveland spent the next several months attempting to get the governor's orders changed, even appealing to officials as far away as Mexico City. Eventually they obtained a permit to trade, but it was so limited that it was hardly worth the effort and they prepared to leave. Just before sailing, they had a stroke of luck that was not only profitable but also determined their next destination. A Spanish ship had recently arrived from California with sea-otter pelts on board which Cleveland, after some dealing, bought, "on such advantageous terms that it would secure our voyage from loss, even if we made no further sales." This piece of business also determined that their next port of call would be somewhere in California, and on the evening of March 16, 1803, the *Lelia Byrd* entered San Diego Bay and dropped anchor.

XII

The following morning, Lieutenant Manuel Rodriguez, commandante of the San Diego presidio, boarded the *Lelia Byrd* to inquire as to its business. The two Americans said, innocently enough, that they badly needed wood, water, and supplies—cattle, flour, salt, and chickens.

To Shaler and Cleveland the story sounded entirely reasonable, but by now Lieutenant Rodriguez was tired of hearing it. Three times since he had assumed command of the presidio, American ships had put in to San Diego claiming to be desperately in need of help. Each time Rodriguez had been friendly and allowed the ships to refit although he also insisted that the laws forbidding trading be obeyed. The most recent of these visits had been that of the American ship *Alexander,* and while it was taking on supplies, Rodriguez heard a rumor that someone had smuggled furs out to the ship. He took a squad of soldiers, boarded the ship, and began a search. In a storeroom just off the mainmast he found almost 500 sea-otter furs. He confiscated them and ordered the *Alexander* to leave San Diego immediately.

It was only a few weeks after this that the *Lelia Byrd* arrived in San Diego, and when Rodriguez came aboard he made it clear by his manner that he was the official representative of the Spanish government and not a man to be trifled with. In doing so he mightily offended Richard Cleveland who said, "such a ridiculous display of 'a little brief authority,' and pompous parade, I never before witnessed."

Still Rodriguez told them they could have supplies provided they sailed as soon as they were loaded. He also allowed them to go ashore, but not to visit the small settlement of San Diego, some three miles from their anchorage just inside Ballast Point. Once these arrangements were made, Rodriguez departed, "with characteristic pomp, leaving on board five of his escort, as he said, to see that we carried on no contraband trade."

After meeting Rodriguez and hearing his conditions for allowing them to remain in port, Cleveland went ashore to look around. Talking to a young Spanish soldier he heard what had happened to the *Alexander*. The most interesting thing, at least to Cleveland, was that the furs had been confiscated and were now in the possession of Commandante Rodriguez. Cleveland immediately called on the lieutenant and offered to make it worth his while to part with the furs. Rodriguez refused to sell, refusing even to listen to such an offer. Cleveland, contemptuous of Spaniards, and also a cynical New Englander who believed that every man had his price, found it difficult to understand. His best explanation was that Rodriguez was willing to make a deal but was afraid he might be caught. Since "they were all spies on each other," Cleveland said, "he dared not indulge his desire of selling them to us." The other explanation—that Rodriguez was an honest man who believed in enforcing the rules—seems never to have occurred to Cleveland.

There were those in San Diego who had no scruples against trading with the Americans, and Cleveland made several deals for furs that would be delivered to the ship the night before it sailed. On March 21, Rodriguez visited the ship, and after inspecting told Shaler that since all the supplies were now on board, he expected the *Lelia Byrd* to sail the next morning. As usual he left several guards behind to prevent any smuggling.

After dark the ship's boat was lowered into the water, and when one of the Spanish soldiers asked why, he was told some men were going to look for a crew member who had not returned. A few minutes later, the launch was also put in the water and this time the guard was told it was going to look for the boat. The boat returned with a few furs, but the launch did not, and Cleveland began to suspect that something had gone wrong. At daylight he could see that the launch and those who manned it, the ship's caulker and two cabin boys, had been captured. The three crew members had been tied hand and foot and were now lying helpless on the beach.

The men aboard the *Lelia Byrd* quickly disarmed the guards and forced them below while Cleveland, with four men, went ashore and rescued the captives at pistol point. Once they were back on board, the crew prepared to sail, but unfortunately there was only a mild breeze. It meant they would be under the guns on Point Loma for a long time, and as they looked ashore they could see a large number of men, afoot and on horseback, racing for the fort.

Shaler ordered the ship's six-pounders lined up on the side toward the shore and then he began the run by the fort. He brought the Spanish guards on deck and stood them in the most exposed spot, hoping that seeing them would keep their comrades from firing, but when the *Lelia Byrd* came within range, shots were fired from both ship and fort. Despite considerable noise, no one was injured and there was little damage, the most serious being a hole in the *Lelia Byrd*'s hull that was later patched with oakum. And the prisoners expressed no hard feelings even when they were herded to the most exposed place on board. As soon as the ship was clear of the fort, they were put ashore, and as the *Lelia Byrd* left them they could be heard crying, "Vivan, vivan Los Americanos."

The *Lelia Byrd* sailed south along the coast of Baja California where Shaler and Cleveland spent the next several weeks trading with the padres at various missions. They obtained more sea-otter furs, some pearls, and even three horses, one a mare in foal. In late May the *Lelia Byrd* sailed, and less than a month later reached Hawaii where they gave the horses to King Kamehameha as a present. Then they sailed for China and in late August 1803 reached Canton.

Shaler and Cleveland sold the furs profitably and also decided to divide their future efforts. The *Lelia Byrd* would be refitted and Shaler, as captain, would take it back to California for another season of trading. They would invest in a cargo of silk and Oriental goods, which Cleveland would accompany back to Boston on the ship *Alert*. After a five-month passage, Cleveland arrived in Boston where "my invoice of silks arrived at a very good market, and were sold advantageously."

It had been almost eight years since Richard Cleveland left Salem to seek his fortune. Now he was back and brought with him a cargo worth $70,000 plus whatever profit he might later get from the *Lelia Byrd*'s second voyage. It had been what he had been searching for all over the world and now he had found it. A few months after his return he married his cousin Dorcas Cleveland Hiller, bought a beautiful estate in Lancaster, Massachusetts, and settled down to spend the rest of his life reading books and tending his flowers.

JOE O'CAIN AND THE RUSSIAN COAST

I

The voyage of the *Lelia Byrd* not only made Richard Cleveland a rich man, it also demonstrated something that was not lost on other Boston traders. Although large numbers of sea otters were available in both Californias, the fact that Shaler and Cleveland had traded successfully on some parts of the coast but had to fight their way out of San Diego showed just how erratically the laws were enforced. And given the cost in both time and money of sending a ship to the Pacific, investors wanted a less capricious system.

Joe O'Cain gave it to them. After being expelled from California, he had gone to Mexico, then to Spain, and eventually to Boston where, in March 1799, he had married Abigail Kimball. His knowledge and experience of the Pacific allowed him to lure the four Winship brothers—Abiel, Charles, Nathan, and Jonathan—into entering the trade. In August 1799, the ship *Betsy,* officially owned by Abiel Winship and Joseph O'Cain, sailed from Boston with Charles Winship as captain, O'Cain as supercargo.

The voyage of the *Betsy* ended in disaster, at least for Winship and O'Cain. Upon reaching San Blas on the west coast of Mexico, they went ashore, leaving the ship under command of the second mate, a man named Brown. A Spanish man-of-war sailed into the harbor, and suddenly there was a flurry of activity aboard the *Betsy.* The anchor was hoisted, the sails were unfurled, and the ship fled from San Blas leaving Winship and O'Cain behind. Possibly Brown leaped into action because he thought the Spanish ship intended to seize the *Betsy,* but more likely he saw a perfect opportunity to take over the ship. He made no real attempt to rescue Winship or O'Cain, but took the *Betsy* directly to China where he sold the furs on board and purchased a cargo of tea for the homeward passage. Eventually he brought the ship back to Boston but the owners always suspected him of cheating them by agreeing to pay a high price for tea, then receiving a kickback from the merchant who sold it to him.

Whatever Brown's motives, the effect of his action was to maroon Winship and O'Cain in San Blas. Within a few months Winship, who was only twenty-three, died of sunstroke, and once again O'Cain was left alone in a Spanish port. This time he was in luck, for a few weeks later, the American ship *Enterprise,* out of New York under Captain Ezekiel Hubbell, entered San Blas harbor. When it left a few days later, Joe O'Cain was on board.

When Hubbell sailed from New York the previous year he apparently intended to do nothing more than engage in routine fur trading along the northwest coast. But now the presence of an experienced Pacific trader in the person of O'Cain offered some new, intriguing possibilities. The first was the possibility of trading with the Russians in Alaska. Some years before O'Cain had been there on board the *Phoenix* and he knew the Russians often had difficulty obtaining supplies. After leaving San Blas the *Enterprise* sailed far to the north to the Russian-American Company settlement on Kodiak Island where they found that O'Cain was right, for the Russians were badly in need of supplies. The ship that usually brought them from Okhotsk had been lost at sea, and a party sent to Unalaska to obtain supplies had not returned. The Russians were not supposed to trade with foreigners, but they seemed to have no choice but to accept arms, ammunition, clothes, and other American items in exchange for two thousand black and red fox furs.

The *Enterprise* was the first American ship to reach the Russian settlements in Alaska, and the opening of business between the two groups was somewhat tentative. They traded but without much trust and the Russians thought the prices the Americans offered were much too low. It must have been clear, at least to O'Cain, that potentially there was more here than simply trading guns and ammunition for a few fox furs. The Americans could provide supplies that the Russians badly needed, their ships gave them mobility throughout the Pacific, and they had access to the Canton market which the Russians did not. The Russians were not entirely without advantages, for they had sea-otter furs, and, more important, they had Aluet Indians who were highly skilled in catching otters not only in Alaska but anywhere they were found.

The possibilities were all there, and by the time O'Cain returned to Boston he had developed a workable plan to present to his partners, the Winship brothers. They enthusiastically provided the financing to build a 280-ton "first-class ship of that day." It was christened, none too modestly, the *O'Cain,* and after being outfitted, it cleared Boston Harbor in January 1803. This time O'Cain was captain of the ship, and upon entering the Pacific, instead of touching in at California or the northwest coast, he sailed directly to Alaska and in late summer of 1803 arrived off Kodiak Island.

Kodiak Island, like most of the Aleutian chain, was usually shrouded in fog, and a ship entering St. Paul Harbor fired its guns as a signal for rowboats to come out and guide it into port. As the *O'Cain* worked its way by the promontory, the men on board could see the wood fort where the inhabitants welcomed an incoming ship by raising the Russian flag and firing an eleven-gun salute. Inside the bay, about half a mile beyond the promontory, was the settlement which, when the *O'Cain* anchored there, contained several buildings. There was a church, a mission, and a school as well as warehouses for furs, storerooms for company provisions, a storage shed where rowboats lay side by side, workshops for the locksmith, the cooper, the tinker, and the blacksmith, and barracks with attached kitchens and cookhouses for company employees. The most important building, at least to a man like O'Cain who came to deal with the Russians, was the residence and attached office of Alexander Andreivich Baranov, chief manager of the Russian American Company.

O'Cain had met Baranov briefly twice before, but now he had come to do serious business with him. At first glance the chief manager was not an imposing figure, for he was short and thin and had a rather pale, sickly look about him. He was also bald with a fringe of reddish-blond hair and sometimes wore, ludicrously, a short, black wig tied to his head with a black handkerchief. Yet he was a capable man who throughout his life had steadily moved farther and farther from civilization until he reached the wild, remote area of Russian America where he seemed to thrive.

Originally he had come from the Russian city of Kargopol, and at fifteen had run away to Moscow where he spent the next several years working as a clerk. Eventually he saved enough money to return to Kargopol, start his own business, marry, and settle down to raise a family. Somehow life as a family man in his old home town was not satisfying and he left for Siberia. In the years to come, he would always send money home to his wife and children, but he never returned to Kargopol, and never saw his family again.

In the Siberian town of Irkutsk, Baranov became the manager of a glass factory. He was also involved in several other industries, and as a result of reports he wrote on them was elected a member of the Civil Economical Society. He had become an important and prominent man, but again he found such a life deadly dull, and again he gave it all up to move farther afield.

Obtaining a supply of goods and liquor, he headed east to trade with the natives of the Kamchatka Peninsula. He established some trading posts among the Chukchi natives along the Anadyr River of northeastern Siberia, one of the remotest areas of the world. After investing everything he owned in the business, he lost it all in 1789 when the Chukchi plundered two of his caravans and destroyed the trading posts. When he went to Okhotsk to report the disaster to the authorities, he met Grigor Shelikov, founder of the Russian American Company who offered him the post of chief manager. Baranov was penniless, and with little opportunity of recovering anything, he accepted the offer. In 1790 at the age of forty-three, he had come to Russian America, even wilder and more remote than the Anadyr River basin. Now, at the age of fifty-six, he had survived thirteen years as boss over Russian fur traders and gangs of Aleut Indian hunters.

Now in 1803, Baranov faced several problems. A few years earlier, in an attempt to open new hunting grounds and to block the northward push of American traders, he had established a settlement at Sitka, naming it New Archangel. In 1802 it had been attacked and destroyed by Kolosh Indians, and as yet he had been unable to mount an expedition to recapture it. It was at this point that O'Cain arrived with a suggestion that would allow Baranov to bypass Sitka temporarily and send an expedition farther south to obtain both sea-otter furs and information.

O'Cain's suggestion was simple. On the voyage out from Boston, he claimed he had discovered somewhere south of Alaska an uncharted island teeming with sea otter. If Baranov would provide Aleut hunters, he would provide the transportation to these new hunting grounds. O'Cain, of course, was not describing a new-found land but only the coast of California, and Baranov undoubtedly knew that. But he cared less about exploration than about sending his hunters to a coast filled with otters. He agreed to supply the hunters, O'Cain agreed to supply the transportation, and after the hunt was over they would split the profits equally.

II

The agreement was between the Russian manager and the American ship captain, but it was the Aleut Indians, men and women, young and old, who had to make the preparations for the trip. The women began sewing waterproof shirts made from animal intestines, shirts that would be almost transparently thin but tough enough to keep a hunter dry in any kind of weather. Then came the making, or patching, of heavy skin parkas, for it was late October and winter had already arrived in Alaska. A man could keep warm by wearing such a parka and he could also pull it over him like a tent and use his stone lamp filled with blubber oil and fitted with a moss wick to provide both heat and light in the almost permanent night of the near Arctic. The fact that things might be different in the land to the south, along the coast of Baja California, probably never occurred to a hunter born and raised on Kodiak Island.

The old Indian men, no longer physically able to go hunting, remembered the necessities and began making spears and darts of bone and stone, whittling paddles, and putting boat frames together. Boys too young to go on the hunt were put to work carrying things, helping stretch the skins over the frames and smearing them with pitch to make them waterproof, learning skills for the day when they, too, would go hunting.

Yet if the old men made the frames and the small boys helped stretch the skins and smear the pitch, the hunters themselves had to give the boat a final check, for in the days to come they would spend most of their lives in their skin bidarkas. Though these boats were small and fragile, the Aleuts piloted them through some of the world's roughest waters, even in pursuit of something as large as a whale. The bidarkas were entirely seaworthy, fully covered except for an opening where the hunter sat. The hatch had a flap which, when tied around his body, kept water from entering and allowing the boat to bob like a cork in the sea. The boats were of different sizes but most of them, particularly those used for sea-otter hunting, had two hatches, the rear used by the paddler, the front by the spear thrower. As the *O'Cain* was loaded for the trip south, twenty bidarkas were taken aboard for the forty Aleut hunters assigned to the ship.

In the months to come these forty men would have to eat, and it would have to be something other than the hardtack and salt beef of an American sailing ship. Company agents began collecting food the Aleuts considered edible—whale meat, whale oil, and most of all youkala, the staple of the Aleut diet, which was made by taking fish, salmon, herring, cod, smelt, halibut, cutting it into strips, and hanging it on a rack until it had dried. Then it was stored for later use.

Once the *O'Cain* was loaded with food and hunting equipment, and the bidarkas were lashed onto the deck, the Aleuts came aboard, led by a Russian commander named Shevtsov. Although he worked in semi-obscurity—his first name is never recorded—he seems to have been a capable man, for Baranov trusted him to control forty Aleut hunters and to keep an eye on O'Cain and his method of counting sea-otter furs. Baranov also ordered him to observe the coast he visited carefully, particularly the hunting grounds, in preparation for the time when the Russians could go south without the help of Americans.

III

The *O'Cain* sailed from Kodiak Island in late October 1803. It was already winter in Alaska and soon it would be almost permanently dark, but not for the hunters on board the ship. By early December—the dead of winter at home—they were off the coast of Baja California where, to an Aleut islander at least, it was summer once again.

They had no more than dropped anchor at San Quintin Bay than Jose Manuel Ruiz, the commandante at Mission Santo Domingo, arrived to inquire as to their business. Once again O'Cain began to spin the well-worn story of distress. He told how he had not touched land in eleven months, how the vessel had been damaged in a wild storm in the northwest, and how he now desperately needed help. None of it was true but apparently it was convincing, for Ruiz reported that the "necessity was real" and allowed the ship to stay for a few days.

Instead of a few days, the ship stayed several months. Not long after it arrived the hunters put their bidarkas in the water. With two men for each boat they used the traditional Aleut system of spreading the twenty bidarkas in a line and moving quietly through the water until someone saw an otter and raised his paddle as a signal. The others converged on the spot, the man in the rear paddling and steering, the man in front holding his spear ready. Usually before he had a chance to throw, the otter would dive and the hunters would surround the spot and wait for it to surface. When it did, they moved in again either spearing it or making it dive before it could fill its lungs with air. Eventually the lack of air would force the otter to surface long enough for the nearest hunter to hit it with his spear. The hunters then hauled the otter in and moved after the next one.

Watching all this activity with great frustration was Jose Arrillaga, governor of Baja California, to whom the arrival of the *O'Cain* had been reported. When the ship stayed beyond a few days he began issuing orders for it to leave but all he received in reply were excuses. Beyond that the only thing he could do was to tell the intruders not to hunt, "and to this," he complained, "they pay no attention." He considered seizing the furs they had stacked on the beach but changed his mind when he saw five cannons trained on the spot. Besides, a few of the tough Aleut hunters always stood guard near the pile of furs. By early March, Arrillaga was complaining to the viceroy that "there is not an otter left from Mission Rosario to Santo Domingo."

The hunt over, the *O'Cain* sailed away and arrived back at Kodiak Island in June. On board were 1,100 furs taken by the Aleuts and, as agreed, these were divided equally with the Russians. O'Cain also had obtained 700 more furs from various missionaries with his own trade goods. These he refused to divide, claiming they were his own personal property, and although the Russians accepted his word, a vague distrust of O'Cain remained. Still, it had been a successful trip, particularly for O'Cain. He soon sailed for China and by early 1805 had reached Canton and by July was back in Boston where, almost immediately, he began planning another voyage to the coast of Russian America.

IV

The presence of O'Cain on the California coast had created a whole new problem for Spanish officials. Throughout the past decade, as foreign ships began reach California, official orders and the actions of ship captains had taught presidio commandantes to suspect any claim made by a foreign ship captain. Admittedly the system was still not perfect. A Spanish commandante on the Lower California coast in early 1804 had been lured into believing Joe O'Cain's story of distress, and as a result O'Cain had been able to slip ashore and trade with the missionaries. Had there been no more to it than that, it would have been only a passing irritant, for the next time the commandante would not have been so easily fooled and, given enough time, every official on the California coast would have known what to expect from an American captain.

It had not ended there, however. Although O'Cain was willing to obtain furs any way he could, the Aleut hunters had freed him from the need to trade with anyone. Spanish orders to their own citizens not to trade with foreigners meant nothing in this situation, and officials had no success in trying to drive O'Cain away. He simply ignored their orders, kept the Aleuts in the water and the furs under the eye of the cannon until he was ready to leave. This was the way of the future, particularly when Spanish officials, irritated by American ship captains who cheated, or ran out of port without paying for supplies, or even fired shots at a Spanish fort, were making it more difficult to trade in California ports. Joe O'Cain had guessed exactly right when he gave up smuggling on the coast in favor of using Aleut hunters.

Just how right O'Cain considered his decision is demonstrated by events in Boston in the summer of 1805. He had arrived home in July bringing the news of his success in California, and within a few months, hardly more than the minimum time required to outfit an expedition, two ships had been prepared for the voyage to the Pacific. The *Peacock* cleared Boston Harbor in mid-September, followed a few weeks later by the *O'Cain.* Joe O'Cain and his partners, the Winship brothers, clearly were trying to keep the business in the family, for the *Peacock* was commanded by Oliver Kimball, a brother of O'Cain's wife Nabby, while the *O'Cain* was now under command of Jonathan Winship, Jr. as captain and his younger brother Nathan as mate. O'Cain himself planned to stay in Boston a few months longer, until the completion of a new and larger ship that was being built for him. Soon after New Year's Day 1806 the new ship, christened the *Eclipse,* was ready to put to sea and in late January it too sailed for the Pacific.

V

By 1806, Russian American Company headquarters were no longer on Kodiak Island. In the two years since O'Cain left Alaska, the chief manager, Alexander Baranov, had been able to defeat the Kolosh Indians and reestablish the settlement at New Archangel. It was here, in the fall of 1806, that O'Cain arrived in the *Eclipse.* The *Peacock* and the *O'Cain,* which had spent the previous year cruising the California coast with Aleut Indians, were also there refitting before heading south for another season of hunting. To Joe O'Cain, however, hunting along the California coast had already become routine, and he now had another plan to suggest to Baranov.

On the way out from Boston O'Cain had stopped in Hawaii where he saw several shipwrecked Japanese sailors who had been picked up at sea and brought to Oahu. If Baranov would give him enough furs to fill the *Eclipse,* O'Cain would sail to Hawaii, pick up the Japanese sailors and take them to Japan. This humanitarian act might induce the Japanese to open a market that was completely closed to foreigners.

The plan appealed to Baranov, for he had a sizable store of furs, most of it brought back from California by the *O'Cain.* Even if O'Cain could not open trade with Japan, the furs could be sold in Canton at a better profit than if they were sent to China by way of Siberia.

He agreed to the plan and provided the *Eclipse* with a cargo of furs worth 300,000 Russian rubles. His distrust of O'Cain apparently lingered, however, for he sent his own agents, two Russians named Bykadrovo and Tropogritskii, to keep an eye on him. Also on board as the *Eclipse* sailed was a Kodiak Indian girl whom O'Cain had given the name Barbara. It was a common practice for a ship captain to take aboard a native girl to be his mistress until he tired of her or found someone he liked better. Apparently O'Cain's relations with Barbara were of short duration for when the ship reached Hawaii she was put ashore and a Hawaiian girl taken aboard in her place.

In Hawaii O'Cain found that the Japanese sailors were gone, and instead of going to Japan he went to Canton. There he learned that China and Russia were on unfriendly terms and that recently two ships had narrowly missed being seized. There were two Russians aboard the *Eclipse* and to avoid trouble in Canton he suggested they wait for him at the Portuguese settlement of Macao. The two Russians protested, but O'Cain insisted, and they were excluded from participating in selling the furs in Canton.

Russian-American officials always felt that the company was cheated during these dealings in Canton. Baranov later complained that the 155,000 rubles paid for the fur was only half what it was worth. He obviously thought O'Cain had worked out a kickback system to pocket the difference himself, although he had no specific accusation and did not indulge in name-calling. Another Russian American Company official, however, showed no such restraint—George Schaffer talked to the two Russians who had accompanied O'Cain and they gave him "several examples of this robber." He also talked to several other people involved in the dealings and finally came to the conclusion that "the expeditions of the ship *Eclipse* under the command of Captain O'Cain met with great losses and supplied proof of the most evil intentions of this rapacious person."

Joe O'Cain did not record his version of these dealings. Undoubtedly he dealt rather sharply, for that was his business, and surely he saw to it that he made a profit, even a sizable one, for that too was his business. But in his own eyes he certainly did not see himself as robbing the Russians, nor did he seem to think that they would see it as such. After the dealings were finished, he loaded his ship with provisions—mostly sugar, rice, and tea—for the return trip to Russian America. If he had done anything wrong he thought that the Russians would either never hear of it or that they would not find it unforgivable.

VI

As O'Cain prepared to leave Canton he was short-handed and willing to offer high wages to lure sailors away from other ships. One man he approached was Archibald Campbell, a nineteen-year-old native of Scotland. Although he was young, Campbell was an experienced sailor, having made several voyages to the Caribbean before sailing aboard an East Indiaman bound for China. When O'Cain offered him good wages, Campbell at first refused. Then O'Cain mentioned that the ship was bound for the northwest coast of America and then the South Sea islands. That, to a nineteen-year-old who had always wanted "to visit those distant parts of the world" was better than high wages and he agreed to desert his ship and come aboard the *Eclipse.* He hid his identity by signing aboard as Archibald MacBride, and to prevent being seized by his former captain, O'Cain hid Campbell and another British sailor in the American factory at Whampoa.

Even then they were almost caught. They were hungry and sent a Chinese out to buy them a loaf of bread. The dollar they gave him was identifiable as coming from a British ship, and instead of buying bread the Chinese went straight to the British captain and offered to lead him to the factory. Campbell and the other sailor saw them coming and went out an upstairs window and ran along the rooftops until they found their way blocked by a warehouse owner refusing to let them pass through. Campbell ran out on a beam, then jumped to the street some eighteen feet below. The fall stunned him, but he soon recovered. The other sailor also reached the street and the two of them made their way to the river where they hired a sampan to take them out to the *Eclipse.* When the East India fleet sailed for home shortly afterward, O'Cain hid them on the *Eclipse* until the British ships were out of sight. Campbell, officially known as MacBride, was safe aboard the American ship, and on May 8 it sailed from Canton.

A month later, on June 6, 1807, the *Eclipse* reached Japan and sailed along the coast until it reached Nagasaki Bay. O'Cain was lacking the shipwrecked sailors he had planned to use to ease his way into the good graces of the Japanese, but he decided to brazen it out anyway. The ship entered the bay flying a Russian flag and was met by a large fleet of boats which surrounded it and led it toward an anchorage. About halfway up the bay the Dutch ambassador, who could speak some English, came aboard and told O'Cain to haul down the Russian colors immediately. There was trouble between the two countries he said, for Russia, disturbed by the rejection two years before of a visit by an official party led by Nikolai Rezanov, had sent an expedition to explore the Kurile Islands and this, in turn, had irritated the Japanese.

Once at anchor, with the Russian flag stowed away and the Russian agents hidden below decks, O'Cain found himself faced with officials who, unlike the Spanish, were both efficient and determined to keep trade barriers intact. Arms and powder were confiscated and the ship was surrounded by guard boats which would allow no one to go ashore. When O'Cain said he had entered the bay because he needed water and provisions, boats were immediately sent out with water, fresh fish, hogs, and vegetables, all of which were loaded aboard the *Eclipse* without charge. O'Cain tried to take advantage of this by laying out a display of trade goods on deck to lure those who had brought the supplies into buying something, but they all refused, saying that they had plenty of everything he had to offer.

After three days in Nagasaki Bay O'Cain decided there was nothing more to be gained and announced that he planned to leave. The arms and powder were immediately restored and he was again surrounded by the crowd of boats which now towed him out of the bay. The ship spent the next week passing through the inland sea in sight of land that young Archibald Campbell found beautiful, "abounding with cultivated fields, woods, villages, and single houses." He also noticed that often, when the ship was in sight of the coast, inhabitants would come down to the shore and make signals, "as if to invite us to land." O'Cain, however, either interpreting the signals differently or made uncharacteristically timid by his reception at Nagasaki, refused to have any more dealings with the Japanese.

After a week the *Eclipse* broke free of the Inland Sea and by the Fourth of July was far to the north. It was Independence Day and to celebrate O'Cain ordered the firing of a salute. When one of the guns misfired, O'Cain attempted to correct the problem himself. He took a powder horn to prime the gun, but as he was pouring powder from it, a spark got into the horn and it exploded, badly burning and mangling his hand.

Two days later those on the *Eclipse* caught sight of the high mountains behind the settlement of Petropavlask on the Kamchatka Peninsula. The fog closed in, however, and it was two days before they were able to enter the harbor. Again, representatives of the Russian American Company found reason to suspect O'Cain's motives. The exact charges are not clear, but they felt that everything on board the ship should have been taken directly to the company's settlements in America. Instead O'Cain had gone to Kamchatka where he disposed of half the cargo. Once again they suspected him of making some kind of private arrangement.

The ship spent a month unloading the cargo, and Archibald Campbell had time to look over the country. The town of Petropavlask, although the main seaport for the entire coast, was disappointing for it was "nothing more than a miserable village." Somewhat more interesting was a tall stone obelisk standing on the north side of the harbor near the governor's house, a monument in memory of Captain Clerke who had died just off the coast and had been buried here. The inscription, however, was badly defaced by the weather and that, plus the rail fence surrounding it, kept Campbell from being able to read it.

In early August, with the cargo now unloaded, the *Eclipse* sailed for America and by September 10 it was approaching the coast. That morning the wind began blowing hard from the south and the ship was under close-reefed topsails. In the afternoon the gale increased to a point where it was necessary to take in the fore- and mizzen topsails, and while the sailors were on the arms one of them spotted land to the north. Quickly the course was altered to the east and by evening the wind had eased off. It seemed that trouble had been successfully avoided, but at ten that night someone gave the alarm that there were breakers ahead. The first mate took the wheel and ordered those on watch to their stations to avoid running aground. But at that moment Captain O'Cain came on deck and countermanded the orders. What lay ahead was not breakers, he said, but only white water, and there was no need to be alarmed or to change course.

The words were barely spoken when the *Eclipse* struck with such violence that those on the off-duty watch, sleeping below decks, were thrown bodily from their hammocks. It was a terrifying experience, for it was dark, they were aground, and the high sea was already beginning to break up the ship. They could only drop anchor, throw the cannon overboard, and stay with the ship as long as it would float. If it went down they would have to save themselves as best they could in the longboat.

At daylight "to our great joy," they saw land in the distance and were able to free the ship enough to let it be driven ashore. O'Cain ordered all the men who could not swim to take to the longboat which was being towed behind the *Eclipse.* When the ship struck again, somewhat off the coast, the boat was brought alongside, took off the rest of the men, and began making its way through the breakers. By noon, they were safely ashore on the small island of Sanak about fifty miles off the tip of the Alaskan peninsula.

It was a bare, desolate, moss-covered island with no trees or even bushes, and beyond the place where they landed high mountains blocked them off from the rest of the island. As far as they could see there were no signs of human habitation, nor did the land provide anything edible. O'Cain and his crew were forced to turn to the sea and, when the tide ebbed, to gather large mussels for food. Finally they found a barrel of sea biscuit soaked with salt water and some beef and pork that had washed ashore from the ship but the weather was so damp they were unable to light a fire and were forced to eat everything raw. They also salvaged enough from the wreck to build a shelter.

Finally on September 28, three bidarkas, each carrying two men, approached. They were Indians from a village on the north side of the island who had seen pieces of the wreckage and had followed the trail around the coast to the source. When they came ashore one, wearing a gold medal around his neck, spoke to them in Russian. O'Cain, from the time he had spent in Alaska, knew a few words of Russian and was able to ask for help. The leader of the Indians immediately sent one man back to the village to bring more men and another to the Russian settlement on Unalaska to inform the commander there of the wreck.

The leader himself stayed with the white men and did what he could. He shared a bladder of whale oil and a basket of berries with the shipwrecked sailors. Although they had eaten almost nothing but raw mussels for three weeks they had trouble gagging down the oil, but the berries were welcomed. One Indian took his bidarka out to sea, caught some fish, and most important of all, lit a fire to cook it with.

The next day a large company of Indians came from the village bringing more food, berries, blubber, oil, and dried salmon. They went to work immediately building huts, and they used their bidarkas to help salvage as much as possible from the *Eclipse,* which after the pounding it was taking had held together surprisingly well. A week later, when the Russian commander arrived from Unalaska, things were under control and when he added his twenty or thirty Indians, what had been an isolated island beach turned into a large, busy village.

Since the *Eclipse* still held together, and since there were now enough people and provisions, O'Cain decided to try to save the ship with the help of the skilled carpenters available among the Russians at Kodiak. He also felt the need to get word of the wreck to Baranov. The longboat was repaired and on November 19 several sailors, including Archie Campbell, pushed off from Sanak Island. It was the last time Campbell would ever see Joe O'Cain.

In the weeks that followed, the longboat sailed along the coast of Alaska until it reached the main settlement of Kodiak Island where a bidarka came out and guided it into port. After spending three weeks with Russian convicts in their barracks, Campbell and the others loaded the longboat with provisions for the trip back to Sanak. In early January 1808 they sailed, but a few days later the heavy weather of an Alaskan winter forced them into a bay on the north side of Kodiak Island, where they were blocked by heavy surf on one side, by high mountains on the other. In trying to force the boat through the surf they wrecked it and in trying to cross the mountains Campbell's feet were frozen. They had to turn back. Finally two Russians succeeded in getting across the mountain and sending help. By the time Campbell reached the Russian settlement his feet were in such condition that both of them had to be amputated.

It was while he was laying in the hospital recovering that he heard that O'Cain planned to use what was left of the *Eclipse* to build a seventy-ton brig which he would man with Russians and Indians. Then Campbell added, "I afterwards heard from some Indians, who had come with despatches from Oonalaska, that the vessel was launched and had sailed from Sannack. What became of her afterwards, I never could learn with certainty, but it was reported that she foundered at sea, and all on board perished."

Kyril Khlebnikov, a man much involved in Russian American affairs in these years, later wrote a biography of Baranov in which he gave a few more details. "During 1808 O'Cain built a small schooner from the fragments of his ship which had been washed up on shore. In it he set to sea on February 26, 1809, but strong winds tore the sails from the schooner and drove her onto the ice of Unalaska Island. The ice damaged her seriously and knocked out her steering. O'Cain, seeing no hope for the vessel, decided to abandon her, and make his way over the ice to the shore, only two miles distant. First he sent off Navigator Bubnov, one Russian and nine Aleuts. When they had all safely crossed the ice O'Cain, two American sailors, and a Sandwich Island woman they had with them, set out to follow in their tracks. But they were not so fortunate as the first group, and all were drowned. The schooner, heavily damaged by ice and rocks, was washed up nearby."

THE LOTUS EATERS

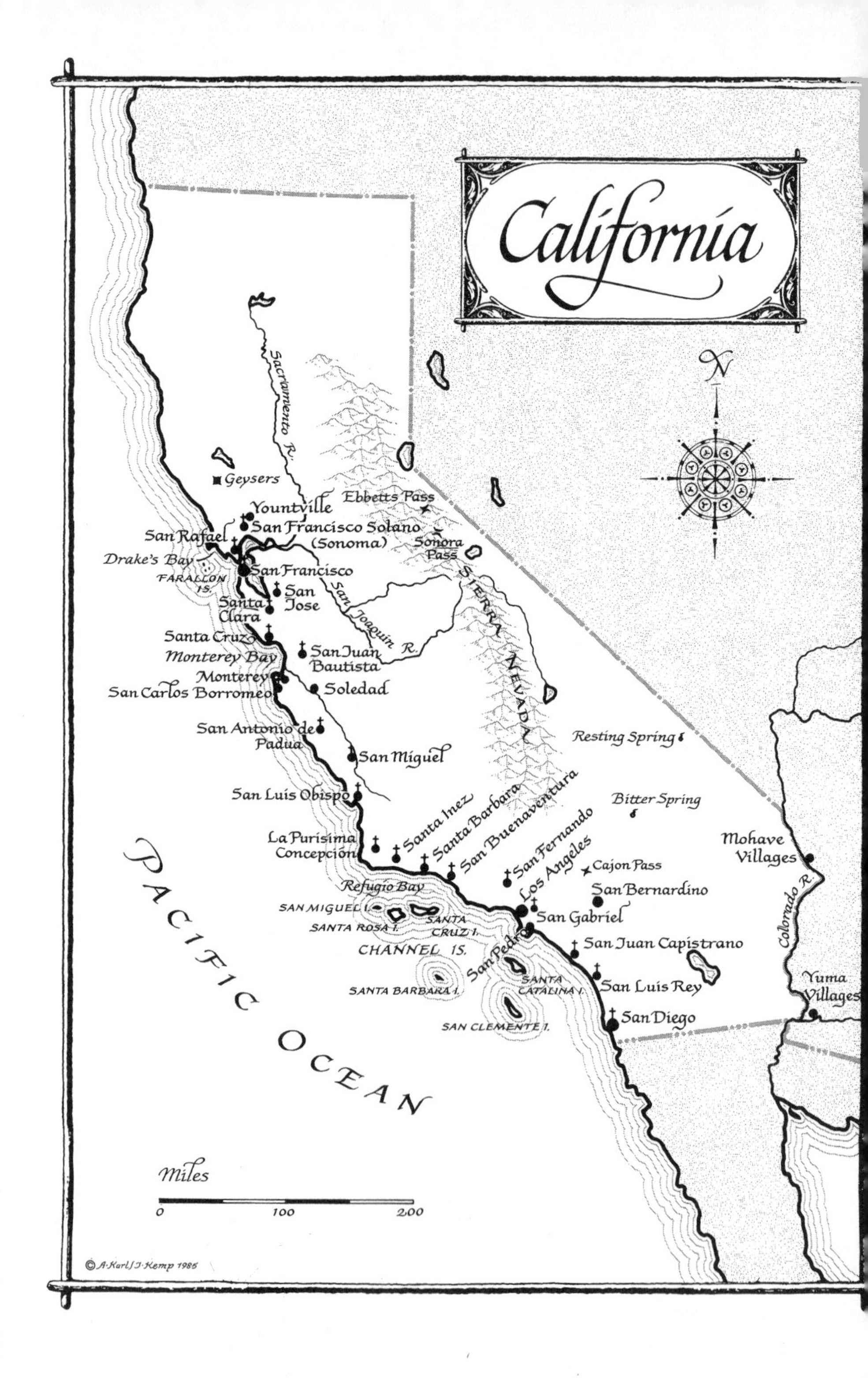
California
N
Sacramento R.
Geysers
Yountville
Ebbetts Pass
San Francisco Solano
(Sonoma)
Sonora
Pass
San Rafael
Drake's Bay
San Francisco
FARALLON IS.
San Jose
Santa Clara
San Joaquin R.
SIERRA NEVADA
Santa Cruz
Monterey Bay
San Juan
Bautista
Monterey
San Carlos Borromeo
Soledad
San Antonio de
Padua
Resting Spring
San Miguel
San Luis Obispo
Santa Inez
Santa Barbara
San Buenaventura
San Fernando
Bitter Spring
La Purísima
Concepción
Los Angeles
Cajon Pass
Mohave
Villages
San Bernardino
Refugio Bay
SAN MIGUEL I.
SANTA ROSA I.
SANTA CRUZ I.
San Gabriel
Colorado R.
CHANNEL IS.
San Juan Capistrano
San Pedro
SANTA BARBARA I.
SANTA CATALINA I.
San Luis Rey
Yuma
Villages
San Diego
SAN CLEMENTE I.
PACIFIC OCEAN
Miles
0
100
200
© A. Karl / J. Kemp 1986

I

The *Eclipse,* brand new when it sailed from Boston in early 1806, was gone now, and its captain, Joe O'Cain, was dead, drowned after the ship he built from its wreckage struck ice in the Aleutians. But the contract system he invented was still very much alive, for even as O'Cain died, other Winship vessels were once again in California waters. They would not have the field to themselves for long, however; other captains in the fur trade were beginning to hear of the possibilities of using Aleut hunters to catch the sea otter.

The Winship brothers were businessmen enough to know good times could not last, for such a successful operation would attract countless imitators who would cut into the profits. In early 1809, a group of men met in Abiel Winship's countinghouse in Boston to consider a new possibility. Present were the owner himself, his two brothers Nathan and Jonathan, both home from recent voyages to the Pacific, and several other Boston merchants who were being allowed to invest in the project in a small way.

The plan announced by the Winships was simple. While Jonathan in the *O'Cain* made a routine voyage with Aleut hunters, Nathan in the ship *Albatross,* old but sturdy, would sail to the northwest with everything needed to establish a permanent colony. Once he reached the coast, he would ascend the Columbia River for thirty miles or so and find a suitable place to settle. Then he would buy land from the Indians and build a fort.

Nathan Winship, as he prepared to sail in the *Albatross,* needed experienced men and chose as chief mate a Virginian named William Smith, who twenty years before had made his first voyage to the northwest in the ship *Margaret.* He had been a carpenter on that voyage, but upon reaching Nootka Sound had been put ashore and given complete responsibility for constructing a small schooner. When it was finished he supervised the launching, took command, and cruised along the coast collecting a thousand otter pelts that later sold for

$30,000. Eventually he rejoined the *Margaret,* abandoned the schooner to some unknown fate, and sailed for home. After a long, slow passage of six months the ship arrived in Boston. William Smith had finished his first voyage around the world.

Within a few months Smith again sailed for the northwest, establishing a routine from which, in the next twenty years, he would seldom vary. He would spend two or three years on a voyage to the northwest coast, Hawaii, China, and on around the world to Boston. Then, after only a few months ashore he would sail again for the Pacific. Some time during this period he married, but that made no visible change in his routine. His only extended stay in Boston came after he returned in 1808 and found that President Jefferson's embargo act prevented ships from leaving port. The act expired early in 1809, however, and soon afterward Smith sailed for the Pacific aboard the *Albatross.*

Also on board the *Albatross* was a young man named William Gale, yet another of those Bostonians seeking his fortune in trade. He had signed on as assistant to the captain and in that capacity, as the voyage progressed, he would become increasingly involved in trading. He would also find time to keep a journal of his experiences during the long years the *Albatross* wandered the Pacific.

One of the first things he noticed was how slowly the ship made its way toward the Pacific. Grass had time to grow on the uncoppered bottom, and it was not until the two hundredth day out from Boston that the ship made its first landfall in the Pacific at Easter Island. Later, it stopped in the Marquesas where Captain Winship, in an attempt to speed up the *Albatross,* hired a gang of natives to dive under and scrape the barnacles from its bottom. That helped, but not very much, and it was not until March, almost nine months out of Boston, that the ship put into port at Oahu to obtain provisions and more men. Then it sailed for the northwest and in late May 1810 entered the Columbia River, worked its way a few miles upriver past the Chinook Village, and dropped anchor.

After a brief exploration Captain Winship selected a site for a new settlement and soon everyone was at work building a fort. In a few days it began to rain. It rained hard all night, the river began to rise, and by morning everything—the fort, the newly planted garden, even the entire point on which it was located—was under two feet of water. There was nothing to do but tear things down and start over on higher ground.

The new fort was no sooner begun than a band of heavily armed Chinook Indians arrived. Although they were outwardly friendly, Winship feared the Indians planned to kill the men who were ashore. Then, with no one to protect the *Albatross,* they would overwhelm it as well. The captain had to do some thinking about the future. Even if he were successful in building the fort, he would eventually have to take the *Albatross* out of the river in order to trade along the coast. And when he did, he would not have enough men both to man the ship and to protect the fort against hostile Indians. The situation seemed hopeless and he abandoned the plan to settle on the Columbia.

William Gale was furious, particularly when some Indian chiefs came aboard for a feast. He said, "It is indeed cutting to be obliged to knuckle [under] to those you have not the least fear of, but whom from motives of prudence you are obliged to treat with forebearance. What can be more disagreeable than to be obliged to sit at table with a number of these rascally chiefs, who, while they supply their greedy mouths from your food with one hand, their bloods boil within them to cut your throat with the other, without the least provocation."

II

The experienced veterans of the trade, Winship and Smith, were not nearly so disappointed, for they knew there were plenty of other opportunities along the coast. After leaving the Columbia River, Winship went to Sitka where he picked up a gang of Aleut hunters and headed for the California coast. This time he added a new twist. Not only would they hunt sea otter, but he would also leave a gang of hunters on the Farallon Islands, off the entrance to San Francisco Bay, to catch seals.

The young trading assistant William Gale was put in charge and for the next year he bossed the gang of hunters and lived in the cold, wet fog and the gore resulting from the clubbing of thousands of seals. When the season was over, the hunters were taken off by the *Albatross* and Gale, now serving as clerk again, computed the take for the past two years. Some 75,000 sealskins had been taken by crews left on the various islands and the *Albatross,* after cruising with Aleut hunters, had as its share 631 prime sea-otter skins and 639 tails. There was also a small assortment of other furs—beaver, raccoon, wildcat, badger, fox, mink, squirrel, muskrat, and mole. There was even one, just one, hide from a skunk.

Once Gale was back aboard, the *Albatross* sailed for China where, using the going price of sea otter at $40 a prime skin and $1.50 a tail, and sealskins at $1.75 each, it was assumed their cargo would bring something more than $150,000. That was in China, of course, and on top of that there was still another profit to be made in Oriental goods shipped to Boston. Seemingly it more than made up for the failure to build a settlement on the Columbia.

Much of the profit on this voyage had come from a new source of income, sealskins, but once again the Winships were not impressed. They were still looking for new areas to develop, and after sending the cargo off to Boston, Jonathan and Nathan Winship returned to Hawaii where they signed a contract with King Kamehameha giving them exclusive rights to the sandalwood trade for the next ten years. Opening that trade would take all their efforts, but they were not willing to give up entirely trading in the northwest and along the coast of California. The veteran William Smith was promoted to captain of the *Albatross* and sent off to America.

Smith would spend the next several years roaming the Pacific. From time to time the *Albatross* was seen at the Russian settlements in Alaska, in the Columbia River, at Drake's Bay, off the Farallon Islands, at Refugio Bay near Santa Barbara, and in various other isolated anchorages all the way to the tip of Baja California. When he had enough furs, Smith would sail for Hawaii, take on a load of sandalwood and proceed to Canton. His route through the Pacific became virtually a routine and he varied it only once when he visited the Marquesas at the request of a Frenchman who had chartered the ship in Hawaii.

It was December 1815 when Smith, on another swing through the Pacific, headed south, this time in company with the ship *Lydia,* commanded by Captain Henry Gyzelaar, a newcomer to the coast. The two ships were separated by a severe storm, however, and Smith and the *Albatross* arrived alone and anchored off Refugio, on the coast a few miles above Santa Barbara. The ship was first seen through a heavy fog just off the Ortega Ranch on January 10. Captain de la Guerra y Noriega, commandante of the Santa Barbara presidio, was notified, and he immediately sent Sergeant Carlos Carrillo and a squad of seven men to arrest anyone attempting to land. Next morning soldiers arrived at Refugio Bay and saw the *Albatross* sitting there. No one came ashore, however, and in the afternoon the ship got under way and began to move slowly down the coast toward Santa Barbara. By dark it had not reached the harbor, and the next morning as it began making its final move toward the anchorage, it suddenly veered away and went back out to sea.

Two days later, just at dawn, the ship reappeared off Refugio. A small boat came ashore and those on board had no more than landed than they were arrested by Sergeant Carrillo. One was Captain Smith himself, and that evening, in the Ortega family's ranch house, he came face to face with Captain de la Guerra, who demanded an explanation of his presence.

It was the same old story. Smith said, through "some words and many signs," that he had no intention of smuggling but had come only because his ship had been driven onto the coast and that he badly needed meat and supplies. He would have come into Santa Barbara, under the guns of the presidio, but the ship was crippled and he was afraid to anchor there because he did not know the harbor. Instead he anchored at Refugio, well known only to smugglers although de la Guerra politely refrained from pointing that out. He asked Smith why he did not go to one of the legal ports of entry and the captain replied that he did not know that was required. If de la Guerra knew of Smith's experience and that he had spent almost twenty years trading in these waters, he again politely did not mention it.

However polite de la Guerra was, he was not at all satisfied with these explanations, and he insisted that Smith order those on board the *Albatross* to surrender it until Spanish authorities reached a decision on the case. Smith refused on the grounds that he was not a smuggler, but he finally agreed to send the ship to one of the channel islands where it would remain for eight days, then return to the mainland to learn Governor Sola's decision. De la Guerra was forced to accept this, and the *Albatross* sailed away. It never returned.

The Spanish commandante had hardly finished his report when another ship put into the cove at Refugio. It was the *Lydia,* and this time Carrillo and his men were there waiting when a boat containing Captain Gyzelaar landed. The sergeant asked, innocently, if he had any goods to sell. Although Gyzelaar was a newcomer to the coast he had been instructed well by Captain Smith, and instantly suspicious, he said no, he was not a trader but he had landed only to see if he could buy provisions. Carrillo said he could supply them and led the captain to the Ortega ranch house where, instead of selling him supplies, he arrested him as a smuggler. De la Guerra was also notified and this time he sent a boat out to the *Lydia* and seized it.

While Smith and Gyzelaar loudly protested their innocence, Spanish officials in California began an investigation into both cases. De la Guerra was ordered to send the *Lydia* to Monterey. Unable to find a man qualified to command it, on the advice of a local padre he put it under command of its own captain, Henry Gyzelaar. Although Governor Sola objected and compared it to asking Martin Luther to protect the church, Gyzelaar was an honorable man and he delivered the ship to Monterey as promised. There an investigation determined that the ship had on board only hatchets and adzes and that it was indeed badly in need of provisions. Sola acquitted the captain of all smuggling charges and ordered the ship released. Soon afterward Gyzelaar, accompanied by Captain Smith, sailed for Hawaii.

Smith took most of his sailors with him, but a few slipped away and disappeared into California. Two Hawaiians escaped the ship's search parties, then asked the mission fathers to instruct them in the true faith. So, too, did a man known only as Bob who was black and thus became the first American Negro in California. Three other men, all from Massachusetts—Marcus Messon of Boston, George Mayo of Plymouth, and Sam Grover of Malden—stayed long enough to be baptized at Mission San Carlos. Beyond this, these men made no impact on California and they never again appear in the records. Probably it was only a matter of months until some other ship arrived and the men, willingly or unwillingly, joined it and left California.

One man who managed to stay was a young Bostonian named Thomas Doak who by early 1816 was clearly unhappy with life on board the *Albatross.* He deserted and through the rest of the year avoided Spanish authorities. Three days before Christmas in 1816, at Mission

San Carlos de Borromeo, he was baptized into the Catholic faith and given the name Felipe Santiago.

III

Each day at first light the silence surrounding Mission San Juan Bautista was broken by the sound of the Angelus bell as it spread across the valley awakening the Indians and calling them to Mass. For the next hour they sat quietly in the mission church and watched as the padre droned his way through the automatic prayers of the assembled neophytes. When it was over another bell rang to announce breakfast. The Indians lined up and invariably, day after day, had their bowls filled with atole, a gruel made of barley that had been roasted, ground, then pounded into paste and cooked without seasoning. Another bell then rang to announce time for work. Some of the Indians headed for their assigned places in the mission, others formed into gangs and were herded into the fields. By the time the sun rose everyone was hard at work.

Caught up in this early morning routine as it unfolded to the ringing of bells was Tom Doak, the American sailor from Boston who had deserted and made his way inland from Monterey to the mission at San Juan Bautista. Geographically he was a long way from home; spiritually he had entered a whole new world. He had been born a New Englander and until recently had been, at least nominally, a Protestant. He was also a man old enough and experienced enough to know his own mind. By the time he reached California he was already past thirty and by then, given the age at which men first went to sea, he could have spent almost twenty years as a sailor, an occupation in which he would have seen much of the world and felt most of the rough edges of mankind.

Now he was a Roman Catholic, baptized and given the name Felipe Santiago at San Carlos Mission. He had stayed there for a short time, then moved to San Juan Bautista to construct a new altar screen. There was always a serious lack of skilled workers in California and supposedly Tom Doak was hired to build the altar screen, the reredo, after another man had demanded the exorbitant fee of six reales (seventy-five cents) a day. Somehow the fathers at San Juan Bautista discovered that Doak, who had been a ship's carpenter, had the skill to undertake the project. Even better, he was willing to work for nothing but his meals and a place to sleep, for being a newcomer he had no settled way to make a living. Having recently jumped ship, it was clearly to his benefit to leave Monterey and go into the interior away from the possibility of being grabbed by his own or some other ship captain.

When Tom Doak first came to San Juan Bautista he was single but he was also a white man, so instead of sleeping in the Indian barracks he had his own quarters. They may not have been entirely comfortable, however, for San Juan Bautista was notorious for its fleas, and visitors frequently complained of them. One man after spending a night there reported that not long after he went to bed he suddenly felt a prickly sensation "as if a thousand needles penetrated my legs and sides." The bed was filled with fleas and when he put his feet on the floor "I felt them jump upon my legs and feet, and reaching down my hand, I swept them off by the dozens." He decided the bed was better than the floor and got back in to spend the rest of the night scratching and fearing "they would surely suck me dry before morning." Yet a man can adjust to anything and Tom Doak, used to the grimness of shipboard life and soon hard at work on the reredos, probably lost little sleep because of the fleas.

When the Angelus bell rang at daylight he was expected to attend Mass, but again as a white man, instead of being crowded in among the Indians he joined the other white men, the mayordomo and the soldiers attached to the mission, in a separate part of the church. Being white also saved him from standing in line with the Indians as they shuffled slowly forward to receive their morning gruel.

Quite likely his breakfast consisted of something more than the monotony of atole. The mission fathers' breakfast of chocolate and toast or biscuits was probably available to the other white men at the mission. Yet if they shared such things, they were consumed separately, for a common sailor like Tom Doak was as far beneath the fathers socially as the Indians were beneath him.

In fact, like most non-Indian laymen at the mission, Doak's specific job was to bridge the gap between the fathers and their neophytes. When the work bell rang after breakfast he had a gang of Indians that formed and followed him to work. The building of the reredo was no small task, for it was to be two stories high, twenty feet wide, and made entirely of wood. Since there were no sawmills in California, each piece had to be hand-hewn from a log, then trimmed and smoothed to fit into the final screen.

Once the outside work of cutting and trimming logs was finished, Doak and his Indian workers moved into the church to build the reredos. Doak himself probably supervised the rougher part of constructing the screen, then personally cut the curves at the top and carved the intricately shaped windows in which the statues of saints were to be placed. When it was finished it had to be painted, a task that fell to Tom Doak. Although he was not a trained artist and was working under difficult conditions, his work was delicate and subtle and impressive enough to satisfy the fathers.

Each morning, while Doak and his men were working, the mission bell would ring and everybody would kneel to say a quick prayer. Sometimes the mission father in charge of temporal affairs would stop by on his way to or from the fields to see that the Indians were at work. At San Juan Bautista it was Felipe Arroyo de la Cuesta, a native Castilian who had been at San Juan Bautista since arriving in California a decade before. He was a tireless worker and in that time he had overseen the construction of the church in which Doak now worked, and he had increased the mission flocks and herds until by now there were more than 10,000 cattle and at least that many sheep. Yet his work did not end there. He also spent much time studying the Mutson Indian language of San Juan Bautista, had reproduced a vocabulary and phrase book, and by now was recognized as having more proficiency in speaking Indian languages than anyone else in California. Father Arroyo also had a fondness for ancient literature from which he often drew names for newly baptized Indians. The names of Doak's helpers on the altar screen could easily have been Plato, Alexander, and Cicero, all names frequently encountered around the mission.

Although Father Arroyo had accomplished much at the mission he was not entirely easy in his mind, for there were problems. Some of his neophytes had recently fled across the hills into the San Joaquin

Valley where they had joined fugitives from other missions. He knew that if they were allowed to stay it would cause trouble. Already, on two separate occasions, bands of runaways had come out of the valley to steal horses and even to murder some of his people.

A less sensational, but in the long run more devastating, problem was Father Arroyo's poor health. He was already suffering from the chronic rheumatism that would eventually confine him to a stretcher. Even now, although he was not yet forty, the pain was enough to sometimes interfere with his work. He persisted, however, spending much of his time supervising the daily temporal affairs of the mission. That in itself was difficult and Father Arroyo would later say of his life as a missionary in California, "I made the vows of a Friar Minor; instead, I must manage temporalities, sow grain, raise sheep, horses, and cows. I must preach, baptize, bury the dead, visit the sick, direct the carts, haul stones, lime, etc. These are things incompatible, thorny, bitter, hard, unbearable. They rob me of time, tranquility, and health of both the body and the soul. I desire with lively anxiety to devote myself to my sacred ministry and to serve the Lord."

Still, someone had to do it, and Arroyo was forced to oversee the Indians in the fields, to keep track of the huge flocks and herds, to supervise the butchering of fifty cattle a week to provide meat, and even to make sure that each day at noon, when the bells rang again, another meal was ready. As in most hard-working agricultural communities, this noon meal was the most substantial and as the line of Indians shuffled forward, each was given a ration of pozole—a thick soup of wheat, corn, beans, and meat. The fathers dined separately on soup, a serving of beef, mutton, or ham and a helping of green vegetables followed by some dried fruit or cheese. Tom Doak, the white working man, probably dined somewhere between the two extremes.

Dinner was followed by a siesta lasting until two in the afternoon. Then the bells rang again, and the Indians returned to their work. Once more Doak and his helpers went to the church where, during the afternoon, they were able to watch and hear the activities of San Juan Bautista's older missionary, Father Esteban Tapis.

Tapis left the temporal affairs of the mission to his younger colleague and devoted himself almost entirely to teaching the children and to directing the mission choir. It was the best of the mission assignments, and Father Tapis had more than earned the right to enjoy it, for he was past sixty, a veteran of twenty-five years in California, and a man who had spent almost ten years as president of the missions. He had never known Father Serra, for he had reached California too late for that, but he had served for more than a decade under Serra's successor Father Fermin de Lasuen. Then when Lasuen died Tapis had been chosen president of the missions and immediately found himself inundated by a mass of administrative details. He had to assign missionaries to their stations, remove them if necessary, make them available to accompany expeditions into the interior, listen to their complaints about the lack of military protection, about the misuse of their Indians by the citizens of nearby towns, and about an endless number of other things. When he was not listening to complaints from his missionaries, he was listening to complaints about them, including one from the people of Los Angeles who claimed that the fathers at San Gabriel refused to attend to the spiritual care of the sick. Tapis, not one to whitewash his fellow missionaries, investigated the case and eventually gave the fathers at San Gabriel a sharp rebuke.

After eight years Father Tapis finally stepped down as president and now at San Juan Bautista he spent his time teaching boys to read, training musicians, and even writing music for the church choir. One of his accomplishments was to pioneer a system in which each singer's part was given different-colored notes so it could be followed at a glance. His presence made San Juan Bautista one of the leading missions in developing musicians and even Father Arroyo, who had a fine singing voice, occasionally stole time from the mission routine to join in the music. Undoubtedly while Doak painted the altar in the church, he heard Father Tapis leading the choir through practice for the coming Sunday.

In mid-afternoon the bells again called everyone to say a prayer, and at five they rang to announce the end of the working day. Then came another hour of prayers and devotions followed by the ringing of the Angelus bell at six, after which supper was served. Once more atole was doled out to the Indians while the fathers ate a light dinner such as roast chicken followed by a cup of chocolate. After that the

Indians could spend some time on their own concerns, and Tom Doak was free to do whatever he liked. Far from home, in a strange land where he was not entirely familiar with the language, he probably spent his evenings quietly absorbing the life around him until at eight when Poor Soul's Bell rang and everyone drifted off to bed.

Some time or other Doak made enough contact with the Californians living near the mission to find a wife. Given the customs of the country, he probably had little to do with it, for in Spanish California it was improper for a man to make a proposal or for a woman to receive one in person. Instead he was expected to work through an intermediary and usually a man sent his father to negotiate with the girl's father. In Doak's case that was obviously impossible, but he could have asked one of the mission padres to intercede in his behalf. They would have known Mariano Castro, father of the prospective bride, for he had long been a thorn in their side.

Castro had obtained a grant of land north of San Juan Bautista and as soon as he was in possession he ordered the padres to remove the cattle grazing there. The fathers refused and appealed to the president of the missions, the father-guardian in Mexico, and eventually to the viceroy himself. The argument with its claims and counterclaims and its endless appeals to higher authority had gone on for years. And in the camaraderie that often arises between opponents in a long-standing dispute, the missionaries responsible for the soul of a newly converted Catholic and the father of an unmarried daughter may easily have reached an agreement. It is possible, even likely, that Tom Doak and his prospective bride, Maria Lugarda Castro, did not even see each other before the wedding. However the arrangements were made, they resulted in a formal marriage, a clear indication that Tom Doak had decided to make California his permanent home. It was also a clear indication that Californians, at least those in the area of San Juan Bautista, were willing to ignore Spanish laws against foreigners and allow him to remain.

IV

Almost four hundred miles south of San Juan Bautista, another foreigner was hard at work in the splendid isolation of southern California. His name was Joseph Chapman, and like Doak, he was from Boston. While still a boy his father had apprenticed him to a shipbuilder, and in the shipyard he had learned both blacksmithing and carpentry. Later he went to sea as a ship's carpenter, spent some years in the Pacific, and by 1818 was on the beach in Hawaii.

He was in Honolulu when the ship *Santa Rosa,* commanded by a man calling himself Captain Turner, arrived. Every sailor in port was instantly suspicious when the ship was sold to King Kamehameha at a startlingly low price. Upon investigation it was discovered that the *Santa Rosa* was a privateer sent out from Argentina to raid Spanish shipping in the Pacific. After rounding the horn, however, the crew had mutinied and the real Captain Turner and several others were set ashore, after which the mutineers fled to Hawaii. Upon hearing this, King Kamehameha ordered their arrest.

Shortly afterward, another ship, the *Argentina,* arrived, commanded by Captain Hippolyte de Bouchard, a Frenchman also sailing under orders from Argentina. As soon as he heard the story of the *Santa Rosa,* he went to Kamehameha and demanded that the ship and those who came on it be surrendered to him. To back up his claim he produced a document from the government at Buenos Aires authorizing him to hunt for and seize the *Santa Rosa* wherever it might be found. It was a forgery, written by Bouchard himself, but it got to the heart of the matter without long, complicated explanations. After extensive discussion, the King agreed to turn the *Santa Rosa* over to Bouchard.

He planned to use the *Santa Rosa* to support his own ship as it raided the Spanish settlements along the California and Mexican coasts. He already had a crew, the captured mutineers, but he needed officers, and he went among Honolulu's community of beached sailors looking for them. As captain he hired Peter Corney, a former officer on a British merchant ship, and as second mate, he chose the American, Joseph Chapman. Some weeks later, after crossing the Pacific, Bouchard launched an ineffectual raid on Monterey. Chapman was captured by the Spanish and when questioned claimed that he had deserted to get away from Bouchard who had forced him to accompany the expedition. It may have been true, or it may have just been a sensible story told by a man who feared he might be executed as a pirate.

Whether true or not, the Spanish accepted Chapman's story and instead of executing or even banishing him, they sent him to the mission at Santa Inez where he was turned over to Father Francisco Uria. Father Uria, a native of Pamplona, Spain, had first come to California as a young man, but after spending some time there had retired to the Franciscan college in Mexico City. By then California had apparently got into his blood, for he soon returned and was assigned to Santa Inez where he had been for the past decade. He was a stout, well-liked man, although he had a short temper and when he lost it was given to foul language. Yet at other times he was known for his sense of humor and his practical jokes which entertained some and irritated others, particularly the victims. One visitor who had dinner with him later said, "the fare was sumptuous, and I was much amused at the eccentricity of the old Padre, who kept constantly annoying four large cats, his daily companions; or with a stick thumped upon the heads of his Indian boys, who seemed delighted thus to gratify his singular propensities." Whatever his strengths or weaknesses, Father Uria, like Father Arroyo at San Juan Bautista, was thoroughly capable of conducting the practical affairs of his mission. And it was this that brought Joseph Chapman to Santa Inez to build a mill.

Since long before the Spaniards came to California, corn had been a mainstay of the Indian diet and for untold centuries it had been ground into meal with a mortar and pestle. As long as the Indians remained in small family groups there were no problems, but when the missionaries gathered large numbers into the missions, the primitive grinding methods were overtaxed. Already in the north at Santa Cruz and San Antonio de Padua and in the south at San Gabriel, the fathers had built water-powered gristmills. These were Spanish-style tub-mills in which the millstone was turned directly, without use of gears, by a horizontal waterwheel. It was much simpler for the missionaries who had little mechanical knowledge and who were working with unskilled Indians to build such mills. Unfortunately they were also very slow and very inefficient. Joseph Chapman was a New Englander, a carpenter, a blacksmith, a jack-of-all trades, and he knew how to build a New England-style gristmill. Not only would it be faster and more efficient, but unlike the Spanish mills it would also be adjustable to different grists and thus be able to grind both corn and wheat.

Chapman went to work building the gristmill, and like Tom Doak in the north he too was awakened at daylight by the ringing of bells, for the routine was virtually identical in all Franciscan missions. And those at Santa Inez, at the same time, almost at the same moment, woke up, went to Mass, lined up for a bowl of atole, another unvarying part of the routine, then formed into work gangs.

Once they were at work, Chapman somehow had to communicate with his workers, and when he first arrived in California he knew little Spanish and even less of the Indian's language. Yet he had spent years on board ships where sometimes a man needed to know almost as many languages as there were crew members. He had no great difficulty working out his own personal language, a mixture of Indian, Spanish, and English words. Once a man heard him tell an Indian, "Ventura!, Vamos! trae los bueyes go down to the Playa and come back as quick as you can *puede.*" Eventually his language became so mongrelized that it was all but unintelligible to those who spoke pure Spanish or pure English or presumably pure Indian. But it was understandable enough to his men, for the missionaries soon learned that Chapman could get more work out of the Indians than all the Spanish-speaking mayordomos put together.

Building of the mill at Santa Inez went well, and as soon as it was finished Governor Sola ordered Chapman to build one at San Gabriel to replace the mission's old, inefficient tub-mill. Before leaving for the south, however, Chapman took the step he had thus far resisted and accepted the Catholic faith. Possibly during his stay at Santa Inez he had become a true believer. Possibly he became a convert so that he could marry, which he did almost immediately after being baptized.

His new wife was Maria de Guadalupe Ortega who at the age of twenty-three was almost entirely alone in the world. She was the eldest of five children but all the others had died when they were babies. Then, when she was eight, her father died, and a few years later, when her mother remarried, she became the one stepchild in someone else's family. Yet no Californian of the time was entirely without connections. Her grandfather had been a well-known soldier, one of her uncles was the owner of the Refugio ranch, and another was an important man in the north.

Soon after Chapman married he moved south to San Gabriel to begin building the new mill. About that time Father Jose Sanchez also arrived, recently assigned to the mission. He was no newcomer to California, for he had spent almost twenty years at the mission in San Diego. He was well-liked, particularly by foreigners, who always got along well with him. He and Chapman soon became friendly and if the American sailor had become Catholic only because it allowed him to marry, he soon impressed the father with his piety. For after he came to know Chapman, Father Sanchez would say that it was "a marvel that one so long in the darkness of baptist faith could give such examples of true catholic piety to older Christians." Joseph Chapman, like Thomas Doak, had adapted himself to the California way of life and to all appearances was entirely satisfied with it.

V

Tom Doak, Joseph Chapman, and a few others like them had successfully managed to slip through the barrier against foreigners that Spain had erected around its colonies. They were the exceptions, and they were allowed to remain because they had arrived by chance, because they possessed badly needed skills, and mostly because they were quiet, unobtrusive, and blended easily into California life. Others who came purposely and who insisted on drawing attention to themselves by trying to trade were still not welcome in Spanish California.

Yet in other parts of the Spanish empire the barrier against trade was beginning to break down. Far to the south, Chile declared its independence, then, in one of its earliest official acts, threw its ports open to trade with the rest of the world. Merchants, most of them from Great Britain, poured in to establish trading firms. It was one such firm that brought a young Englishman named William Hartnell to Chile in 1819. A few years earlier his life had been seriously disrupted by an unexpected disaster.

At the age of sixteen Hartnell, the son of an apparently well-to-do businessman, had been sent to Germany to study at the College of Commerce in Bremen. Before he could finish his studies, however, his father died, and Hartnell inherited nothing. His father's holdings were less extensive than they appeared on the surface, and what there was had been eaten up when, not long before his death, he had signed a note for a friend who had gone bankrupt. Hartnell was forced to drop out of school and return to England. And in the economic slump that followed the end of the Napoleonic Wars, he was unable to find a job.

In the area around his home in Lancashire, already becoming grimly industrial, he found nothing, and he eventually moved to London where his uncle, Edward Petty, took him in. Although Petty was able to provide him with a place to stay and food to eat, he was not a wealthy man nor could he supply a job. Hartnell continued to search the city of London, day by day and office by office, for any kind of employment. After three long years he had still found nothing.

Finally his Uncle Edward remembered an old schoolmate named James Brotherston, head of a large trading firm with offices in the major English cities and agents in all sorts of strange places around the world. An interview was arranged and Hartnell was hired as a clerk for John Begg and Company, Brotherston's agent in Santiago, Chile. In early 1819, after signing a contract in which he promised to work for the company for the next three years, Hartnell sailed for South America.

Hartnell arrived in Chile soon after it had declared its independence and opened its ports to British traders. Thus there was considerable business for a firm like John Begg and Company at the time Hartnell took up his position in Santiago in 1819. At first it was a lonely life, for he knew no one but his employer who was a man who worked almost constantly and demanded the same of his clerks. Apparently Hartnell fell into Begg's rigid routine, for within six months he was promoted over the heads of three senior clerks to the post of cash-keeper. He was particularly proud, he said in a letter home, of the fact that always before Mr. Begg had kept track of the cash himself.

During the time Hartnell worked in Santiago, the wars for independence continued, particularly in the north where, throughout 1820, there was a constant struggle between Royalist and Patriot forces over Peru. By early 1821 the Patriot forces seemed near victory and John Begg decided that, as soon as Lima fell, he would head north and personally supervise the opening of an office there. He also asked his young clerk, William Hartnell, to accompany him.

In July 1821 Peru declared its independence and shortly afterward opened trade to foreigners. Soon John Begg and Company's ships—the *Queen Charlotte, Caledonia, Araucano, Constancia, Embargo, Goldrina, Indian Oak, Olive Branch, John Begg* and several others, were working in and out of ports all along the west coast of South America. Mostly they loaded large cargoes of cocoa, but traders representing John Begg also took on hides, corn, cotton, Chilean hams, Peruvian shawls, Indian curiosities, and whatever else South Americans could offer in exchange for British manufactured goods—woven cloth, wool, canvas, crockery, hardware, and liquor.

Much of Hartnell's job consisted in keeping track of these ships and making endless inventories of the goods they carried. It was hard work, performed under the close supervision of Mr. Begg, and there was little time for anything but work. What time he could spare he used to cultivate new friends in Lima. One was Hugh McCulloch, a fellow clerk in the company office; another was a young woman from England named Miss Lynch whom he called his "English Rose." Given Hartnell's past, it was hardly a surprising friendship. In Germany there had been Lene Mueller, his "little sweetheart" whom he promised to return and marry one day; in Santiago there was "Dulcinea" whom he called his "intended wife"; now, in Lima, there was Miss Lynch, his "English Rose."

They attended dances, they went to parties, they picnicked, and they strolled together along the Alameda, always accompanied by a chaperone. Soon they were engaged to be married and Dulcinea, the "intended wife," was forgotten like Lene Mueller before her. Now he was betrothed to the English Rose, yet the promise of marriage also brought problems, for despite the explosion of business and profits for the company, Hartnell was only a clerk working for a salary. His three-year contract would expire at the end of 1821 and he would thus be free to take advantage of a scheme that was offered to him.

His fellow-clerk Hugh McCulloch had been carefully watching events in the north and had come to the conclusion that Mexico was as ripe for new traders as Chile and Peru had been in the past few years. He suggested that the two of them pool their resources, form their own company, McCulloch and Hartnell, and contract with John Begg to be his company's representative in the north. The two agreed, then approached John Begg for financing.

He accepted their proposal and drew up a contract in which he would associate with his two clerks in "trade on the coast and country called California in Spanish North America." Since McCulloch and Hartnell had little money and were almost unknown outside the company, Begg was virtually able to dictate the terms. He would provide the necessary funds and shipping for McCulloch and Hartnell who would spend all their time gathering, preparing, and shipping cattle hides, tallow, and anything else that seemed promising. The price for this produce, and for all the trade goods sent north, would be determined solely by John Begg and Company which also reserved the right to make a final and binding decision should any dispute arise as to profit and gains. Begg also reserved the right to cancel the agreement at any time during the next five years. On the other hand, McCulloch and Hartnell were forbidden to withdraw for the first three years and even after that they could not trade in California, directly or indirectly, until the five-year contract expired in 1827. Obviously John Begg had everything his own way and the two clerks, being young and poor, had no choice but to agree.

After the formal contract was signed, and the two prepared to leave for California, Mr. Begg relaxed enough to write them an informal letter about business. It contained fatherly advice, most of it pointless; suggestions of how to economize, most of it obvious; and information on prices in California, most of it wrong. Yet surely McCulloch and Hartnell, being young and beholden to Begg, had to pretend to be soundly impressed by the old man's wisdom. They also had to endure silently the final indignity of sailing for California in the ship, *John Begg,* named, of course, after the old man himself. In March 1822 they sailed for Callao, leaving behind Peru, the company, the old man's advice, and in Hartnell's case, the "English Rose."

VI

In March 1822, about the time the *John Begg* sailed from Peru, dispatches arrived in California announcing that Agustin Iturbide, a Royalist colonel, had declared Mexico independent and established an imperial regency that he would govern pending the arrival of a new ruler from one of the royal families of Europe. All those in California were called upon to accept this new government by swearing an oath of allegiance and also sending a deputy to attend future meetings of the Mexican Cortes.

In response to a summons from Governor Pablo de Sola, the ten leading religious and military men in California met in Monterey and on April 9 drafted a resolution in which they recognized California as part of an independent Mexico and promised to obey the laws of the new government. Two days later they met again, this time in the governor's home, and officially took the oath of allegiance to Mexico. The same oath was given to the troops in the plaza, after which Father Mariano Payeras, the highest-ranking Franciscan in California, preached an appropriate sermon. The day ended with the firing of guns, the shouting of *vivas,* and a celebration in honor of independence.

The next day, with the formalities and celebrations out of the way, these ten men met once more, this time to decide how to choose a delegate to the Mexican Cortes. They agreed, unanimously, that an election should be held. Those living in each of the presidial districts of San Francisco, Monterey, Santa Barbara, Los Angeles, and San Diego would choose an elector who, in turn, would vote for the delegate. By late May the five electors met in Monterey and voted to send Governor Sola to Mexico as California's representative. It is not entirely clear how this was arranged, but certainly it allowed Sola, a native-born Spaniard who had come to rule in the name of the Spanish King, to retire honorably from California.

Sola, however, was still serving as governor in Monterey when McCulloch and Hartnell arrived there in June 1822. They discussed their business proposal with him and found that not only would he permit them to trade, he was even anxious to help. He wrote personal letters to each of the commandantes encouraging them to welcome the Englishmen and to listen carefully to their proposal. It was an opportunity, he said, they had long been seeking, and if those in California did not "leave off slackness" and seize it, they deserved to be treated as vagrants.

The two young traders also discussed their business with Father Payeras, the representative of the mission system, and soon there was a letter from him as well, addressed to "Reverend Fathers, Apostolic Preachers and Ministers of our Missions." It announced that Hugh McCulloch and William Hartnell, "both Protestants" and partners of John Begg of Lima, would soon be calling at each mission to ask the fathers to sign a three-year commercial contract.

Payeras then outlined the specific terms of the contract. The company—Macala and Arnell as the Spanish wrote it—would send at least one ship a year to California to take all the hides offered as well as up to 300 tons of tallow. They would pay, in either cash or goods, $1 for each hide, $80 a ton for tallow, $3 a fanega for whatever wheat they took, plus other prices, all carefully spelled out, for suet, lard, soap, and pickled beef. Each mission was free to accept or reject the agreement, but whoever signed it must do so for the full three years during which they would trade exclusively with McCulloch and Hartnell.

Payeras then added a personal comment in which he looked, rather realistically, at the mixed blessings that would come from increased trade with the outside world. It would, or at least it should, do little to change the "frugal fare and sad shroud" of the missionaries, and at the same time it would bring in sinners, annoying kinds of people, and all sorts of problems. Still, he added, it meant progress for the poor Indians who were their charges, for it would greatly increase the wealth and influence of the missions. That, he said, should outweigh any inconvenience to the fathers themselves, and therefore he urged its acceptance.

Armed with the blessings of both the governor and the prefect of missions, the two men set out to visit California, McCulloch going south, Hartnell north. In the long run McCulloch would prove the better businessman, but in the summer of 1822, as he traveled from mission to mission, he was hampered by the very attributes that would make for his success. He was all business, brusque, always in a hurry to get things done, and contemptuous of any time-wasting activities. Yet most of the missionaries, used to long empty periods of time without a visitor, wanted a chance to show their hospitality, to talk at length with an educated man, and to hear the news of the outside world. It was a system almost perfect for William Hartnell, less businesslike, fond of wine and conversation and willing to accept the easygoing ways of the Californians. By the end of the summer, Hartnell had agreements from all but a few of his missions. McCulloch had signed almost none.

VII

Possibly there was another reason for McCulloch's lack of success, for only a few weeks after he and Hartnell reached Monterey another ship, the *Sachem,* out of Boston under command of Henry Gyzelaar, arrived in California. Soon its supercargo William Gale was traveling from mission to mission offering $1.50 rather than a $1.00 for each cattle hide.

Both these men were thoroughly experienced Pacific traders, and for the past five years they had served on several ships together, Gyzelaar as captain, Gale as supercargo. Now they were back again, in the same capacities aboard the *Sachem.* This time, however, instead of seeking sea-otter furs or sealskins, they were in search of cattle hides.

The change had come mainly because William Gale, after all his years in the Pacific, had returned to Boston convinced that there were real opportunities in the California cattle-hide trade. He began searching for backing and eventually found a group of merchants who were willing to outfit the *Sachem.* Among them was the firm of Bryant and Sturgis, headed by William Sturgis, himself no stranger to the Pacific.

More than twenty years before, William Sturgis, as a sixteen-year-old boy, had entered the Pacific as a common sailor aboard the *Eliza.* By the time the voyage was over he was third mate, and not long after returning to Boston he was given command of his own ship although he was still a teenager. He spent the next decade at sea, trading over much of the world, and by 1810 was back in Boston where he joined John Bryant to form Bryant and Sturgis. After that Sturgis himself no longer went to sea but supervised the sending of an almost endless number of ships around the Horn seeking furs, sealskins, sandalwood, and now, upon the urging of William Gale, cattle hides.

Upon arriving in California, Gale discovered that obtaining cattle hides would be more difficult than he had envisioned. The *Sachem* had arrived just a few weeks after the *John Begg* and as Gale went from mission to mission he found that many had already promised to sell all their hides to McCulloch and Hartnell. There was nothing to do but to persist and to offer higher prices to those who had not committed themselves. Slowly through the rest of the year Gale began to put together a cargo, but by the spring of 1823, when McCulloch sailed for South America with his first shipload of hides, the *Sachem* was still far from full. It was not until the following October that Gale was finally able to sail for Boston. By then his rivals, McCulloch and Hartnell, were beginning to run into troubles because William Hartnell was distracted from business by a series of personal problems.

When the *John Begg* sailed from California the previous spring, McCulloch had gone with it, for the two partners had agreed that he would handle the South American end of the business while Hartnell would be the firm's representative in California. It should have worked, for McCulloch, the brusque, no-nonsense businessman would be dealing with the parent firm of John Begg and Company, while Hartnell would be trading with Californians whose slow, easygoing style of doing business matched his own temperament. Yet upon his return to California McCulloch soon discovered he had to do much of the trading. When Hartnell met him in San Diego, there was no sign of trouble until McCulloch gave him a packet of personal letters from England. After reading them Hartnell began to drink heavily and, much to the disgust of his partner, was often incapable of doing business.

Hartnell was a deeply troubled man although at first no one knew exactly why. One of the letters was from his sister Mary telling him that Uncle Edward Petty had suffered serious financial reverses and was too old to recoup them. Such news would have been disturbing, for this was the uncle who had taken him in after his father died and who had also provided the contacts through which he had obtained the job that had taken him to South America and eventually on to California. Still, even though he owed him much, Hartnell had not seen him in almost five years and in the past had never been overly concerned with those he left behind. Yet for some reason the news caused him to lose himself in an alcoholic fog.

Hartnell's despair was not lost on his friend, the San Luis Obispo missionary Father Luis Martinez, who had accompanied him to San

Diego to look over the latest goods brought back by McCulloch. While in San Diego the two roomed together and it was soon apparent to him that Hartnell was suffering inner turmoil. Eventually when the business in San Diego was finished, Martinez invited Hartnell to accompany him back to San Luis Obispo to spend some time, without liquor, quietly meditating at the mission. Hartnell did so, and after a week he was able to sit down and write to his brother in England, pouring out the whole story of what had caused so much agony.

After swearing his brother to secrecy he began his confession. While in England, just after he had returned from school, he had stayed with a man in Liverpool and had secretly taken some money that was left lying around. Later, while staying with another friend in Paddington, he had done the same thing. Worst of all, after Uncle Edward had taken him in and virtually supported him in London for several years he had taken "at several times certain sums of money." Hartnell added, however, "this can't be called an actual robbery as I always intended some time or other to repay them and never till now had it in my power." Besides that, he had always felt that his uncle would never miss the money. But now, with money of his own, and his uncle faced with business reverses, he had no choice but to confess and send what money he could to make amends.

Although Hartnell tried to put the best face possible on the affair, it was clear he had taken more than just loose change left lying around the house. To the man in Paddington he sent two pounds, to the man in Liverpool ten pounds, and to his Uncle Edward forty-eight pounds. Large as these amounts were—the payment to his uncle would come to several hundred dollars in today's currency—this was not the amount of money taken but only "interest for the time they had *lent* their money." Given the amount of money involved, surely those from whom he had borrowed missed it but had chosen to say nothing about it. And possibly the knowledge that in England several men, including his main benefactor, thought of him as a thief, was what hurt more than anything else. The confession and sending the unsought interest seemed to ease Hartnell's conscience enough that when he returned to Monterey he was able to resume his normal business affairs.

At the same time—as usual—Hartnell had not been in the country long before he found a new love to replace Lene Mueller, Dulcinea, and most recently, the English Rose. Now in California it was Teresa de Jesus Guerra y Noriega, daughter of Commandante Jose de la Guerra of Santa Barbara. She was not quite fourteen when Hartnell met her while passing through on his way north. The meeting occurred after he had received his sister's letter, but apparently his despair and guilt were not so overwhelming that he failed to notice the commandante's daughter. Soon Father Martinez was referring to her as "the loved one who fills your thoughts."

As Hartnell came out of his depression he convinced himself, as he had done so often in the past, that he wanted to marry, but in Mexican California that was impossible for he was not a Catholic. Father Martinez, who had played a major role in helping him ease his conscience, was also interested in saving his soul, about which he seems to have had many doubts. When he invited Hartnell to the mission, he said he could not only meditate but "satisfy Jesus Christ our Lord." But then he added, "or perhaps I should say *my* lord for I do not know that he is yours." This doubt was even heightened when it was reported that Hartnell actually had a copy of one of Voltaire's works in his Monterey home. This so alarmed Prefect Sarria that he asked Governor Arguello to see that the book was destroyed before anyone could read it.

Soon after his mental recovery, however, Hartnell began to study the Catholic creed and in October 1824 he was officially baptized into the church. Besides his own given name he added, possibly as penance for past crimes, that of his Uncle Edward Petty and thus was officially known in California as William Edward Petty Hartnell. There were signs, both at the time and in the years to come, that he took his conversion more seriously than the lip service paid by most foreigners. Also, it gave him the right to become a citizen of Mexico and to own land, both of which would be valuable in conducting his business.

It also allowed him to marry. This time he did not move on to some new field before the wedding could actually take place, and on the last day of April 1825 he and Teresa de la Guerra were married in Santa Barbara. It was a huge wedding, as befitted the daughter of one of California's most important men. When it was over, Hartnell took his bride to Monterey where he again took up his task of being the resident partner of McCulloch and Hartnell.

DANIEL BOONE COUNTRY

I

In late September 1820 as summer again turned into fall, more than a half-century had passed since that day in May 1769 when Junipero Serra had celebrated Mass at a newly founded mission in Baja California, James Cook had watched an odd scene among the natives on the island of Tahiti, and Daniel Boone had made camp in the wilderness somewhere on the road to Kentucky. Thirty-six years had gone by since Serra quietly died in a small room at Mission San Carlos Borromeo in Carmel, and almost forty-two years since Cook was clubbed to death on a beach in Hawaii. But on that first day of fall in 1820—fifty-one years, four months, and eight days after that spring Sunday of 1769—Daniel Boone was still alive.

He was eighty-five now, only a few weeks short of his eighty-sixth birthday, and although history would identify him almost exclusively with Kentucky, he had lived in Missouri for the past twenty-one years. He had gone there in 1799 to take up land at Femme Osage when the country west of the Mississippi still belonged to Spain. He was sixty-five years old then, and his move out of Kentucky marked the last in a long series of failures.

Even before he left for Kentucky in the spring of 1769, Boone owed large amounts of money, and much of what propelled him west on that hunting trip was the desire to escape from his burden of debt. Partly it worked, for during the next two years he was beyond the settlements, beyond the reach of courts and creditors, and free to roam a new land full of game. There was something to eat almost everywhere: nuts, fruits, berries, and more than enough meat—wild turkey, venison, elk, buffalo, and even bear bacon with enough grease to cook it all. Beyond that there were plenty of hides to be carried back to the settlements and sold for enough to free a man from all his debts and even provide something for the future. But on his way home after two years in the wilderness, he passed through Cumberland Gap and, just a few days from home, was set upon by a band of

Indians who took everything he had. When he reached the settlements he was poorer than when he had left two years before.

This strange mixture of success and failure was to plague—or bless—all of Daniel Boone's later life. Often he would escape the confines of the settlements and live the lone, free life of the wilderness. Once a party of hunters in the Green River country of Kentucky heard an eiree, wailing sound and found Boone, all alone, stretched out on a deerskin singing to the sky. Yet there were bad times, too, for unlike Junipero Serra, who spent his entire life within the Franciscan order, or James Cook whose career was made possible by the British Navy, Boone was never quite able to come to terms with the established world in which he lived.

Possibly it was his independence—the kind that allowed him to sing, not for an audience, but for himself alone—that caused some men to worship him, others to fear and distrust him. It may have been the thing, too, that made him stand out from others, for when John Filson, an itinerant school teacher, published a history of Kentucky in 1784, he included as an appendix the story of a frontiersman entitled, "The Life and Adventures of Col. Daniel Boone." Filson, as he passed through Kentucky in the early 1780's, could have chosen any number of men to glorify. But instead of Benjamin Logan, Simon Kenton, James Harrod, or even Boone's own brother Squire, he chose Daniel Boone. It may have been nothing more than mere chance, but usually fake heroes created by chance disappear with the sunset, and Boone's reputation, despite many attempts to undermine it, has remained alive ever since the publication of Filson's book.

It was also that stubborn streak of independence, that willingness to go it alone, that cost Boone his chance to become a wealthy Kentucky landowner. At first, his wilderness skills, his knowledge of the country, his ability to spend long periods of time alone in the woods, put him far ahead of more timid souls, and by 1786 he had filed claims on almost 100,000 acres. But locating land to claim is one thing, and validating it in court is another, particularly since various officials had issued warrants on four times as much land as actually existed in Kentucky. All these conflicting claims created a new kind of wilderness through which lawyers, politicians, and bureaucrats moved easily, shuffling papers, quibbling over technicalities, and often flattering each other, exchanging favors, and scratching each other's backs when they itched and sometimes when they didn't. A frontiersman like Boone lost his bearings completely and soon was stripped of every acre he owned. Consequently, in 1799, at the age of sixty-five he left Kentucky and went west to take up land in Missouri.

II

The troubles that drove Boone out of Kentucky were soon repeated in Missouri. He had been invited to settle in Spanish territory by Lieutenant Governor Trudeau, who granted him 8,500 acres at Femme Osage. Four years later, however, the United States took control as a result of the Louisiana Purchase and once again the land commissioners and the lawyers arrived. This time Boone had kept careful records and seemingly had no worries. But he had built his cabin, not on his own land, but on that owned by one of his sons; he had not traveled all the way to New Orleans to have the grant confirmed by the Spanish Governor of Louisiana; and he had not cultivated any of the land, for he was a hunter not a farmer. The American land commissioners, using these technical violations of Spanish land law, invalidated the claim and once again Boone lost all his land.

Some years later the United States Congress in a well-publicized move restored 850 acres to Boone. But two Kentuckians, having read of this in the newspapers, arrived in Missouri with twenty-year-old claims against Boone and he had to sell all his land to satisfy them. The unkindest cut, however, came from an orphan child whom he had rescued from the Indians, taken into his home, and eventually given some land in Kentucky. She was grown now and married, and one day her husband arrived in Missouri saying that the claim Boone had given her had been invalidated and therefore he ought to make good the loss. By now Boone had lost all his property and was dependent on his children. The man persisted. Finally, in disgust, Boone said, "You have come a great distance to suck a bull. And I reckon you will have to go home dry."

But there was always the wilderness, and for years after his arrival in Missouri Boone continued to trap and to hunt. No one knows exactly how far he traveled in these years, although he must have penetrated well up the Missouri River, for in the spring of 1816 he was seen at Fort Osage in western Missouri where he stayed for two weeks. Later a resident of the fort wrote a letter describing Boone at eighty-five (actually he was only eighty-one) as somewhat short and stout, of vigorous mind and "pretty well informed." The letter carried the tone of awe of a man who had actually seen a legend in the flesh.

He identified Boone as "the first settler of Kentucky," then added, "he has taken part in all the wars of America, from before Braddock's war to the present hour. He held respectable state appointments, both civil and military, has been a colonel, a legislator, and a magistrate . . ." But despite all this, the man said, "this singular man could not live in Kentucky when it became settled." Even now, he added, "The Colonel cannot live without being in the woods. He goes a-hunting twice a year to the remotest wilderness he can reach and hires a man to go with him, whom he binds in written articles to take care of him, and bring him home, dead or alive." It was clear that he preferred the woods, "where you see him in the dress of the roughest poorest hunter."

The letter-writer was also impressed with what Boone, at the age of eighty-one, planned to do in the future. He told those at the fort, "I intend, by next autumn, if I can obtain permission, to take a party of Osage Indians, and visit the salt mountains, lakes and ponds, and see the natural curiosities of the country along the mountains." He was talking about the Rockies, for he added, "The salt-mountain is but 5 or 600 miles west of this place." Probably the trip was never made; not too long after his visit to Ft. Osage he suffered a paralytic stroke from which he never really recovered.

The fame of Daniel Boone was such that even when he was at home in Missouri he attracted many visitors. By now several more books had been written about him, some of them full of lies that irritated him. But most of his reputation was still based on Filson's original narrative, supposedly a first-person account of Boone's adventures. That, he claimed, was entirely accurate, and despite the high-flown language in which his story was told, he often talked as if he had actually written it himself. He loved to hear it read aloud, when he would chortle happily, "All true! Every word true. Not a lie in it."

Filson's book made him America's best-known wilderness hunter, and Boone himself later added to the legend by claiming he had moved out of Kentucky in search of elbow room when he discovered that his nearest neighbor lived only seventy miles away. By the time he settled in Missouri he was famous, not only as a man, but as the personified symbol of a way of life that even then was being destroyed. An eastern writer, commenting on the rapid settlement of Missouri, used Boone's reputation for seeking wilderness solitude to make his point. The colonel, he said, "lately seated himself so far up the Missouri as to possess a well grounded hope that a teeming population would not again compel him to seek a new abode." So rapidly was Missouri filling with people, however, that Boone, "to enjoy his favorite manner of life, may yet be driven to the Rocky Mountains and even there be disturbed in eight or ten years."

Even then the price of fame was having to endure those who came to look, to question, to pry, to obtain material for their books. His fame even brought a well-known artist, Chester Harding, to paint his portrait. In June 1820 Harding left St. Louis and traveled upriver looking for Boone. In spite of the man's enormous fame he had difficulty finding him, for the closer he got the less people seemed to know of him. Finally, within two miles of Boone's home he asked for directions from a man who said he didn't know a Colonel Boone. The man's wife, however, interrupted to say, "Why, yes you do. It is that white-headed old man who lives on the bottom near the river." Harding drew the obvious conclusion that "a prophet is not without honor save in his own country."

Harding found him living in one of the cabins of an old blockhouse built years before for protection against the Indians. "He was lying in his bunk, near the fire, and had a long strip of venison wound around his ramrod, and was busy turning it before a brisk blaze, and using salt and pepper to season his meat." When Harding told him why he had come Boone hardly knew what he meant, but after it was explained he was willing to sit for the artist.

By now Boone was a very old man—he told Harding he was ninety although, as always, he added several years to his age. He was also too feeble to hold his head up and his friend Reverend Welch stood behind him to steady it. Still, the old man took an interest in Harding's painting, talked with him and even occasionally was able to parry the painter's questions. Once, when Harding asked if during any of his long hunts he had ever got lost, Boone answered, "No, I can't say as ever I was lost, but I was *bewildered* once for three days."

Harding's portrait was the only one painted from life, and it was finished none too soon, for by now Boone had little time left. He was an old, old man who had survived most of those who had been dear to him—his son James, just sixteen when Boone found his body after he had been tortured to death by Indians; his son Israel, who died in his arms after having been hit in the chest by a bullet at the Battle of Blue Licks; still another son, William, who died, peacefully, while still an infant; his brother Edward, shot from ambush while he and Daniel were out hunting; his friend John Floyd, who was killed by an Indian in Kentucky; even his biographer John Filson, who was killed by Indians in Ohio. Sudden death even continued on into Missouri and into the third generation, for during the war of 1812 his grandson James Callaway was killed.

Finally, in the spring of 1813 his wife Rebecca, to whom he had been married for fifty-six years, died during maple sugar time. She had been, right up to the end, a sturdy old woman, and she had just spent a week in the woods boiling sap. Then she took ill, returned to her daughter Jemima's house, and within a few days died and was buried on a high hill overlooking the Missouri River.

Several of Boone's children were still alive and living in Missouri, and in these last days of his life he seems to have lived with them all. Some people who visited him found him at Jemima's, others at his son Jesse's, and still others at his son Nathan's. Quite likely after Rebecca died he had no particular home, but rather a room in the homes of his various children, each of whom agreed to take care of him when it was their turn.

Finally, the old man's time had come. The summer of 1820 was over, the fall had arrived, and Boone was at his daughter Jemima's when he began to feel ill. A physician who was married to one of his granddaughters attended to him, and soon he began to feel better. Eventually he felt so good that, even though the doctor advised against it, he mounted his horse and rode off to Nathan's. There he had a large helping of sweet potatoes, one of his favorite foods, which brought on an attack of acute indigestion. He took to his bedroom in the front of Nathan's large stone house, and there, three days later, he died. His fourteen-year-old grandson Albert Gallatin Boone, who was with him at the time, later said that he "passed off gently, after a short illness, almost without pain or suffering." The next day the body was placed in a cherrywood coffin Boone had made for himself, and was moved to Flanders Callaway's barn, one of the few buildings large enough to handle the crowd that attended the funeral. The sermon was preached by the Reverend James Craig, husband of another of the granddaughters. There was little he needed to say about the old man's life, for it was already known to much of the world. Instead he talked mostly about Boone's essential decency and ended by saying, "He was a good man."

III

The Missouri in which Daniel Boone died in 1820 was far different from what it had been when he first settled there in 1799. Then it had been an isolated, unimportant part of the Spanish Empire with only a few thousand people scattered over a wide territory. By 1820, however, it had become part of the United States, had grown to some seventy thousand people and was on the brink of being admitted to the Union as a state. Congress had already passed the enabling act, a constitution had been drawn up, and in late August, an election was held to choose new state officials. On September 19, although not yet officially admitted by Congress, the legislature of the new state met at the Missouri Hotel in St. Louis. A week later, on September 26, it adjourned briefly out of respect for the passing of the old pioneer Daniel Boone.

The center, culturally, economically, and politically, of this new state was the city of St. Louis which by 1820 held almost six thousand people. It was well on its way to becoming a major urban area and as such was a prime market for a printer like John Paxton who, in 1821, published the first St. Louis city directory.

Paxton opened his directory with a brief portrait of the city itself. He listed all the streets, from the narrow cluttered paths along the riverfront to the wide avenues on the hills behind the city. He also enumerated the dwellings, 651 in all, the most imposing of which was the new St. Louis Cathedral with its sacred vases, ornaments, and paintings by Rubens, Raphael, and several other "modern masters of the Italian, French, and Flemish Schools." Paxton, however, was most interested in the commercial side of the city. In adding up the entries he had collected he found no less than forty-six establishments which "carry on an extensive trade with the most distant parts of the Republic in merchandise, produce, furs, and peltry." Then he went into detail as to all the other occupations in St. Louis beginning with 57 grocers, 27 lawyers, 13 doctors, and on through the bricklayers, the carpenters, the carriage makers and wheelwrights, the blacksmiths, the tailors, the tanners, the saddle and harness makers, the gunsmiths, and everything else a major city should have.

Paxton, besides portraying the city he knew at the time Missouri was admitted to the Union, also momentarily froze in time a group of people. Some of them, like Auguste Chouteau who had been present at the city's founding, or Don Carlos de Lassus, one-time Spanish Lieutenant Governor of Missouri, had once been famous but were now nearly forgotten. Others like Thomas Hart Benton, listed simply as "attorney at law, north F above Church, near Bennet's," were almost unknown but would one day be famous men.

Another such man was William Ashley, a newly elected state official who, when Paxton published his directory, was listed as "lieutenant-governor of the state, South B, above South Main." Unlike Benton, he would never go far in politics, but in trying to finance his political career, he would have an enormous impact on the western part of America.

By 1821 Ashley was in his early forties and had been in Missouri for almost two decades. In the early years he had lived in Ste. Genevieve and Cape Girardeau, and had done some hunting, some mining, and like any good Missourian, a good deal of land speculating. He had also become an officer in the militia, and during the war of 1812 commanded the sixth regiment of Missouri militia. Eventually the state would commission him Brigadier General, thus giving him the title "General Ashley," by which he was usually known. After the war he spent several years manufacturing gunpowder at a saltpeter cave in the interior of Missouri, but when his partner was killed in a duel, he moved to St. Louis where he began speculating in real estate. He also entered politics and in 1820 was elected lieutenant governor of Missouri.

That office, which he had accepted only because it was a stepping stone, required little time or effort, and he could devote his energies to making the necessary money to build a major political career. He entered into partnership with Andrew Henry, the owner of a lead mine who, years before, had been involved in one of the early attempts to open trade on the upper Missouri River. After two years of trouble and almost constant attacks by the Blackfeet, Henry had given up and returned to Missouri to resume his life as a lead miner.

Now, in partnership with William Ashley, he was willing to try again. The two men formed a company, and in February 1822 began by running an ad in various Missouri newspapers. The first appeared in the Missouri *Gazette:*

TO ENTERPRISING YOUNG MEN

The subscriber wishes to engage ONE HUNDRED MEN, to ascend the river Missouri to its source, there to be employed for one, two or three years—For particulars, enquire of Major Andrew Henry, near the Lead Mines, in the County of Washington, (who will ascend with, and command the party) or to the subscriber at St. Louis,

Wm. H. Ashley

February 13, 1822.

Thus Ashley became the first to advertise widely in Missouri newspapers to procure men to go west. It was an intelligent thing to do, for Missouri at the time was filled with enterprising young men who were thoroughly qualified to take up the new kind of life Ashley was offering. Many of them were the sons of that generation of frontiersmen swept west during the great migration that had so rapidly populated Missouri. And although the St. Louis lawyers, merchants, and speculators would dominate the state politically and economically, and also profit most from the fur trade, it was these frontiersmen who settled Missouri and who, with their sons, provided the backbone of western trapping.

The first of the frontiersmen, like many French traders before them, attracted little attention as they pushed west. Before 1800, while the country beyond the Mississippi still belonged to Spain, hunters crossed the river and entered Missouri. There were only a few of them and they came long distances to hunt. After the Louisiana Purchase, many more came to Missouri and took up life in small cabins just beyond the last line of settlements.

By 1820, as a new generation came of age, Missouri was filling up and the game was disappearing. It had happened before, and most of these young men could look back to ancestors who had once hunted in Kentucky and Tennessee and before that in Virginia and the Carolinas. But now, the new, strange, unforested country of the plains and the distances involved in reaching the mountains made it much more difficult for a man to push west alone. When Ashley's ad appeared—and in frontier Missouri a man need not be able to read to get wind of the news—it provided a perfect opportunity for those whose whole background had prepared them, not to farm, not to live in the settlements, but to hunt game.

Some of these naive young hunters from the wilderness, possibly never having seen a city, may have made their way to the lead mines of Washington County to look up Major Andrew Henry. Those who went to St. Louis to see Ashley soon found themselves in a strange new world. It was a river town, and as such was usually filled with boatmen, who, after manhandling a keelboat upriver against the current, had come ashore to drink the whiskey, to find the whores, and to fight with each other. Once that was over they always needed another job, and it was easy enough for Ashley to find men to pole his keelboats up the Missouri.

Like bars everywhere, those in St. Louis were also frequented by men who were down on their luck. Most were no longer young, but somehow they never found what they were looking for, and they never settled down. Usually they were not much interested in hunting or trapping, but either in their desperation or when they were in a drunken fog they could be lured into signing up. And when Ashley's ad failed to provide the necessary recruits, several of these men more or less unwittingly joined the migration west.

Yet St. Louis, as a new, rapidly growing city, also attracted a better class of men who were young and ambitious and who were looking for an opportunity to go west. One such man was Jedediah Smith, who arrived in St. Louis in the spring of 1822, just when Ashley's ad appeared in the *Gazette.* Originally, Smith was from New York where he was born in 1799. When he was twelve, his family migrated west, first to Pennsylvania, then to Ohio. In 1821 he had left home and gone to Illinois where he worked for a year before coming to St. Louis. Now, at the age of twenty-three, he asked to join the expedition going west. Ashley was impressed with him and he was hired. In May 1822 Jedediah Smith, accompanied by other enterprising young men like himself, as well as wild, young hunters from the back country, and even the dregs of St. Louis taverns, began his first trip into the west.

IV

In November 1826 Indian messengers arrived at San Gabriel with the astounding news that a band of foreigners had arrived at one of the mission's outlying ranchos. By then, foreigners should have been nothing new in California, for since Mexico had become independent more and more traders had arrived to do business. All those foreigners, however, had come by sea, and Californians had considered themselves protected on the east by the great wall of seemingly impenetrable desert. Now, suddenly, a band of men had come out of that desert.

There were fifteen of them and they appeared in San Bernardino after having come through the mountains. In the valley they met friendly, Spanish-speaking Indians who guided them to their settlement. The Indians killed a tender young cow and soon "there was great feasting among the men as they were pretty hungry not having any good meat for some time." Eventually, two missionaries arrived from nearby San Gabriel, and when they returned to the mission they were accompanied by the leader of the party.

Jedediah Smith had seen much since that day four years before when he left St. Louis as one of Ashley's band of enterprising young men. He had spent the summer of 1822 ascending the Missouri and the fall and winter with Major Andrew Henry at his post at the mouth of the Yellowstone. By the following spring he had proved himself to the extent that Henry chose him to carry an urgent message to Ashley in St. Louis.

Thus Smith was also a member of the party that ascended the river in 1823, this time personally commanded by William Ashley. It was on this trip that Arickara Indians attacked the party and Ashley lost thirteen men. During the battle, Smith was notable for his coolness under fire, and when it was over he volunteered to go overland to the mouth of the Yellowstone to obtain reinforcements from Major Henry. Within a month he was back with more men, but the ensuing attack on the Indian village accomplished nothing, and Ashley found himself blocked from ascending the river by hostile Arickaras. He decided to send a party directly west to explore, and the man he chose to lead it was Jedediah Smith.

It was a history-making expedition. There were a dozen or so men in the party, and from Fort Kiowa on the Missouri below the Arickara villages, Smith led them due west. They followed the White River, then went directly crosscountry until they reached the Black Hills, passed through them, and eventually reached the Wind River where they spent the winter in camp with a band of Crow Indians. During that winter, the Indians told them of a river just over the mountains to the west where the beaver were so plentiful that to catch them a man need only walk along the banks with a club. At the trappers' insistence, the Indians took a buffalo robe, and on it made a map of the surrounding country, using piles of sand to represent the mountains. With the topography in mind, and after one false start, Smith and his men, in mid-March 1824, found their way over South Pass and down to the Green River.

When Smith reached the Green River in the spring of 1824, William Ashley's fortune was made. Up to that time returns had been so poor that in the fall of 1823 his partner Andrew Henry had dropped out. Ashley, desperate, decided to make one more attempt, and it was then that he received word of the new discoveries in the west. He took a band of men and immediately headed for the Green River country. The next two years were enormously successful and in 1826 Ashley, now a wealthy man, sold the company to three fur trappers—David Jackson, William Sublette, and Jedediah Smith.

It was as a direct result of the formation of this new company that Jedediah Smith was in California. In 1826, as trappers gathered at the rendezvous on Bear Lake, northeast of the Great Salt Lake to dispose of their winter catch, obtain supplies, and carouse wildly for a few days, the partners made a major decision for the coming year. Two of them, Jackson and Sublette, would follow the usual practice of taking trapping parties north into the Green River country for the fall hunt, even though they were well aware that the beaver supply in that area was not endless and that their activities, and those of the Hudson's Bay Company coming from the northwest, would soon trap it out. But Smith planned to lead his men into the unknown country to the southwest to look for new beaver streams. Possibly, too, he might in this unexplored country find the River San Buenaventura, rumored to lead all the way to the Pacific.

V

In mid-August 1826, with the rendezvous over, Smith led his band of trappers southwest in search of new beaver country. By now he had proved himself thoroughly capable of leading tough, hard-swearing, hard-drinking frontier hunters through the wilderness. Yet Smith himself was a quiet, religious man, who even in his early days in the fur trade was not afraid to express his beliefs. During a funeral for one of the men killed at the Arickara villages, one old trapper remembered that "Mr. Smith, a young man in our company, made a powerful prayer which moved us all greatly." Nor did he ever lose his faith, for after all those years in the fur camps, he still believed and wrote home saying, "Oh, the perverseness of my wicked heart! I entangle myself too much in the things of time. I must depend entirely upon the mercy of that Being, who is abundant in goodness and will not cast off any, who call sincerely upon him." Yet for all this Smith was remembered in the mountains not with contempt but with respect as "a very mild man and a Christian; and there were very few of them in the mountains."

Given Smith's beliefs, it is not surprising that he chose as his second-in-command Harrison Rogers, another of the few Christian gentlemen in the mountains. Little is known of Rogers except that, like so many other mountain men, he came from Missouri. But he too was a believer who, in the course of keeping a journal which listed all the endless difficulties of wilderness travel, suddenly burst forth with "Oh! God, may it please thee, in thy divine providence, to still guide and protect us through the wilderness of doubt and fear, as thou hast done heretofore, and be with us in the hour of danger and difficulty, as all praise is due to thee and not to man, oh! do not forsake us Lord, but be with us and direct us through." With that off his chest, he returned to his laconic account of the day-by-day difficulties they faced.

Yet if two Christian gentlemen were the leaders, the rest of the expedition consisted of men who often behaved like errant Sunday School boys. When chosen by Smith, none of them had any real reputation and only Arthur Black had any known past. Even that was based more on legend than fact, for according to tales told by mountain men in later years, Black had saved Smith from grizzlies on two occasions. If one of those was during the time Smith led his first party west, then Black had been with him from the very beginning and was still with him as he left Bear Lake bound for the southwest. All the rest were simply vague, shadowy men who happened to have been at the rendezvous and who emerge from obscurity only because they were chosen by Smith. Whoever they were, they were soon causing trouble for the leaders, and later Harrison Rogers would say, "our own men are contentious and quarrelsome amongst themselves and have been ever since we started the expedition." Yet given the life they led and the fatigue, both mental and physical, their constant arguing is understandable.

The company traveled southwest until they reached Utah Lake, then followed first the Sevier River and later the Virgin until they reached the Colorado, which they descended to the Mohave villages. Almost all of it was desert country and they crossed it during the hottest time of the year from late August through September and into October. There were no buffalo and little other game, and they lived mostly on dried buffalo meat, which, even though Smith had brought almost half a ton, ran out long before they reached California. Once they met some friendly Paiute Indians who provided them with corn and pumpkins but nothing else. Finally they reached the Mohave villages where they found more food and where they were able to rest for two weeks.

Then began another desert crossing, this time to reach the Mexican settlements in California. They followed the Mohave River over the age-old trade route between the Colorado River and the coast. Once again it was dry, sterile country which Smith described as one of "complete barrens." Guided by Indians who knew where to find water, it still was often necessary to travel from morning to night without finding a fresh source. Water in the river they were following disappeared and reappeared so frequently that Smith named it the Inconstant River.

It is little wonder that when the band of trappers crossed the mountains and descended into the San Bernardino Valley they were impressed by the large herds of cattle, sheep, and horses grazing in "handsome bottoms covered with grass similar to ours." Little wonder, too, that they thoroughly enjoyed their first meal of fresh meat, or that, a few days later, Harrison Rogers wrote, "The men all appear satisfied since there was new regulations made about eating."

While the men were still feasting on the day of their arrival in California, Smith and the two missionaries went to San Gabriel. He immediately wrote Rogers to bring the rest of the men to the mission and when they arrived Rogers found life there even better. "I was introduced to 2 priests over a glass of good old whiskey and found them to be very joval friendly gentlemen." After that they had a supper consisting "of a number of different dishes, served different from any table I ever was at. Plenty of good wine during supper, before the cloth was removed sigars was introduced." In his diary, he added, "I expect we shall remain here some days."

The two priests welcoming them to San Gabriel were Father Geronimo Boscana and Father Jose Sanchez. Boscana, who had recently transferred from San Juan Capistrano, apparently had little to say in front of the Americans, for neither Smith nor Rogers would remember him as anything more than an anonymous missionary. Father Sanchez, on the other hand, made such an impact on the two men that Smith would eventually name a mountain after him and Rogers would call him the "greatest friend that I ever met with in all my travels."

Sanchez was then in his late forties, a large, stout man who had come from his native Spain to California in 1804. He had spent his early years as a missionary at San Diego, then after a brief time at Purisima had come to San Gabriel where he had been since 1821. Possibly one reason he got along so well with the trappers was that he was known as a great sportsman himself and was a good shot with both rifle and fowling piece. He was also a good story-teller, full of anecdotes, and almost every foreigner who visited his mission was made to feel at home.

Certainly Smith and Rogers felt thoroughly welcome at San Gabriel. After good whiskey, good food, and good cigars on the night of their arrival they retired, to be awakened at sunrise with a request that they join the missionaries for a cup of tea and some bread and cheese. Later, at noon, they were invited to have a glass of gin and water and some bread and cheese before sitting down to a full dinner. The next day there was a wedding, and although the two Americans protested that their clothes were too poor for them to attend, the priest insisted, and once again they sat down to an elegant dinner of roasted and boiled meat and chicken, accompanied by wine and brandy, with grapes for dessert. Since this was a special occasion, an Indian band provided background music. All this, of course, was for the leaders, but the men were not neglected, for they were furnished with cooking utensils and enough rations to last them for several days.

A few days later Father Sanchez also presented Smith with 64 yards of material to make clothing for the men who, after all their travels, were nearly naked. Smith divided it equally among them, giving each man three and a half yards, enough to make himself a shirt. Rogers, at least, tried to show his gratitude by giving Father Sanchez a buffalo robe only to have the priest reciprocate by giving him a very large blanket.

Smith, too, tried to repay the favors by putting two of his men, Silas Gobel and James Reed, to work in the mission blacksmith shop making a bear trap for Father Sanchez. Not only did he return a favor, but he also gave two of his bored and contentious men something to do. Apparently it came none too soon in the case of Reed, for just the day before he had said or done something to irritate his captain and Smith told Rogers, "he had to give Read a little floggin yesterday evening on account of some of his impertinence." It seemed to have done some good, Rogers said, for "he appeared more complasant today than usual."

It was a sign that despite the ease and comfort of life at San Gabriel, those who had joined the expedition to trap were dissatisfied, and a few days later Rogers wrote in his diary, "Mr. S. and all hands getting impatient." Smith, as soon as he arrived, had written to Governor Echeandia explaining his reasons for being in California and asking permission to pass through the country to the bay of San Francisco. As yet there had been no reply, and finally Smith decided to lay his request personally before the governor. On December 9 he left for San Diego, leaving Harrison Rogers in charge of the men at San Gabriel.

VI

While Smith was gone Rogers did his best to keep the men occupied and out of trouble. The blacksmiths, Gobel and Reed, were kept at the mission forge making horseshoes and nails for the day the expedition would take the trail again. When Father Sanchez told Rogers about the trouble he was having with thieving Indians, the two blacksmiths were put to work making a large trap to catch those who were stealing fruit from the mission's orange grove. Two other men, Arthur Black and John Gaiter, worked for the missionary on the understanding they would receive a horse in return for three days' work. Rogers and Martin McCoy sometimes went hunting, once killing several brants and a duck, another time killing a wolf and wounding a deer. It helped pass the time, but, Rogers said, "all hands appear to be anxious to move on to the north." And a few days later he noted that the men were again "contentious and quarrelsome."

Rogers found what escape he could in the company of Father Sanchez. He ate with him, "our fare at table much the same as at first, a plenty of everything good to eat and drink." Sometimes he played cards with the father and other visitors to the mission, although apparently with little success, for he noted they were all "pretty expert." He was also drawn into a conversation with Father Sanchez about religion.

Rogers, who had been brought up a stern Calvinist, apparently thought that the main interest of all Catholics was to lure him away from his faith. Certainly there is an air of surprise in his journal when, soon after arriving in California, he wrote, "They all appear friendly and treat us well, although they are Catholicks by profession, they allow us the liberty of conscience, and treat us as they do their own countrymen or brethren." And there it remained for several weeks until one evening, at supper, Father Sanchez began to question Rogers about his religious beliefs.

If Father Sanchez expected a brief, noncommittal answer from an ill-informed, lukewarm Protestant, he must have been surprised at Rogers' fervor, which remained even as he recorded his answer in his journal. "I very frankly informed him that I was brought up under the Calvinist doctrine, and did not believe that it was in the power of man to forgive sins. God only had that power, and when I was under the necessity of confessing my sins, I confessed them unto God in prayer and supplication, not to man."

A few weeks later Rogers elaborated on his religious knowledge in a New Year's message to Father Sanchez. It began, "Reverend Father, Standing on the threshold of a New Year, I salute you with the most cordial congratulations and good wishes." Then he traced the history of the spread of the Christian gospel, mentioned Jesus, Jonah, the twelve apostles, Paul, and even St. Justin the Martyr. It was a definite attempt to demonstrate that he was not just an ignorant hunter. As such it was impressive, although Rogers, after mustering all his witnesses, could only come to the somewhat lame conclusion that "the gospel was preached in every part of the globe which was then known." All this deepened the friendship between the two men as did the fact that Rogers, during Smith's long absence, continued to use his own men to help the missionary.

Just after New Year's Joseph Chapman arrived at the mission to meet the hunters. Rogers found him to be "a very ingenious man; . . . he gets many favours from the priest, by superintending the building of mills, black smithing, and many other branches of mechanism." In this particular case he was making charcoal and Rogers assigned some of his men—Robert Evans, Manuel Lazurus, John Hanna, and John Wilson—to help build a coal pit and to cut the wood to burn in it.

Two days were spent working with Chapman in the charcoal pit.

Then on January 6, Epiphany, there was a large celebration at San Gabriel to which all the men were invited. They were allowed to join the mission soldiers in firing a salute, after which they were given bread, cheese, and large amounts of wine. After all the boredom of the last weeks it was a chance for them to blow off steam and it nearly ended in disaster. Some of the men got drunk and two of them, James Reed and Daniel Ferguson, got into a fight. Some soldiers, in trying to break it up, struck Arthur Black, "which come very near terminating with bad consequence." Rogers, however, heard the disturbance and was able to pacify his own men before it turned into a full-scale war.

The next day the celebration continued with Father Sanchez amusing himself by throwing oranges among the Indian women and watching them scramble for their share. Then, that night, there was a large fandango that lasted until nearly daylight. It was that same night that a young Indian woman came to Rogers' quarters and asked him "to make her a blanco Pickanina." Rogers, the pious Calvinist, refused, saying, "I was ashamed, and did not gratify her or comply with her request, seeing her so forward, I have no propensity to tech her."

A few days later Smith returned from San Diego, where he had gone to see Governor Jose Maria Echeandia and to explain his reasons for being in California. Echeandia was himself a relative newcomer to California, and although he understood those who came by sea to trade for cattle hides, he was highly suspicious of Smith because he had never heard of such a thing as beaver trapping. To emphasize the fact that he and his men were hunters, Smith sent word to Rogers to pick out eight of the best beaver skins and send them to San Diego to show the governor. Echeandia remained suspicious, however, for there were no precedents concerning foreigners who came by land and he was reluctant to make an independent decision. Finally, Smith showed him a license signed by General William Clark and also got several ship captains to sign a document attesting to his honesty and to the purity of his motives. Echeandia at last agreed that Smith and his men could replenish their supplies and leave California, but they could not go north toward San Francisco Bay. Instead they must leave over the same route by which they had arrived.

Smith returned to San Gabriel on January 10, and the frustration and boredom disappeared immediately as the men prepared to leave. For the next week some of them joined Smith traveling back and forth between San Gabriel and the pueblo of Los Angeles to obtain horses. One of the blacksmiths made a branding iron, others used it to brand the horses while still others were put to work getting the traps ready for packing. It was a busy time, and for once Rogers could write, "time is passing off swiftly."

Yet even though they were finally preparing to leave, Rogers must have had mixed feelings because he had spent much of that long wait dreaming. From the beginning he had been taken with San Gabriel's location in a valley with "pretty streams of water running through from all quarters, some thousands of acres of rich and fertile land as level as a die in view, and a part under cultivation, surrounded on the N. with a high and lofty mou., handsomely timbered with pine, and cedar, and on the s. with low mou. covered with grass."

He also noted the huge herds of horses, cattle, and sheep, the fields of wheat and corn, and the large number of Indians available to do the work. He even calculated the income of the missions from its many products—hides, tallow, soap, wine, brandy, wheat, and corn. Finally, in one burst of enthusiasm, he said that if the mission were properly managed it would be worth a "mine of silver or gold."

If Rogers' dream included staying in California to manage the mission for Father Sanchez, it was never to be. Instead, on January 18 the hunters left the mission bound for the east and traveled as far as the Indian settlement where they had arrived several months earlier. It was only a few miles from San Gabriel, and once the men had settled down in camp, Smith and Rogers rode back to the mission to have a final farewell dinner with Father Sanchez. When it was over he gave each of them a blanket, and also gave Rogers a cheese and a gourd filled with brandy for the trail ahead. Then the two men returned to camp and the next morning began moving toward San Bernardino where they would make their preparations to leave California.

As the band of trappers rode away from San Gabriel, two men were left behind. One was Daniel Ferguson who, as the expedition prepared to leave on the morning of January 18, could not be found. Possibly after two months of easy California living, the life of a trapper no longer appealed to him. Possibly, too, there was some lingering resentment—or fear—of the blacksmith James Reed with whom he had fought a few weeks before. Whatever caused him to hide, he did it well enough that Smith could not find him and was forced to go without him. The corporal at the mission promised to keep on searching and when he was found would send him back to Smith. But Rogers said, correctly, "I expect we shall not see him again."

The other was John Wilson who was discharged the day before they left San Gabriel. Although there is no indication that he was a troublemaker, Smith was obviously trying to get rid of him. A week later Wilson caught up with the expedition, saying that the authorities would not allow him to stay. Rogers with some irritation wrote in his diary that they were "obliged to let him come back to us; he remains with the company but not under pay as yet; I expect he will go with us." This time Rogers was wrong, for somehow the difficulties with the authorities were ironed out, or ignored, and Wilson was left behind in California.

VII

Governor Echeandia had ordered Jedediah Smith to leave California by the same route over which he arrived, but these instructions were open to a certain amount of interpretation, at least as far as Smith was concerned. To him, California was only the settled region near the coast and once he was beyond it and into the San Bernardino Mountains he felt that he had complied with the governor's orders. Therefore, instead of again entering the Mohave, he angled northwest through the mountains and eventually descended into the San Joaquin Valley.

Smith's choice of direction may well have been determined by some of the stories he had heard at San Gabriel. Both he and Harrison Rogers had told Father Sanchez about their travels and had even gone so far as to draw a map of the country they had crossed. Apparently, in return, they were told of the country to the north, for on one occasion Rogers reported hearing that two days above San Fernando there were "plenty of beaver at a lake." He also heard that beyond there, at a place called "Two Larres," there were, again, "plenty of beaver."

These stories of innumerable beaver in the valley turned out to be true, for by April 1827, when Smith had worked his way as far north as the American River, he had some fifteen hundred pounds of fur. He was ready to leave California and take the furs to the rendezvous, and he and his men turned east and began following the canyon of the American River into the Sierras. It was already May, but there was no sign of spring in the high mountains. There was only deep snow in which the horses bogged down and in which five eventually died. There was nothing to do but to turn around and follow the river back down into the warmth of the San Joaquin Valley. Smith moved south seventy-five miles to the Stanislaus River where he and his men went into camp.

All this movement had been closely watched by Indians in the valley and soon rumors reached the Spanish settlements of white men in the interior. In the coastal areas of California any news from the valley was almost always bad, for the Indians there often raided the horse herds of the settlements and also provided a haven for runaway Indians. Now the thought of American trappers goading them on was positively alarming. From San Jose, on May 16, the president of the missions Father Narcisio Duran wrote to Ignacio Martinez, comandante of San Francisco:

"This is to inform you that last night and this morning about four hundred souls ran away from this mission to their villages at the Tulare." The reason, he said, was that a band of Americans was roaming the country encouraging them, and "offering them protection to abandon the missions and Christian obligations and return to their villages to live and die gentiles." He also expressed his belief that this might "be the beginning of such troubles and happenings in other missions. I believe them to be the same people who were in San Gabriel and who have come all along the chain of missions causing trouble."

There was more hysteria than accuracy in the letter, and somehow word of these feelings reached Smith, who from his camp on the Stanislaus wrote Father Duran to calm his fears. He explained that he had wanted to leave the country but had been unsuccessful in crossing the mountains. As soon as the snows melted, he would leave, for he was a long way from home and anxious to be on his way.

Duran, however, refused to accept the letter and it was delivered instead to Commandante Martinez who sent it to Governor Echeandia. Martinez also investigated the trouble at San Jose and found that it was being caused by a mission Indian who was using the Americans as a pretext to encourage his fellow neophytes to run away. The trappers themselves, apparently, were entirely unaware of the whole business.

Still, as far as Governor Echeandia was concerned, they had remained in California in direct violation of his orders and he decided the time had come to be firm. Martinez was ordered to send a squad of soldiers to inform Smith that he had no right to be where he was, frightening the whole country, and that he must be on his way. If he so desired he could bring his men into San Jose where, after being disarmed, they could await instruction from Mexico or the first ship that could take them to Oregon.

When the soldiers reached the American camp, Smith was not there and Harrison Rogers was in command. Apparently he was able to convince the soldiers that the orders did not apply to him, for they made no attempt to bring him in but left the entire party at their camp on the Stanislaus.

VIII

In the meantime Smith was on his way east. He had decided that because of the deep snow it would be impossible to take the heavily loaded horses across the Sierras early enough to reach the rendezvous in July. He left the furs and most of the party behind while he went east to recruit men to help trap the valley north all the way to Oregon. Smith, with just two other men, Robert Evans and the blacksmith Silas Gobel, plunged into the Sierras. They went up the north fork of the Stanislaus, crossing Ebbets Pass, and dropping down into the Nevada desert. After a long, difficult, and almost waterless passage, they reached Bear Lake where Smith's partners, Sublette and Jackson and their bands of trappers, had already gathered. "My arrival," Smith said, "caused a considerable bustle in camp, for myself and party had been given up as lost. A small Cannon brought up from St. Louis was loaded and fired for a salute."

Ten days later Jed Smith was on his way to California again. This time he had eighteen men, one of whom was Silas Gobel, the blacksmith who had made the trip east from California with him. Robert Evans, however, was not. On the way east, as they were passing through the salt desert of western Utah, Evans had given out and had lain down under a tree to die. Smith and Gobel, realizing that staying with him meant that they too would die, went on and before long stumbled on a spring. Smith filled a small kettle with water and took it back to Evans who drank four or five quarts and asked Smith why he hadn't brought more. It was enough, however, to enable him to travel again, but he wanted no more of the desert and did not join the second expedition to California.

Smith, too, apparently had his fill of the waterless desert he had crossed on the way east. The year before in California he had told Echeandia he did not want to leave over the route by which he reached California—the Sevier, Virgin, Colorado, and Mohave rivers—because it was too dry and barren. But now he was following exactly that same route, for the desert he had crossed coming east, he found, was even worse. This time, however, he did not plan to go into the settled areas of San Bernardino or San Gabriel but rather cross directly from the Mohave Desert into the San Joaquin Valley. Then fate in the form of the Mohave Indians intervened.

In mid-August Smith reached the Mohave villages where he planned to cross the river and enter the desert. When he was in these same villages less than a year before, he had encountered no trouble and there seemed no reason to expect any now. He spent a few days resting horses and men, traded with the Mohaves for new horses, bought some corn and beans for the trail ahead, and even gave presents to some of the chiefs.

Yet there was smoldering anger against white men among the Mohaves, and although Smith was told why, he did not at the time understand how it could involve him. A Spanish-speaking Indian named Fernando, who had served the previous year as Smith's interpreter, told him that some time after the earlier party had crossed the river, another band of white men had entered the Mohave country from the south. They had quarreled among themselves, and some of them had continued up the Colorado River while the rest turned east. But before they divided, there had been trouble with the Mohaves and there was a battle in which some Indians were killed. The story was interesting to Smith, for it gave him the answer to something that had been puzzling him. Farther north, in Ute country, he had seen tracks of horses and mules and had been told by the Indians that they had been made by a band of starving white men. Now it became clear that those men were undoubtedly part of the band that had come up the Colorado from the south.

To the Mohave the most important part of the story was the death of several of their warriors, but apparently it did not occur to Smith that they intended to exact revenge from him. When the time came to cross the Colorado River, he showed no signs of expecting trouble. He divided his forces, taking half the men across on rafts, leaving all the horses and the other half of the men on the river bank to await a second trip. Almost immediately those left behind were attacked by the Mohaves who killed all ten, including the blacksmith Silas Gobel. Smith and the others on the raft were also attacked but survived, although Thomas Virgin was badly wounded when an Indian smashed him on the head with a war club.

Smith, with no horses left, took most of the supply packs he had brought over on the rafts and sank them in the river. He saved a few, and these he spread out along the bank hoping to gain some time while the Indians came to loot. Then he and the eight other survivors, carrying what they could on their backs, headed into the desert. Before they had gone more than a few hundred yards, the Indians were already closing in, and Smith decided to return to the river. There, in a grove of cottonwoods, he and his men built a makeshift breastwork from what small trees they could hack down with their knives. As they waited for the attack, some of the men asked Smith if he thought they could defend themselves, and he said he was certain they could, but in his journal he admitted, "that was not my opinion." Finally, however, a few Indians ventured within range of at least a long shot, and Smith ordered two good marksmen to fire. Both hit their targets, and as the two Indians fell the rest ran off "like frightened sheep," and Smith said, "we were released from the apprehension of immediate death."

Although momentarily free of the fear of being killed, Smith and the survivors were still in a difficult position. They had few provisions, no horses, no guides, no way to carry water, and no place to go but into the searing late summer heat of the desert. But Smith had been here once before and knew vaguely the way to California. Led by him they traveled from spring to spring, mostly at night, and after nine and a half days they reached the San Bernardino Valley where they killed some cattle for fresh meat. After resting several days and using what goods they had carried on their backs, they traded for horses to replace those they had lost. Smith also wrote a brief note to Father Sanchez thanking him for the cattle taken from the mission herds, and explaining that he had not intended to return to California but had been forced to do so by an Indian attack. Then Smith rode north toward the San Joaquin Valley.

As he went he left two men behind in southern California. One was Thomas Virgin who, despite his serious head wound, had managed to struggle across the desert with the rest. Now he obviously had reached the limit of his endurance, for not only was he wounded, he was not a young man. Although no one ever gave his specific age, Harrison Rogers always referred to him, respectfully, as "Mr. Virgin," while Smith on two occasions called him "old." To these two young men, *old* could mean almost anything, but whatever his age, Virgin was badly in need of rest and Smith left him behind in southern California to recuperate.

The other man left behind was Isaac Galbraith, who had accompanied the party as a free trapper rather than as an employee. He was known as "a crack shot" and everyone who ever saw him said he was "gigantic." He was also a long-time friend of Thomas Virgin's. Two years before, at the rendezvous of 1825, the two appeared together in the account books as they sold their furs and then, still together, purchased a supply of coffee and sugar as well as powder, knives, flints, fishhooks, and some scarlet cloth. In 1827 they had both joined Smith, and when Virgin was left behind, Galbraith asked that he also be allowed to remain. Since he was a free trapper there was no objection and he stayed at San Bernardino.

Smith and the rest of the men rode north into the San Joaquin Valley and on September 18, 1827, reached the camp on the Stanislaus. There Smith found that Rogers and the other men had spent "what hunters call a pleasant summer." There had been no trouble with the Indians, the climate had been good, and there was plenty of game, mostly deer, elk, and antelope. Smith learned, too, of the soldiers' visit and that they had left without bothering Rogers or his men. Possibly that encouraged Smith to go to San Jose to obtain more supplies. More likely it was a matter of desperation, for Smith well knew that his "last and only resource [was] to try once more the hospitality of the Californians."

Smith, with three men, rode to San Jose, where he was met by Father Narciscio Duran, who greeted him in a far different fashion from that of Father Sanchez at San Gabriel. Duran, of course, knew of Smith, for it was he who had complained about the hunters the previous spring and who had also refused to receive Smith's letter. Now he either "could not or would not understand me when I endeavoured to explain the cause of my being in the country." Smith was not allowed to continue to Monterey to see the governor; his horses were taken and he was conveyed to "a dirty hovel which they called a guard house." There he was allowed to write a letter to the governor.

Smith could think of no reason for Duran's enmity "unless perhaps it might be that he was apprehensive of danger to the *true faith,* for which reason he was anxious to stop my fishing around the country (for such he termed my traveling . . .)." It was a reasonable explanation, although it does not fully take into account the problems that Duran himself was facing.

In 1825 Duran had been elected president of the California missions, but while in office he had opposed Governor Echeandia's plan of emancipation of the Indians. In doing so he had angered Mexican officials who, when another election was held, notified the college of San Fernando that Duran was no longer acceptable as president. When the new election was held in June 1827, the office of president went to Smith's old friend Father Sanchez of San Gabriel, and Duran was returned to his position as a simple missionary at San Jose. The whole business, which had happened only three months before Smith arrived, apparently left Duran bitter and depressed. Those who had known him at other times in his life said he was generous and cheerful, but another visitor in the year 1827 remembered him as unable to see things except "through a funereal veil: never has a soul held less cheerfulness than Fray Narciso's."

Smith's letter to the governor did bring some results. Commandante Martinez arrived from San Francisco, questioned Smith, and finding no evidence that he was a spy, agreed to help him in his attempt to see the governor in Monterey. While awaiting permission to leave San Jose for the capital, Smith was visited by two Americans, John Rogers Cooper and Thomas Park. Park was new to California, having just arrived as supercargo on the brig *Harbinger,* and he could do little more than commiserate with Smith. Cooper, however, was an old California hand and had just recently been baptized and become a citizen of Mexico. He promised to do everything in his power to help.

It took two weeks to obtain the permission, and when Smith was finally allowed to leave San Jose he was guarded by four soldiers. Arriving in Monterey late one evening, Smith was unceremoniously thrown in the calabozo where he remained without food until almost noon the next day. When he was released and taken to the governor's house, he was met at the door by Echeandia who immediately asked him if he would like something to eat. Smith, having been deprived of food, greedily accepted. The governor began to talk, but although Smith knew some Spanish, he did not think he could fully understand the governor without an interpreter. The discussion was broken off temporarily, although Smith was able to obtain permission to reside at Captain Cooper's home and to move freely about Monterey.

The next evening Echeandia and Smith met again, with an interpreter, William Hartnell. For some reason, Echeandia, a cold man who was suspicious of foreigners like Smith and even Cooper, had considerable trust in Hartnell and this attitude would eventually work in Smith's favor. At first, however, everything looked hopeless. There were several meetings at which they talked through Hartnell. "The governor would sometimes say Mr. Smith must go to Mexico; at other times, Mr. S. and party must be sent off by water; again he would say, 'Send fetch in the party here,' and continued in the equivocating manner for several days." Clearly the governor wanted to get out from under the situation without making a decision.

It was Hartnell who finally suggested the way out. The English, he said, had a law by which, in times of emergency, four ship captains could appoint someone to act as temporary consul. Possibly the Americans had a similar law that might be used in this case. Several American ship captains were in port, and although some of them doubted that such a law existed, they were willing to pretend that it did, particularly when Echeandia indicated he would accept such a solution. Captain Cooper was appointed temporary consul and he immediately set to work on the problem. There were still several disagreements, and at one time the negotiations almost broke down over Echeandia's insistence that the rest of the trappers be ordered to come into Monterey. Smith refused at first, but after obtaining the governor's promise they would not be imprisoned, he ordered Rogers to bring them in, not to Monterey, but to San Francisco.

At another meeting with the governor Cooper agreed, under penalty of forfeiting his own property, to guarantee Smith's good conduct. The governor found this acceptable and agreed that Smith could have his choice of three things: he could remain in California until orders came from Mexico; he could go to Mexico himself; or he could take what men he had and leave California —permanently. Smith chose to leave.

On November 15, 1827, Smith sailed from Monterey bound for San Francisco on board the ship *Franklin* commanded by Captain John Bradshaw. After all the weeks in the capital and after all the trouble with the governor, Smith was free again but he had little chance to enjoy it. They sailed in early afternoon and by evening such a gale was blowing that he was thoroughly seasick. Two days later, however, he was in San Francisco where the commandante, Luis Arguello, was satisfied with his passport and offered him no more trouble. His men were there, too, and in good condition, and thus Smith began his final preparations to leave California.

IX

His first move was to dispose of the 1,568 pounds of beaver fur the party had collected by selling it to Bradshaw at $2.50 a pound. It relieved him of having to pack it all the way back to the rendezvous, and it gave him enough money—nearly four thousand dollars—to refit his expedition. Over the next several weeks he used it to obtain horses, mules, arms, ammunition, and supplies.

As he made preparations, he found he could not get the necessary work done in San Francisco and despite the difficulties he had once had with Father Duran, he moved down to San Jose. Somehow the two men worked out their differences, for Smith was able to obtain a room for himself and two more for his men and also to make arrangements to use the mission blacksmith shop for a week to get ready to take the trail.

Smith, as he prepared to depart, was also somewhat concerned about the two men left behind in southern California. Finally, on December 6, Isaac Galbraith arrived in San Francisco, but he brought no news of his long-time friend Thomas Virgin. Instead of remaining with Virgin he had apparently gone hunting, for Smith now paid him two hundred dollars, probably for beaver fur he had collected. Certainly Galbraith had not shared his old friend's life over the past several months, for when Virgin reached San Jose a week later he told Smith that he had spent most of that time in jail. Often, he said, he was "without anything to eat and strictly forbidden to speak to anyone and abused in almost every way." Eventually he had been released, and when he joined the party, Smith said, "I was quite glad to see the old man again."

Isaac Galbraith, however, may not have been so glad to see him, for the two seem to have had a falling out either earlier in southern California or now in San Francisco. After a friendship that had kept them trapping together for several years, they had now reached a parting of the ways. Virgin clearly intended to go with Smith, while Galbraith, the free trapper, elected to stay behind in California. Smith lost not only Galbraith but Wilson and Ferguson, who had dropped out of the previous year's expedition, as well as the ten men who were killed by the Mohaves. He was indeed short-handed and would have liked to increase the size of the party. Several men were willing to join, but Echeandia had forbidden the taking of any men other than those who had come with him. Smith did manage to add two men, Richard Leland and Louis Pombert, of whom little is known except that Leland was an Englishman who was an excellent horseman and

Pombert was a Canadian who drifted from trapping band to trapping band. The history of how they came to California and the life they led there before joining Smith is an absolute blank. Possibly their very obscurity made Smith feel safe in defying the governor and adding them to his band of trappers.

Finally they were ready to go and on Christmas Day Smith rode back to San Francisco to talk to Commandante Arguello, who had been ordered to see him out of California. Once more there was trouble. Smith had been ordered to cross to the north of San Francisco Bay at Carquinez Straits, which was too wide to swim with horses, and he had been unable to obtain a boat. He offered to solve the problem easily by ascending the river to a place narrow enough to swim, but Arguello would neither allow this nor provide Smith with a boat. He insisted that nothing be done until further instructions could be obtained.

At this point Smith's patience snapped. He pretended to agree and rode back to his men still waiting at San Jose. There he wrote to Echeandia bitterly protesting the treatment he had received, and without waiting for an answer and without permission, he and his men left for the north. It was December 30, the last day but one of 1827, and it was pouring down rain, but Smith was thoroughly content as he "returned again to the woods, the river, the prairae, the Camp & Game with a feeling somewhat like that of a prisoner escaped from his dungeon and his chains." Smith, finally, had seen the last of California.

California, however, had not quite seen the last of Smith's trappers. About three weeks later the party was trapping on the San Joaquin, having some success in spite of a shortage of traps. It had also been raining fairly steadily, the country was flooded, and Smith ordered the men to kill some elk and use the hides to make bull boats. James Reed and Louis Pombert were assigned to one boat, and at first they did well, coming in one day with twenty-two beaver. Then they were sent out to trap again and told to rejoin the party in a week, but they did not reappear. They had deserted, taking eleven traps with them.

Surely the mistake had been in assigning these two men to the same boat. Pombert was something of a drifter, and Reed, who had been flogged by Smith, and who had fought with Daniel Ferguson, was obviously a troublemaker. Nobody knows what happened between them as they spent that week in the mountains trapping, but for some reason they did not rejoin the party. Soon afterward Pombert was back in San Jose where Smith had first found him. James Reed was not with him and, in fact, never again showed up anywhere in California. He disappeared from the records which, given his inability to stay out of trouble, seems unlikely unless he was dead. Possibly, after going into the mountains with Pombert, he did not make it out again.

THE NEW CALIFORNIANS

I

When Jed Smith led his men out of California in late 1827, Governor Jose Maria Echeandia could begin to relax. The problem of the American trappers that had plagued him for more than a year was solved, and the governor was now free to return to San Diego, which he much preferred to Monterey. Two years before, when he had first come to California, he had stopped in San Diego to recover from the long and difficult voyage. He soon became convinced that the mild climate there was good for his delicate health, and rather than continue north he ordered his predecessor, Luis Arguello, to come to San Diego to turn the office of governor over to him.

Much to the irritation of his deputies in Monterey, Echeandia spent the next year governing California from San Diego. He made no attempt to change the location of the capital officially, and when California's representative body, the diputacion, met in the summer of 1827, he went north to attend. Although he did not especially like Monterey, the meeting itself had gone well. He had dominated the delegates, maintained control over all the sessions, and the program that emerged had been entirely his. And now he was free to leave Monterey and return to the warm sunshine of San Diego.

Admittedly, travel was a problem for Echeandia, for he was a poor traveler. On the way north to Monterey he had indulged himself in a long rest stop at Santa Barbara. Now, on his way back, he planned to stop there again, and after arriving in early December he settled down for a stay that stretched into several months.

He was still there in March 1828 when word reached him that California had once again been invaded by trappers. He wrote to the commandante at San Diego, "Eight armed men have appeared at a frontier post with a *guia* of the N. Mex. custom house as a passport. Arrest them and seize their arms." Shortly afterward he sailed from Santa Barbara for San Diego.

By the time he got there, whatever inner peace he had found during the past months had been destroyed. The relief he felt when Smith left ended with the appearance of this new band of men, and the relaxation of the long rest in Santa Barbara had been shattered by the rigors of the sea voyage to San Diego. Then, when he landed, he found still another problem, a personal one, that shattered whatever vestiges of peace were left.

During his earlier stay in San Diego he had become enamored of Josefa Carrillo, daughter of a prominent family. In fact, there were many in California who thought his insistence on living in San Diego rather than in the capital was due not to its better climate, as the governor claimed, as much as it was to the opportunity to pursue the young lady. Echeandia, however, had a major rival for her affections in the person of Henry Delano Fitch, an American ship captain who had recently come to San Diego. Possibly Echeandia, even though he was governor of all California, never really had a chance against the young American. Certainly his trip north to Monterey had removed him from serious contention, and by the time he returned, Senorita Carrillo had promised to marry Henry Fitch. The wedding had not yet taken place, and now that Echeandia was back in San Diego, he planned to do whatever he could to prevent it.

That, however, was a personal problem, and for now it had to be put off in favor of the official problem of the American trappers who had been captured and brought to San Diego. Eight of them were escorted to the governor's office to explain their reasons for coming to California. Two, Isaac Slover and Sylvester Pattie, were older men, the rest were young trappers, some barely out of their teens. Nominally Pattie was the leader, but he was too ill to give a clear account of why the party had come to California and one of the others stepped forward to tell the governor their story.

The previous fall, the report went, they had obtained a permit in Santa Fe and left for the west to trap. Starting from the copper mines in southern New Mexico they had followed the Gila River downstream until they reached the Colorado. There the party had quarreled and separated. One group had turned north up the Colorado, the other, these eight, had begun descending the river. As they floated downstream, they had enormous success trapping, and by the time they reached the mouth of the river they had large packs of fur. But they also were in a trap. They had no horses and they could not push their canoes upstream against the river's current. They had buried the furs and with great difficulty had crossed the desert until they reached a mission in Baja California from which they were escorted north to see the governor. All they wanted now were some horses and the right to return to the mouth of the Colorado to dig up their furs and bring them to California where they could be sold to some ship captain.

Echeandia was in no mood to be reasonable. Not only was he exhausted from his trip and irritated by the loss of his lady Josefa Carrillo, but he was tired of hearing Americans claim they had come to California only accidentally and in desperation. Twice in little more than a year he had heard that story from Smith; now he was hearing it again from another band of trappers. This time he decided it was all a pack of lies. As far as he was concerned, he said, they were spies for the Spanish king who had come to look over the country and find its weaknesses so he could send troops to reconquer California.

It was, of course, a ridiculous charge, and Echeandia may have made it because he momentarily lost his temper. Or he may have wanted to see, seriously or with tongue in cheek, if he could get some kind of reaction from the Americans. If that was his intention he was not disappointed, for they exploded at the accusation of being royalist spies. They were, they said, "born and bred full blooded republicans" who would die before they would be spies for the Spanish king. One of them launched into a description of American institutions, only to be cut off by the governor who said he did not want to hear any more of their long speeches, did not want to hear any more of their lies. He ordered them returned to the guardhouse.

Eventually the governor cooled down and began making arrangements to allow the trappers to go to the Colorado and retrieve their furs. Sylvester Pattie, however, was still too ill to travel and the seven others remained in San Diego awaiting his recovery. He never made it. In late May he died and was buried in San Diego. Shortly afterward several of the trappers returned to the river only to find that the spring flood down the Colorado had ruined all the furs. Two of them, Isaac Slover and William Pope, went back to New Mexico, the others settled in California.

One of the trappers, Sylvester Pattie's son James, had not gone with the others to retrieve the furs. It may have been because, as he claimed, the governor held him hostage for the return of the rest of the party. More likely it was because he also was too ill to make the trip. Unlike his father, he recovered and was available in San Diego to serve as Echeandia's interpreter when the governor ran into still another problem with a foreigner.

Even as Echeandia was trying to work things out with the trappers in San Diego, he received disturbing news concerning the American ship captain John Bradshaw. Six months earlier, while still in the north, he had watched as Bradshaw sailed from Monterey in the ship *Franklin.* At the time he was happy enough to see him go, for on board the ship was Jed Smith, and in taking him away, Bradshaw removed a problem that had long plagued Echeandia.

Now, six months later, both the governor and Bradshaw were in San Diego. At first their relations were cordial. In early May Echeandia gave Bradshaw a permit extending to him all possible trading privileges and also allowing his supercargo, Rufus Perkins, to travel by land from mission to mission seeking trade. Soon afterward Echeandia received word that Bradshaw, who had recently been in Baja California, was suspected of smuggling there. Other reports indicated he had also avoided paying customs duties by illegally transferring goods from another ship to his own, and also, in defiance of the governor's order, had landed on Santa Catalina Island. Echeandia ordered an investigation. He also ordered Bradshaw to land his cargo and deposit it in a San Diego warehouse as security pending the outcome of that investigation.

Echeandia's order caught Bradshaw ashore in San Diego away from the security of his ship, and he immediately agreed to obey the governor. He asked if he could return to the *Franklin* to personally arrange the landing of the goods, and Echeandia gave his permission. That was a mistake, for it soon became obvious that Bradshaw, now back aboard his ship, was going to defy the governor. Echeandia wanted to send soldiers aboard to seize the ship but had no boat and before he could find one, the *Franklin* was gone. On the morning of July 16 it cut its cable and began running out of the bay. There was little the governor could do but watch as it passed the fort at the entrance, the sailors on board shouting defiance at the Mexican flag. The soldiers in the fort opened fire, sending forty cannon balls after the ship, but with little visible effect.

For Echeandia the troubles with foreigners seemed never to end. He was no more than free of the trappers and of Bradshaw, than an American named Charles Lang was arrested in a small boat just off the coast of California. He was brought into San Diego where Echeandia launched an official investigation into his reasons for being there. Lang, when questioned, claimed he had come to California to establish a ranch, build a house, and devote himself entirely to farming. The investigating officers, however, seemed to think that the things he had with him in the boat—two trunks of dry goods and a barrel organ—were better suited to trading than to farming, and the governor ordered them confiscated. Lang soon left San Diego bound for Mexico and never returned to California.

Echeandia was constantly being harried by foreigners causing trouble of one sort or another. Sometimes they arrived illegally by land, other times they came legally by sea but then tried to evade the payment of legitimate customs duties. And as Echeandia spent much of his official time dealing with these difficulties, the personal problem caused by the American Henry Fitch's intention to marry Josefa Carrillo was coming to a head.

On April 14, 1829, Padre Menendez of the presidio of San Diego baptized the young American trader Enrique Domingo Fitch. The new middle name, Domingo rather than Delano, was for his godfather Domingo Carrillo, Josefa's uncle and also an aide to Governor Echeandia. Fitch was now free to marry in the Catholic faith, and in fact arrangements had already been made for Father Menendez to perform the ceremony the following day.

By evening on the fifteenth, all the preparations had been made, and members of the Carrillo family and several friends had gathered for the wedding. Then, even as Father Menendez began the service, Domingo Carrillo suddenly appeared and in the name of the governor forbade the ceremony. Surely Echeandia had known of the wedding plans at least since Fitch's baptism the previous day, but now at the last moment he apparently could not stand the thought of it and sent his aide to intervene.

Whether the governor could legally prevent a wedding is open to question, but it makes little difference for his orders so frightened Menendez that the padre refused to continue with the ceremony. He did, however, remind Fitch that there were Catholic countries beyond the governor's reach where the couple could be legally married. There were, at the time, several ships in port, including Fitch's own *Maria Ester,* and the *Vulture,* whose captain Richard Barry was one of the wedding guests. For some reason, probably because of the governor's suspicions, the couple did not go on the *Maria Ester* but slipped aboard the *Vulture* and sailed away. Echeandia was left with the knowledge that his scheme had failed and that they would soon be beyond his power as governor and free to marry without interference.

II

Many of the foreigners who had to do business with Echeandia came to dislike him intensely. So, too, did many of the old-time Californians who had to serve under him. Yet he was something of a radical at least in his attempts to reduce the power of the missions and missionaries, and as such he quickly became a hero to the new generation just coming of age in California. In later years one member of that generation, Mariano Vallejo, would praise him extravagantly, while another, Juan Bautista Alvarado, would give him credit for teaching them all the true principles of republicanism. Such testimony demonstrates Echeandia's considerable influence, for these two young men, along with their close friend Jose Castro, were members of influential California families of the past, and they would soon come to dominate its government themselves.

All three had been born in Monterey—Vallejo in 1808, Alvarado in 1809, and Castro in 1810—and they still lived there when their new hero Echeandia first arrived in Monterey to attend the diputacion in 1827. By then all three were attached in some way to the government. Vallejo, like his father and older brother before him, had entered the army and after serving four years as a cadet had recently been promoted to the rank of alferez. Juan Alvarado, also the son of an army officer, had shown no interest in the military and had become secretary of the California diputacion. Jose Castro, equally uninterested in the army, had obtained a similar though lesser position as secretary of the local Monterey ayuntamiento.

Holding these positions, plus their loyalty to the governor, would cause them trouble when, in 1829, the soldiers in Monterey revolted against Echeandia's government. One night when the three were sleeping in the same room, a band of soldiers burst in, arrested them, and took them to jail. They were thrown into a dark, dirty cell with the lowest kinds of criminals and spent the rest of the night sitting, half-dressed, on the dirt floor. As several more prisoners were brought in, the three Monterey youths pieced together the story of an uprising by soldiers who without firing a shot had seized the presidio and disarmed all the officers.

Once in control, however, the soldiers had little idea of what to do next and finally decided to invite a man named Joaquin Solis to be leader of the revolution. Solis, living on a ranch near Monterey, had originally been sent to California as a convict for crimes committed during the Mexican wars of independence. During those wars he had been chief lieutenant of Vicente Gomez, known widely as "el capador"—the gelder. Gomez was notorious as a thief, a killer, and a man who tortured all Spaniards who fell into his hands. Yet Gomez' services to the cause of independence had been so great that, like Solis, his only punishment had been banishment to California. A few years after they arrived, Gomez had been killed in a brawl and Solis, his chief lieutenant, took his place as a hero to those who looked up to such men. When the revolution began in Monterey it was Joaquin Solis who was invited to take command.

His first act was to give the whole thing an air of legitimacy by drawing up a document justifying the actions of those who had revolted against the governor. On the night of November 15 the paper was read aloud in Monterey to a group of foreign merchants. The pronouncement itself was extremely long-winded and surely no one took seriously the almost endless account of massive wrongdoing by the governor or the glittering promises of the revolutionaries. Whether or not they took it seriously, the foreigners indicated to Solis their approval of his document, although as one of them later claimed, they did so only "from motives of courtesy."

The foreign merchants in Monterey were certainly in a difficult position. They had to walk a narrow line between the rebels who controlled the capital and the governor who, having returned to San Diego, was in possession of the rest of California. It required experienced leadership, and John Rogers Cooper stepped forward to provide it. He had spent some years as a sea captain trading in the Pacific before selling his ship and coming ashore to establish himself as a merchant in Monterey. He soon became a leader in the foreign colony and the burden of guiding the merchants through this trying time fell on him.

From the beginning, apparently, he hoped to keep the revolt from turning into a blood bath from which there would be no retreat. Soon after Solis took control, Cooper and several other foreigners approached him and negotiated the release of those who had been arrested. Among them were Alvarado and Castro, both civilians, who were freed in exchange for a promise that they would no longer oppose the revolt. Vallejo, as a soldier, was not allowed to go free, but was placed aboard the ship *Brookline* and sent off to San Diego to join Governor Echeandia.

Cooper, attempting to keep things as cool as possible, soon found it easier to deal with the rebel leader than to control some of his own people. Several hotheads among the foreigners, mainly those who had had trouble with Echeandia, now wanted to join the rebels in attacking him. Cooper and several other foreigners who had spent much time trading in Latin America were firmly opposed to such rash action. They thought the best thing now was to give the rebels a lot of advice and a little bit of money, but active participation should be withheld until they saw which side was going to win.

For the next several weeks those in Monterey watched and waited as Solis led his army north as far as San Francisco. Since he had the only sizable group of armed men in the area, he met no opposition and received at least nominal submission from all settlements in the north. Having accomplished that, he returned to Monterey where he made plans to march south to meet the real enemy, Governor Echeandia, who was waiting with an army at Santa Barbara.

Soon after Solis left Monterey for the south, Cooper heard a disturbing piece of news from his father-in-law Ignacio Vallejo. Although Solis had been publicly promising full trading rights to all foreigners, in private, Vallejo said, he was saying that they would either have to support his rebel government or he would drive them out. Hearing that, Cooper and several others who had been vaguely supporting Solis, decided they should now demonstrate their support of the governor by warning him of the revolt. Since it was already several weeks old and Echeandia had organized an army and marched it from San Diego to Santa Barbara, the message can hardly have been news to him. Still, it gave the foreigners a foot in each camp and they could now sit back and await the outcome of the battle in the south.

Eventually news arrived in Monterey that the two armies had met near Santa Barbara. Although the accounts differed in specifics, they all agreed that cannon had been fired but no one had been hurt. According to one story, the two armies were so far apart that cannon balls, by the time they reached the enemy, were so spent they could be caught by hand. A Scots doctor who was there wrote to Cooper, "You would have laughed . . . The two parties were in sight of each other for nearly two days, and exchanged shots but at such a distance that there was no chance of my assistance being needed."

It was all very amusing to the foreigners, but they soon realized they still faced a serious threat. Some accounts claimed that the rebels, after firing all their ammunition, had made an orderly retreat, others that they had fled at the first sound of cannon fire. Whatever had happened, it was obvious that the rebels had lost, that they were returning to the north, and that Monterey now lay right in the path of a large band of defeated and disgruntled soldiers who in their frustration might well loot the town.

The time had come to take sides, and John Rogers Cooper took the lead in organizing a force to protect the capital. According to one story, a barrel of rum was rolled out and those whom Solis had left behind in control of the capital were invited to celebrate their leader's victorious retreat. Once they were drunk they were locked up and the foreigners took possession of the town. Then as members of Solis's army straggled into Monterey they too were taken into custody. Solis, however, did not come to Monterey but went to his ranch where he tried to hide and was soon arrested. When Echeandia, after a long, slow march finally reached the capital, he found it had already been captured by its foreign residents who now turned it over to him. A few months later, in early May 1830, Solis and fourteen other ringleaders of the rebellion were sent to Mexico as prisoners on the American bark *Volunteer.*

III

The revolt of the soldiers at the presidio in Monterey was the first uprising of any importance in California, and as it began, Mariano Vallejo, Juan Alvarado, and Jose Castro were in the midst of it. But beyond being captured by rebels on the opening night, they played no part in the revolution or its suppression. It was the foreigners, led by Cooper, who defeated the rebels, then welcomed Governor Echeandia and his army when they marched into the capital.

The three young men from Monterey also remained relatively quiet during the next several years of political turbulence in California. A new governor, Lieutenant Colonel Manuel Victoria, was sent to replace Echeandia, but he soon made himself highly unpopular and was driven out by another revolt. Once he was gone former Governor Echeandia, living in retirement in San Diego, tried again to take control of the government only to be faced with a counterrevolution led by Captain Agustin V. Zamorano who had come to California as Governor Victoria's secretary. Neither side much wanted to fight, however, and after firing a barrage of plans and pronuncimientos at each other, they found a basis for compromise. Echeandia would remain in control of the military in the south, Zamorano in the north, while both of them simply ignored the diputacion. With that the two sides withdrew to their respective areas to await the coming of a governor from Mexico who, it was hoped, would put an end to the differences.

The new governor, Jose Figueroa, arrived in early January 1833 and began a term that was remarkably free of trouble. It was during this brief, quiet reign that each of the three young men from Monterey began his rise to prominence in California. Jose Castro was a member of the diputacion and was able to move steadily upward in government because Figueroa was willing to work with that representative body. The diputacion was also important in the career of Juan Alvarado because his role as secretary brought him into contact with Figueroa and gave him experience in the problems facing California governors.

The man who moved the farthest ahead, however, was Mariano

Vallejo. By the time Figueroa arrived, Vallejo had become comman-dante of the presidio at San Francisco. The new governor, however, had bigger plans for him. Feeling the need for some kind of frontier post as a buffer against the Russians in the north, he appointed the twenty-seven-year-old Vallejo to the post of Military Commander and Director of Colonization of the Northern Frontier and assigned him the task of settling the Sonoma Valley. In the summer of 1835 Val-lejo, with a small squad of soldiers, arrived in Sonoma and began work on the settlement that would eventually make Vallejo the most pow-erful man in northern California.

Not only did the careers of the three young men advance steadily during Figueroa's time but all California benefited from his quiet or-derly administration unmarred by any serious political turmoil. All things must end, however, and the halcyon days of Figueroa's reign ended in the late afternoon of September 19, 1835, when the gover-nor died in Monterey. Soon, California was again torn by political turbulence which in the following year led to the overthrow and ex-pulsion of Governor Mariano Chico, who had been sent out to replace Figueroa.

By then, Juan Alvarado, at the age of twenty-seven, was well es-tablished within California government. Two years before, in 1834, after several years as secretary of the diputacion, he had been elected a member in his own right and now, in 1836, he was chosen presi-dent. It was a position that would soon bring him into conflict with Nicolas Gutierrez who had become interim-governor of California upon the expulsion of Chico.

It seems strange that difficulties should develop with Gutierrez, for a few months earlier, upon the death of Figueroa, he had briefly ruled California as interim-governor with no trouble. Yet much had changed in the few months since he last ruled. He had first become governor upon the death of Figueroa, a much-respected man, whose calming influence on the Californians had been such that they accepted Gu-tierrez easily. Now he was succeeding Chico who, in his contempt for local citizens and his flaunting of his "niece" at public functions, had so irritated Californians that they would have opposed almost anyone simply because he was governor. Chico's behavior had also done much to reintensify the anti-Mexican feeling among Californians, and

Gutierrez could never overcome the fact that he, himself, had been born in Spain and was an army officer sent to California by the government of Mexico.

Thus there was considerable hostility toward the interim-governor, creating an ideal situation for a young man like Juan Alvarado who had political ambitions of his own. Somehow he provoked an argument with Gutierrez, goading him into losing his temper and threatening to place Alvarado, the president of the diputacion, in irons. At this point, Alvarado walked away, and when Gutierrez cooled down he realized he had been trapped into making a serious mistake. As soon as he could, he sent a message to Alvarado asking him for another interview. By then Alvarado had already left Monterey and gone to San Juan where, with his old friend Jose Castro, he began to plan a revolt.

In announcing their intentions they ignored, as good revolutionaries should, the personal quarrel and drew up a list of illegal and despotic acts of the governor. Some of the charges were not true, others were unimportant, but they provided a cause to rally around and won Alvarado much support from fellow Californians. Then, knowing the need for military aid, Alvarado set off for Sonoma to obtain the backing of another old friend, Commandante Vallejo.

Juan Alvarado, having just begun a career as a revolutionary leader, would soon learn just how changeable were the winds of support for a man involved in such activities. As he rode north to see Vallejo, he had every reason to expect complete support from him. Only a few months before, the two had been among those who had planned to overthrow Chico and introduce home rule to California, and for Alvarado the expulsion of Gutierrez was just a logical extension of that plan. When he arrived in Sonoma he launched into an enthusiastic recital of the rebellion only to be brought up short by the cold silence of his old friend and schoolmate.

When he did respond, Vallejo explained that of course he was in favor of such a move, but he thought this rebellion possibly was a bit premature. After all, Gutierrez's behavior, which was so objectionable to Alvarado, might not seem quite so serious to the supreme government in Mexico. Might it not be better, Vallejo suggested, to wait for some more flagrant violation by the governor before behaving so rashly? Besides, he added, affairs on the frontier at present were such that he could not ask his men to leave their families exposed to the danger of Indian raids. The rebels could expect no help from him, for he simply could not spare any troops to help overthrow the governor.

For Alvarado it was a shattering blow, and as he rode back south he decided the only thing to do was to forget the rebellion until Vallejo was ready to cooperate. At San Jose, however, he met several fellow conspirators, including Jose Castro, and they convinced him to go ahead with the revolt. They gathered together what few men they could and began to move south, announcing that they were the vanguard of a large army soon to follow under Commandante Mariano Vallejo. Later Alvarado would write Vallejo saying "it was necessary to employ this ruse, for in this belief many people joined us."

Alvarado also increased the size of his military force with a band of foreigners led by Isaac Graham, a fur trapper who had come to California in 1834. Even before Alvarado had gone north he had briefly talked to Graham in the grog shop of Tio Borondo in Monterey. Quite likely Graham was there to sell liquor, for by 1836 Graham had established himself at a distillery in the Pajaro Valley about twenty-five miles from the capital. There, using skills he had probably learned as a boy in Kentucky, he turned out large amounts of whiskey. His business attracted a clientele, and already the distillery was known as a noisy and disreputable gathering place for runaway sailors and ruffians of all kinds. There was always a ready supply of men around the place, and Graham could easily attract them with his whiskey to any cause he thought worthy of support. And after Alvarado, in the conversation in the grog shop, promised both excitement and land, Graham formed them into a band of revolutionary soldiers. Graham himself and a few other former trappers were good shots, most of the runaway sailors were not, but such was the reputation of American hunters that the Californians identified them as a company of crack shots. In that capacity they joined Alvarado's small army and in early November 1836 marched on Monterey.

After dark on the night of November 3, the revolutionary army, about a hundred men under Jose Castro, arrived in Monterey. Spreading out on the hills around the town they built numerous campfires until it looked as if the capital was surrounded by a huge army. Faced with this Gutierrez had little chance. He was not particularly popular anyway, and now he seemed to be opposed by a large army. Besides, there were rumors that the rebel forces were filled with American sharpshooters. Others maintained that another large army under Vallejo was approaching Monterey. Before morning most of the townspeople of Monterey had announced their support of the rebellion and many had even actively joined the ranks of the revolutionary army.

Many of the foreign merchants in Monterey and even some of the captains of ships in the harbor joined the cause. Some thought they read the situation correctly and were able to predict the eventual winner. Others, with the example of Texas before them, looked on this as an opportunity to tear California away from Mexico. In fact, Isaac Graham claimed he had joined the rebel army because both Alvarado and Castro promised that if the revolution was successful, they would declare California independent.

Faced with all this opposition, both domestic and foreign, Gutierrez, alone except for a few loyal officers and soldiers, retired to the presidio where he was soon under siege. He was given the chance to surrender but when he delayed answering, the rebels fired a cannonball that scored a direct hit on his home. At the time, he and his officers were conferring in the courtyard, and when the cannonball crashed through the house they bolted in all directions and were not seen again for an hour. Then they sent a message refusing to surrender, which so angered the rebel forces that they began to dismount and form into lines to storm the walls. When Gutierrez and his followers in the presidio saw this, they sent another message offering to surrender, and soon afterward they were allowed to go aboard the *Clementine* lying at anchor in the harbor. Five months earlier the same ship had carried away Governor Chico; now it had returned to Monterey to carry another exiled governor back to Mexico.

Although Juan Alvarado had played a major role in causing this rebellion, he had remained behind the scenes. When Gutierrez departed, Jose Castro, official commander of the rebel army and also the man who had replaced Alvarado as president of the diputacion, took control until that representative body could elect its own interim-governor. There were other more immediate issues facing the diputacion, and it quickly met to declare that this was a rebellion against the former governor, not against Mexico itself. The Americans had no chance to use the Lone Star flag that some of them had already made.

The diputacion also appointed a new military commander for California, Don Mariano Guadalupe Vallejo, whose name, if not his person, had been a major factor in the rebellion. There were still problems with the Indians in the north, but this time, when Vallejo heard that the rebellion had succeeded and that he had been appointed military commander, he was able to arrange a visit to Monterey. It was there, on November 19, that he was sworn in as the Commandante General of California.

Now Juan Alvarado, protected from the charge of treason against Mexico and guaranteed the support of Vallejo, could officially come forward and reap the benefits of the revolution he had planned. On December 7, 1836, the diputacion officially chose him governor, *ad interim,* of California. The revolution was now complete and the young men from Monterey were in control, Juan Alvarado as civil governor, Mariano Vallejo as military commander.

THE CATTLE-HIDE COAST

I

The frequent revolutions and changes in government that plagued Mexican California from the late 1820's onward seldom bothered the foreign traders. Sometimes, as when the soldiers in Monterey rose against Echeandia, they found themselves caught in a situation in which they had no choice but to intervene. But mostly they were able to ignore the internal political squabbles and concentrate on the cattle-hide trade which, since Mexico had become independent, had grown enormously and opened great new opportunities. Ironically, William Hartnell, the man who had done so much to start that activity, by the late 1820's could see nothing but the ruins of a business on which he had once pinned all his hopes.

It had all caught up with him rather suddenly. As recently as 1826 he had seemed to be in excellent shape. His business appeared to be doing well, particularly since many of the missionaries still preferred his easygoing way of doing business. He was married and settled down now, and during 1826 his wife Teresa had given birth to their first child, a son christened Guillermo Antonio. Soon afterward Hartnell wrote to his father-in-law, Jose de la Guerra, "Mi muy querido Padre! Albricias! Joyful news! You have another grandson—on the 31st of March Teresa gave birth to a little Englishman. . . . I love him deeply because I believe he is truly mine and each day my love increases for the Mother who gave him to me. Teresa had an auspicious delivery—the moon rose for the first time as though especially to honor the occasion."

Yet beneath an outward appearance of success, the seeds of Hartnell's failure were already planted. In spite of being a trader, he had never really cared much for the competition of business. His success during his early years in California had come mainly because his temperament was closely attuned to the ways of the country. Eventually, however, that same temperament—friendly, generous, and too trusting of other people—would destroy him, for it made him a virtual lamb among the wolves of California trade. It caused him trouble with his business rivals, men like Cooper and Gale, and, what was worse, it created difficulties with his own partners John Begg and Hugh McCulloch.

Old Mr. Begg in Peru had always been free with both his advice and his censure and now he wrote to criticize Hartnell for not collecting a cargo of horsehair which was selling at a high price. Hartnell replied, pointing out that, as usual, Begg knew nothing about conditions in California. There, Hartnell wrote, a man would rather give you the horse he was riding as a gift than to allow its tail to be cut off. Admittedly they did dock the tails of mares, but there was such a demand for horsehair in California to make halters, bridles, reins, and lariats that there was little left for export. Hartnell's reply made little difference, for by now Begg had cooled toward the business in California and, other than writing critical letters, was virtually ignoring it.

Begg's attitude cannot have been entirely unexpected, but Hartnell was distinctly shocked when he learned that his other partner was also paying little attention to company business. McCulloch had established his own stores in Peru and was devoting all his effort to running them. Finally Hartnell exploded and in a letter told his partner, "Instead of devoting all your time and attention to this concern as you bound yourself to do, I am informed that you never bother your head at all about it, having two other flashy establishments that engross the whole of your attention."

McCulloch had also on several occasions sold company goods through his own store and charged a commission, further angering Hartnell. He wrote, "It appears that you wish that I who am toiling from year's end to year's end and getting bald and blind in the concern should pay you for doing what is no more than your bounded duty."

Obviously, Hartnell's business problems could not be handled at long distance by correspondence. In addition to trouble with his partners, the five-year contract with John Begg and Company was due to expire and Begg had indicated he was not interested in renewing it. Hartnell would have to go to Peru to settle his business affairs. In late 1827 he took his wife, his son William, and a new baby named Nathaniel, to Santa Barbara where they would stay with his wife's parents, then boarded the ship *Fulham* and sailed for Peru.

There he found everything changed. It had been five years since he had been in Lima. Several revolutions and counterrevolutions had taken place, and control of the government had changed innumerable times. In the foreign business community, the companies were still the same, but most of Hartnell's old friends had been replaced by new, unknown people from Europe. But there was one familiar face in Lima, that of his one-time fiancée, the English Rose, Miss Lynch. She was still unattached, and the old fire seems to have been rekindled, for soon news of the affair reached the California coast. David Spence, who worked for Hartnell in Monterey, wrote him asking "By the by, how did you escape that English wifie of yours? I have as yet keeped it all quiet." But if Spence had kept it quiet, there were others who did not, for, he said, he had recently heard from Mrs. Hartnell that "some good friend has been kind enough to let her know about your being prisoner in Lima."

The main reason Hartnell was in Peru, actually, was to settle his business affairs, and once he was able to face his partners personally it took little time, for they all wanted the same thing. John Begg and Company, itself in serious financial trouble, had no desire to continue its association with McCulloch and Hartnell. McCulloch, too, with his own business in Peru, had no objection to breaking up the company and leaving the California trade to Hartnell who, by now, preferred to pursue it on his own. The only thing left was to settle accounts and dissolve the partnership.

The company had lost money, and when the loss was calculated and distributed among the partners, Hartnell's obligations amounted to $18,885. On May 1, 1828, a letter went from Lima to California, announcing the dissolution of McCulloch, Hartnell, and Company and notifying all concerned that William Hartnell would continue the trade on his own. Soon afterward Hartnell sailed for California after telling friends in Lima that his only ambition was "to pay off my debts as quickly as possible . . ."

At first the undertaking seemed easy. A few years earlier Hartnell had loaned a considerable amount of money to Mexican officials in California to help them pay long-overdue salaries. Mr. Begg had criticized him even though it was his own money and the loan had been made to establish good will. Now he needed cash and, somewhat naively, he asked the government to repay him. When it did so he would have more than enough to settle all his obligations. Instead of responding, Governor Echeandia ignored his request.

This first hint that things were going wrong was quickly followed by several others. Hartnell had arrived back in California with trade goods just in time to face new trade restrictions ordered by the governor after an American ship captain had defied him. By then, too, William Gale had arrived in the *Brookline* and was providing stiff competition.

One hope of saving it all remained. Before leaving Peru Hartnell had reached an agreement with Daniel Coit, an American who was to send a ship direct from New York to California. When it reached the west coast Hartnell would serve as supercargo, handling the trading, for which he would receive one-third of the profits. This would provide enough to pay off his debts, and knowing the ship was on its way, he wrote to various missionaries asking them to save their trade for him. To one he wrote, "I assure you in all seriousness that if I do not come out well with this cargo I am ruined without fail."

Yet much of 1829 passed and the ship did not arrive. While a frustrated Hartnell waited, William Gale went from mission to mission telling the fathers it was unlikely the ship would ever come and buying most of the hides they had been saving for Hartnell. In September the ship *Danube* finally arrived and Hartnell found it carried a splendid assortment of goods that, despite Gale and the *Brookline,* might still make for a successful trading season. Then, suddenly, while the ship stood off the southern California coast a storm came up and it was driven ashore and wrecked on the rocks off San Pedro.

Hartnell wrote to John Begg, saying, "I have no longer any prospect of being able to fulfill my engagements to you, and request that you will appoint someone to wind up our affairs and make a bankrupt of me at once. I am perfectly willing to give up everything I possess to satisfy my creditors that is all I have it in my power to do."

Hartnell's life as a trader in California was over.

II

While William Hartnell was in the last stages of trying to save his business, Alfred Robinson, a young man from Boston, arrived in California to enter the cattle-hide trade. He was aboard the American ship *Brookline* when, as the fog cleared on a winter afternoon in 1829, it began working its way past Point Pinos and into Monterey Harbor. There was little breeze, and long before the ship reached an anchorage night had fallen. Robinson could see very little and hear only the occasional cry of the leadsman in the chains and the dip of oars as the boatmen towed the ship into port. Then suddenly there was a flash on shore, followed by the report of a cannon and the whizzing of a ball as it crossed the bow of the *Brookline.* Immediately the captain shouted "Let go the anchor," and soon the ship was standing dead in the water.

Within minutes a boat brought a customs official who greeted the Americans politely and also said he was pleased they had come to trade. But after a few minutes he told them that an American ship, the *Franklin,* had defied the authorities and run the gauntlet past the fort in San Diego. The whole business, he explained, had so exasperated the governor that he had restricted foreign ships to Monterey and San Diego. All other ports were closed to them.

Suddenly, without prior notice, all the trading plans for California were seriously threatened. It came as a shock to Alfred Robinson, a clerk for Bryant and Sturgis. Although only twenty-one, he had worked in the company's office in Boston for several years and had made three trips to the West Indies as ship's clerk. Now he had come to California for the first time and these new, unforeseen restrictions made him predict the voyage would be a total failure.

His momentary panic is not entirely surprising, for he was both young and new to the business. Presumably the very reason he had been sent on such a voyage was to learn not to be overwhelmed by unexpected problems but to find a way to handle them. Fortunately for Robinson his mentor was the *Brookline*'s supercargo, the old California hand, William Gale.

Even Gale, for all his experience, wondered how to handle the situation. He decided to send a letter to Governor Echeandia explaining that the ship had been fitted out in Boston on the assumption that there had been no change in California's commercial regulations. Since there had not been sufficient time, he said, for word of the *Brookline*'s impending arrival to reach California, it was only fair that the governor relax the rules in this instance.

Once the letter was sent, there was nothing to do but wait for an answer. While the sailors went ashore to fill the water casks, cut wood, and pack beef in barrels to be stored in the hold, Gale and his young clerk called on the various members of the Monterey business community. In this way Robinson made his first friends in California, many of them Englishmen and Americans who had married California women and settled in Monterey. He was particularly impressed by William Hartnell who, although on the very brink of financial disaster, was still maintaining appearances. According to stories of other traders, he had large contracts with the missions and was doing an extensive business all up and down the coast.

The reply Gale received from San Diego contained some minor concessions by the governor. The port of Santa Barbara was opened to the *Brookline,* but when the ship called there, or at Monterey or San Diego, customs duties would have to be paid on the entire cargo, and there would be no refund if any of the goods were re-embarked. Such an arrangement was entirely unsatisfactory to Gale, and, after talking to various friends in Monterey, he decided to go to San Diego to see Governor Echeandia in person.

By late March the *Brookline* was at anchor in San Diego. Gale and Robinson found the governor in his house on a slight rise where he could look out to sea and also watch everything going on in the presidio square of San Diego. The governor himself, Robinson found, was tall and thin, and if his troubles with foreigners caused him to dislike them he gave no sign of it, for he received the American traders with "true Spanish dignity and politeness." He even went so far as to give them permission to trade in ports that were closed and also to travel overland from mission to mission.

Once official business was settled, Gale was free to invite San Diego people to come aboard the *Brookline* to trade. The ship had a trade room, fitted with shelves and counters like a country store, that appealed to the visitors who came aboard. One of them, Father Antonio Peyri from Mission San Luis Rey, after looking over all the goods on display, made large purchases, testifying, Robinson thought, to "how vastly he had been pleased."

When business began to slow down in San Diego, Gale sent the *Brookline* on to San Pedro while he and Robinson traveled overland by horse. They visited Father Peyri's mission at San Luis Rey, then went on to San Juan Capistrano where they created a mild stir. When they arrived several Indian boys were hanging around the mission gate. Two or three of them approached the visitors rather closely, saying nothing but looking intently at Gale who wore thick glasses that magnified his eyes. After staring for a long time they darted away shouting, in Spanish, "Four eyes, four eyes." It delighted Robinson, who promptly adopted the nickname and told the story widely, for, as he said, from that time on Gale "was ever known throughout the whole coast by the nickname of 'cuatros ojos.' "

The two men spent the night at San Juan Capistrano and then continued north to Father Sanchez' mission at San Gabriel. It was Saturday night when they arrived, the bells were tolling the hour for prayer, and Robinson could see hundreds of Indians kneeling on the ground. As the tolling stopped they rose and the bells took on a more joyous note as the coming of the Sabbath was announced.

Next morning, even though the two Americans were up before six o'clock, they found services under way when they reached the church. Robinson was particularly impressed by the music provided by an Indian choir accompanied by others playing flutes and violins. The musicians waited for Father Sanchez at the mission door after the services and escorted him to his quarters where they played waltzes and marches until presents were distributed among them.

Robinson, like Harrison Rogers before him, was impressed by both Father Sanchez and his mission. The father himself was kind and generous, giving freely of whatever he could to make a traveler feel comfortable. And his mission offered many resources to draw on—extensive gardens containing "oranges, citrons, limes, apples, pears, peaches, pomegranates, figs, and grapes in abundance." The grapes, Robinson was told, were used to make as many as six hundred barrels of wine and two hundred barrels of brandy each year, bringing in a considerable amount of money. Storehouses and granaries were full of grain and the mission square itself was "usually heaped with piles of tallow and hides."

The atmosphere was different when Gale and Robinson went to San Fernando to meet Father Francisco de Ibarra. Although the Indians at the mission liked the padre, and others in California found him witty and charming, he must have done something to offend Alfred Robinson. The American described him as short, fat, and ugly, and a man who knew it all. "In his own opinion," Robinson said, "no one knew so much as himself; nothing was so good as that which he possessed." He was also cheap, setting a sparse dinner table which "seemed perfectly in accordance with the narrowness of his mind." Father Ibarra and the Americans certainly did not hit it off, and when the time came to trade, he refused to accept their terms even though, Robinson said, he had a vast number of hides that had been kept in storage so long that many were ruined. Robinson felt the padre well deserved his nickname, "cochino"—hog.

Gale and Robinson did not linger at San Fernando but soon returned south, first to Los Angeles, then to San Pedro where they found the *Brookline* lying at anchor. Going aboard, they sailed to Santa Barbara, the next port of call. Gale had made many California friends on his earlier trips, and he had brought gifts for the family of Don Jose de la Guerra. He invited Robinson to go with him when he delivered them and the two went to call at the family's stately home. Guerra was in Mexico at the time, but the Americans were entertained by his wife Dona Maria Antonia, who served them chocolate while her daughters scurried around distributing gifts the visitors brought. Before too many more years passed, Alfred Robinson would be married to one of these daughters, but at the time there was no way he could have guessed it, for as the Guerra girls opened their presents, the one who would some day be his wife was only eight years old.

Robinson and Gale spent the next several weeks working out of Santa Barbara, ranging north to the missions of Santa Inez and La Purisima and south to San Buenaventura. Then they sailed back to San Pedro, loaded the hides they had left there and took them to San Diego where they delivered them to the hide house to be prepared for shipment back to Boston.

After about ten days in San Pedro, the *Brookline,* with Gale and Robinson on board, sailed for San Francisco. As they entered the bay they passed the Farallon Islands where they could see huts and a dozen or so people whom they took to be Russian seal hunters. It brought back memories to William Gale who twenty years before had spent a whole season with Aleut hunters clubbing seals on the islands. Gale still remembered that bloody work, for, Robinson said, "he assured me he had assisted in collecting during one season, over eighty thousand skins from this same island."

Until now Robinson had spent his time in California under the careful supervision of William Gale. At San Francisco, where the *Brookline* anchored for several weeks to collect hides, he was given his first chance to work alone. He and Gale went together to Mission Santa Clara at the south end of the bay, but after purchasing hides there, Gale went on to San Jose and turned over the details of moving the hides back to the ship to his clerk. Robinson rode back overland to the presidio at San Francisco, rented some launches, brought them to Santa Clara, then oversaw the loading and transporting of the hides up the bay to the *Brookline*'s anchorage.

Gale apparently was entirely satisfied with Robinson's performance, for a few months later, when the *Brookline* returned to San Diego, he was allowed to function on his own again. While Gale took the ship north for another trading run along the coast, Robinson stayed behind to sell goods in an improvised store in the Dominguez home in San Diego. For the next three months he spent his time selling what he could, breaking the monotony of isolated, small-town California life sometimes by riding off into the surrounding country to hunt, other times by riding down to the hide house to watch the men work. When Gale returned with the ship, the store was closed, the goods reloaded, and once again Robinson accompanied Gale as he traded along the coast.

Robinson's ability to work without supervision allowed Gale to make a major decision. When he came to California on this voyage his intention, apparently, had been to remain as Bryant and Sturgis's resident agent on the coast. For some time, though, his health had been poor and with little medical help available in California he decided to return to Boston with the *Brookline.* Before leaving he appointed his twenty-three-year-old clerk company agent in California. Robinson settled in Santa Barbara, which he seemed to prefer to San Diego or Monterey, and it was there, in the summer of 1830, that he watched the crew on the *Brookline* make preparations to leave. Then, as he later remembered, "With a heavy heart, and swimming eyes," he said goodbye to the ship's officers, to his old friend and mentor William Gale, and particularly to "all hope of seeing my home, my 'native land' again for years."

III

In August 1834 the brig *Pilgrim* lay at anchor in Boston harbor while the employees of the firm Bryant and Sturgis prepared to clear the ship for the coast of California. By now such preparations were almost routine, for since opening the cattle-hide trade back in 1821, Bryant and Sturgis had sent ship after ship into the Pacific. Trade goods bound for California were routinely loaded aboard the *Pilgrim* until it was ready to sail. On the day before sailing, William Sturgis himself came aboard to make sure everything was in order.

Unlike many ship owners, Sturgis not only checked the cargo and gave instructions to the captain but descended into the forecastle to talk to the common sailors as they were stowing their sea chests. Being an old hand in the Pacific trade, he tried to give them some idea of what lay ahead, telling them the kind of clothes they would need, and making sure they had a lamp and a few other minor items to make them comfortable. Such information was welcomed by those who, although they were experienced sailors, had never been to California. It was especially welcome to a young man named Richard Henry Dana, who, when he signed on board the *Pilgrim,* was just a few days past his nineteenth birthday. He had never been to California, he had no experience as a sailor, and there was almost nothing in his past to prepare him for life in the forecastle.

He was a member of a prominent family that could trace its ancestry back to 1640 when the first Dana settled in Boston. Like all the Danas before him, he had entered Harvard University at the age of sixteen. After his sophomore year he had spent several weeks vacationing at Plymouth, but when he returned home, he came down with a severe case of measles. Although the illness lasted only a few days, it had so weakened his eyes that at first he could hardly bear the light of day. Eventually his vision improved enough for him to get around, but any attempt to read caused intense pain. He was forced to drop out of school and remain at home, unable to read or do anything else that involved much use of his eyes. His brother was also at home with eye trouble, and his father, concerned about his two sons and worried about financial problems, was deeply depressed. Soon his eighteen-year-old son Richard lapsed into his own moody depression.

Finally the young Dana decided to go to sea, although he knew that any kind of foreign travel as a tourist was beyond his father's financial capabilities. The family, however, was well connected, and among their many Boston friends were the Bowditches, including Nathaniel, mathematician and publisher of *The Practical Navigator.* His son, J. Ingersoll Bowditch, who was about to sail as supercargo on a ship bound for Calcutta, offered to take Dana as a companion, giving him free passage to India and back and a room on shore as long as they were there. Dana, however, feared that as a passenger with nothing to do during the long months at sea, he would damage his eyes further by attempting to read. That, plus "the attractiveness of the romance and adventure of the thing," made him determined to go before the mast as a common sailor. And after some difficulty he was able to procure a berth on the brig *Pilgrim* bound for California.

IV

Thus the former Harvard student began a new kind of education. The tight dress coat, silk cap, and kid gloves of a Cambridge undergraduate gave way to the sailor's loose duck trousers, checked shirt, and tarpaulin hat. Dana was painfully aware that the mere change of clothes meant little for, he said, "A sailor has a peculiar cut to his clothes, and a way of wearing them which a green hand can never get. The trousers, tight round the hips, and thence hanging long and loose round the feet, a superabundance of checked shirt, a low-crowned, well-varnished black hat, worn on the back of the head, with half a fathom of black ribbon hanging over the left eye, and a peculiar tie to the black silk neckerchief, with sundry other minutiae, are signs, the want of which betray the beginner at once."

Green as he looked in his new sailor clothes, it was a beginning, and before the *Pilgrim* had been long at sea, Dana began learning not only how to wear them but also how to function as a sailor. On the first night at sea he was on watch, and as he stood on deck he was much affected by the quiet beauty of the sea, the bright stars, and the clouds blowing past the ship. Suddenly, an officer shouted to trim the yards, and Dana, looking at the more experienced sailors, could see they were worried about the dark clouds rapidly approaching. The order was given to reef the topsails, and in the pitch dark of a night at sea, Dana went aloft for the first time.

Later he said that he did not think he could have been of much use, for he was sick several times on the topsail yard. Yet somehow he managed to go out on the yard and hang on tight until the order was given to go below. This, however, he found was no great favor, for by now he was thoroughly seasick, and the smell of the bilge, churned up by the rough sea, only made him feel worse. He was completely miserable, and all he could think of was that this was only the first night of a two-year voyage.

The seasickness continued for several days until the ship's cook told him how to end it. " 'Now,' says he, 'my lad, you are well cleaned out; you haven't got a drop of your long-shore *swash* aboard of you. You must begin a new tack,—pitch all your sweetmeats overboard, and turn to upon good hearty salt beef and sea bread, and I'll promise you, you'll have your ribs well sheathed, and be as hearty as any of 'em, afore you are up to the Horn.' " For Dana, at least, the cure worked, for he added, "I cannot describe the change which half a pound of cold salt beef and a biscuit or two produced in me. I was a new being."

He had his sea legs and he soon began to adapt to his duties as a sailor. He was able to spring aloft into the yardarms with ease and he learned there was much more than that to a sailor's life. Instead of being idle most of the time he had an endless number of things to do: examining all the ship's rigging, tightening it, replacing it, spinning yarn to be used throughout the ship, and when all was done, scraping rust from the chain cables. He also began to learn something about the ship's hierarchy and about the most important man on board, Captain Francis Thompson.

As the *Pilgrim* sailed from Boston Harbor in late summer 1834, Thompson was just thirty years old, already a veteran of the California trade, having commanded the *Roxana* on a two-year trip into the Pacific. That had been a difficult voyage, and after reaching California he had written to his mother about the tedious 192-day passage out. "I had hard luck the whole passage, and especially off Cape Horn. For 5 weeks I was beating and banging off that horrid place. It seems as though all the Furies of the infernal regions were let loose. Tremendous Gales, Snow and Hail continually, night 18 hours, sun 9° high and sometimes not seen for a week." It had given him pause to think about his life's work, for he added, "Any person thinking there is pleasure, in going to sea, I would advise them to double Cape Horn the season I did. I think they would change their opinion." Later, after more troubles, he added, "I sometimes wish I could live my life over again." Once the voyage was completed, however, he spent only a few months ashore and now was again on his way to California.

Thompson, like all ship captains of the time, had learned to behave like a god aboard ship and to impress his men with the fact that their entire lives lay totally under his control. The first Dana saw of him after the *Pilgrim* sailed was when he appeared on deck and gave a short speech. He said, " 'Now, my men, we have begun a long voyage. If we get along well together, we shall have a comfortable time; if we don't, we shall have hell afloat—All you've got to do is to obey your orders and do your duty like men,—then you'll fare well enough;—if you don't you'll fare hard enough—I can tell you. If we pull together, you'll find me a d—d clever fellow, if we don't, you'll find me a d—d rascal. That's all I've got to say.' "

Thompson knew that to maintain his god-like role as captain he must keep as much distance as possible between himself and his crew by working mainly through his officers. This soon proved difficult, for his first mate, Andrew Amazeen, was far too lenient. Like most of the sailors, Dana liked Amazeen and thought him the most honest, upright, and kindhearted man he had ever met. Unfortunately, these were not qualities to make him a good ship's officer, for as Dana himself realized, "he was not the man to call a sailor a 'son of a b---h' and knock him down with a handspike." Captain Thompson was a hard-driving man, "made of steel and whalebone," who Dana, during the entire time he was with him, never saw sit down while on deck. Seeing that the first mate was too easygoing, and fearing that discipline was becoming too relaxed, Thompson began to interfere in everything, drawing the reins tighter and becoming harsher in his discipline. Quite naturally the crew sided with the first mate, which only made the captain more hostile. "He saw that everything went wrong—that nothing was done 'with a will' and in this attempt to remedy the difficulty by severity he made everything worse."

The tension continued to build through much of the voyage until the ship was well into the Pacific just short of California when it finally surfaced. The crisis began over almost nothing—a change in the bread issue to the crew—making them think they were losing a few bites each. The men were in turmoil, and since the captain would not condescend to explain why the bread issue had been changed, the entire crew, led by John Linden, a Swede who was both the oldest and best sailor aboard, went aft to talk to him.

They stated their grievances—"as respectfully as we could," Dana thought—but Captain Thompson lashed out, saying they were getting fat and lazy, and that only because they didn't have enough to do they had time to find fault. Apparently some of the crew talked back and Thompson, losing his temper began to shout, " 'Away with you! go forward every one of you! I'll *haze* you by J---s! I'll work you up! You don't have enough to do! if you ain't careful I'll make a hell of heaven! . . . You've mistaken your man by God! I'm Frank Thompson, all the way from 'down east! I've been through the mill, ground, and bolted and come out a *regular built down-east johnny-cake,* good when its hot d--d good, but when its cold, d--d sour and indigestible; and you'll find me so!' " At this the crew retreated in disarray, although the phrase, "down-east johnny-cake," became a byword for the rest of the voyage.

The problem was solved when, after the captain cooled off, the first mate explained the men's request, which was reasonable enough. They were called aft and had to listen to another harangue in which all the blame for the misunderstanding was thrown on the crew. They tried to hint that the captain had exploded so quickly they had no time to explain, but he would not hear it. The whole thing blew over and a few days later the *Pilgrim* arrived off Santa Barbara.

Captain Thompson went ashore at Santa Barbara to see both Alfred Robinson, the California agent for Bryant and Sturgis, and his brother Alpheus Thompson, who had settled in Santa Barbara and married a daughter of the prominent Californian Carlos Carrillo. He returned to the ship with Robinson, his brother and his sister-in-law Francisca, and with them aboard sailed for Monterey. Both Robinson and Alpheus Thompson were old California hands who knew the cattle-hide trade, and undoubtedly they told Captain Thompson he was going to have trouble finding a cargo because of the scarcity of hides. Soon the disappointing news filtered down to the crew that instead of the eighteen months or two years they had planned on, they now faced at least an additional year before the voyage would be finished.

Apparently the delay was just as distressing to Thompson, for after the ship cleared Monterey and began working its way back south to pick up hides, he was even more difficult than usual. By the time they reached San Pedro, Dana said, "the captain seemed very much out of humor. Nothing went right, or fast enough for him. He quarreled with the cook and threatened to flog him for throwing wood on deck." But mainly his anger began to center on a sailor named Sam who was slow-moving and slow of speech. Dana thought him a decent enough sailor, but the captain took a dislike to him, claiming he was surly and lazy.

One day while lying at anchor at San Pedro the crew heard the captain, who was down in the hold, suddenly begin shouting. Upon checking, Dana found that the captain in a loud harsh voice was asking Sam if he would ever be insolent again. Sam, in a low, choked voice, was denying that he had been insolent. Thompson shouted, " 'answer my question or I'll make a spread eagle of you. I'll flog you by G-d.' " At that Sam answered, " 'I'm no negro slave,' " and the captain said, " 'then, I'll make you one,' " and shouted to the mate, " 'seize that man up, Mr. Amerzene! . . . Make a spread eagle of him! Ill teach you all who is master aboard.' "

As the order was being carried out, John Linden, the Swedish sailor who had led the crew in their protest over the bread, stepped forward and asked, " 'what are you going to flog that man for, sir?' " Thompson ordered him seized and put in chains. Then, swinging the rope himself he flogged Sam six times, yelling as he did so, " 'Will you ever give me any more of your jaw?' " He was greeted only by silence.

After Sam was cut down, John Linden was strung up, and when the Swedish sailor asked if a man couldn't ask a question without being flogged the captain replied, " 'No . . . nobody shall open his mouth aboard this vessel, but myself.' " Then he began to flog Linden. By now he was in a frenzy, dancing around the deck as he swung the rope and shouting, " 'If you want to know what I flog you for, I'll tell you. It's because I like to do it!—because I like to do it!—it suits me! That's what I do it for!' " As the flogging continued, Linden groaned, " 'Oh, Jesus Christ! Oh, Jesus Christ.' "

" 'Don't call on Jesus Christ,' " shouted the captain; " 'he can't help you. Call on Frank Thompson! He's the man! He can help you! Jesus Christ can't help you now.' "

By now Dana was thoroughly sickened and he wrote later, "at these words, which I shall never forget, my blood ran cold. I could look on no longer. Disgusted, Sick, and horror-struck, I turned away and leaned over the rail and looked down into the water."

V

Some time later the *Pilgrim* sailed from San Pedro and in a few days entered the harbor at San Diego where several ships were in port, including Captain John Bradshaw's *Lagoda.* As the *Pilgrim* tried to anchor, Captain Thompson bawled out, " 'let go the anchor,' " but for some reason it failed to stop the ship. Then he yelled, " 'pay out chain.' " That too failed and the ship kept drifting until it smashed broadside into the *Lagoda.* Little damage was done, except to Thompson's pride, for the cook on the *Lagoda* had seen the *Pilgrim* coming and had called everyone on deck so that the entire crew, men and officers alike, saw the crash. As Thompson tried to clear the *Lagoda,* he bumped into another ship anchored near by, then started drifting down on still another, the *Ayacucho,* whose captain, John Wilson, came aboard the *Pilgrim* and made some gentle suggestions that brought the ship safely to anchor.

Later that evening Dana and another sailor rowed their captain over to the *Lagoda,* and as they came aboard the mate shouted down the companionway to his own commander, " 'Captain Thompson has come aboard sir!' " Quite distinctly they heard Bradshaw shout from his cabin, " 'Has he brought his brig with him?' " The expression became a standing joke for all on board the *Pilgrim.*

Not long after the ship anchored Dana's life changed completely when he was put ashore in San Diego to work at the hide house. While the ship and Captain Thompson sailed back up the coast for more hides, Dana remained behind to help cure the hides already obtained. Working with him was Thomas Russell, who would boss the operation; a giant Frenchman named Nicholas, "the most immense man," Dana said that he had ever seen; and four Sandwich Islanders. Only Dana had come from Boston with the *Pilgrim.* The rest had been hired in California.

Curing the hides and preparing them for final stowing aboard the ship was no simple task. When the cattle were killed and skinned, the procedure was to stake the hides in the sun so they would dry without shrinking. They were then picked up and loaded aboard the ship which took them to San Diego where they were given final treatment by the hide-curing crew.

The first step in curing was to soak the hides by tying them down in small piles along the shore and letting the tide come in and cover them. After forty-eight hours they were taken out, wheeled on barrows up to vats filled with brine where they were thrown in and allowed to soak for another forty-eight hours and then taken out and laid on a platform for twenty-four hours. They were stretched and staked out on the ground while they were still soft and wet, so the hide-curers could go over each one with a knife, cutting off all meat and fat that could rot and destroy the hides when they were tightly packed aboard the ship.

The whole operation was so arranged that there were hides in all states of preparation. Every morning twenty-five hides were ready for each man to go over with his knife. Since the original skinning had been done quickly and carelessly, cleaning the hides was no simple task. Dana, on his first day, was so slow and awkward he could do only eight. A few days later he doubled his number, and after two or three weeks he was able to keep up with the others and do the allotted twenty-five a day.

After the meat and fat was cut off, the hides were staked out in the sun, bringing out the grease that had to be removed with a scraper.

The hides were carefully folded, hair side out, to dry, and finally placed on a long, horizontal pole, five at a time, and beaten with flails until all the dust was knocked out of them. Last of all, they were stored in the hide house to await loading aboard the ship.

Hide-curing was hard work, for it involved wheeling heavy hides to the beach and back, throwing them in the brine, wading knee-deep in the vats to press them down, and continually stooping over to stake them out, to clean them, to scrape them, and finally to unstake them. Yet Dana, somewhat proudly, found himself becoming hardened to the work, and the relative independence of his life compensated for the other difficulties. Russell, the boss, spent most of his time sleeping and eating, and thus the rest were free to do as they pleased as long as they got their twenty-five hides cured each day. They learned to rise early, get to work, and have the task finished by about two in the afternoon so they could be free to do whatever they wanted.

During the long afternoons and evenings Dana became friendly with his fellow workers, particularly the Sandwich Islanders, or Kanakas, as they were almost universally called in the Pacific. Since most white men would make no attempt to learn their Hawaiian names, the Kanakas, when they left the Islands, were usually given a new name after whatever came to mind. The four Dana knew were Hope, named after a ship he had served on; Thom Davis, after his first captain; Mr. Bingham, after a white missionary in the Islands; and Pelican, because he looked like one.

In the months he worked with them Dana found the Hawaiians to be "the most interesting, intelligent, and kind-hearted people I ever fell in with." Still he could not help teasing them, particularly Mr. Bingham who spoke very little English and who was missing two front teeth, supposedly knocked out by his parents as a sign of grief at the death of King Kamehameha I. Dana thought him "the best hearted old fellow" he had ever met, but soon found that the one way to anger him was to tell him he had lost his teeth when he ate Captain Cook. At that, he would become excited and say, " 'Me no eat Captain Cook! Me pikinini—small—so high—no more! My father see Captain Cook! me—no!' " The other Kanakas were also angered by the charge and pointed out endlessly that although New Zealanders were cannibals, Hawaiians were not.

Dana and his companions had been curing hides ashore for several weeks when one day at dinner they heard the cry, "Sail ho!" At first no one paid much attention, for they had learned the cry did not necessarily mean the arrival of a ship; it was just as likely to mean an ox cart coming down from town or, frequently, an attractive woman—or any woman—walking by the hide houses. This time, however, the cry became so general up and down the beach that they looked and saw not one but two sets of sail coming into the harbor. The one in the lead was a ship, the other a brig, and as they drew closer they could be identified as the Italian ship *Rosa* and the Mexican brig *Catalina.*

In the next few weeks the crews of the two vessels spent most of their evenings ashore and the social life of the men at the hide houses improved greatly. They spent their time going from house to house visiting and listening to tales in all kinds of languages. If they wanted to converse they usually ended up speaking Spanish, for everyone knew a little of that. Dana decided that virtually every nation under the sun was represented and listed the nationalities of those he knew. There were, he said, "two Englishmen, three Yankees, two Scotchmen, two Welshmen, one Irishman, three Frenchmen (two of whom were Normans, and the third from Gascony), one Dutchman, one Austrian, two or three Spaniards (from old Spain), half a dozen Spanish-Americans and half-breeds, two native Indians from Chili and the Island of Chiloe, one Negro, one Mulatto, and about twenty Italians, from all parts of Italy, as many more Sandwich Islanders, one Otaheitan, and one Kanaka from the Marquesa Islands."

Finally the time came for the ships to sail, and the night before they departed there was a big party at the *Rosa*'s hide house. Songs of every nation and tongue were heard, the Germans singing, "Och, mein lieber Augustin!" the French roaring "the Marseilles," the Englishmen and Scotsmen singing "Rule Britannia," and "Wha'll be King but Charlie?" the Americans making a not very successful stab at "the Star-Spangled Banner," and the Italians and Spaniards singing national anthems that might as well be Greek for all Dana could make of them. By the time he left, they were all singing at once, for "the aguardiente and annisou was pretty well in their heads." The ships sailed the next morning, and the men at Dana's hide house went back to the relative quiet of hide-curing.

Soon the crew finished curing and stowing all the hides and had nothing to do until the *Pilgrim* brought more. As the quiet increased and Dana was almost desperate with boredom, he took his Bowditch, which was always with him, and went through it again, this time working out each of the navigation problems. Then, with no sign of the *Pilgrim,* Dana began to search the sea chests of other crew members for something to read. He found himself reading children's stories, shipping calendars, even a joke book which he read straight through one day as if it were a novel. When he thought all possibilities were exhausted he found in the bottom of an old sailor's chest *Mandeville, a Romance* by William Godwin in five volumes. For the next two days he was up early and late reading with huge enjoyment. "It is no extravagance," he added, "to say that it was like a spring in a desert land."

The *Pilgrim* finally arrived, bringing more hides as well as a rather startling change. As usual, when the ship entered the harbor, the cry, "Sail ho!" went up and as Dana looked toward the *Pilgrim* he saw, and heard, "there was a new voice giving orders, and a new face on the quarterdeck—a short, dark-complexioned man, in a green jacket and a high leather cap." Soon the beach was alive with gossip and those on shore could barely wait for the ship's boat to come ashore with an explanation. When it did, Dana learned that another Bryant and Sturgis ship, the *Alert,* had arrived in California. It would take on board all the hides already collected and when it was full would return to the east coast leaving the *Pilgrim* behind to obtain another load. Captain Thompson, wanting to return home sooner, had switched commands with the captain of the *Alert,* Edward Faucon, the man in the green jacket standing on the *Pilgrim*'s quarterdeck. The *Pilgrim* had brought more hides and Dana and the others went to work again.

About a month later, the cry, "Sail ho!" was heard along the beach once more, this time for the *Alert,* which entered San Diego Bay and "having the tide in her favor, came up like a race horse." Dana was particularly interested, for he already knew that this, rather than the *Pilgrim,* would be the vessel on which he would return to Boston. Earlier, Captain Faucon had told him that the owners, at the request of Dana's father, had written to Captain Thompson and told him to bring Dana home on the *Alert.* When it prepared to sail back up the coast seeking more hides, Dana asked to be taken aboard so he could become familiar with the new ship and new crew. Thompson agreed, provided Dana could find someone to take his place. Several men aboard were willing to spend time ashore rather than under the watchful eye of the captain and mates, and Dana had no trouble finding a replacement. He was aboard the *Alert* as it sailed from San Diego in early September 1835.

VI

The *Alert* spent the next several months sailing along the coast visiting the regular hide-gathering ports until January 1836, when it came to anchor at Santa Barbara. It arrived just in time for one of California's major social events, the wedding of Ana Maria, daughter of Santa Barbara's most prominent citizen, Jose de la Guerra y Noriega, to Alfred Robinson, California agent for Bryant and Sturgis.

Dana already knew Robinson from earlier trips along the coast and he did not particularly like him. He gave no real reason but claimed he was not alone, for he said he "was very much disliked by the crew one and all." Possibly Robinson did lord it over the sailors—or maybe just over Richard Henry Dana—and certainly he was the boss's representative, never very popular with those farther down the scale. Whatever the cause, Dana and several other sailors, on their earlier voyage north, had seen an opportunity to get even when they were sent ashore in the ship's boat to bring off Robinson and several California gentlemen who were going to Monterey in the *Alert.* There was no officer with them, and the sailors knew their passengers were too unfamiliar with seamanship to know whether the boat was being handled properly. They did not come all the way up to the beach, making the gentlemen wade in the water to get on board. They then waited for a particularly large breaker and swung the head of the boat into it, sending a huge wave crashing into the stern, drenching everyone. The Californians all leaped out, shaking themselves, swearing, and protesting against trying it again. It was with great difficulty that Robinson could convince them to come back aboard. Eventually they did, and this time the sailors were more careful and the boat slid out through the breakers without trouble.

Even Captain Thompson did not particularly like Robinson. Still, he was an American, a New Englander, and the agent of Bryant and Sturgis, and when the *Alert* reached Santa Barbara in time for the wedding, the captain used all his efforts and those of his crew to enhance the celebration. The ship's cook spent three days ashore making pastries and cakes, while the rest of the crew took some of the best stores ashore for the celebration, a move that may explain why neither Robinson nor the captain was popular with the crew.

On the day of the wedding Thompson arranged to have a salute fired from the guns on board the *Alert.* Dana, stationed at the starboard after gun, watched as the bride, dressed completely in black, went with her sister to the confessional. An hour passed, and suddenly the great doors of the mission church opened, the bells rang out, and the bride, now dressed in white, came out accompanied by her new husband and followed by a long procession. A signal went up from shore, and the first gun on board the *Alert* boomed out its salute, followed by twenty-three more. The shots came at fifteen-second intervals, an impressive feat, Dana thought, for a merchant ship with only four guns and a dozen or so men, none of whom was a professional gunner.

Dana was a member of the boat crew that went ashore to bring the captain back. They were allowed to go early enough to attend the fandango following the wedding. It was held at the bride's family home, the largest in Santa Barbara, where a tent capable of holding several hundred people had been pitched in the courtyard. As Dana and the boat crew approached, they heard violins and guitars, and upon entering the tent found it so jammed with people it was almost impossible to dance. The music was lively, and somewhat surprisingly Dana recognized some popular American tunes which he now suspected had come originally from the Spanish. He was disappointed in the dancing, particularly that of the women. They stood erect, their hands at their sides, their eyes on the ground, sliding around with no visible means of motion since their feet were out of sight beneath their long dresses. Their faces had no expression, and they "looked as grave as though they were going through some religious ceremony."

The Emigration of Daniel Boone, *by George Caleb Bingham*

Jedediah Smith, *by Frederic Remington*

Mariano Vallejo

William Hartnell

Mission San Francisco Solano at Sonoma

Isaac Sparks

George Nidever

George Yount

Juan Bautista Alvarado

Isaac Graham

A more romanticized portrait of Isaac Graham

Thomas ("Peg-Leg") Smith

Walkara and his brother

James Beckworth

John Bidwell

Charles Wilkes

Thomas ap Catesby Jones

Monterey at the time of Commodore Jones's invasion, 1842

San Francisco during Richard Henry Dana's second visit, 1856

Richard Henry Dana

George Yount

Mariano Vallejo

The men did better, he thought, as they danced more spiritedly in circles around their nearly stationary partners.

The best, the man who performed the most graceful dancing Dana had ever seen, was Don Juan Bandini. He was a small man, dressed in white knee-britches, a short dark silk jacket decorated with bright figures, white stockings, and thin morocco slippers on very small feet. His slight graceful stature, Dana thought, was perfectly suited to dancing, and he "moved with the grace and daintiness of a young fawn. An occasional touch of the toe to the ground seemed all that was necessary to give him a long interval of motion in the air." Later, after the wedding supper, when the waltzing began, he was again prominent, this time dancing with Dona Maria de los Angustias, sister of the bride. They swept through what Dana, the prim New Englander, saw as a series of "beautiful, but to me, offensive figures." Whenever they were on the dance floor, no one else tried to compete, and sometimes they spent as much as half an hour dancing alone as the rest of the crowd waved handkerchiefs and hats, and from time to time leaped from their chairs to shout encouragement.

At ten that night, when the boat crew had to take the captain back aboard the *Alert,* the fandango was still going strong. In fact, the next afternoon when some of the men went ashore they found that although the crowd had thinned out considerably, the musicians were still playing in the tent. That evening the crowds picked up again and the fandango continued for three whole days, reduced to a few diehards in the daylight hours, then picking up again each night until the sailors on board "got almost tired of the monotonous twang of the instruments, the drawling sounds which the women kept up, as an accompaniment, and the slapping of hands in time with the music in place of castanets."

Not long after the wedding the *Alert* left Santa Barbara for another cruise along the coast, ending its voyage in San Diego where it spent several weeks loading the hides stored in the warehouse. At last it was time for the *Alert* to sail for Boston, and it came none too soon for Dana. Earlier, when he first reached California in the *Pilgrim,* he had been worried at the news that it would take an extra year or more to obtain a cargo. He had planned on only a two-year voyage and the extra time would upset his plans for the future. He said, "three or four years would make me a sailor in every respect, mind and habits as well as body." Besides, he would be so far behind the rest of his university class that he would never be able to catch up and his hopes of entering the legal profession would be shattered. He was considerably relieved when the *Alert* arrived with instructions to return him to Boston.

He was aboard the *Alert* now as it was in the final stages of loading at San Diego. Anchored nearby was the *Pilgrim,* which had come into port, unloaded hides, and was preparing to sail the next morning for another long trip up the coast. Dana was thinking of how long and hard that voyage would be and congratulating himself on having escaped when he was ordered to report to the captain's cabin. There he found Captain Thompson, Captain Faucon, and the agent Alfred Robinson. Thompson did the talking.

Abruptly he said, " 'Dana, do you want to go home in this ship?' "

" 'Certainly, sir,' " Dana said, " 'I expect to go home in the ship.' "

" 'Then,' " said he, " 'you must get some one to go in your place on board the *Pilgrim.*' "

This sudden announcement stunned Dana, and for a moment he was unable to reply. He knew it would be almost impossible to find anyone on the *Alert* willing to spend another year in California. He also knew that the company had sent orders to bring him home on the *Alert,* and Captain Thompson himself had told him he would be returning to Boston in it. He thought it was cruel that he had not been warned about a replacement until now, just a few hours before the brig sailed. When he recovered from the shock, he put on a brave face and told the captain that he had a letter in his sea chest telling him that the owners had ordered Thompson to bring him home in the ship.

At that the captain exploded, showed Dana the crew list of the *Pilgrim,* from which his name had not been erased, and told him he must be on board the next morning with his sea chest and hammock or have someone else ready to go in his place. Furthermore, he would not hear another word about it. Dana, still fearing that "two years more in California would have made me a sailor for the rest of my days," repeated his argument.

He got away with it and he was intelligent enough to know exactly why. "It would have all availed me nothing," he said, "had I been 'some poor body,' before this absolute, domineering tribunal." Fortunately, he was a man who had "friends and interest enough at home to make them suffer for any injustice they might do to me." Thompson apparently had second thoughts when he discovered that Dana would not remain unless forced to do so. The captain sent for another member of the *Alert* crew, Ben Stimson, and told him he must remain in California with the *Pilgrim.* English Ben, as he was known to the crew, had originally come on the *Pilgrim,* but desperate to get home, had arranged an exchange with a man on the *Alert.* Now he found himself having to stay with the *Pilgrim.*

Dana was free to go home on the *Alert* but trouble now came from another source. Ben was a favorite of the crew and they were upset that he was being forced to stay. They told Dana, "the captain has let you off, because you are a gentleman's son, and have got friends, and know the owners; and taken Ben, because he is poor, and has got nobody to say a word for him!" It was true enough and Dana, who prided himself on being accepted by the crew as just another sailor, knew it would drive a wedge between himself and the others during the long voyage home. That, plus sincere sympathy for Ben's plight—it could have been his own—caused him to find another replacement. He offered to give six month's wages, plus all the clothes, books, and other things he would not want on the voyage home, to any man who would remain. Finally a sailor named Henry May—"Harry Bluff" to the crew—decided to accept it, for he was the kind "who did not care what country or ship he was in, if he had clothes enough and money enough."

The deal was made and on May 8, 1836, Dana was on board the *Alert* as it left San Diego and the California coast. Four and a half months later, after surviving a violent storm off Cape Horn, the ship arrived in Boston Harbor where Dana would be able to resume the life he had left behind two years before. The effect of his arrival home, however, was not quite what he had expected. He said, "A year before, while carrying hides on the coast of California, the assurance that in a twelvemonth we should see Boston, made me half wild; but now that I was actually there, and in sight of home, the emotions which I had so long anticipated feeling, I did not find, and in their place was a state of very nearly entire antipathy."

THE LAST OF THE TRAPPERS

I

During the same years that Boston traders, coming by sea, made their greatest impact on California, increasing numbers of trappers began to arrive by land. By the late 1820s stories told by those who had been to California with Jed Smith or with the Patties were circulating among western trappers. And they all agreed that life there was good, that all the rivers were filled with beaver.

Among those who heard the stories was George Yount who by 1830 was trapping in the northern mountains. It was new country to him, for usually he spent his time hunting in the southwest. And like most of those who made Taos, New Mexico, their headquarters, he had come from Missouri where he had grown up and received his baptism by fire in the war of 1812. His outfit had been commanded by Colonel Nathan Boone and Major Daniel Morgan Boone, who, he proudly remembered, were sons of "the great Dan Boone." He also remembered that once, during the war, his outfit passed through the village of La Charette where "we saw the old man himself."

After the war Yount worked as a teamster, did some farming, and like almost every other Missourian, speculated in land. In 1818 he married Eliza Wilds from Kentucky. "She was the oldest of eight children, herself not more than fifteen of age." Later, Yount wrote, "And now I was what the world calls a happy man. In body and mind I felt my superiority over many. Fortune favored me." But he also admitted he had much to learn "by hard experience." And "the lessons came fast and quick."

Before his marriage he had been able through hard work and saving to accumulate $1,000 which he had deposited with an older man who had placed the money in a small trunk, locked it, and kept the key. Since he was an important man known to his fellow citizens for his honesty, Yount did not bother to ask for a receipt. After he was married, when an opportunity arose to make an investment, he called on the much-respected pillar of the community, the trunk was opened, and several hundred dollars were found to be missing. There was nothing he could do without a receipt or a witness to the fact that he had deposited any money.

His family was terribly disappointed by his naiveté. "My young and sensitive wife," Yount said, "suffered more than I from the world's chilling frown," and her father clearly demonstrated his lack of faith. A neighbor offered to provide Yount with enough money to reestablish himself if his wife's father, also rich and able, would provide an equal amount. "But," Yount said, "my father-in-law coldly refused," although he did offer to take him and his family in as tenants. Instead "I sold all my herds and loose property, paid all my debts save one which the generous creditor refused to receive, bestowed on my wife all that remained, declined my father-in-law's solicitations to become his tenant, and resolved to restore my fortune elsewhere." The generous neighbor gave him a job as a teamster and in 1826 Yount drove a wagon down the Santa Fe trail.

Once in New Mexico Yount worked briefly at William Workman's still, then joined an expedition that trapped the Gila and Colorado Rivers, only to have all the furs confiscated when the party returned to Santa Fe. The next year he went back into the Gila country with another band of trappers. He claimed he was the leader, although James Pattie always claimed his father was in command. Perhaps it was that argument that finally caused the party to break up, with the Patties and several others going to California while Yount and the rest returned to New Mexico.

Despite the conflict it had been a successful hunt and Yount, remembering the loss of furs the previous year, stopped on the Jemez River, well short of the settlements, and cached all the fur before going into Taos to investigate. There he found his former employer William Workman, the still owner, deeply involved in smuggling. Hidden in the still house, where Yount had once helped turn out "Taos lightning," was the entrance to an underground passage leading to a "grand subterranean cache, where goods to an enormous amount were being secretly deposited."

Not only was Yount able to smuggle his own furs into Taos but since he had a considerable knowledge of the surrounding country, he was invited to join the smuggling operation. He was promised great profits—"offers to almost any amount"—and hearing that, he began to dream of his triumphal return to his family in Missouri with enough to live on for the rest of his life. Thus he joined what he would later call "these works of darkness" and became a smuggler. He lived through many hardships and more adventures than he really cared to have, but somehow the promise of great rewards never came. Finally he went to those who had made the glittering promises, "looked them in the face and alluded to that pledge . . . They smiled in contempt and turned away with cold indifference." Eventually Yount decided it was his own fault for, he said, "It was a just retribution. . . . I had no right to embark in that illicit employment for any consideration . . ."

He had, however, managed to save enough from his own trapping venture to send some money to his family in Missouri and with the rest to organize a trapping expedition to the north. It was on this trip in 1830 that, somewhere in the northern mountains, he met Jedediah Smith and, more important, a man named Arthur Black.

II

He was the same Arthur Black who had followed Jed Smith through much of his career. Although he was a shadowy figure, he apparently was with Smith when he discovered South Pass and when he trapped the Green River country for the first time. Mountain tradition, too, always insisted that it was Black who had saved Smith, not once but twice, from being killed by grizzlies. However much of this early legend is true, it is clear that Black was one of those who accompanied Smith to California and was still with him when the party left for the north. And now he was the only man who could tell, firsthand, what had happened when that band of trappers was suddenly attacked by Indians on the Umpqua River. Jed Smith and two others had survived, being out on the trail when the attack began. Only Arthur Black of all those who were in camp that morning had lived.

Black's story was simple. On the morning of July 14, 1828, he and the rest of Smith's men were preparing to break camp. Smith, when he left to look over the trail ahead, told his men not to allow any Indians to enter the camp. Such a warning should have been unnecessary, for several of these men were veterans of the Mohave attack, and all of them had been present during a tense confrontation just two days earlier when an Indian had stolen an ax and Smith had grabbed him, tied him up, and put a noose around his neck until the ax was returned. The strategy worked, but it greatly offended the man who had been seized—a chief—and he began to argue that the white men should be killed. Another, more respected, chief opposed it and was able to prevent an attack. Despite this, the men apparently thought Smith was being too careful, like an old woman, and they ignored his orders. Soon there were almost a hundred Indians wandering around the camp.

Later, Hudson's Bay Company officials heard the Indians' version of what happened next. One of those in the white men's camp was the same Umpqua chief who two days before had prevented an attack. All he did, he later said, was to climb on one of the trapper's horses to ride around the camp. But suddenly he was faced by an armed man—it was Arthur Black—who ordered him off the horse and threatened him with a gun. He was affronted and his good will toward the white men was destroyed. The attack followed almost immediately.

Black, when he later told his story, admitted he had told the Indian to get off his horse but denied that he had threatened him with a gun. Besides, Black's version involved not horses, but women. There had been no trouble, he said, until squaws were admitted into the camp. Then, while Harrison Rogers was trying to force a woman into his tent, he knocked down her brother who had rushed to her defense and, Black added, "seeing the opportunity favorable, as some of the people were asleep, others eating and none on their guard they rose in a body." Two Indians grabbed Black's rifle and as he struggled to keep it they slashed him on the hands with their knives. Another Indian ran up and swung an ax at his head, but he dodged and took most of the blow on his back. He gave up trying to save his gun, dropped it, and darted into the woods. As he ran he caught one last glimpse of the camp. Thomas Virgin had two Indians on him, Tom Daws was in the river with Indians in a canoe after him, while someone who Black couldn't identify was on the ground being butchered by a horde of Indians with axes. Only Black got away, and after wandering in the woods for four days he encountered some friendly Indians.

On the evening of August 8, 1828, just after dark, the people at Fort Vancouver heard a great commotion at the gate made by a crowd of Indians who were shouting something about an American. The fort's commander, John McLoughlin, ordered the gate opened and a white man came in so affected that, for the moment, he could not speak. At last he recovered enough to talk. He was Arthur Black, he told McLoughlin, and "he was, he thought, the only survivor of 18 men, conducted by the late Jedediah Smith, all the rest, he thought were murdered."

McLoughlin immediately sent Indian runners to the various tribal chiefs threatening punishment to anyone who harmed a white man and offering rewards to anyone who brought a survivor into the fort. He also equipped a well-armed party of forty men to search for and rescue any who might have survived the attack. Just before the party left, three men arrived—John Turner, Richard Leland, and Jed Smith himself.

The three of them, on the morning of July 14, had left camp early to look over the trail ahead. Since the whole area was swampy, they ascended the river in a canoe paddled by one of the Indians instead of following the land trail. They went a few miles, then turned back toward the camp, but as they approached they could see no one. Suddenly, an Indian appeared out of the brush on the river bank, yelled something to the man paddling the canoe, who instantly turned, seized Smith's rifle and dived into the river as the Indians on shore opened fire. Smith frantically paddled the canoe to the opposite bank and climbed a ridge where he could see the camp. There were no signs of life, and that, plus the fact that no one had come out to investigate the gunshots, convinced him that all had been killed. He and the other two set off toward the north where eventually they found some Tillimook Indians who guided them to Fort Vancouver. It was not until they reached there that they learned Arthur Black had also survived.

Even as Smith arrived at Fort Vancouver, John McLoughlin, knowing what trouble his own trappers would have if this attack went unchecked, was already preparing an expedition to the Umpqua country. Led by Alexander McLeod, the assignment was to go to the area, recover what they could of Smith's property, chastise the Indians, and restore as much order as possible. He was given an expedition consisting of twenty-two trappers, fourteen Indians, as well as Smith and his three men.

As they pushed up the river pelted by almost constant rain, they heard that the Indians, made confident by their easy victory, planned to ambush them. It was only a rumor, however, and the Indians fled before them until they reached Smith's old campsite where, McLeod said, they found "the Skeletons of eleven of those Miserable Sufferers lying bleaching in the Sun." There should have been fifteen, and for a time there was some hope that the others had survived. But in talking to the Indians it soon became definite that these, too, had died, although their bodies were never found. The skeletons were buried, and McLeod went from tribe to tribe regaining as much of Smith's property as he could. When he finally returned to Fort Vancouver he had, among other things, three horses, two mules, seven traps, a rifle, a rifle barrel, some beads, and a copper-covered kettle. He also had Harrison Rogers' journal, the last entry of which was dated July 13, 1828.

> Sunday, July 13, 1828. We made a pretty good start this morning, directing our course along the bay, east and travelled 4 miles and enc. 50 or 60 Inds in camp again to-day (we traded 15 or 20 beaver skins from them, some elk meat and tallow, also some lamprey eels). The traveling quite mirery in places; we got a number of our pack horses mired, and had to bridge several places. A considerable thunder shower this morning, and rain at intervals through the day. Those Inds. tell us after we get up the river 15 or 20 miles we will have good travelling to the Wel Hammett or Multinomah, where the Callipoo Inds. live.

The next day he was dead. Not only was he dead but Arthur Black accused him of causing the whole thing by chasing Indian women. When Jed Smith heard Black's version of the attack, he refused to believe that it began by Rogers trying to force an Indian woman into his tent. Rogers' religion, his attitude toward life, and his friendship with both Smith and Father Sanchez give considerable credence to Smith's doubts. Quite likely Black was trying to deny his own responsibility for causing the death of his comrades. Besides, after all these years of following Smith, he seemed to have become disenchanted with him as a leader. At least George Yount, after talking to Black in the northern mountains, said, "This was Smith's second defeat by Indians . . . In both instances the disaster was attributable to carelessness."

By the time Yount met him, Black was just spinning yarns, for he told Yount a story that was highly unlikely, although certainly designed to capture his listener's attention. According to Black—or so Yount remembered it years later—Smith's party, while hunting in California, "had discovered gold there in great abundance." Smith himself had carried away a large lump of gold that was lost during the attack on the camp and hence he was unable to substantiate the story. Still, there was much gold there and, he told Yount, California was "the finest country in the world." Soon Yount returned to Taos, sold his furs, and joined a party of trappers bound for California.

III

Jedediah Smith was one of the few who survived the Indian attack on the Umpqua River that killed most of his men and destroyed much of his work of the past two years. He also managed to escape financial disaster, for when he rejoined his partners, Jackson and Sublette, he found that they had done well enough at trapping to more than offset the losses of Smith's California expedition. Then, during the winter of 1829–30, Smith led a band of trappers into the Blackfoot Country. For once he had good luck, and when the three partners were reunited at the rendezvous of 1830, they had a great harvest of furs from a successful winter hunt. It was at this point that the three men apparently decided they had pushed their luck far enough, for they sold the whole company to another group of trappers and left the mountains for good, taking with them a long line of wagons filled with furs that one newspaper later guessed, somewhat wildly, might be worth as much as $150,000. By October 1830—just a little more than two years since disaster overtook him on the Umpqua—Jed Smith arrived in St. Louis, a wealthy, victorious businessman.

His success was not destined to last, however. The following spring, Smith joined the annual caravan bound for Santa Fe. Originally, he had planned only to stake his brothers in the Santa Fe trade, but he had ended up investing so much money that he finally decided to accompany the expedition himself. In early May 1831 the wagon train left for New Mexico and several weeks later, after ascending the Arkansas River, reached the point where it was necessary to leave the river, turn south, and make the forty- or fifty-mile dry crossing to the Cimarron.

As the caravan entered the plains, flat and unmarked except for a bewildering maze of buffalo trails, a hot wind was blowing from the south, scorching the plains and drying up what few sources of water there were. By the third day the teams were near perishing and a last desperate search was made for water. Men were sent in all directions, and Jed Smith and Tom Fitzpatrick rode off toward the south. They came to a deep hole, which should have contained water but was dry. Smith told Fitzpatrick to wait for the wagons to come up, and while he was waiting, to dig for water. He rode on south to investigate some broken country about three miles away and was soon out of sight. He was never seen again.

Six weeks later, on the fourth of July 1831, the caravan entered Santa Fe. Its members had survived the dry crossing, having found water and gone into camp to rest. They had also spent some time searching for Smith but were eventually forced to give up and continue on toward the Mexican settlements.

Soon after they arrived, a small group of Comancheros—New Mexicans who each year went out onto the plains to trade with Comanches—rode into Santa Fe. Among the things they had obtained from the Indians were a rifle and pistols which were identified as having once belonged to Jed Smith. They also had a story of how the Indians came to have possession of them, and as much as could be made out after passing from Comanche to Spanish-speaking New Mexican to English-speaking trader was this:

A Comanche hunting party of fifteen or twenty men was hiding near a water hole waiting for buffalo to come to drink. A lone white man came riding up, dismounted, drank, and gave his horse some water. As he was standing beside the horse, the Indians suddenly appeared. There was no way to escape now, and the white man began making peace signs. The Comanches, however, ignored them and fanned out, making quick darting moves to frighten the horse. The horse wheeled suddenly, and as the white man turned his back in an attempt to control it, one of the Indians fired and hit him in the shoulder with a musket ball. He spun back and fired his rifle into the crowd of Comanches, killing the leader of the party. Then he dropped the rifle and reached for his pistols, but before he could get them out, the rest of the Indians were on him, cutting him to pieces with their lances.

Not only was Jed Smith dead but so were almost all those who had gone to California with him. Some had been killed by Mohaves while trying to cross the Colorado River, others had died during the attack by the Umpquas. A few had survived, however, among them the giant free-trapper from Kentucky, Isaac Galbraith, who had dropped out of Smith's band of trappers before it left California to go north. He soon found his way to Monterey where he liked to hang around Captain Cooper's store. It was there that Alfred Robinson found him with several other hunters who were boisterously firing at a target while Galbraith stood by loudly bragging of his skill as a marksman. Much to the amusement of the hunters, Robinson was invited to fire at the target—a small piece of paper about the size of a dollar bill stuck on a board with a pin through the center. Robinson stepped back the required forty paces and fired. A loud shout went up from the trappers. He had not just hit the target but had driven the pin in the center clear through the board. It was a lucky shot, but it made Galbraith extremely jealous and he challenged Robinson to a head-to-head contest. Robinson declined, knowing he was no match for a man "who amused himself daily by shooting off the heads of little 'chenates' (blackbirds) at the distance of twenty paces."

Possibly it was these displays of markmanship that interested Captain William G. Dana, for if Galbraith could shoot the head off a blackbird, surely he could do the same to a sea otter. Dana, another of those New England traders who had recently become a naturalized citizen of Mexico, approached Galbraith with a proposition. Although the Kentucky hunter had the necessary skills to catch sea otters, he did not have a license to hunt which only a citizen, like Dana, could obtain. The two agreed that Dana would provide the license, Galbraith would do the hunting, and they would split the profits. In this way the landlocked beaver hunter took to the sea in pursuit of otters. His success was considerable although he often complained about doing all the work and receiving only half the profits.

Dana was certainly satisfied with the deal, for when the opportunity arose to obtain another hunter he jumped at it. The new hunter was George Yount, who, although only recently arrived from New Mexico, already had a reputation in California as a crack shot. From his trapper's garb he had also been given the name "Captain Buckskin," and Dana, hearing of him, sent a message asking if he would be interested in hunting otters. For Yount the offer came at just the right time, for he had not reached California until it was too late to undertake a spring beaver hunt in the San Joaquin Valley, and he was casting around for some other money-making activity when Dana's message arrived.

Yount made the hundred-mile ride from Los Angeles to Santa Barbara where he met Captain Dana and learned the specifics of the offer. Dana would obtain the necessary license, furnish transportation in his ship to the hunting grounds along the coast and on the channel islands, and supply the canoes and the provisions for the actual hunt. Yount would do the hunting, and in exchange would receive half the proceeds from sale of the fur. It seemed reasonable to Yount and an agreement was reached.

At the time the agreement was signed, Dana's ship was not in port, and while Yount waited for it in Santa Barbara he met several people, many of whom were sailors. As a trapper from Missouri he knew nothing of the sea and, in fact, had never seen the ocean until he arrived in Santa Barbara. His ignorance was so great that it vastly amused his seagoing friends who, to further his education, arranged to take him out in a small sailing ship on a day when the sea was particularly rough. After they put out from Santa Barbara the ship began bouncing so much that Yount had trouble standing up while, one by one, his friends started getting seasick. About the only one who wasn't sick was Yount himself—he spent the time examining the strange, fascinating world of a sailing ship before sitting down to a shipboard dinner which he thoroughly enjoyed.

Dana's ship eventually returned to Santa Barbara, bringing the rest of his sea-otter crew—Isaac Galbraith, an unidentified mulatto, and two Kanakas who were used as retrievers to bring the otters back after they were shot. Yount joined them, and the entire party was ferried across to Santa Rosa Island where they began to hunt. As Yount took to his canoe he saw stretching before him hundreds of sea otters on the surface of the water. But when the killing started Yount—Captain Buckskin, the crack shot—missed. Then, much to his astonishment he missed again, and then again, until he had missed fifteen straight times. Much confused, Yount went ashore and after examining his rifle and experimenting with it, discovered that he had accidentally disturbed the sight. He repaired it, and the next morning took to the canoe again where he quickly redeemed himself by killing ten otters without a miss.

Once that problem was solved, Yount developed a routine that allowed him to take large amounts of fur. Each morning as he entered the canoe he carried two rifles, and also laid out powder, ball, and patch in such a way that he could reload quickly. Then he would sit in the canoe as the two Kanakas paddled him through the sea until they came within easy shot of an otter. He would fire, and almost instantly one of the Hawaiians would plunge into the water and bring back the animal. If another shot offered itself, he would make it with the second rifle, and by the time the otter was retrieved by the other Kanaka, he would be reloaded and ready to fire again.

The same efficiency did not rub off on Galbraith and the mulatto who served him as both retriever and watchdog. One day the mulatto was left to watch the boat but fell asleep and it drifted away. Much to his disgust, Yount was forced to take his boat and the two Kanakas and spend valuable time trying to retrieve Galbraith's canoe. They had no luck and with the loss of the boat Galbraith became very ill-natured, thus interrupting the efficient pursuit of business.

Then Yount ate some kind of herb he found on the island and became ill with cramps and vomiting. In itself it was only a case of temporary poisoning from which he soon recovered, but it had a more serious effect on his superstitious Kanakas. Connecting the loss of the boat with the poisoning of Yount, they became convinced that the devil was on the side of the island where they were camped and they insisted on moving to the other side. Yount humored them, but they had no more than made a new camp than a big storm began to gather out to sea. They quickly put everything in order to weather the storm, and just as they finished they saw a large ship approach, drop anchor, and lower six boats which began making for the island. The Kanakas were wild with excitement and fear, and it was all Yount could do to calm them while he tried to figure out what to do about the intruders.

With rifle in hand he met the newcomers on the beach and found that they were from a trading vessel that was scouring the coast for furs. By now the storm had reached the island, the sea was running high, and the men from the ship decided that they would spend the night ashore rather than try to return. Under these circumstances Yount decided the best thing was to be friendly and hospitable, although Galbraith "maintained a sour and cold dislike." When the storm abated, Yount was invited aboard the ship while Galbraith was ignored. Galbraith was in "a very uncomfortable mood," and finally insisted on abandoning the whole project. Eventually relations got so bad between the two that Yount agreed to end the hunt, return to the mainland, and report to Captain Dana. Although he would have preferred to stay longer, he still had not done too badly, for he took with him seventy-five skins which brought him "the snug little sum of Two Thousand Two Hundred and Fifty-Dollars—the fruits of his first expedition in pursuit of Sea Otter."

IV

Soon after returning from this expedition, Yount decided to strike out on his own. Instead of relying on Captain Dana to supply canoes, he made his own by using the design of a Plains Indian bull boat. In the absence of buffalo hide he stretched seal skin over the framework. If not as manageable as a canoe, at least it floated, and Yount used it to hunt through the channel islands. And now he was able to pick his own companions rather than have a difficult man like Isaac Galbraith forced on him.

One of those who joined him was Lewis Burton, who had come from New Mexico in the same party as Yount. Burton was a good hunter, but he had one habit that was sometimes maddening, for he was a nonstop talker. According to Yount, "waking or sleeping his tongue was never idle."

The strangest thing about Burton was that while asleep he delivered long narratives, orations, and even sermons, but when he awoke he remembered nothing of what he had said. Even more peculiar was his ability to sing in his sleep. When he was awake, he had no musical ability whatever, and according to Yount could not even carry a tune. When asleep, however, "he was one of the most melodious musicians—In vocal music his somniliquism was most exquisit."

Burton could also tell the future, or so he claimed one time while he and Yount were hunting on San Clemente Island. One evening, after the day's hunt was over, the two lay awake in camp with Yount, as usual, listening to his incessant talk. When he suddenly launched into prophecy, Yount interrupted to ask him how he knew. Burton replied, "such is fate; the Devil tells me so." Then he went on to predict Yount's future, telling him "what would befall him in the future; what calling he would be compelled to pursue, and to what humiliating servile employment he was destined." At Yount's urging he told his own fortune, saying, "I must sit in an armchair, and there remain indefinitely."

However adept he was at reading a distant future, Burton was unable to read the immediate future, as he demonstrated one beautiful Sunday morning while they were still on San Clemente Island. During an early breakfast Burton said, "this is a charming day and we must be early in our boats and no time must be lost." Yount agreed and they pushed off to hunt otters. Within a few hours, however, clouds covered the sky, the wind rose, and "the sea was thrown into convulsions, and the waves rolled most terrific." Both Yount and Burton, as well as their Kanaka boatmen, fought to return to the island, but were pushed further out to sea by the high winds and heavy sea. After several hours' struggle, the wind shifted, they were driven into a small cove and thrown up onto the beach. After it was over and they were safe, Yount and Burton agreed that they had been punished—then forgiven—for their violation of the Sabbath and they "resolved never more to violate the Fourth Commandment of the Decalogue; but ever thereafter to remember the Sabbath day to keep it holy."

Eventually the hunting trip to San Clemente Island ended, and Yount went north to Monterey. At Cooper's ranch he met another trapper, George Nidever, who agreed to join him in a hunt in the north. They sent their equipment, including Yount's special boats, north to San Francisco Bay on a Russian ship and went overland themselves. Using Kanaka boatmen they paddled their skin boats around the north end of the bay hunting otters.

It was a successful hunt, but in the area where the San Joaquin and Sacramento rivers converge and run toward the bay, they came on a succession of terrible sights. The previous year a band of trappers had found whole villages wiped out by a violent fever. Now it was cholera that had reached the interior valley of California with even more devastating effects. Later Yount said that when he ascended the river, "all was silent as the house of death—Here and there wandered a scattered few, in sullen and mournful indifference to everything around them—They were unwilling to hold any intercourse with the white man, half suspecting him of some agency in the calamities that had befallen them."

The tragedy was brought much closer to the white hunters one evening when, while making camp, they heard a child crying. At first they ignored the sound, thinking they were near an Indian family, but it continued all the time they were pitching their tent and building a fire. Finally they could stand it no longer. With darkness approaching Yount went on with the camp chores while Nidever investigated. He soon returned and told Yount that he had found some deserted Indian huts, in one of which lay a three-year-old girl, all alone and quite naked. Thinking that she had been left temporarily by her parents they decided not to interfere, but throughout the night they heard the cries from time to time. The next evening when they visited the hut again, they found the child had neither been cared for nor fed. She was by now, Yount said, "a most pitiable spectacle, much emaciated, and covered with vermin . . ."

Yount decided the child had been abandoned and he took her to his boat, fed her, then with difficulty gave her a bath and wrapped her in some of his old clothes. Later, as he and Nidever continued up the river, they met a band of Indians and Yount tried to turn the child over to them but they refused to take her and urged Yount to throw her in the river. Since it was clear enough what would happen if she was left with them, Yount kept "the forlorn object in his boat, and with him in all his wanderings afterward."

V

Actually George Yount's wanderings soon ended. Although he had done well hunting sea otters, it was clear that, like the beaver business, it too must end one day. Besides, he discovered that his ability to make shingles, another talent picked up as a young man in frontier Missouri, was much in demand. He gave up hunting and settled down in Sonoma where he began putting a shingle roof—the first ever seen in California—on a new home being built by Mariano Vallejo.

Yount was roofing Vallejo's house and offered George Nidever a steady job making shingles but he refused, saying he "was not in the habit of working for wages," and went to Santa Barbara where he resumed otter hunting. Nidever and another man made arrangements to use William Dana's license and went to Santa Rosa Island to hunt. Having no canoes, they hired a Kanaka at sixteen dollars a month to retrieve whatever they shot. It was not a particularly successful hunt, for after only a few weeks the second man fell ill and had to return to the mainland. Nidever stayed six more weeks, during which time he killed only a few otters.

The next year he met a more capable man in Allen Light, a black man who had served as steward on a ship before deserting in California. Nidever and Light, who was often known as Black Steward, again used Dana's license and made two successful trips along the coast north of Santa Barbara. These two were soon joined by a third man, Isaac Sparks, who had come to California with a band of trappers from New Mexico. He had taken up otter hunting, although with no money to invest he had to begin in the smallest possible way. He had no boat, no Kanaka retriever, in fact nothing but the rifle he had brought with him from St. Louis. He would walk along the shore with it, shoot otters, strip off his clothes, swim out, and retrieve them himself. Sparks made enough money this way to hire a swimmer and later to build a small boat. Eventually he took on two partners, Job Dye and Lewis Burton, the nightsinger, and the three of them built their own ship and went on an otter-hunting expedition. They were unable to get along, however, and after they returned, Sparks broke away and joined Nidever and Light to hunt in the channel islands.

Hunting these same islands were Aleut and Kodiak Indians brought from the north by American ship captains. The Indians did not particularly like competition, and both Yount and Sparks had weathered some tense moments with Indian hunters during their early days in the islands. Recently, Sparks and Light had been driven into the interior of Santa Rosa Island by some Northwest Indians who stole their supplies. Then, in early 1836 Light, Sparks, and Nidever became involved in a full-scale battle with the Indians.

It began early one morning in January when the three men, each in a canoe with a Kanaka boatman, went out to hunt in a heavy fog. They had just spotted an otter, and using the usual triangular formation and firing shots, were driving it toward land, when suddenly Light shouted, "Northwest Indians!" Coming out of the fog were five or six canoes, each carrying two or three men who were using the sound of the shots to guide them to the hunters. The three Americans and their Kanaka paddlers quickly forgot the otter and began to pull for the shore. They made land and scrambled up the beach amid a hail of buckshot from the Indians' guns. The Kanakas kept on running, but Light, Sparks, and Nidever scrambled into the brush and opened fire on their pursuers. Several of the Northwest Indians were hit, and this was enough to halt their canoes and force them to back out of range. As the fog lifted during the day those on shore could see the brig which had brought the Northwesterners to the islands.

The standoff continued all day and on through the night. Next morning the men on shore saw the canoes being lowered again and watched as they maneuvered back and forth along the coast, trying to look as if they were hunting. Everybody knew they were trying to find the place where the American hunters kept their supplies, a large cave with an entrance facing the beach. After a while someone shouted that the Indians had landed near the cave, and once again the hunters opened fire. A Northwest Indian was killed and the rest returned to their brig. For two days the brig lay becalmed off the island, but no one tried to come ashore. On the third day a breeze came up and the ship sailed away. "This defeat," Nidever said, "was a severe blow to the Northwest Indians, who for several years had been the terror of the coast. This was the first reverse they had met with."

Although it was Northwest Indians who had actually attacked the island, they were not the true terror of the coast. They were there only because they had been brought south by ship captains, in this case Captain John Bancroft. Bancroft, whose brig *Convoy* had appeared so ominously out of the fog to Nidever and his companions, was a contrabandista, an illegal hunter of otters along the coast. Usually these vessels looked like warships, with several guns, nettings to avoid being boarded, and an oversize crew to fight off any assailants. Such ships carefully avoided the California ports and slipped along the coast and among the islands, frequently sending out canoes with Indian hunters to take whatever otters they could.

The people involved in such trade were not particular about how they did business. When the men on the brig *Convoy,* anchored in the fog off Santa Rosa Island, heard the guns of competing hunters, the easiest solution was to send several canoes of Indians to take care of them. The strategy failed, but that did not particularly bother Captain Bancroft, and when the wind rose again, rather than lose any more men in pursuing those ashore, he sailed away to hunt elsewhere. After a few more months on the California coast, the *Convoy* returned to its home port of Honolulu.

Apparently such cruises were still highly profitable, however, for after returning to Hawaii, Bancroft obtained a new ship, the *Llama,* and used it to make several more voyages along the coast, sometimes as far south as Cedros Island off Baja California. Beyond that, his exact movements are not clear, for Bancroft kept his activities as quiet as possible. If he or his Indians again found and attacked other bands of hunters, there is no surviving testimony. Either those who were attacked escaped and said nothing or Captain Bancroft's men destroyed them, effectively eliminating the evidence.

In the fall of 1838 as Bancroft made still another sweep of the California coast, trouble developed. He had stopped on the northwest coast to pick up hunters and obtained a crew of twenty-five Kaigani Indians from Dall Island in the lower Alaskan panhandle. A veteran of the trade, Bancroft should certainly have known that a ship crowded with Indian hunters would be none too easy to control. Nonetheless he took his new wife with him, a half-Hawaiian girl, the daughter of a Hawaiian mother and an old American settler named Oliver Holmes. Although she was native herself, or possibly because of it, she was extremely prejudiced and continually showed the hunters her contempt. Captain Bancroft also drank heavily and was harsh with his Indian hunters, none of whom took kindly to any kind of discipline. By the time they reached the channel islands everyone was in a bad mood.

A bitter argument broke out between Bancroft and the Indian hunters, who suddenly exploded into revolt, shooting the captain and killing him. His wife, who was below, rushed on deck and threw herself across the body to shield it. The firing continued and she was struck in the leg and foot. A white crew member was shot in the head and killed. After that, the Indians vented their anger by abusing the captain's body, then calmed down and left the remaining white men alone, although they forced the first mate to take them back to their native village on Dall Island.

Early one morning a few weeks later, a ship flying its flag at half-mast was seen off Diamond Head. It was the *Llama,* and when it reached port those in Honolulu heard the story of the attack and saw firsthand evidence in Bancroft's wounded wife. She lived only a few weeks after reaching Hawaii, and according to one man, "her life might have been saved had she consented to submit to a surgical operation which was proposed, but she declined to have it performed."

The attack shocked not only those who had known Captain Bancroft and his wife, but it also had repercussions in the business community of Honolulu. The number of otters had obviously decreased significantly, and there were hints that Mexican officials, aware of the attacks on such local hunters as Sparks, Nidever, and Light, were preparing to take action against contraband ships. Added to this was the threat of losing part, or even all, of one's investment through the uprising of Indian hunters. It no longer seemed worthwhile, and on the day the *Llama* arrived in Honolulu, a man who was there wrote to Thomas Larkin in Monterey saying, "Sparks may now have the range of the whole coast without interruption as there will be no more fitted out from here."

VI

Thus Isaac Sparks, George Nidever, and Allen Light became the dominant men in what was left of the otter trade. All of them had started out hunting under Captain Dana's license, but that was no longer necessary, because Nidever and Sparks had become citizens of Mexico in 1837, followed by Light two years later. About that time Governor Alvarado wrote to Light addressing him as the "compromosiario pral"—chief representative—of the "national armada" engaged in hunting along the coast, an impressive title for the man known as Black Steward, and a more than elegant description of the bunch of canoes he used in otter hunting.

If the title and description were overblown, the special task given to Light was real. Governor Alvarado had heard that a contraband ship was somewhere on the coast, and because of Light's long experience, he was assigned the task of investigating. He was given full discretion to use whatever methods he thought best to end the intrusion including, in the case of resistance, the use of force "even to the point of placing the mentioned vessel and crew at the disposition of the governor." The rumored ship was, of course, the *Llama* and Light would never have a chance to carry out his instructions, because by the time he received them the ship had left the coast and limped its way back to Honolulu, never to return to California.

Meanwhile, Isaac Sparks and George Nidever, both now citizens of Mexico, began to accept California domestic life. Nidever, when he was not hunting, lived in Santa Barbara, and there he married Sinforosa Sanchez and settled down in a large adobe close to the ocean. Sparks also lived in Santa Barbara, operating a store between his otter-hunting trips. He did not enter so easily into domestic life, however, for he was often "in no end of trouble by reason of his amorous irregularities." One case involved a young unmarried woman with whom he was living. Apparently the liaison was of long standing, for she had already borne him two children. But for some reason city officials in Santa Barbara suddenly became outraged and threatened to fine him $19 if he did not end this scandalous behavior. The problem was solved by exiling the woman to Los Angeles.

In these last years the spectacular profits of the early days were no more. Too many sea otters had been destroyed and no longer could a hunter kill enough to make a fortune in a single season. There were no untouched hunting grounds anywhere in the west, although the distant coast of Baja California still held promise. Yet that was a long way from California and could not easily be reached by a few men in a fleet of canoes. They needed larger boats, more equipment, more supplies—in other words, a much larger investment. Sparks, Nidever, and Light turned to the American merchants to obtain capital for their operations. Together they formed a tightly organized business which, if it did not make a man sensationally rich overnight, it did, when combined with store-keeping or ranching, give a man and his family an adequate income.

VII

George Yount later remembered that "early in the Spring of 1836 he found himself no longer a wanderer." After all the years of traveling the west in search of beaver, then sea otter, Yount now found himself the owner of a large ranch. Early in 1836 he had been granted the Caymus Rancho, almost 12,000 acres in the Napa Valley, and when the weather cleared, he began building his home. With him was a hired servant, the little Indian girl whose life he had saved—she would have been about five by now—and his old friend, the rifle he had carried through all his travels. During all these twenty years, he later told his biographer, he had never passed a night without this weapon of defense by his side.

The road to ownership of this large ranch had begun when, two years before, Yount had made shingles for Mariano Vallejo's new home in Sonoma. In one way the relation was strange, for the employer,

Commandante Vallejo, military commander of all California and virtual ruler of the area north of San Francisco Bay, was only twenty-six. His employee, until now a drifting hunter, was forty. Still the two got along well and Yount once described Vallejo as a noble, generous, and high-minded gentleman. Vallejo also admired Yount's many abilities and his character and saw to it that he was baptized, naturalized as a citizen, and finally granted Caymus Ranch in 1836.

In the years to come Yount would build a big log and adobe house as well as a saw mill and flour mill. First, though, he built a Kentucky-style blockhouse which, he said, "combined a convenient dwelling house with a strong fortress." It was an intelligent move, for in 1836 Yount's new ranch was on the frontier, well beyond the Spanish settlements and exposed to Indian attack. When trouble came it usually came from the north, and one of the reasons Yount had been granted this land was because Vallejo wanted to build a line of defense.

Yount was expected to do something more than sit in his blockhouse, as was apparent one morning not long after he settled in the valley. A messenger arrived from General Vallejo with an order "to repair to him with the least possible delay, to join him in an expedition against the Indians who had assumed a hostile attitude." Yount, leaving his servant and little girl at the blockhouse, went to Sonoma where he found Vallejo preparing a major expedition against Indians who lived on the Russian River. It was a large force, made up of mounted soldiers armed with "Mexican Muskets and Rifles," friendly Indians carrying bows and arrows, spears, and war clubs, and followed by a baggage train of pack horses and mules carrying provisions and ammunition.

The march was long and tedious but the assembly eventually arrived at the Russian River and the Indians seemed totally unaware of their approach. Vallejo divided his forces, taking charge of one part himself, sending another under the command of his brother to the rear of the village, and assigning Yount and some other hunters to serve as a scouting and flanking party. Then, with the village surrounded and the Indians still unaware, the attack was launched "at early dawn, of a clear and brilliant morning."

As Mariano Vallejo's troops advanced from one side and his brother's from the other, many Indians were killed. "Between two fires they fell like the leaves of Autumn," Yount remembered and added, "Endeavouring to escape upon the flank they were met by Yount and his scouts." A few escaped to the mountains, but when the battle was over most of those who had not been killed were taken prisoner. Then Vallejo turned his own Indians loose on the village as Yount and the rest watched. "They sacked and burnt the towns of the vanquished foe, heaped the dead together promiscuously and burnt them, and indulged in the usual demonstrations of savage exultation." Vallejo declined to restrain them, claiming it was necessary that the wild tribes respect the Mission Indians and "stand in awe of them," an attitude which could not be expected if they tamely retired without celebrating their victory.

The general did, however, forbid the torturing of captives, although less from humanitarian motives than from fear of damaging their usefulness as workers. According to Yount, these captives were to be taken to the mission where they would be taught Christianity, agriculture, and the arts. The mission at Sonoma was now secularized and this training would not be provided by the church but by the man who controlled it, Mariano Vallejo. And while the captives were being trained, Yount admitted, "they must submit to a kind of servitude, to be 'hewers of wood and drawers of water' for the establishment."

After the campaign Yount returned to his ranch and for the next year there was little trouble with the Indians. He used the time to continue developing the ranch, constructing more buildings and enlarging his herd of livestock. By Christmas 1837 he had done so well that he had 170 head of cattle plus horses and other small livestock. But when he held a roundup and corralled his cattle, he discovered that his herd contained only half that number. He found out that Indians had stolen the missing animals and driven them off into the mountains. To Yount this was tantamount to a declaration of war, and when he reported the loss to Vallejo, the general agreed.

Another expedition was sent out, but this time the Indians were too alert to be caught asleep in camp. They attacked Vallejo's column, and during the course of the battle Yount's cap was shot off and two horses were shot from under him. The Indians were at last beaten off, several prisoners were taken, and the expedition returned to Yount's ranch to rest before continuing on to Sonoma, where it disbanded. Not long afterward a band of Indians arrived to attack Yount and lay siege to the blockhouse but they were driven away.

In the long run, however, Yount's troubles with the Indians were solved not by any military expedition but by an epidemic of smallpox. Some time in 1837 word reached Vallejo that smallpox had broken out at Fort Ross, and not long afterward it appeared at Sonoma. By May of the next year, Vallejo was writing of the "horrible contagion which has carried off, during the last few months, hundreds of human beings, especially among the natives." Thousands of Indians died and in the valley where Yount lived the Napa Indians were virtually annihilated. The frontier retreated, leaving the blockhouse unused and unneeded as George Yount settled into the life of a quiet rancher in the Caymus Valley.

THE INVASION OF THE HORSETHIEVES

I

Juan Bautista Alvarado, the idealistic young man who became governor of California at the age of twenty-seven, was soon disillusioned. He had barely assumed office when a revolt broke out in Los Angeles, and while he was in the south trying to put it down, another erupted in Monterey. This one was led by some of his original supporters who had now turned against him. It was short-lived, for Alvarado's old friend Commandante Vallejo quickly marched down from his headquarters at Sonoma, recaptured Monterey, arrested the rebel leaders, and banished them from the capital.

It would not be long, however, before Alvarado began to have differences with Vallejo, for the rise to power and eminence soon drove the boyhood chums apart. Several minor issues were involved, but at the heart of the matter was the question of who controlled what in California. After Alvarado and his followers expelled Interim-Governor Gutierrez, the government in Mexico bowed to the inevitable and, instead of sending a replacement, officially recognized Juan Alvarado as the new governor of California. The same orders officially appointed Mariano Vallejo commandante-general.

Each man interpreted these appointments in a different way. Alvarado saw his role as governor as meaning that he was in charge of the civil government, and that everything else, including the military, was subordinate to that. As far as he and his advisers in Monterey were concerned, the commandante-general should pay attention to the northern frontier and leave the government to them unless they needed his military support. Vallejo, on the other hand, thought that his position as military commander made him equal to and independent of the governor. Once, when the governor called upon him to provide troops to quell some sort of disorder, Vallejo refused until he was told, specifically, the nature of the trouble so he could personally determine whether he was supporting or abusing the law. When one of Alvarado's assistants heard this, he disgustedly told the general to forget the request and they would find help elsewhere.

As trouble developed between the two, there were many who were only too willing to help drive the wedge deeper. Alvarado's advisers, particularly his old friend Jose Castro and his secretary Manuel Jimeno Casarin, were hostile to Vallejo and continually advised against giving the "autocrat of Sonoma" too much power. Vallejo was frequently told stories of graft among the "Monterey clique," and that Alvarado was drinking heavily, often too "ill" to function and therefore having to turn the government over to his secretary.

Another issue caused more trouble between the two men. By now, conditions in the California missions had reached a point near scandal. Several years earlier, under Governor Figueroa, the missions had been secularized and administrators appointed to handle the transition from religious to secular institutions. Then Figueroa died and California was torn by several revolutions. During these years of turmoil little attention was paid to the missions and many of the administrators looted them for their own benefit. By the time Alvarado stabilized the government to a point where he could attend to something besides rebellion, he found himself inundated by charges that the missions were being plundered by government officials. In January 1839 he appointed William Hartnell to the post of Visitador General of missions and assigned him the task of inspecting all the missions from San Diego to Sonoma.

Ten years had passed since Hartnell had failed as a trader, and neither his attempts at ranching nor at schoolteaching had brought him much in the way of money. The $2,000 a year he would receive as inspector of missions would be welcome, although he found during his tour of California missions that he would more than earn it. He began at San Diego where he found the Indians in "a very naked condition," then moved on to other missions where conditions were even worse. In a few places, such as San Gabriel and San Fernando, the missions were run efficiently and the Indians seemed relatively content. But by and large the dismal tale continued as Hartnell rode north. In some instances mission records were poorly kept, in others much of the mission land had been turned over to private ranchers, and in still others the administrator was harsh and cruel, giving the Indians nothing but threats and blows in exchange for their work.

Hartnell's biggest difficulty, however, came from Mariano Vallejo.

By the fall of 1839, having spent much of the summer traveling the length of California, Hartnell reached the northernmost missions at Sonoma and San Rafael. He had nothing to say, good or bad, about the mission at Sonoma, tacitly admitting that it was under Vallejo's complete control. At San Rafael, however, his criticism was pointed. Once again he found the mission accounts in poor condition, this time because the administrator, Timothy Murphy, could not read or write. Most of the mission lands had disappeared as several men, including Vallejo's brother-in-law, John Rogers Cooper, had been given grants.

Usually Hartnell tried to avoid trouble, particularly with one as powerful as Vallejo, but in this case he either misjudged the general's interest in San Rafael or saw no way to ignore the situation. In his report he recommended that the administrator be replaced, and when Governor Alvarado accepted the recommendation, Hartnell went to San Rafael personally to take the office from Vallejo's friend, Timothy Murphy. Suddenly Hartnell found himself confronted by an enraged general who ordered him arrested. By the next day Vallejo had regained his composure and he released Hartnell with apologies, but refused to allow Murphy to be replaced. Eventually Hartnell became so disgusted with the situation that he resigned. No one was ever appointed to replace him, the office of mission inspector was abandoned, and the whole thing was forgotten.

II

This long series of difficulties had a profound effect on Juan Bautista Alvarado. When he first took office he was young and idealistic, but much had changed in a few short years. He was still young, in his early thirties, but he was no longer very idealistic, for he had seen too much. Old friends in California had turned against him as soon as they saw better opportunities elsewhere. Men appointed as administrators looted the missions they were supposed to protect. Even his oldest friend Mariano Vallejo refused to take him seriously as governor and treated him like a child who should do exactly as he was told by his superiors.

All these concerns, combined with the daily pressures of the office of being governor, began to wear him down and he sought escape. The stories Vallejo heard of the governor's behavior, although exaggerated, were not entirely the invention of Alvarado's enemies. He was drinking heavily, often to the point of being unable to function, and the story that he often turned the office of governor over to his secretary because of "illness" was true.

One event that Alvarado missed in late summer 1839 was his own wedding. On August 24 he was married to Dona Martina, the daughter of Francisco Castro, in a ceremony performed by Padre Jose Gonzales at Santa Clara with Jose Antonio Estrada standing in for the absent bridegroom. Alvarado claimed that the press of official duties kept him away, but others insisted it was once again because of "illness." Eventually his new bride arrived in Monterey where the marriage was celebrated with fireworks and festivities lasting several days.

Given the governor's mental state at this time, it is not difficult to see how he became first irritated, then suspicious of those foreigners who had once supported him. Their leader, Isaac Graham, had proved less than a model citizen. The distillery he had established at Natividad attracted all kinds of troublemakers, mostly deserting sailors plus a few dropouts from fur-trapping expeditions who did not always confine their drinking and carousing to the area around the still. Once the administrator at San Miguel Mission, two days' ride south of Natividad, complained that a group of men led by Graham had forced their way into the women's quarters at the mission. The administrator gave no details, no official charges were filed, and nothing came of the incident other than the decision to end group housing and send all the women back to their individual families. Later, an official complaint was filed against Graham charging him with illegally killing cattle on the ranch of a neighbor. He was convicted and sentenced to eight months in jail. Some time after his release, he and his partner Henry Naile tried to organize a party to return to New Mexico, but they gave up when they could not find anybody who wanted to join them.

Graham and Naile continued to run the distillery at Natividad, and the foreigners who hung around them often drifted into Monterey where they sometimes harassed Alvarado to the point of distraction. Later he told Alfred Robinson, "I was insulted at every turn by the drunken followers of Graham; and when walking the garden they would come to its wall, and call upon me in terms of the greatest familiarity, 'Ho! Bautista, come here, I want to speak to you.' 'Bautista here, Bautista there,—and Bautista everywhere.' "

Drunken sailors showing off by being familiar with the governor were irritating enough, but Alvarado's deeper suspicions were roused by another group of foreigners. Some of these men, including Graham himself, insisted they had been promised independence as a reward for their earlier support. Instead, after winning his revolution, Alvarado had made peace with the government in Mexico, and those who had helped him were left with nothing. Alvarado was not ignorant of this sentiment for independence among at least one segment of foreigners nor was he unaware of what had already happened in Texas. Then, rumors began to circulate of a foreign plot to overthrow the government and Alvarado reacted.

III

It was three o'clock in the morning when the pistol went off next to his ear and the ball passed through the handkerchief he had tied around his neck.

Isaac Graham leaped out of bed as several more shots were fired at him, some at such close range that the powder flashes set his shirt on fire. It was too dark to see anything, and Graham was hit only once, in the left arm. As his assailants backed away to reload, he could see there were too many to fight, and he tried to bolt from the room. He did not reach the door before they were on him, hitting him with whatever they could and eventually using their combined weight to ride him down. Then, while he lay on the floor struggling, one of them pulled a knife and tried to stab him. The knife missed, passing between Graham's body and arm and sticking in the ground. Before the intruder could try again the others dragged Graham out of the room and up the hill at the rear of his house. There stood Governor Alvarado's old friend and supporter Jose Castro who reached out and with the back of his sword hit him over the head hard enough to knock him down.

A rope was fastened to one of his arms and passed to a man on horseback who wound the other end around his saddle horn. The rest took hold of his other arm and tried to jerk his shoulder out of joint, but the rope broke. Graham, convinced they were going to kill him, asked for time to commend his soul to God. He was told, "You shall never pray till you kneel over your grave."

The assailants took him back to his room, so he could put on his pants. In his struggle he had forgotten about the other man sleeping in his room—Henry Naile, his friend, partner, and almost constant companion since they had come west to trap a decade earlier. Now back in the house he saw Naile "pale from loss of blood and vomiting terribly. He had had a lance thrust through his thigh, and a deep wound in his leg, which nearly separated the cord of the heel."

Alfred Morris was also sleeping at Isaac Graham's distillery that night. He and another of Graham's employees were sleeping in the stillhouse, not far from the room where Graham and Naile slept. He too was awakened in the early morning hours by loud knocking at the door. Morris asked who was there, in English and again in Spanish. He was answered by Nicolas Alviso, a man who lived nearby. Morris told him to wait and he would open the door as soon as he could light a candle and get dressed. He had only time enough to put on his trousers when he heard Alviso shout to his followers to break down the door. Morris heard shots from the direction of Graham's house and the tramp of horsemen behind the stillhouse. He also heard someone shout, "Where is Graham? Tear the devil in pieces," and someone else yell to set the building on fire.

Morris fired at the men trying to break down the door, but missed. They returned the fire, hitting him once in the left side with a musket ball. Then all but Alviso fled and Morris aimed his rifle at him and exploded three caps but could not get the rifle to fire. It was enough to make Alviso run, however, and Morris disappeared into the thick willow swamp at the rear of the stillhouse.

It was pouring down rain but occasionally the moon would come out from behind a cloud and Morris could see about forty men attacking the distillery. Once he heard Jose Castro shout at them, later he heard them break down the door of the stillhouse, and he saw William Garner, an Englishman who was acting as their guide.

He did not see Graham or Naile, both of whom had been put in double irons, carried about half a mile out into a field and left in the rain under guard while the rest went back to plunder the house. One of the captors approached Graham with a drawn sword and demanded that he tell him where the money was buried. When Graham said there was none, the man cursed and turned away. Possibly, if he had persisted he might have had some success, for Graham had buried some money, although "I determined they should never enjoy it." At last Graham was put on a horse and taken to Monterey where he was thrown into jail. Naile was too badly wounded to travel and was left behind at the still.

Morris spent the rest of the night and all the following day hidden in the swamp, traveling after dark eight miles to the farm of David Littlejohn where he hid for two more days. Then, with an Indian guide and a horse provided by Littlejohn, he set out for Job Dye's distillery near Santa Cruz. Dye was not there, but Henry Cooper who was in charge welcomed him and allowed him to stay for three days until Dye returned.

A ship commanded by Alpheus Thompson was expected at Santa Cruz, and Morris wanted Dye to make arrangements to sneak him aboard when it arrived. Dye promised he would try, but he sent Morris into the hills above the distillery to hide until arrangements could be made for his escape. Five days later an American and a Canadian came to him and said his only hope was to surrender. All the authorities wanted was to ask him what he knew about an intended revolution. Because they promised he would not be put in irons or in prison he surrendered and was turned over to Captain Antonio Buelna who with a squad of soldiers was to escort him to Monterey.

In his flight from the stillhouse, Morris was clad only in a shirt and pants and had left everything else behind. Now, since it was only a few miles out of the way he asked permission to return for his clothes and Captain Buelna agreed. But little good was done, for Morris found his trunks broken open and all his clothes stolen.

He did, however, have an opportunity to see Henry Naile, lying in bed looking ghostly pale from loss of blood. Naile began to cry and said he had received a lance wound through the thigh and a deep saber cut in his leg. He also claimed his assailant was not a California soldier but the Englishman, William Garner. The conversation was short and Morris had to leave Naile because Captain Buelna insisted they must continue on to the capital. Reaching Monterey the next day Morris found it "occupied by soldiers and the prisons filled with foreigners." He was immediately put in irons, and after an interrogation lodged in jail.

As Morris had already discovered, he and Graham were not the only foreigners arrested. On the evening of April 6, 1840, David Spence, a native of Scotland but now a citizen of Mexico and the alcalde of Monterey, received an order from the governor to arrest every Englishman and American in town except the merchants Thomas Larkin of Boston and James Watson of London. Throughout the next day soldiers brought in foreigners until by evening only a few were left at liberty in Monterey.

The order had also been sent to other parts of California, and there was a general roundup of foreigners, particularly in the redwoods where several gangs of lumbermen were surrounded, then arrested. There was no repeat of the violence at Natividad, however, and most of the foreigners surrendered quietly and were taken to the capital. For the next several weeks small groups of foreign captives continued to arrive in Monterey. They were put in jail, but hardly a day went by without someone being released, either through the influence of Spence or Larkin or even some native Californian who suddenly discovered that the husband of one of his daughters was among the prisoners.

One of those released quickly was the merchant Nathan Spear who had been arrested in San Francisco, taken to Monterey, and set free almost immediately by Governor Alvarado who had once worked for him as a clerk. Others did not spend even that long in confinement. At Sonoma, Mariano Vallejo had just returned from a campaign against the Indians to find a message from the governor ordering him to take his forces to Monterey to put down a plot in which, supposedly, American settlers were planning to massacre Californians. Vallejo obeyed, but he made no effort to arrest George Yount, having just returned with him from the campaign in the north.

Down in San Diego, George Nidever, Isaac Sparks, and the rest of their sea-otter hunting party also escaped arrest. During the early months of 1840 they had been out of contact, hunting along the Baja

California coast. Then, needing provisions, they returned to San Diego where they anchored their ship and Sparks went ashore to buy supplies. He had barely touched land when a Mexican woman warned him to be careful because all Americans were being arrested and driven out of the country. Sparks did not believe her, but when he reached town he met the alcalde who had received orders to arrest him and all those who were with him. Sparks told the alcalde he could carry out the order if he wanted to, but that if he arrested him, the other hunters would come to town and release him, by force if necessary. Since the alcalde had no soldiers to back him up, he did not bother Sparks any further.

When Sparks returned to camp and told the others what had happened, they all agreed they should resist, if necessary, any attempt at arrest. About a week later, they heard that the ship taking the prisoners to Mexico was on its way to San Diego. They dropped down the coast to a small bay about twenty miles below San Diego where they made camp and prepared to defend themselves. Three days later the ship passed by just a few hundred yards offshore but made no attempt to arrest the hunters even though George Nidever, at least, was sure they had been seen.

IV

As the ship *Joven Guipuzcoana* sailed past the hunters' camp it was filled with Englishmen and Americans, under arrest and in chains, on their way to Mexico and exile. Although many of those arrested had been released through the efforts of influential friends, the ship still had fifty foreigners on board, mostly the hard core of the disreputable lot that hung around the still at Natividad. Among them was their leader, Isaac Graham, but not his partner Henry Naile, still unable to travel because of his wounds.

These foreigners had been brought to this state of affairs partly by their own activities and partly by the fears, both real and fancied, of Governor Juan Bautista Alvarado. The first official notice that foreigners were under suspicion came during a meeting of the junta on April 4 when a member said that public statements made by certain foreigners indicated they were involved in some kind of plot against the government. Governor Alvarado immediately rose to say that he did indeed have evidence of such a plot, and although he refused to disclose the source of his information, he said the conspirators were being watched closely and the plot could not possibly succeed.

Exactly what if any evidence Alvarado had in hand is not at all clear. By early April rumors of a foreign uprising were widespread in Monterey—everyone seemed to have heard them. Beyond that, it is difficult to find any solid evidence. In early April Father Jose Juarez del Real at Mission San Carlos sent a letter warning the governor of an intended uprising on the part of some American settlers. Supposedly the plot had been revealed to him in the confessional by a foreigner at the point of death and the father sent an informal warning but could not make a legal statement. This warning could not have been the cause of all the concern in Monterey, for by the time it was received rumors of such a plot were already circulating through the capital. Besides, Real's reputation for honesty was not particularly good.

The other major witness claiming to have evidence that foreigners were planning to overthrow the government was William Garner, the Englishman. His testimony, like Real's, came late and, in fact, was not given until after Governor Alvarado had already assured the junta that he had evidence of the plot. Shortly after the meeting of the junta, Garner appeared before Alvarado and confirmed that foreigners, led by Isaac Graham, were planning a revolution. Garner was sure, for he himself had been involved in the planning.

There are several stories about why Garner was so willing to testify against his friends. Alvarado and Vallejo claimed he did it because he was friendly to the Californians and wanted to help them avoid trouble. Others thought that he had been trapped into revealing part of the plan, then forced to tell the rest on the threat of being shot. Those he testified against, however—Graham, Naile, and Morris—never had any doubts about his motives. They claimed he was a dishonest man, a former Botany Bay convict who had been bribed to perjure himself by California officials hoping to obtain evidence against political opponents.

Not only is the exact source of the charges against Graham and his followers obscure but the testimony does not reveal exactly what they were suspected of having done. The beginning, supposedly, had something to do with a horse which Graham had trained to race and which had beaten several horses owned by prominent Californians. The American, Thomas J. Farnham—unreliable, simplistic, and anti-Californian—claimed that one of the losers was Jose Castro, "a villain with a lean body, dark face, black mustachios, pointed nose, flabby cheeks, uneasy eyes, and hands and heart so foul as to instinctively to require a Spanish cloak, in all sorts of weather to cover them." Another loser, he claimed, was Governor Alvarado himself, who lost so much money that he was heavily in debt to Graham.

Alfred Robinson, a far more reliable witness, agreed the trouble began over a race horse. In his version, Graham arranged to run the horse against one owned by a man in San Diego. The true owners drew up an agreement concerning the race and somehow, Robinson said, "This document was construed into a plan for overturning the government—a plan to plunder, and destroy, what was left of the Missions—a plan to deprive the Californians of their lives and country." Robinson was aware he was stretching credulity, for he added, "as ridiculous as this may appear to the reader, nevertheless, it is a fact to which I can testify from information I received on the spot, shortly after its occurrence."

His story lends weight to Farnham's claim that foreigners being questioned about the revolutionary plot were asked, "What meant that advertisement for a horse-race, put forth by Graham?" At least one man answered by saying, "It meant what such advertisements have meant for the last five years: a wish on the part of Graham to run his American horse in California."

Shaky as all this was, Alvarado was convinced he had evidence of a revolutionary plot and therefore he acted. He ordered Jose Castro to raise a force to arrest foreigners living between Monterey and San Francisco. Similar orders were sent to military commanders in the south and also to General Vallejo in Sonoma. In his message to the general, Alvarado went so far as to claim that foreigners planned not just to overthrow the government but to commit murders, robberies, and other horrible crimes.

Alvarado's reaction was, of course, totally out of proportion. He ordered a sweeping roundup of foreigners to prevent "murders, robberies, and other horrible crimes," based on little more than rumors, an advertisement for a horse race, and some vague testimony by untrustworthy men. None of this even vaguely supported the claim that there was a serious foreign plot to overthrow the government of California. A bunch of drunken, deserting sailors hanging around a still hardly constituted a serious band of filibusterers. It is even more difficult to see such a plot being planned and led by Isaac Graham, whose main abilities in the past ran to cattle rustling and invading nunneries. Nor is such a plot necessary to explain Alvarado's actions in ordering the arrests. Drinking heavily, often unable to function, faced with the thousand pressures of governing, betrayed by many of his old friends, and personally harassed by overfamiliar, drunken foreigners, he was prey to even the flimsiest of rumors. And so, it seems, the basis of the whole thing was nothing more than a figment of his imagination.

And yet, just about the time Alvarado ordered the roundup of foreigners to forestall a revolution, a band of Americans, well mounted and heavily armed, left Fort Davy Crockett on the Green River bound for California.

V

By the year 1840 the western fur trade was all but dead. In the past decade newcomers to the mountains—Benjamin Bonneville, Nathaniel Wyeth, and most of all the American Fur Company—had provided stiff competition for the Rocky Mountain Fur Company, lineal descendant of William Ashley, and Smith, Jackson, and Sublette. The increased number of trappers had gone everywhere, even to California, looking for beaver, and before long there were no untrapped streams left. There was not enough business to go around and one by one the participants bowed out. The Rocky Mountain Fur Company was gone, as were Bonneville and Wyeth, all of them forced out by the American Fur Company. Faced with a continually diminishing supply of beaver, even that giant was having trouble maintaining itself against the bigger monopoly from the north, the Hudson's Bay Company.

The decline was most evident when the mountain men gathered at the annual rendezvous. Once these had been wild, free celebrations where in a few summer days and nights a man could spend his entire year's earnings. But then a man could plan to go back into the mountains and, if he survived, be reasonably sure of making plenty to spend at the next rendezvous. Now what was once a near-certainty was not even a likelihood, and only those who watched every penny could hope to maintain themselves in the mountains. So tame had the rendezvous become by 1839 that well-behaved mountain men gathered to hear a sermon preached by a missionary on his way to Oregon. Admittedly, some listeners got drunk afterward, but that was the exception, for a visitor at the same rendezvous said, "There was little drinking of spirits, and almost no gambling."

Trappers also were kept in a state of uncertainty by the constant rumor that the American Fur Company would no longer send supply trains into the west. In 1839 it was only a rumor, but in the summer of 1840 it became a reality when the company announced its last caravan. The rendezvous was dead, as was the day of the mountain man which traced its beginning back to the arrival on the Green River of Jed Smith and a band of trappers less than twenty years before.

Although the old system did not entirely disappear until 1840, it had been dying for several years. And rising to take advantage of what trade was left in the west was a system of privately owned forts located in places where they could easily be reached by supply wagons from the east and by trappers coming out of the mountains to the west. Some of these posts—Fort Hall on the Snake, Fort Laramie on the North Platte, Bent's Fort down on the Arkansas—became both important centers of trade and major stopping points on the trails west. Others came into existence, struggled through a few difficult years, then passed into oblivion.

One such place was Fort Davy Crockett on the Green River just above the mouth of the Vermilion in the valley known as Brown's Hole. The natural setting in a small valley surrounded by high mountains was impressive, but beyond that there was little to admire at the post. Although grandly called a fort, it was nothing but a small one-story building made of wood and mud, with some connecting wings but no walls to keep out intruders. It had no supplies to offer travelers and instead of cows there were a few goats. So poverty-stricken was it that trappers doing business there called it Fort Misery.

As might be expected, those who hung around the fort were equally unimpressive. The owners—William Craig, Phil Thompson, and Prewitt Sinclair—were remnants of the earlier fur trade in which they had all played an obscure part. Although occasionally a well-known trapper like Kit Carson would spend a few months hunting out of the fort, most of those who lived there were as obscure as the owners. And all of them faced the problem of making a living now that the fur trade was over. They could have gone back east and taken up farming as some had done; they could have gone to California and become ranchers, or carpenters, or even clockmakers, as other trappers had done. Yet none of that appealed to this band of men who were looking for more than just a way to make a living. They wanted something that would provide excitement and danger and at the same time keep them in the west. They were ripe to join one of the big horse-stealing raids to California.

VI

Once, years before, the Ute Indians had been meek, withdrawn people who spent their summers in the high country, then each fall followed the deer and antelope down out of the mountains. As they went they hunted on foot, slowly accumulating enough hides and meat to last them through the winter which they spent in the lower, open regions of the Great Basin.

The coming of the horse changed all that. Soon after the Spanish settled in New Mexico, horses began to arrive in the Ute Country and the tribe broke out of its quiet mountain routine. Deer hunts were replaced with forays onto the plains for buffalo which soon became the mainstay of Ute life. These trips to the east also brought them into contact with hostile plains tribes—the Arapaho, the Cheyenne, the Sioux, the Kiowa, and the Comanche. As the Utes encountered and fought these enemies, they began to change from a meek mountain people into a tribe led by confident, aggressive mounted warriors. And these warriors, using both their newly acquired horses and their newfound confidence, began to travel far more widely than they had. Instead of the careful routine of moving from the same mountain valley each summer to a set place to winter in the Great Basin, Utes began to range over the west from the Spanish settlements of New Mexico in the south to the Wind River country and beyond in the north. As they went they sought mostly the horses on which their new life depended. Sometimes they traded for them, more often they raided other tribes or stole them from the Spanish settlements in New Mexico.

This new tribal life was thoroughly established by the early nineteenth century when a Ute named Walkara was born somewhere on the Spanish Fork River. Like all Ute boys he was virtually brought up on horseback and soon became a superb rider. Yet to Walkara and his fellow warriors a horse was something more than a means of transportation. It was a sign of wealth and prestige and soon, like other young Utes, he was riding out onto the plains and down into the Spanish settlements of New Mexico. Then one day he led a raiding party that went all the way to California to steal horses.

Early residents of the San Bernardino Valley soon learned to dread the coming of the moon that each year brought the Utes and their "Chief Cuaka." Sometimes the settlers would chase them and the Utes would scatter up the various canyons in the San Bernardino Mountains, leaving the pursuers with no main trail to follow. Later they would reassemble in the desert, then follow the Mohave River to the east. Once, however, a particularly tenacious band of men continued the pursuit and when Walkara reached the Colorado River the horses refused to enter the cold water. Knowing the Californians were close behind, he turned back and with a few warriors drove the herd back to meet those who were chasing him. Assuming that none of them would know what the Ute leader looked like, he passed himself off as an Indian who had rebelled against Walkara, taken the horses from him, and brought them back to their rightful owners. He maintained he was entitled to be compensated for his efforts and rewarded for his honesty. The Californians agreed, paid him for his trouble, and gave up the pursuit.

Walkara, born at the height of the tribe's horse culture, grew to manhood just as white fur trappers began to appear in Ute Country.

One of the first was Tom Smith, a wild young man from Kentucky who had come to New Mexico after running away from home and the drunken father who frequently beat him, once so severely that he was laid up for a week. Yet it was his schoolmaster rather than his father who finally drove him from home. The teacher, enraged at something Smith had done, demanded that he take off his coat to receive a beating. Instead, Smith grabbed a dogwood poker, slugged the schoolmaster "below the belt" and sent him reeling across the room. That night Smith ran away from home, then drifted through jobs as flatboatman on the Mississippi, farmer in Missouri, frontier hunter, and Indian trader among the Osage, until, finally, he reached Santa Fe.

Not long after arriving in New Mexico, Smith and a man named Maurice Le Duc drifted north to trap along the Green River. They were just two men in Indian country, and soon a band of Utes stole several of their horses. The two of them, or so Smith claimed, simply marched into the Ute village and demanded their horses back. Their courage so impressed the Indians that they returned the horses and allowed the white men to go on their way unmolested.

It was some years later, on another trapping expedition, that Smith received the name Wa-ke-to-co, "the man with one foot," from the Utes. The name came from an incident when he was with a band of trappers camped near the headwaters of the Platte. A shot fired from ambush hit Smith in the left leg, shattering both bones just above the ankle. As he took a step toward his rifle, which was leaning against a nearby tree, both bones stuck in the ground and he fell. He managed to reach the gun and fired in the direction from which the shot had come. For the next hour, the trappers fought a pitched battle, killing nine Indians and wounding several more. Some time during the battle, Smith tied a buckskin thong around his leg to control the bleeding. After the Indians were driven off, he asked his fellow trappers to cut off his foot. They refused, claiming they didn't know how.

Smith asked the camp cook for a butcher knife and with it cut through the torn muscles around the wound. All that held the foot on was the Achilles tendon, and Milton Sublette took the knife from Smith and cut through it. Sublette also wanted to sear the stump with a hot iron, but Smith refused and instead used buckskin thongs to tie off the arteries and stop the bleeding. Then he bound the wound in a dirty shirt and waited. Everybody expected him to bleed to death, but within twenty-four hours the bleeding had stopped, and after another day's rest in camp Smith was strong enough to travel in a litter swung between two horses.

Before long Smith noticed that one of the bones protruding from the stump was loose. Using a pair of bullet molds as forceps, he and Milton Sublette were able to extract it. A few days later, the party fell in with a band of Utes who knew Smith and, seeing that he was hurt, wanted to help. They began a healing ritual that opened with chanting and wailing. The women and children gathered around him, chewed roots into a paste and spit it on the wound. This remedy was repeated for several days, and either because of it or in spite of it Smith improved. Later, the other protruding bone fragment was removed, again with the bullet-mold forceps. One of the trappers also made a wooden leg for him, and he became known among the white men as "Peg-Leg" Smith.

He would continue to trap for several more years, but the difficulty of getting around on one foot, plus the decline of the fur trade, led him into a new business. Some time in the 1830's, using his long association with the Utes and forming a firm friendship with Walkara, he began to accompany the horse-stealing raids to California, where he soon became known as El Cojo—"the crippled"—Smith. Now, in 1840, he was ready to ride southwest once more.

Smith was not the only trapper to join Walkara and his band of Utes as they headed toward California. Phil Thompson, one of the owners of Fort Davy Crockett, also joined, as did several of those who hung around the fort. So, too, did old Bill Williams, who like Smith had arrived in Ute country soon after the New Mexican settlements were opened to Americans. By the late 1820s he was living more or less permanently among the Utes, and in the 1830s had joined one of the horse-stealing raids. Now, in 1840, he was ready for another trip to California. But he was fifty-three years old, and like many aging men, had the desire to pass his knowledge along to a younger man. As he set out on the raid, he was followed by a protégé, young Calvin Jones, who had recently run away from home and joined a wagon train. Somewhere he met Bill Williams who took him on as an unofficial trainee and now, just past his eighteenth birthday, he was on his way to California as an apprentice horsethief.

Still another trapper to join Walkara's party was Jean Baptiste

Chalifoux. Originally from French Canada, he had been brought as a child to St. Louis where he grew up among the French community in which most of the men were involved in the fur trade. He had gone west while still young and by now, approaching fifty, had spent twenty years trapping the mountains from the northern Rockies down into Mexico. He, too, had reached Ute country quite early and had known both Smith and Williams from the time, fifteen years before, when they had all trapped together under Ceran St. Vrain.

Chalifoux was more than just an ordinary fur trapper, and his presence with this band of raiders suggests they may have been interested in something more than simple horse stealing. In recent years he had spent time in California where, as the leader of a mixed band of French Canadians, Americans, Mexicans, and Indians, he had sometimes dabbled in California politics. When southern Californians rebelled against Alvarado they got in touch with Chalifoux who, sensing the opportunities of being on the winning side in a revolution, joined the cause. Before he could become actively involved, however, Alvarado put down the rebellion and Chalifoux and his men faded back into the mountains.

A few months later, when Juan Bandini began another revolution against the governor, he sent a man to invite Chalifoux to join the rebel forces. Chalifoux agreed, but before he and his men saw action, Bandini and Alvarado settled their differences and once again Chalifoux was denied the chance to fight. But this time he and his men did not disappear back into the mountains. They threatened their own revolution if they were not paid for their services under Bandini. Alvarado sent money but also ordered them to leave the territory immediately. Instead, in October, they stole some horses from the ranches around Santa Inez and a month later stole more from San Luis Obispo. They wintered in the San Joaquin Valley and the following spring rode east toward New Mexico with nearly 1,500 horses.

No more is known of Chalifoux in California until two years later when Mariano Vallejo, irritated by raids of frontier Indians, sent troops into the Sierras. It was a successful expedition, the troops retaking some horses, rescuing several women who had been kidnapped, and arresting fourteen thieves. Among them was "the notorious bandit Chief Califa." Not long after his arrest in late 1839, he was released—it is not clear by whom—and reached Ute Country in time to join the big band of horsethieves on their way to California.

Was it possible that there was more to this raid than stealing horses? Had Chalifoux, while in California, somehow worked out a plot with Isaac Graham? Was it possible, heretical as it might sound, that the raid was planned with his captor Vallejo as part of an elaborate, secret attempt to undercut Alvarado with whom the general had lately had so many differences? There is no conclusive evidence, but Chalifoux certainly was not reluctant to get involved in revolutions for he had done so twice in the past. There is also the undeniable fact that at exactly the time Alvarado claimed he had uncovered a foreign plot against his government there were, indeed, armed foreigners approaching California. And in the actions of the mulatto, Jim Beckworth, there is another piece of supporting evidence.

Beckworth had been in Ute country while the expedition was being organized but was sent ahead of the others into California. According to a story later told by an old fur trapper, Beckworth, while pretending to look over the possibilities of sea-otter hunting, spied out the land, and when Peg-Leg appeared in Cajon Pass, he was "ready at hand to consul, guide and assist him." The story implies that Beckworth had come to spy out horses, but if so he was a poor choice. He had spent little time in California, he was unfamiliar with the country, and such experienced thieves as Smith, Chalifoux, and Walkara hardly needed help in finding California's horse herds.

On the other hand, Beckworth was an ideal man to send as a spy to see what was happening among the Californians. He was little known in California, and posing as a neophyte sea-otter hunter, he would be free to visit places where foreigners congregated and listen to their stories and rumors. And if keeping track of the California political situation was his main task—or even if it wasn't—he could hardly have missed the big news of 1840 when the government began rounding up all foreigners. He certainly would have told the raiding party when they arrived in California—if it was a band of filibusterers coming to support a foreign takeover of California—that their cover was blown, that there would be no uprising, and that all that was left was to make this another expedition to steal horses.

VII

Whenever and however the members of the expedition reached their decision, by the time they came down out of Cajon Pass and into the populated valleys of southern California their sole purpose was to steal horses. And soon ranches and missions stretching from San Luis Obispo on the north to San Juan Capistrano in the south were aware of their presence.

The first alarm was heard at Santa Barbara in late April when officials received word from the north that more than a thousand horses had been stolen at San Luis Obispo. Not only that, but the thieves also got away with some of the best saddle horses in the area. These were stolen when a band of men—mountain legend claims they were Utes led by Walkara himself—one night slipped into a corral where the best stock was held, let down part of the rail fence, and ran them out. Others—and again legend says Peg-Leg Smith was there—tied up several servants and carried off saddles and various other horse trappings. People who encountered the thieves that night said they were bragging about even bigger crimes they planned to commit.

A few weeks later the administrator of San Gabriel Mission notified the alcalde in Los Angeles that three bands of tame mares had been stolen. Then word arrived of mission horses being taken from ranches near San Bernardino, from those near San Juan Capistrano, and from several others in the Los Angeles basin. The horsethieves had divided into separate bands and were collecting horses all up and down California.

The coming of the horsethieves from the east was nothing new in California, for during the past decade they had arrived each year almost like clockwork. And usually the ranchers had done little about the raids because their herds were so large they could afford to ignore the losses. Yet each year the raids grew worse and now, in 1840, several thousand horses had been run off, affecting virtually every ranch in the south. Their patience finally snapped, and there was a flurry of unexpected activity among the quiet, easygoing ranchers of southern California.

The day after the first reports reached Los Angeles, Ignacio Palomares, who owned a ranch near Cucamonga, left with twenty-three men to pursue the thieves. The following day, Felipe Lugo, Justice of the Peace in Los Angeles, sent a message to the mayordomos at all the ranches ordering them to provide men to reinforce Palomares. Anyone failing to respond, he warned, would be fined twenty pesos. The strategy worked, for within a day, a second band led by Juan Leandry also left for the east. A few days later Tiburcio Tapia, prefect of Los Angeles, who also owned a ranch east of town, decided to organize still a third group. Since by now virtually every able-bodied man had already been drafted, he even threw open the Los Angeles jail and ordered the prisoners to join the chase.

Originally the raiders had held most of the stolen horses in a canyon near Cajon Pass where they had amassed a herd of almost five thousand. There was no hope of lingering there, however, for if the horses were not pushed across the Mohave before summer came, it would be several months before such a large herd could be driven through the desert. Therefore in mid-May, only days after the big raids, they began to drive the horses up the pass and into the Mohave. Right behind them came the California pursuit parties.

The first Californians into the desert were those in the hastily organized band led by Ignacio Palomares. They were easily defeated, however, their horses were taken, and they were left to walk back to San Bernardino. Palomares filed a report which, despite its wordiness, was very vague as to exactly what had happened. It only indicated that the Californians were barely into the desert when they met and fought a heroic battle with the horsethieves in which one white man and one Indian were killed. The report differed radically from another version of these same events told in later years by Calvin Jones, the eighteen-year-old follower of Bill Williams.

According to Jones, the raiders were aware that they were being followed, and they kept a close eye on their pursuers. When evening came the Californians went into camp, and Williams, looking back from a height of land, noticed they had not posted any guards. During the night he and Jones sneaked back to the camp and stampeded all the horses. The next morning they went into the Mexican camp and offered to round up the horses if they would turn over all the best animals and give up the pursuit. Palomares, having no real choice, agreed and even went so far as to give Jones his own horse, complete with saddle and extra provisions.

The thieves still were not quite free of pursuit. When Juan Leandry, who was hurrying to reinforce Palomares, heard that he had been defeated, he stopped in Cajon Pass and waited for another, larger, party that was on its way from Los Angeles. Two days later this band, led by Jose Carrillo, arrived and the combined forces numbered eighty men. It was a formidable group, but as was common in California at the time, the men were poorly armed, having only forty-nine rifles plus a few pistols that were usable only at a range of a few yards. The rest would have to rely on swords, spears, and sabers in the unlikely event that they got close enough to engage in hand-to-hand combat. Not only was there a lack of rifles but they had few cartridges, less than ten rounds per gun, and Carrillo decided to wait for a supply of ammunition from Los Angeles before continuing.

When the ammunition arrived, Carrillo and his band of pursuers rode into the desert after the thieves. Tracks revealed that the trappers were heading north driving a herd of at least three thousand horses. The pursuers rode hard and by the following morning reached Bitter Springs, where they stripped down the expedition, leaving all their baggage and extra horses, and hurried on the trail. Eventually they caught a glimpse of one of the raiders, a man who had been left behind as a lookout, and they chased him as far as some nearby mountains, but there he escaped. About four in the afternoon dust clouds off in the distance told them the horses had been divided into several herds.

The pursuit continued on through the night, and late the following day at Resting Spring, the pursuers surprised a camp of about twenty-five men who formed a rear guard of the raiding party. As the Californians rode in, or so Juan Leandry claimed, the thieves bolted, fleeing in such disarray that they abandoned everything—saddles, clothes, even cooking utensils. Leandry also said that he found in the pocket of a coat a list of names showing that the thieves were all citizens of the United States. By now, he added, the Californians' pursuit had forced the thieves to push the stolen horses so hard that the trail was littered with bodies of animals that had given out.

The Californians' horses were also worn out and Carrillo was forced to give up the chase. They turned back to Los Angeles having had no success in recapturing any of the stolen horses. Still, according to Leandry, they had won a victory of sorts. The rapid pursuit had forced the thieves to drive the horses at full speed through the desert without stopping for water. At Bitter Springs, not even the midway point in crossing the Mohave, they had already lost at least half the herd, and Leandry thought it unlikely that many of the others would survive the drive to the Ute villages or the New Mexican settlements. At least, he said, the robbers had gained little from the raid.

Whether or not he was right depends entirely on which version you listen to, for mountain legends ascribe several different fates to this band of horses. According to one they were driven to Fort Bridger where they were sold at good profit. Another claims they were sold at Santa Fe, while another insists it was Bent's Fort. One man said that the following year he saw at least some of the horses as far east as the Big Blue River in Kansas. There he met Phil Thompson who was driving the horses and who told how he had been among those who had gone to California to steal them. He added that "in passing the cheerless desert, between the Sierra Nevada and Colorado, the heat, dust, and thirst were so intolerably oppressive, that full one half of their animals died. The remainder however, were brought to rendezvous and variously disposed of, to suit the wants and wishes of their captors."

According to all these versions at least some of the horses survived and were sold at a profit. Others claimed that the raiders gained nothing, for either the desert killed all the horses, or they were run off by various Indians as the trappers passed through their country on the way east. Finally, there is one last story about Bill Williams which claims that most, but not all, the horses died. It ends by saying that "Bill turned his surviving share into Bent's corral and settled for a barrel of whiskey."

CIVILIZATION

I

In late 1840, as fall turned into winter along the lower reaches of the Missouri River, the young schoolteacher John Bidwell met a trapper who claimed he had once been to California. Bidwell, newly arrived from the east, never quite got it straight who he was, calling him only "a Frenchman named Roubidoux." To those who knew the west he was the trapper Antoine Robidoux, one of six brothers whose family had been involved in the fur trade from the earliest days of Missouri. The eldest brother, Joseph, ran the family business on the Missouri while several of the younger brothers, including Antoine, helped open trade with Santa Fe, then trapped west from New Mexico, eventually going all the way to California. But like everyone else, by 1840 they found the fur business all but dead and came east to see their brother Joseph at his trading post on the Missouri River just a few miles above the town where John Bidwell taught school.

Robidoux described California in such glowing terms that the young schoolmaster was "resolved to see that wonderful land." He organized a meeting at Weston, Missouri, and invited Robidoux to address the assembled crowd. Anyone who expected the old mountain man to be tongue-tied in talking to such a group had forgotten that he had spent years among trappers who loved to spin yarns around their evening campfires. Quickly he captivated his listeners with his description of California as a land of eternal spring, boundless fertility, and a place filled with huge herds of cattle and wild horses. There were even oranges that could be picked right off the tree.

When the audience was given a chance to ask questions Robidoux handled them effortlessly. The authorities, he said, were friendly, and the people were so hospitable that a man could travel all over California and never pay for food, lodging, or horses. Even the Indians were friendly, he said. Someone then asked if there was any fever or ague there. "I remember his answer distinctly," Bidwell said. "He said there was but one man in California that ever had a chill there, and it was a matter of so much wonderment to the people of Monterey that they went eighteen miles into the country to see him shake."

The meeting was a resounding success, and it came at just the right moment in the life of John Bidwell. The previous year he had left his family home in Ohio and come to Platte County, Missouri, where the rapid growth in population made it relatively easy to find a job teaching in a country school. That provided him with an immediate income, and in the confused land system he discovered some long-range possibilities. Many of the settlers had staked out their farms and built their homes before surveying teams arrived in the area. Now, the surveyors had begun to lay down official boundary lines which did not coincide with the haphazard approach of the Missouri settlers. Sometimes the lines ran through a man's barn, other times they split his home right down the middle. Many were willing to sell cheaply rather than involve themselves in all the confusion and legal hassle necessary to maintain their claim. Bidwell took advantage of this situation and "by paying a small amount for a little piece of fence here and a small clearing there, I got a claim, and proposed to make it my home."

He was new to the tangled world of western land claims, however, and he soon found that his hope of maintaining ownership was thoroughly naive. While he was gone on a trip to obtain supplies, a man took advantage of his absence to jump his claim. Public opinion was against the claim jumper, and some influential men tried to get the man at least to divide the claim and give Bidwell eighty acres. He refused, and there was nothing anyone could do, for technically the law was on his side. The law said that to claim land a man must be either twenty-one or a family man and at the time Bidwell was neither. It also said that a man must reside on his claim and Bidwell, although he had made some improvements, had never actually lived on it. More to the point, possibly, was the fact that the claim jumper was known as a bully who, supposedly, had killed a man in Calloway County. Everyone was afraid of him. Bidwell could find little support, and he gave up. It was soon after this that Bidwell met Robidoux and invited him to the meeting where he spoke so glowingly of the wonders of California.

After the success of the meeting Bidwell, like the schoolteacher he was, formed a committee to investigate the possibilities of migrating west. Out of this grew the Western Emigration Society which through the following winter corresponded with interested people all over Missouri and even as far east as Kentucky and as far south as Arkansas. Soon they had the names of at least five hundred people interested in going to California.

It is impossible to say how many of these were serious and how many were only mildly curious, but a letter published in a Missouri newspaper caused almost everyone to lose interest overnight. The letter, written by Thomas Jefferson Farnham, had originally appeared in a New York newspaper after his return from California in early 1841. Farnham, who had been in Monterey soon after the arrest of Graham and the roundup of other foreigners, gave an almost hysterical account of the way foreigners were being mistreated by Californians and concluded that it was dangerous for Americans to go there. Missouri merchants, who had long worried about the exodus of so many people, saw to it that the letter was reprinted in newspapers all over the state. Those who had promised to go rapidly changed their minds until Bidwell was the only one left. "Indeed," he said, "the man who was going with me and who was to furnish the horses, backed out and there I was with my wagon."

He did get one break, however, with the arrival of George Henshaw from Illinois. His appearance at Weston, Bidwell said, was "almost providential," for he came at the last possible moment before Bidwell, still with no animal to pull his wagon, had to start for the rendezvous point at Sapling Grove, Kansas. Henshaw had only ten or fifteen dollars in his pocket, but he was riding a fine black horse. Bidwell convinced him to trade the horse for two oxen to pull the wagon and a one-eyed mule to ride. With that they set out, joined by one other wagon and four or five people. It was a rather sad caravan compared to the huge migration that Bidwell had once imagined.

Yet if the people of Weston were too frightened to go west themselves, they had not lost interest in the project. At least half the town turned out to see them off and follow them down the road for a mile or so. Some even went along for four or five miles before they turned back to their homes in the small Missouri town.

Bidwell with his small party reached Sapling Grove in early May only to find just one other wagon waiting for them. During the next several days more wagons straggled in until a party of sixty-nine men, women, and children had gathered, ready to take the trail to California. It was not a very prosperous band of migrants, for although they had the necessary supplies and teams of oxen, mules, or horses to pull the wagons, there were no dairy cattle and, according to Bidwell, it was doubtful that one hundred dollars in cash could be found among the entire party. Still, "all were enthusiastic and anxious to go."

Before taking to the trail, those in the caravan felt a need for some kind of organization and a meeting was held to elect a leader of the wagon train. John Bartleson, who was not particularly qualified for the job, was elected because he said if he wasn't chosen captain he wouldn't go. Since he had seven or eight men with him, and since the party was already small, his platform impressed the voters and he was elected.

II

The caravan was almost ready to leave when a late arrival brought news that a company of Catholic missionaries, on their way to the Flathead Indians, would arrive in another day or so. If the assembled migrants would wait, they could travel with the missionaries and their guide, an old Rocky Mountain fur trapper. At first there was opposition from some who objected to waiting for a slow-moving band of missionaries. But no one in the wagon train at Sapling Grove had the faintest idea of how to get to California. Bidwell said, "we sobered down and waited for them to come up; and it was well we did, for otherwise probably not one of us would ever have reached California because of our inexperience."

The fur trapper who led the party of missionaries into camp the next day was Thomas Fitzpatrick, who had been with Jed Smith when he first crossed South Pass and reached Green River. Since then he had done a good deal of trapping in Indian country, and on several occasions had led supply caravans west from St. Louis to the rendezvous. All that had ended in 1840, and now, a year later, at the age of forty-two, he was leading a group of missionaries and, accidentally, the first band of emigrants along the trail. These emigrants—

schoolteachers, farmers, merchants—had little experience in the kinds of things they would encounter and the advantages of having a guide like Fitzpatrick soon became evident. Not only did he guide them but, as Bidwell pointed out, "when we came in contact with Indians, our people were so easily excited that if we had not had with us an old mountaineer the result would certainly have been disastrous."

The first Indian scare came just two weeks after they set out and before they had even reached the Platte River. Nicolas Dawson, a young man who had gone out hunting alone, suddenly came rushing into camp without his mule, his rifle, his pistol, and without most of his clothes. Excitedly he described how he had been surrounded by thousands of Indians and robbed of all his belongings. The tale frightened the emigrants and despite Fitzpatrick's attempt to keep them calm, every man whipped up his mules, or horses, or oxen, into a full gallop. Fitzpatrick raced ahead of the wagons and when they reached a stream that momentarily stopped the stampede, he forced them to form a hollow square instead of continuing to run pell-mell across the prairie.

When the Indians appeared they turned out to be a band of Cheyenne which contained, not thousands of warriors, but just forty men. And as the emigrants watched they came up and went into camp within a hundred yards of the barricaded wagon train. Undoubtedly there were excited emigrants who wanted to open fire immediately, but Fitzpatrick pointed out that if the Indians were hostile they would not have come in as they had. He and another hunter went to talk to them.

They were soon back with Dawson's mule, his rifle, and the story of what had happened to him. The Cheyenne said that they had no intention of hurting him or taking his mule or rifle when they met him on the plains. In fact, they said, they made all the necessary signs that they were friendly, but he had become so excited that they had to disarm him so that he would not shoot them. They were perfectly willing to return the mule and the rifle, but they had no idea what had happened to his pistol or his clothes which, they claimed, he had torn off himself. With that the story ended except in the minds of those who knew the young man and ever after called him "Cheyenne" Dawson.

A week or two later another, more serious incident involved George Shotwell who had come from St. Louis to join the party. While breaking camp at the forks of the Platte one morning, he pulled his rifle out of the wagon muzzle first and it accidentally fired. He was shot near the heart and, according to Bidwell, "lived about an hour and died in full possession of his senses."

Beyond these events little happened as the caravan followed the Platte to its forks, then ascended the northern branch past Chimney Rock and Scott's Bluff until, in late July, it reached Fort Laramie. From there it continued on west, crossing the North Platte at a place where the river ran swiftly and where, during the difficult crossing, a wagon was upset and a mule swept away and drowned. By now flour and sugar barrels were almost empty and there was nothing to do but live off the country. The travelers stopped for several days to hunt, but they had waited too long and were on the western edge of buffalo country where the herds had thinned out. Eventually they were able to kill enough buffalo and dry enough meat, and they continued on, crossing South Pass on July 18 and reaching the Green River five days later.

It was the same river that had been wild and untouched by white men when Jed Smith reached it seventeen years before. Now it was trapped out, the last rendezvous was already a year in the past, and a band of emigrants in their covered wagons was camped on the river itself. While there they met, symbolic of this changed world, a band of fur trappers with whom they spent a day in camp. They did a little trading, mostly the emigrants' alcohol for the trappers' dressed hides, buckskin clothes, and moccasins. They also did some talking, particularly about the route ahead, and the trappers agreed it would be impossible to take wagons to California. Hearing that, several men turned around and headed back to Missouri.

The rest continued on and a few weeks later at Soda Springs they too reached a parting of the ways. On the morning of August 11, after traveling six miles, they came to a point where the trail divided and the missionaries with Fitzpatrick as their guide turned toward Oregon. Several members of the remaining party, realizing they would have to find their way to California without a guide, decided they too would do better to go to Oregon. Thirty-three emigrants, however, including the schoolteacher John Bidwell, were adamant that they were going to California whatever the difficulties.

III

In California, at almost exactly the same moment, the U.S.S. *Vincennes* entered San Francisco Bay and dropped anchor off Yerba Buena. It was the first of several vessels of the United States Exploring Expedition which had spent the past three years in the Pacific under the command of Captain Charles Wilkes. It had reached the northwest coast in the spring of 1841, and from there Wilkes had sent the *Vincennes* on to California. Several weeks later Wilkes himself arrived in San Francisco with the rest of the fleet—the *Porpoise,* the *Flying Fish,* and the *Oregon.*

This expedition had been authorized by Congress after years of pressure by various interest groups. There were the mercantile interests—the whalers, sealers, fur traders, cattle-hide traders—who had opened much of the Pacific on their own and who now wanted the United States Government to enter the Pacific officially. There were also those who thought that United States prestige demanded that it enter the ranks of scientific exploration alongside the Englishmen Cook and Vancouver, the Frenchman La Perouse, and the Russian Kotzebue.

For years Congress ignored these requests, but when John Quincy Adams became President he used his authority as Commander-in-Chief to send the U.S.S. *Peacock,* commanded by Thomas ap Catsby Jones, on a tour of the Pacific. Jones' tour was not a scientific expedition but only a single naval vessel showing the American flag in the Pacific. Soon after it returned home United States officials began to read reports of an English expedition to Antarctica, a French expedition into the South Pacific, and a British ship, the *Beagle,* which was also making scientific observations in the Pacific. The United States must do something if it did not want to fall far behind the European powers in scientific exploration. Congress appropriated $15,000 for such an expedition and also allowed the use of an equal amount of naval stores for the purpose.

Thomas Jones, promoted from Commander to Captain, was assigned the task of organizing the expedition and leading it into the Pacific. At first preparations went smoothly as Jones gathered a fleet consisting of a frigate, two barques, a schooner, and a storeship. He also wrote to various learned societies asking what they would like the expedition to accomplish, and dispatched a naval officer to Europe to buy the necessary scientific instruments. It all took time, and in December 1836, when the Secretary of the Navy made his annual report to Congress, he had to admit that the expedition was not yet ready to go. Congress, which had taken more than twenty-five years to pass a bill authorizing the expedition, indicated its irritation at the length of time it was taking to get organized.

New troubles arose to create further delays. It was difficult to staff the ships, for Captain Jones was not a popular officer and the list of those who refused to serve under him reached eight lieutenants, three surgeons, two pursers, and a midshipman. Jones, on the other hand, objected to several qualified officers assigned to the expedition and demanded their removal. Eventually, however, all the officer berths were filled and the fleet went on a brief shakedown cruise. A new problem arose. Captain Jones claimed that all the ships behaved beautifully but the commander of one of the small ships said it was a poor sailor and not fit to be part of the expedition. A major controversy ensued which was settled only when a specially convened Navy Board inspected the fleet and reported that, although better vessels might have been selected, Jones' ships, with some minor repairs, were capable of carrying out their assigned task.

In November of 1837 Jones was at last given his sailing instructions. Instead of hoisting sail, however, he responded with a whole new set of objections. He did not like the personnel recently assigned to the fleet; he was unhappy with the date on which he had been ordered to sail; he even objected to the specific wording of certain portions of the order. It all made him ill, he said, and therefore he was going to resign because of poor health. Attempts to dissuade him were unsuccessful and the Secretary of the Navy came to the conclusion that Jones was seeking an excuse to leave the expedition. The Secretary wrote, "I do not believe that for a year past he has intended to go out on this expedition. His failure, however, will make infinite confusion, as no one will take the command in such vessels as he has had constructed, or such arrangements as he has made."

It was an accurate prediction. The command was offered to several naval officers, all of whom declined. Finally President Van Buren, anxious to see the expedition sail, took it out of the hands of the naval secretary and turned it over to Joel R. Poinsett, Secretary of War. Poinsett reorganized the expedition, trimmed the size of the scientific corps, and replaced some of the old, lumbering vessels with smaller, faster ships. Then, after several officers refused, he gave command of the entire expedition to the junior lieutenant Charles Wilkes, an accomplished scientist. Finally in August 1838, more than two years after Congress had authorized it, the expedition sailed from Norfolk, Virginia.

By early 1839 the ships had rounded Cape Horn and entered the Pacific Ocean where they spent the next three years. Much of the time they followed the track of Captain Cook's voyages now almost three quarters of a century in the past. They visited Tahiti, Australia, sailed far enough south to enter the ice fields of Antarctica, then turned north to Hawaii and finally to the northwest coast of America. By the time the expedition reached San Francisco Bay in late 1841, it was nearing the end of its assigned task.

Possibly it was a combination of weariness, the desire to go home, and the knowledge that most of the area had already been explored that led Captain Charles Wilkes to write a report that was sketchy and often contemptuous of California. Upon entering the bay, Wilkes had brought his ship up to Yerba Buena, which he found to be singularly unimpressive, consisting of only a few buildings—a store, a warehouse, a blacksmith shop, a combination billiard parlor and bar, and the poop cabin of an old ship that was now serving as a residence. Wilkes had also disliked the people and was very cold and reserved to the few who were allowed to meet him. An American in Yerba Buena at the time found him to be "rather severe and forbidding in aspect, not genial and companionable and not popular with his officers."

One man who was often invited aboard the Wilkes flagship, however, was Nathan Spear, the Yerba Buena storekeeper who was providing the expedition with supplies for the trip home. Spear first entered the Pacific at the age of seventeen more than twenty years before. Then, after two more trips, he settled in Monterey where he traded for several years before moving to San Francisco. Because he could swap stories about the various islands of the Pacific and also provide information about California, he was one of the few men that Wilkes welcomed aboard.

Undoubtedly it was Spear who provided him with the material for the historical part of his report in which he summarized events in California since Mexico took over in 1822. Although his raw material was reasonably accurate, he distorted much of it by his lack of any deep understanding and by relying mainly on his ear which led him into frequent misspellings—Captain Noningo; Governor Echandia; San Juan Capista; Zonoma; and many more. Mostly, the report consisted of secondhand, hearsay evidence, and his account of the Graham affair was obviously a sensationalized version told by someone who considered Graham a "resolute, strong, and brave man."

Wilkes had an opportunity to meet one of the characters from California history in the person of Mariano Vallejo. The commandante general, accompanied by his brother Salvador, visited the *Vincennes* and was welcomed aboard with a salute and with all the naval courtesies due a person of his rank. Wilkes revealed his true feelings when he described Vallejo as having absolute control of San Francisco Bay, and added, "he is not over-scrupulous in demanding duties of the vessels entering the port of San Francisco; and until he has been seen and consulted, a vessel trading here is liable to an indefinite amount of duties. A portion of the payment adds to his wealth, and how much goes to the government is not known; enough I was told, in some cases, to save appearances, and no more." Wilkes cites no evidence although quite likely this view of Vallejo came from his many conversations with the storekeeper Nathan Spear.

Later Wilkes and some of his officers went north to "Zonoma" where they visited the home of General Vallejo. The general told some stories that Wilkes thought showed "a striking disregard for the lives, as well as the property and liberty of the Indians and *gente de razon.*" Wilkes also claimed that many Californians valued Indians' lives no more than that of wild cattle and added, "the commandant-general is frequently said to hunt them, and by his prowess in these expeditions he has gained some reputation."

Although Vallejo's own stories may have helped form Wilkes' opinion, more likely he was adapting something he heard from Nathan Spear. In the summer of 1841, not long before Wilkes reached California, Salvador—not Mariano—Vallejo had led a punitive expedition to Clear Lake where he attacked several Indian villages. When word reached Yerba Buena its residents were horrified. A young American said, "I remember that Spear spoke of it as nothing but butchery for which there was no justification, and the officers of Wilkes' expedition regarded it in the same light."

After Wilkes and his officers returned from Sonoma the four ships of the exploratory fleet raised anchor and sailed for home. Three days later, on November 4, 1841, John Bidwell and the rest of the caravan from Missouri straggled in to John Marsh's ranch in the shadow of Mt. Diablo, about thirty miles due east of San Francisco Bay.

IV

When the emigrant caravan reached Soda Springs the previous August, its members had been faced with a difficult decision. Originally their destination had been California, but now the missionaries were going to Oregon taking the guide, Thomas Fitzpatrick, with them. Those who wanted a guide would have to go to Oregon, those who wanted to go to California would have to do so without a guide. After some soul-searching, the caravan divided almost equally between the two destinations.

One of those who chose California was John Bidwell who wrote, "we were now thrown entirely upon our own resources. All the country beyond was a veritable *terra incognita,* and we only knew that California lay to the west." Even Fitzpatrick, in all his travels, had never been to California and could give them only the vaguest idea of which way to go. They decided to send four men to Fort Hall to obtain information about the trail ahead.

What these men found out was not particularly encouraging. They were told that those trying to get to California should go southwest to the Great Salt Lake, then strike more or less west until somewhere in the desert they would find a river sometimes called Mary's River, sometimes Ogden's River, and they could follow it much of the way to California. If, in striking west from the lake, they drifted too far north they would get into broken country filled with deep canyons in which they would wander around and eventually die. If they went too far south they would enter a desert region in which all the animals would die for lack of grass and water.

For the next month the California contingent traveled southwest through the dry, barren country north of Salt Lake. Once, after a long, tiring stretch without water, they were forced to stop for several days to rest and to allow the overworked oxen to recover. Two men were sent ahead to search for the river they were to follow, but when they did not return after several days, the rest of the party began slowly moving west again. Eventually the two men rejoined them, saying they had found what they thought was Ogden's River, but they had reached it only by crossing a mountain range over which it would be impossible to take the wagons. The only thing to do, they said, was to circle the mountains instead.

The next several days were spent pushing the wagons south along the eastern base of the mountains, then through a pass, then north again along the other side of the mountains. Finally, on September 15, they gave up and abandoned the wagons, which were almost empty anyway, and what few goods and supplies remained could be packed on the animals which, free of the wagons, could travel much more rapidly. Besides, they were running out of food and without the wagons they would be free to eat the oxen and even the horses and mules.

The decision was no sooner made than another problem arose. No one knew anything about packing. Earlier, when they had camped with a band of fur trappers they had seen the type of pack saddles they used. Now, using their memories, they tried to recreate them. It did not work very well, for according to Bidwell, "the difficulties we had at first were simply indescribable." He continued: "The trouble began the very first day. But we started—most of us on foot, for nearly all the animals, including several of the oxen, had to carry packs. It was but a few minutes before the packs began to turn; horses became scared, mules kicked, oxen jumped and bellowed, and articles were scattered in all directions." Eventually, by trial and error, they improved their packing technique, although through the rest of the trip packs often fell off and had to be replaced.

Even with the problems with packs, the stripped-down caravan moved more rapidly as it reached the south fork of the Humboldt, descended it to the main branch, then followed the river to the southwest until it sank into the desert. Somehow they missed the Truckee River Valley, filled with fresh water and grass, and traveled southwest across the desert until they came to the West Walker River which they followed into the Sierras. After crossing the divide near Sonora Pass, then began to descend the difficult, almost impassable, canyon of the Stanislaus River.

It was as they descended the Stanislaus that John Bidwell had an experience he would later remember with much more interest than he felt at the time. It was about dark when he came to a fallen tree and, trying to get around it at its head, found the way blocked by brush. Going around the other end, he found that the tree trunk was immense, towering at least twenty feet above his head. At the time he was too concerned with the difficulties of travel to think much of it, but in later years he went back to the Calaveras Grove of the Sequoias, identified it, to his own satisfaction at least, as the same place, and laid claim to having been "the first white man who ever saw *sequoia gigantea.*"

By now they were almost to the .edge of the San Joaquin Valley, although, according to Bidwell, "we did not even know we were in California." They thought they still had a long way to go, particularly when one day they looked ahead and saw in the far distance a range of mountains. The sight virtually destroyed hope, for they assumed they would have to travel through mountain country until they passed beyond that distant range. Then everything changed. They had been looking at the Coast Range from a perspective that blocked off a view of the San Joaquin Valley, and suddenly the canyon opened up and they saw the valley just below them. There they found an Indian who, from what they could understand, knew a Dr. Marsh and offered to guide them to his ranch. Two days later, on November 4, they arrived at the first settlement they had seen since reaching California.

Arrival of the emigrants at Marsh's ranch caused a wave of fear to sweep through California. They had arrived in an almost desperate condition, without wagons and having abandoned much of their equipment and lost or eaten most of their pack animals. Yet somehow rumors in California had transformed this group of ragged emigrants into a large, well-armed band of invaders coming to start a revolution. When some of the emigrants approached San Jose, they were met by a band of soldiers led by an officer who arrested them and escorted them to the town jail. Since they understood little Spanish, they could not get an explanation, but they were treated well and finally given to understand that their arrest was only a formality.

Mariano Vallejo was at Mission San Jose at the time, and the responsibility for making an immediate decision fell upon him. He had the prisoners brought to the mission where they were only loosely confined and he sent a messenger to Dr. Marsh asking him to come to San Jose to explain the intentions of these foreigners. After listening to Marsh, and after giving the matter considerable thought, Vallejo granted the emigrants temporary passes until they could take the necessary steps to legalize their residence in California.

Once that was accomplished the newcomers scattered throughout California, some taking up farm land, others entering business. The young schoolteacher John Bidwell moved north to New Helvetia where he went to work for Johann Sutter. Then, when Sutter purchased Fort Ross from the Russians, he sent Bidwell to supervise the dismantling of the fort and the transportation of its equipment to Sutter's Fort. It was a job that would keep Bidwell busy most of 1842.

V

It was also in 1842 that Captain Thomas Jones returned to the Pacific. By then it had been four years since he resigned his command and, pleading illness, had gone to live on his plantation in Virginia. Once the impending expedition sailed, however, and there was no further danger of his being reassigned to it, his health improved and he asked to be returned to active duty. His requests were ignored until Abel Upshur, a fellow Virginian, became Secretary of the Navy in 1841. He appointed Jones commander of the Pacific Squadron and in January 1842 the U.S.S. *United States,* flying the pennant of the new commander, sailed from Norfolk, Virginia, bound for the Pacific Ocean.

Upshur, in the orders he gave Jones upon sailing, specifically instructed him to protect American commerce in the Pacific and added that the weakness of local governments and their irresponsibility made it likely that he would have to visit west coast ports occasionally to protect American citizens. He did not name any specific enemies but certainly Jones was familiar enough with the problems of the Pacific to have no trouble identifying them.

There was Mexico, which blamed the United States for the loss of Texas to which it was not at all resigned. The arrest and expulsion of foreigners from California, and some of the highly sensational accounts that had appeared in the United States had created considerable animosity toward Mexico. It seemed entirely possible that at any moment the United States and Mexico might go to war which, many thought, would play directly into the hands of the British. Great Britain was involved in a serious argument with the United States over Oregon, and many Americans thought Britain had undue interest in both Texas and California and was waiting for an excuse, like the outbreak of war, to seize them.

It was this attitude that caused Jones, a few months after his arrival in the Pacific, to become very suspicious of British naval activities. The American squadron was at anchor in Callao when the British ship *Dublin,* carrying Rear Admiral Richard Thomas, entered the harbor. Soon afterward two British warships that were anchored there slipped out to sea under sealed orders. A few days later Captain Jones, while attending a funeral at the British consulate, heard that Admiral Thomas in the *Dublin* would soon put to sea on a highly secret mission. Then a trading vessel arrived from Mexico with dispatches for the admiral who, after reading them, immediately sailed in the *Dublin* for an unknown destination.

Captain Jones, his suspicions thoroughly aroused, also received dispatches from the same ship which, when he read them, heightened his fear. Among them was a newspaper article claiming that Mexico had sold California to Great Britain for seven million dollars. Several documents concerned trouble between the United States and Mexico and a cover letter from the U.S. Consul at Mazatlan said, "It is highly probable there will be a war between the two countries." By the time Jones received them, however, the reports were already several months old and since then, there had been nothing but silence. But then several British ships had sailed from Callao for a secret destination. Putting it all together, Jones concluded that war had broken out between Mexico and the United States and the British fleet had sailed north to take possession of California.

Jones called a full meeting of squadron captains and laid the dispatches before them. After listening to Jones they concurred with his assessment and agreed he should try to anticipate the British by seizing California. On September 8, the *United States,* the *Cyane,* and the *Dale* put to sea, the first two bound for California, the third headed for Panama with messages for the Secretary of the Navy in Washington.

As they sailed north, one hundred men picked from the ships' companies were given muskets and each day they practiced firing at a bottle hung from the foretopmast until they became accomplished marksmen. The gun crews also practiced firing at a floating target made of two empty whiskey barrels lashed together with a flag flying between. All this gave rise to sensational rumors among the men, until the captain called the crew aft to explain both their destination and their purpose.

By mid-October the two ships were nearing Monterey and the men were given more explicit instructions in an order outlining the conduct of those who would go ashore. No one was to insult or offend any of the inhabitants, there was to be no plundering, and the men were not even to enter a house under any pretense without express orders from an officer. Captain Jones said, "during the battle and strife, every man must do his utmost to take and destroy but when the flag is struck, all hostility must cease, and even become the *protectors* of all, and not the oppressers of any."

At dawn the next morning they rounded Point Pinos and entered Monterey Bay. Much to Jones' relief, there was no sign of Admiral Thomas or the British fleet, but only a small Mexican vessel that was trying to leave the harbor. Jones, thinking that an American ship might be fired on, raised the British flag, then sent a boat to board the small bark, which proved to be the *Joven Guipzucoana.* Its commander was Joseph Snook, an Englishman, who when taken before Captain Jones said he was totally unaware of any war between the United States and Mexico. Further questions, however, showed that he had been out of touch with the world and had heard no news from Mexico since May. Clearly, he was not in a position to know, and his statement that there was no war was discounted. Jones took his ships, now flying the American flag, and pushed in close to the presidio—"a dilapidated work mounting eleven guns." Then he waited.

Eventually a boat flying the Mexican flag and carrying two officers approached the flagship. Representatives came aboard, but were so frightened that they were almost incoherent, and it was impossible to obtain any information other than that they too claimed to be ignorant of any war. Their nervousness made Jones even more suspicious, and he sent for one of the officers of the merchant ship *Fama* which was in the harbor at Monterey flying an American flag. The mate came aboard and said that his ship had recently been in Hawaii and although he heard nothing specific about war, there had been rumors that Great Britain did, indeed, plan to take over California. That stiffened Jones' resolve, as did the activities on shore where horsemen could be seen gathering while others ran back and forth with messages as they apparently prepared to defend the capital.

"The time for *action* has now arrived," Jones said, and at four o'clock on the afternoon of October 19, Captain James Armstrong was sent ashore under a flag of truce to demand that Monterey be surrendered to the United States. He presented his ultimatum to Governor Juan Bautista Alvarado who was given until nine o'clock the following morning to respond. Alvarado was placed in a strange position for officially, at least, he was no longer governor. Earlier in 1842 Manuel Micheltorena, a Mexican army officer, had been appointed to succeed him. Micheltorena had arrived in southern California in September, but he had remained in Los Angeles and had not yet come to Monterey for the official transfer of power. Surely Alvarado would have liked to turn this mess over to him, but communications being what they were, there was nothing to do but handle it himself.

Alvarado went through the motions of determining whether Monterey could be defended. At six that evening he formally asked the presidio commander, Captain Mariano Silva, to report on the condition of the fortifications. Silva also observed the proper formalities by waiting a full hour before reporting back that they "were of no consequence as everybody knows." After that, a meeting of leading Monterey citizens determined that resistance was impossible and about midnight an envoy was sent aboard the *United States* to arrange the final terms of surrender.

At 7:30 on the morning of October 20, Mexican officials came to sign the surrender documents. A few hours later 150 men from the American fleet landed and marched into Monterey. The Mexican flag was hauled down and the American flag was raised while the assembled Americans on shore gave three cheers and the musicians played "Yankee Doodle." In response, the *United States'* and *Cyane*'s crews, watching from the rigging, returned the cheers while the band played the "Star-Spangled Banner." Governor—or ex-governor—Juan Bautista Alvarado saw none of this, for he had already retired to his rancho in the country. So, too, had many other Californians, for by early evening a resident of Monterey reported, "All is tranquil; and the town is almost deserted, for many of the officials have fled to the country."

It was a strange little war and it was soon over. The next day Captain Jones, who throughout the preliminaries had remained aboard the *United States,* now came ashore in person to inspect the fortifications. Thomas Larkin, who served as interpreter during the negotiations, had always doubted there was any war and he repeated these doubts when Jones landed. Two American officers, sent to look through the papers of various Mexican officials, reported that they had found documents dated as recently as late August. The papers proved that the rumor of war, as well as the rumor that California had been ceded to Great Britain, was false. The war was over.

At 3:45 that afternoon Jones, after consulting with his senior officers, issued orders to lower the American flag flying over Monterey. The Mexican flag was again raised, the American warships in the harbor honoring it with a thirteen-gun salute. The troops were reembarked, and the Mexican vessels that had been seized, including the *Joven Guipzucoana,* were returned to their captains. All of it—the invasion, the surrender, the reversal, the retreat—had been carried on in a most civilized manner. And when it was over, Captain Jones concluded that "notwithstanding what has happened since our arrival here, no incident has occurred to interrupt for a single moment the most friendly intercourse between the inhabitants of the town and the officers of the squadron."

Captain Jones, despite whatever embarrassment he felt, remained in California for more than a month, partly to make sure there were no retaliations against Americans because of his recent blunder and partly to investigate the damage done to Americans who had been arrested in 1840. He invited Isaac Graham aboard the flagship to present their claims, but beyond collecting statements and forwarding them to the Secretary of State in Washington, he accomplished little.

After six weeks in Monterey the American ships sailed north to San Francisco Bay. While there Captain Jones sent a message to General Vallejo indicating a desire to visit him. Vallejo promptly replied that he would be honored to have such a distinguished guest and included instructions on how to reach Sonoma. He sent soldiers and servants with horses to the Sonoma Creek landing to meet the captain and his party. The American officers never arrived, however, for somehow they got lost and precipitated an event that was a fitting end to this splendidly ludicrous little war.

Jones and his fellow officers, coming up the bay in a boat, failed to recognize Sonoma Creek and landed at Huichica Creek instead. Late in the afternoon, making their way overland toward Sonoma, they encountered a squad of soldiers who apparently had not been told of any distinguished visitors, for they promptly took them prisoner and brought them before Salvador Vallejo and Chief Solano at a nearby Indian camp. The officials, too, were unaware of the status of the visitors, for they took personal command and marched them to Sonoma and locked them in the garrison barracks.

They arrived about midnight. General Vallejo was awakened and told that his brother and Solano had captured a number of prisoners wearing strange uniforms. Fearing the country was being invaded, he dressed hurriedly, buckled on his best sword, and rushed off to the barracks where he found Captain Jones and several American officers. Vallejo apologized profusely for the mistake and surely Captain Jones, of all people, understood how such things could happen. About two in the morning a large breakfast was set before the Americans and then they were allowed to go to their rooms and sleep until seven when they were awakened to witness a parade of Vallejo's troops and to hear a thirteen-gun salute fired in their honor.

After touring the country with Vallejo as guide, the officers returned to their ship and sailed back to Monterey. From there Jones went south to Los Angeles where he met the new governor, Manuel Micheltorena, and attended a banquet followed by a grand ball. Then he sailed on to Hawaii where he spent a full month, delaying his return to his home port of Callao where he would have to face the consequences of his mistake. But finally he had to leave, and when the *United States* sailed from Honolulu one of its crew members was a young sailor named Herman Melville. Later, Melville would write a book, *White Jacket,* about this voyage and in it Captain Thomas ap Catesby Jones would appear only thinly disguised under the title, "the commodore."

VI

It was December 1842 by the time Jones finished up with the aftermath of his invasion of Monterey and moved on to see the rest of California. At the time, it appeared that he left it little different from what it had always been. Yet from the perspective of more than a century, it is clear that by 1842 a major watershed had been reached in California.

At the end of that year Juan Bautista Alvarado officially stepped down from the post of governor he had held for six years. His successor, Manuel Micheltorena, had remained in Los Angeles insisting that the governorship be turned over to him there. Alvarado, however, had no desire to make the long difficult trip south and instead used a technique he had developed to perfection while he was governor. Whenever he was unable or unwilling to appear, he would appoint his secretary, Manuel Jimeno Casarin, acting governor and send him in his place. Now, one last time, Jimeno Casarin found himself acting governor, and in that capacity he carried the position to Los Angeles where he turned it over to Alvarado's successor. At four o'clock on the afternoon of December 31, 1842, Manuel Micheltorena was sworn in as the new governor of California.

It was the end of an era for Alvarado and the rest of those young Californians who had taken over the government with so much hope six years before. They had their chance to create a strong government that was at least semi-independent of Mexico, but somehow they had failed, and now they had no choice but to turn California over to a Mexican general who was followed by an army made up mostly of exiled convicts. Soon that army would revolt against him, drive him out, and make not Alvarado but Pio Pico governor of California. It was not so much the dawn of a new era as it was a brief, chaotic epilogue to the era that ended here.

Other eras were ending as well. Since before the turn of the century sea-otter hunters, in the wake of Captain Cook, had been coming to the west coast of America. Now, most of the otters were gone, and the business had declined to a point where it was hardly worth sending ships into the Pacific. Almost all the hunting was done by a few men—Isaac Sparks, George Nidever, Allen Light—who were financed by such American merchants as Alpheus Thompson, John Coffin Jones, Jr., and Henry D. Fitch. It was a tight little group which, because of its experience and knowledge, could survive where others had failed.

The cattle-hide trade had also brought many ships onto the California coast, but it too was now far less profitable. In 1840 the ship *Alert,* commanded by William D. Phelps, sailed from Boston bound for California. It was the latest in a long line of ships sent by the firm Bryant and Sturgis, which had pioneered the cattle-hide business twenty years before when California was first thrown open to foreign traders. Like all its predecessors, the *Alert* spent the next two years cruising the California coast taking on hides until its hold was full and it was ready to leave. Then, in December 1842 it sailed for Boston, taking with it Alfred Robinson who had been the firm's agent in California for thirteen years. He was no longer needed, for the company was closing out its interest in the west coast cattle-hide trade. Others would keep the trade going for a time, but the pioneer had abandoned the field. The *Alert* was the last ship Bryant and Sturgis would send to California.

Indicative, too, of the changes that had come to fur trapping in California was the visit in late 1841 and early 1842 of Hudson's Bay Company officials, including Governor-General George Simpson, and the Chief Factor of the Pacific Coast John McLoughlin. They came to visit the company's new store at San Francisco which had been opened the previous summer by William Rae, McLoughlin's son-in-law. Simpson, McLoughlin, and the other officials made the usual tour of the north—San Francisco, San Rafael, where they spent a night with Timothy Murphy, then on to Sonoma for two nights at the home of Mariano Vallejo. When they sailed away they left Rae in charge of the store which, backed by the organization and experience of the Hudson's Bay Company, could squeeze a little profit from the beaver trade.

There was little left for those who preferred the old days of the free trapper. Even the horsethieves seem to have been curtailing their activities, for although there are stories in 1841 and 1842 of "El Cojo" Smith in the interior valleys, they are only vague rumors. There are no more reports of serious thefts after the great raid of 1841. Those coming by land to California, men like John Bidwell, were looking for much more sober, respectable ways to make a living.

By 1842 it is a world in which sea-otter hunting, fur trapping, the cattle-hide business are no longer controlled by freewheeling pioneers trying to make a quick fortune but by businessmen using careful organizational methods to render a small, long-term profit. It is a world no longer visited by contrabandistas hunting illegal furs but by carefully organized, government-sanctioned exploring expeditions, no longer visited by bands of horsethieves but by a column of sober farmers looking to settle down. It is a world, too, all but lost to the Californians who demonstrated their inability to protect it by failing to muster even token resistance when it was conquered by a pompous navy captain conducting his own private farce.

VII

It is not quite yet the United States. But it is no longer the Outer Coast.

EPILOGUE

RICHARD HENRY DANA REVISITED

I

On July 20, 1859, the steamship *Star of the West* cleared New York Harbor bound for Aspinwall on the Isthmus of Panama. Among the passengers was Richard Henry Dana, a middle-aged Boston lawyer who, having nearly collapsed from overwork, was now beginning a voyage around the world. It was almost exactly twenty-three years since the young sailor Richard Henry Dana had left California bound for home and Harvard University. At the time he had been wildly happy, but upon arriving in Boston Harbor and realizing that his career as a sailor was over, he suddenly found himself in "a state of very nearly entire antipathy."

Whatever lingering feeling for life at sea Dana had was soon forgotten, for as a Dana he was expected to graduate from Harvard and enter the legal profession. He was able to relive his experiences in California as he wrote his book, *Two Years Before the Mast,* but soon after it was written he was admitted to the bar and opened a law office on Court Street, just across from the state and federal building in Boston. A year later he married Sara Watson in Hartford, Connecticut and began to raise a family.

There was, a few years later, a brief moment of nostalgic return to his days at sea. In early May 1843 Dana heard that the ship *Alert,* 125 days from San Diego, was entering the harbor. He hurried down to the wharf where, when he saw the ship hauling in, he was overwhelmed with memories. "She looked just as she did when I made her my home, being painted in the same manner, with the same rigging & spars. There was the same new missen rigging upon wh. we worked at Monterey, the same blocks thro' wh. he had hauled rope so many months, the wheel at wh. we had stood hour after hour, & every other familiar sign."

Dana went aboard and visited his old berth in the forecastle, where he fell into conversation with the sailor who had occupied it for the 39 months of the voyage. He gave Dana two sea shells he had picked up on the coast of California. In the cabin Dana talked briefly to the ship's captain, William D. Phelps. Most of the crew were too busy for conversation, but later two members came to Dana's office and spent the afternoon talking about California.

They told him of many people he had known while on the coast—of Captain Henry D. Fitch, who had eloped with Echeandia's intended and who was still alive and rich in San Diego; of Don Juan Bandini who through his actions as administrator of one of California's missions had managed to repair his shaky financial condition; of Mariano Vallejo who was still in office as commandante and still popular with foreigners. They told him, too, of the changes that had come to California, many of them having to do with the relations between Californians and the ever-increasing number of foreigners. One of the sailors could personally describe the trouble caused by two events to which he had been eyewitness. He had been in Monterey when Captain Jones burst into town, captured it for the United States, then beat an embarrassed retreat. He had also been one of the American sailors arrested and deported to Mexico during Governor Alvarado's roundup of foreigners. He and the rest had been badly treated, he told Dana, but they had finally been released through the effort of the British consul who, he admitted, had exerted as much effort on behalf of the Americans as he had for his own countrymen.

The worst change of all was in the cattle-hide trade. What had once been an infrequently visited coast was now full of ships seeking cargoes and consequently trade was very dull. It had taken the *Alert* almost forty months to fill its hold. The *Tasso,* after eighteen months on the coast, was less than half full and now had to face the competition of the Boston ships *California, Barnstable,* and *Admittance,* all of which had arrived about the time the *Alert* left. Not only that, but several other ships owned by Californian and Hawaiian merchants were also trading along the coast. It was a hopelessly overcrowded market and Bryant and Sturgis, owners of the *Alert,* had decided to abandon the California hide trade.

Yet for all that, some things had not changed at all. San Pedro was as bad as ever, and Santa Barbara and Monterey had changed very little. At San Juan Capistrano, one of the sailors said, the stake to which Dana had fastened his rope still stood at the top of the cliff down which he had slid to free the hides. All this brought back memories and by the time Dana and the sailors were finished they had talked away the whole afternoon.

A leisurely afternoon spent remembering the past was a rarity for Dana. He had become an extremely busy man. He had developed a successful law practice and was outspoken in favor of Free Soil at a time when, even in Boston, it was still unpopular to do so. On several occasions he defended fugitive slaves, and during one highly inflammatory case he was attacked on Court Street by a hired thug wielding an iron bar, who stunned him but did no serious damage. He also became involved without much success in politics, did some writing, a considerable amount of lecturing, and in 1855 was among the prominent literary figures who founded Boston's Saturday Club. During these years his family continued to grow until by 1858 he and his wife had six children ranging from Sarah who was sixteen to Angela who was one.

Dana's law practice increased to a point where he was forced to give up most of his other activities. He stopped lecturing, did little writing, rarely took a vacation, and seldom left Boston except on business. In 1859 he did take advantage of a short period between court sessions to make a trip to Cuba. Instead of moving at a leisurely, relaxed pace, however, he raced from place to place trying to see as much as possible in the brief time he had. Then, when he reached home he immediately went back to work while, at the same time, furiously writing a fifty-thousand-word account of his trip—*To Cuba and Back: A Vacation Voyage*—which was in print within two months after his return to Boston.

Not long after this, in the midst of a trial, Dana went into Parker's Restaurant, bolted down some cold corned beef, and had such a severe attack of indigestion that he fainted. Although no permanent damage was done, Dana realized the episode had occurred because "I have over-worked for the last ten years—undertaking to do everything and study everything." His doctor confirmed this, saying that "my system is out of order, both nervous and bilious, & that I need long rest & recreation. Of all plans proposed, none suits me so well as a voyage round the world. This has been the dream of my youth & maturer years, & I am actually happy in being able to realize it." On July 20, 1859, he was aboard the *Star of the West* as it cleared New York Harbor.

II

Before daybreak on August 1 the ship arrived at Aspinwall. By 9 a.m. the passengers were aboard the train crossing the isthmus and three hours later they were in Panama where they boarded the steamer *Golden Gate* for the trip to San Francisco. It was Dana's forty-fourth birthday, a memorable one for, he said, "on my birthday cross a Continent. In morning, afloat on Atlantic, in evening afloat in Pacific."

Two weeks later, on the evening of August 13, the ship made the headlands off San Francisco and entered the Golden Gate by moonlight. Dana was instantly struck by the changes. One of the sailors he had talked to back in 1843 told him that Yerba Buena, a single house when Dana was there, had increased to a village of almost a hundred buildings. But he was not prepared for the huge city that now, ten years after the gold rush, stood in its place. Dana, in a letter home, guessed the population at more than 70,000, overestimating it by almost 20,000, although surely when he arrived it seemed larger than it was. For it was Saturday night in San Francisco, the steamboat landing was jammed with people, and it was not until well after midnight that Dana was able to reach his room at the Oriental Hotel.

Dana, who had written a book on California before most Americans even heard of it, found that he was a famous man in San Francisco. His return to California after all these years created considerable stir, there were several notices in the newspapers, and a local liquor dealer offered him a free supply of the best wines for as long as he stayed. Representatives of the Mercantile Library invited him to lecture and those from the Pioneer Society asked him to deliver an oration at their anniversary celebration. Apparently, Dana's recent collapse from overwork had frightened him enough to slow his pace for he declined all honors, including the free liquor, and maintained as much privacy as possible. Even that was difficult and almost every night he dined with parties of prominent San Franciscans who wanted to meet him.

After a week in the city he took the steamer *Senator* south to Santa Barbara and San Diego, places that during his earlier visit had been, to him at least, more important than San Francisco. He had barely left the bustle of the city and stepped aboard the steamer than he met an old friend from his earlier days on the coast. It was Captain John Wilson, the old Scotchman who had commanded the *Ayacucho* which was lying at anchor, all by itself, when Dana, aboard the *Pilgrim,* first arrived at Santa Barbara in 1835.

Back then Dana, a nineteen-year-old common sailor, had been in awe of Captain Wilson. One night while the two ships were at anchor a southeaster began blowing and it had become necessary to slip the cable attached to the anchor and run out to sea. Dana claimed his own captain did so only after seeing the *Ayacucho* preparing to leave and had suddenly remembered that Wilson was an old hand on the coast and knew all the weather signs. Later when the storm was over, both ships returned to Santa Barbara to pick up their anchors. Again, Wilson demonstrated his skill and later Dana said, "this picking up your cables is a very nice piece of work. It requires some seamanship to do it, and come to at your former moorings without letting go another anchor. Captain Wilson was remarkable among the sailors on the coast, for his skill in doing this."

Now, twenty years later, the young sailor was a middle-aged lawyer and the old captain had retired from the sea and was one of the richest ranchers in California. They were equal now, and undoubtedly Wilson had read or at least heard of the good things Dana had said about him in *Two Years Before the Mast.* The two men spent much of the trip south talking over old times. One story that both of them surely remembered was about the time when Captain Thompson in the *Pilgrim,* trying to come to anchor in San Diego, had run into the *Lagoda,* then had begun to bear down on the *Ayacucho.* It was John Wilson, captain of that ship, who had come aboard the *Pilgrim* and quietly given the necessary orders to bring it safely to anchor.

After a full day's run to the south the *Senator* put in at Santa Barbara, the place where Dana in 1835 had caught his first glimpse of California. It was here, too, a year later that he had attended one of California's major social events, the wedding of Alfred Robinson to Ana Maria, daughter of Jose de la Guerra y Noriega. Dana had not treated Robinson kindly in *Two Years Before the Mast,* and Robinson had replied in kind when he wrote his own book, *Life in California.*

Whatever irritations remained, they were now forgotten as Dana found that Robinson was living in Santa Barbara and went to call on him.

Back in 1842 Robinson had left California and returned to Boston aboard the *Alert.* It was the arrival of that ship in March 1843 that so excited Dana, but if he and Robinson talked either then, or later, there is no mention of it. Robinson remained in the east for some years, but unlike Dana he was unable to settle back into Boston life and in 1849 returned to the west coast as the representative of the Pacific Mail Steamship Company. Now, ten years later, he, his wife, and his eight children were living in the old Noriega house in Santa Barbara. Dana, after spending some time with Robinson, also visited Dona Maria de las Angustias, the sister of Robinson's wife, whose graceful dancing at the wedding Dana had described in his book. He had spoken of her as a handsome woman and now he found that she was still fine-looking. She was also very appreciative of what he had done, for his description of her had made her a celebrity in California.

The next day Dana reboarded the schooner and continued to San Pedro where he saw again "the point—the beach—the hill! this was our hated spot—place of toil & exposure." Now there was so much trade that a landing had been built and the steamboat went clear up to the head of the creek to discharge its passengers. Dana made a quick side trip to Los Angeles where he saw, among other people, Don Juan Bandini, the dancing partner of Dona Angustias at Robinson's wedding. Then he returned to San Pedro and took the steamer on to San Diego where he had spent so much time during the earlier voyage.

As the ship approached the entrance to the bay Dana instantly recognized Point Loma but noticed that now it had a lighthouse. That was only the first of many changes, and as the ship approached the beach where the hide houses once stood Dana saw they were all gone. So was the old ship landing, and the steamer continued on toward the dock at the new San Diego at the head of the bay. Dana, overcome by nostalgia, asked to be put ashore on the beach and spent the next several hours wandering over the area, meditating. "Causes eno' for reflection," he said, "23 years ago, curing hides, cutting wood—4 houses full of men—all gone—most dead." Finally he found the site of an old Kanaka oven, but all that was left were a few bricks.

After that he walked up to town as he had done so many times in the past.

Physically the village of San Diego looked much the same, but Dana soon discovered there was almost no one there that he remembered. The man who had owned the store, Henry D. Fitch, who, Dana heard, had grown rich, was dead now, as was Tom Wrightington who actually ran the store for Fitch. Wrightington, Dana was told, had died when he fell from his horse while drunk and was eaten by coyotes. The only person Dana could find from those earlier years was Jack Stewart, a shipmate on the *Alert* who now, with his wife and family, lived a quiet life in San Diego.

In the absence of anyone to reminisce with, Dana obtained a horse and rode out to the mission where he found the saddest changes of all. Everything had fallen into decay, the buildings were delapidated, the aqueduct was in ruins, and the large, beautiful gardens were now overrun with willows and cactuses. Dana poked around in the ruins for a time, then in one last burst of nostalgia returned to town riding his horse at a full run "as Ben S & I did back in 1835." That evening Dana boarded the steamer for the return trip to San Francisco and later wrote, "Steamed out of S. Diego—last look of Beach, hills, point &c." Three days later he was back in San Francisco at the Oriental Hotel.

Dana, having paid his respects to the past, spent the next two weeks seeing a California that was completely unknown back in the 1830s. He took a river steamer as far as Stockton, then boarded a coach for the trip into the Sierras to see the Big Trees and Yosemite Valley. As he traveled through the foothills he saw endless signs of the mining that had created so much of this new California. Everywhere the country was rooted up and men were digging and washing dirt in gold pans and rockers. Once, the six-horse coach on which he was riding was forced to turn off the highway to go around a ditch dug in the middle of the road by a man looking for gold.

Riding a horse through the mountains near the Mariposa grant he met the ranch's owner, John C. Fremont. Dana, who had supported Fremont's bid for the presidency in 1856, was cordially welcomed and Fremont insisted that he briefly interrupt his trip to accompany him on an inspection of his quartz mills and return to his home for lunch with the Fremont family. Dana ended up staying the night, leaving the next morning for a trip to Yosemite. After touring the valley, he returned to Mariposa, spent another night with Fremont, then returned to San Francisco. By now he had spent his allotted time in California, and although he would have liked to see hydraulic mining at work, the time had come to move on. On the morning of September 10, 1859, he boarded the clipper ship *Mastiff* bound for Hawaii.

III

Five days out and a thousand miles off the coast of California, the *Mastiff* caught fire. For Dana, who on his ocean travels until now had been a passenger, it was an opportunity to be actively involved again in life at sea. It became necessary to abandon the *Mastiff*, and fortunately an English ship, the *Achilles,* was near and could take aboard the passengers and crew. Because there were not enough officers to command all the *Mastiff*'s boats, Dana volunteered to take charge of one. Although his boat leaked and he had to keep one hand busy bailing it out, he made several trips between the two ships helping to remove, safely, all the passengers and crew and much of the baggage. Then he returned to his role as a passenger, this time aboard the *Achilles,* which finally put into Honolulu Harbor on September 27.

Dana spent the next week in Honolulu touring the island and enjoying the near-perfect weather. He had brought many letters of introduction from New Englanders to their friends and relatives in the Islands, and this gave him access to Honolulu's most distinguished residents. As in San Francisco he was soon absorbed into the social life of the city, and it culminated on the afternoon of October 3 when, wearing full formal attire, he went to the palace for a private audience with King Kamehameha IV himself. Dana saw the King, who was in his mid-twenties, as tall, handsome, and very easy to talk to. He spoke perfect English and they conversed for half an hour, during which Kamehameha commented on Dana's book, then went on to tell stories of his own visit to the United States and Europe. The fact that Dana was able to have a private audience with the King created considerable stir, and virtually every leading man in Honolulu tried to claim responsibility for having arranged it.

On October 5, after a week in Honolulu, Dana sailed on the little schooner *Mary* for the big island of Hawaii. The accommodations were poor, the ship was slow, and it spent one whole day becalmed off Maui where Dana watched some whaling ships going into Lahaina to join several others already at anchor there. After five days at sea, the *Mary* reached Kawaihae on the northwest side of Hawaii and Dana went ashore.

Once again, as he had in Honolulu, he called on various people, many of them missionaries, to present his letters of introduction. Although he was frequently invited to lunch, dinner, and tea, Hawaii was still mostly rural and there was little of the formal, organized social life of Honolulu. He was free to spend more time seeing the attractions, the best of which was Kealakakua Bay. Approaching it by land on horseback he first saw it from the top of a hill that overlooked the entire valley and bay. From there he had a "beautiful view. Very rich & green, with stretches of black lava, & Kealakakua, looking more thoroughly Hawaiian than any place I have yet seen. Just as it does in the pictures in Cook's voyages, & there, across the Bay, under the cocoa nut trees, is the place where he fell."

Dana descended the hill into the little village of thatched huts where the people all looked "primitive and half-barbarous." Despite appearances, there was both a church and a school in the village and Dana was later told that a higher proportion of these people could read and write than in many parts of the United States. It was here, too, that Dana met Captain Cummings, a native of New Hampshire who had once been master of a whaler but was now living with his Hawaiian wife in the small village at Kealakakua Bay. He was the only white man for twenty miles around and consequently did almost all of the area's business, serving as shopkeeper, harbor master, customs collector, and anything else that needed doing. All these duties did not greatly interfere with his quiet, relaxed life for there was little trade except for an occasional whaler that put in to obtain potatoes, fresh fruit, and water.

Dana was so delighted by Kealakakua Bay that he stayed an extra day. When he first arrived he had noticed children tumbling in the surf and had seen old, gray-haired men come dripping out of the sea. Now he joined them and found the temperature of the water absolutely delightful. No wonder, he said, Hawaiians were such good swimmers, for if he lived there he would spend most of his time in the water.

Still he was able to tear himself away from the surf long enough to make a historic pilgrimage. He hired a canoe and had the natives paddle him across the bay to the place where Captain Cook had been killed. Once there he walked along the beach, shaded by coconut trees, and relived the past. "Here he fell. There lay his boats, firing on the natives who used stones and darts. Broke off piece of the rock. Just above the rock, is the stump of a tree . . . with inscriptions in commemoration of Cook's death." That had been eighty years in the past and not only Cook was dead but so were George Vancouver, John Ledyard, William Bligh, James Burney—every one who had been there that day. The last survivor, among the officers at least, was Marine Captain Molesworth Phillips and even he had been dead for more than twenty-five years.

As Dana left the island of Hawaii to return to Honolulu aboard a whaling ship, his own past caught up with him. While the ship lay off Kawaihae taking on supplies, a native pilot came aboard and introduced himself to Dana as someone who had known him long ago in California. He had been a boy aboard the *Ayacucho* and although he was sixteen then and forty now, Dana easily recognized him. They spent some hours talking over old times and Dana heard what had happened to all the Kanakas he had come to know so well while working at the hide house in San Diego. His favorite, old Mr. Bingham, was still alive over on the island of Kauai but, sadly, all the rest had either died or disappeared, never to be heard of again.

IV

Originally Dana had intended to sail directly from Hawaii to Canton but when he returned to Honolulu he found that no ship bound for China was expected to call there in the near future. Rather than wait endlessly he decided to return to San Francisco where he would have a much broader selection of clipper ships bound for the Orient. He sailed from Hawaii aboard the bark *Architect,* and on December 11, 1859, was once again in California.

Checking the sailing schedules he found "No vessel up for China. Fear long delay." Still, he added, "Glorious weather here—like our warm October weather, & grapes, pears & apples in market, & flowers growing in open air." There was nothing to do but enjoy the delay, and each day for the next week he hired a horse and rode out to see the sights. One day he visited the presidio, another the mission, still another a camp of Digger Indians on the outskirts of town. Each evening after his return, he would dine with one or another group of San Francisco's well-known residents.

After about a week, Dana decided to extend his rambles and on December 20 took a steamer up the bay to visit the Mare Island Navy Yards. On board this vessel he met John B. Frisbie, a prominent businessman, Frisbie's father-in-law, General Mariano Guadalupe Vallejo, and "above all old Mr. Yount, the famous pioneeer & woodsman, the first settler in Napa Valley." They all insisted that Dana visit Napa and he quickly agreed for he had heard that the Napa Valley was the pride of California. Besides, he said, "old Yount is alone worth a journey there."

Upon arriving at Mare Island, Dana toured the facility, spent the night, and the next morning was up so early that he arrived at Frisbie's home in Vallejo in time for breakfast. Frisbie, a native of New York, had been in California for little more than a decade, but being married to a daughter of General Vallejo, he had taken on enough of the old customs to serve Dana frijoles for breakfast. During the meal Dana had a chance to talk more fully with the general whom he had met back in 1836 when Vallejo had come aboard the *Alert,* anchored in San Francisco Bay. Vallejo said that he, too, remembered the encounter and even repeated some of their conversation to prove it.

At that time, Vallejo, aged twenty-eight, had been commandante of the presidio of San Francisco and was well on his way to becoming the most powerful man in California. Now, at fifty-one, he had no power at all and was just another aging Californian caught in an alien world. His world, the one he had so thoroughly understood, began with the arrival of Junipero Serra and Pedro Fages in 1769. He had been born into it about the time most of the early problems had been solved and a new society had begun to emerge on a distant edge of the Spanish empire. As a boy he had watched some of the first foreigners arrive in Monterey, as a teenager he had seen California break away from Spain and become an isolated part of Mexico, and as a man he, better than any other Californian, had used that isolation and those foreigners to accomplish his own ends. But somewhere things had gone out of control, the foreigners had taken over, his world had been destroyed, and now he was the foreigner. And Dana who once knew him in his glory now saw him in his despair.

Between what Vallejo told him as they sat over breakfast and what he heard from others, Dana was able to put together a brief account of what had happened. He said, "The Vallejos, Guadaloupe & Salvador, owned nearly all Napa & Sonoma, having princely estates, but have little now, Guad. by bad management, & Salvador by that & gambling. Gen. V. got the capital placed here, on condition of putting up publ. b[uildings] at his own exp. Did so, expended $100,000, but after 2 sessions was moved to S. Jose, & the town fell to pieces, the houses . . . moved off &c." Now, however, Dana noticed the town of Vallejo had revived and was growing, but he doubted that the general would gain anything from it, although Frisbie, who owned all the land, certainly would. At least Vallejo, unlike many other old Californians fallen on hard times, had his son-in-law John Frisbie, the prominent Anglo businessman from New York, to take care of him in his old age.

Later that day Dana boarded a coach for Napa and that evening arrived at George Yount's ranch, "a principality," Dana said, "of some 12,000 acres, from mountain to mountain." Unlike Vallejo, and many others who came during the Mexican period, Yount had been able to hang on to all his land, which was somewhat surprising for he had always lacked any real sense for business. He had recently married a middle-aged widow who took care of his affairs, keeping the accounts, paying the bills, and making sure that he was not cheated. That freed Yount for more important things like telling stories, which he did that evening as he sat with Dana in the old log house where he still lived.

What Dana heard that night was the story of Yount's life, which in many ways was just a later-day version of Daniel Boone's story.

Yount was born in North Carolina not too many years after Boone left there bound for Kentucky. His family continually moved west following the trail first blazed by Boone until eventually they too reached Missouri where Yount, during the war of 1812, joined a band of mounted rifles commanded by one of Boone's sons. And once, as his company passed through the village of La Charette, Yount had actually seen old Daniel Boone himself. After the war he had gone west to hunt and trap and now, almost forty years later, he entertained Dana with stories of his fights with bears and panthers and Indians.

He also told Dana how he was the first white man to settle in the Napa Valley when it was still filled with Indians and grizzly bears. He had fought frequent battles with Indians, some of them, he told Dana, right where the house they were in now stood. Once Indians had besieged him for several days before he was able to beat them off. In those early days he had also had many encounters with grizzlies, and he claimed that over the years he had killed hundreds of them. Once, he said, he and a Spaniard had killed eight in one day.

The most gripping story that Yount told that night was of a dream he had once had. One night he dreamed that he was walking in a strange place in the mountains when he came upon a band of people who were snowed in, starving to death, had eaten their pack animals and were beginning to eat their own dead. Yount awoke but when he fell asleep again he had the same dream. Once again he awoke, then fell asleep and had the same dream a third time. Finally he told it to others and although he had never crossed the Sierras by the northern route, when he described the place he had seen, those familiar with the area recognized it. Rescuers were sent and found the Donner party in exactly the condition Yount had described.

Although Yount, disturbed by stories he heard of the Donner party's condition, may well have had such a dream after the fact, the version he liked to tell was clearly impossible. Even Dana, although he carefully transcribed the story as Yount told it, expressed some doubts. He was convinced, however, that Yount sincerely believed it and thought the message had been divinely sent. And, he added, "Yount is a man of unimpeachable integrity, & moderate & reasonable in his views, & does not exaggerate."

The next day, carrying a bottle of George Yount's homemade, nonalcoholic wine, Dana set off to visit the Geysers. He spent a delightful two days traveling through the hills north of Yount's, talking to people who lived in this out-of-the-way place, and finally visiting the Geysers. But in the afternoon of the second day it began to rain and it poured all night and was still raining heavily the next morning. Dana was told the streams were so swollen he might have to spend several days there. He found a man who knew of a ford that was still passable and Dana and another man left, traveling as best they could through the heavy rain, muddy roads, and swollen streams. They were trying to reach Yount's ranch again, but by late afternoon, as they approached a small store two miles from the ranch, they decided to stay there, for it was getting dark and they were not sure they could find their way. Much to their delight when they arrived at the store they found a wagon from Yount's just preparing to return and they followed it, arriving at the ranch house about seven in the evening.

It was Christmas Eve and they were cordially welcomed by Yount and his family. There was no attempt at a formal celebration, however, for Mrs. Yount had just returned from a trip and was very tired. Instead, Yount once again told stories of his early days in the west.

This time he told about an old hunter named Hugh Glass. The story of Glass's miraculous survival was already well known, but instead of reading it Dana was glad to hear it told by an old trapper who had once known Hugh Glass personally. And later he jotted down an outline of the story as told by George Yount in his log cabin on Christmas Eve 1859. He wrote, "Wounded by a grissly, shoulder torn, neck open, windpipe open, one flank gone. Major —, Command. of the party, obliged to leave him, pd. man & boy $4.00 to stay with him & bury him when he died. came in, after 2 days, reported dead and decently buried. Glass ate berries in reach, drank water, killed rattle snake, cut off head & tail, pounded up & ate rest. So, for 2 mos. Crawl a little, walk with cane. At last, got into fort. 'how far to fort?' 'Well, 200 miles, or so.' Man & boy given up to him to punish. 'If God forgive them, I will.' "

Richard Henry Dana, who during his life had risen from the crew's quarters of a sailing ship to the upper reaches of Brahmin Boston society, recognized George Yount for something more than just an entertaining story-teller. In his *Journal* he said, "There is a simple, natural courtesy in Y.s manners, wh. is delightful . . . He is a gentleman, roughened by 40 years' hardy adventure & not a boor half polished."

On Christmas Day 1859 Dana left Yount's and the following day was back in San Francisco where, upon his return, he wrote, "this trip makes me less regret my revisit to California."

Two weeks later, on January 11, 1860, he sailed from San Francisco aboard the bark *Early Bird* bound for Hong Kong. He never returned to California.

Notes

Given the nature of this book I have not felt the need for detailed notes citing the source for each specific piece of information. My main intention was to tell an uninterrupted story of men living on the Outer Coast, and I assume that those interested in such an approach would not welcome the constant intrusion of footnote numbers luring them away from the narrative for a discussion of the books I have read.

I have assumed, however, that there will be readers who, at some point, find themselves interested enough in a subject that they may wish to pursue it further. For them I have appended a brief indication of the sources for each chapter. Since the number of books written about California, Serra, Cook, Boone, and all their historical descendants is almost beyond count, I have made no attempt to list every book on the subject or even all those I have used. Instead, I have simply indicated what I consider the main starting point for each subject, leaving it to the zeal of the readers to find the way from there to the heart of the subject. Hopefully they will find it as fascinating a journey as I have.

Full citations may be found in the bibliography.

MAY 14, 1769

Serra: Bancroft, *Hist. Calif.* Vol. I; Palou, *Hist. Memoirs,* Vol. II; Tibesar; Palou, *Life;* Geiger, *Life and Times* and *Franciscan Missionaries.*
Cook: Beaglehole, *Journal,* Vol. I and *Life;* Banks.
Boone: Bakeless; Elliott; Draper.

THE SPANISH MAIN

Part I: Bancroft, *Hist. Calif.* Vol. I; Tibesar; Geiger, *Life and Times* and *Franciscan Missionaries;* Palou, *Hist. Memoirs,* Vol. II.
Part II: Warren Cook; Geiger, *Franciscan Missionaries;* Thurman; Cutter.
Part III: Bancroft, *Hist. Calif.* Vol. I; Nuttal; Tibesar; Fages; Priestly.

Part IV: Geiger, *Life and Times* and *Franciscan Missionaries;* Tibesar; Palou, *Life.*
Part V: Bancroft, *Hist. Calif.* Vol. I; La Perouse; Ogden, *Calif. Sea Otter.*

CAPTAIN COOK'S AMERICA

Part I: Beaglehole, *Journal* and *Life;* B. Anderson; Godwin; Boswell, *Ominous Years.*
Part II: Beaglehole, *Journal,* Vol. III and *Life.*
Part III: Beaglehole, *Journal,* Vol. III and *Life;* Ledyard; Burney.
Part IV: Beaglehole, *Journal,* Vol. III and *Life;* Godwin.
Part V: Boswell, *Laird of Auchinleck;* D'Arblay [Burney]; Beaglehole, *Journal,* Vol. III and *Life.*
Part VI: Beaglehole, *Journal,* Vol. III; R. Straus; Wheatley; Portlock; Dixon.
Part VII: Greenberg; Ormsby: Colnett; Morse; Howay, "List of Trading Vessels"; Pethick; Warren Cook.
Part VIII: Portlock; Dixon; Howay, "List of Trading Vessels"; Nicol.
Part IX: Portlock; Dixon; Meares; Nicol.
Part X: Morse; Warren Cook; Pethick; Howay, *Dixon-Meares;* Beth Hill.
Part XI: Warren Cook; Manning; Howay, "List of Trading Vessels."
Part XII: Warren Cook; Manning; Bancroft, *Hist. Northwest;* Colnett, *Journal* and *Voyage.*

INTERNATIONAL WATERS

Part I: Bern Anderson; Godwin; Vancouver; Warren Cook; Manning; *Gentleman's Magazine,* May, 1790.
Part II: Vancouver; Warren Cook; Meany; Menzies, . . . *Journal of Vancouver's Voyage;* Bern Anderson.
Part III: Warren Cook; Menzies, . . . *Journal of Vancouver's Voyage;* Vancouver; Bern Anderson.
Part IV: Bern Anderson; Menzies, ". . . Calif. Journal"; Bancroft, *Hist. Calif.* Vol. I; Geiger, *Franciscan Missionaries;* Warren Cook; Vancouver.
Part V: Bancroft, *Hist. Calif.* Vol. I; Nuttal; Warren Cook; Vancouver.
Part VI: Bancroft, *Hist. Calif.* Vol. I and *Hist. Alaska;* Andrews; Howay, "List of Trading Vessels."

THE COAST OF BOSTON

Part I: Sparks; Augur; Ledyard; Watrous; Burney; Boyd; Hallet.
Part II: Howay, *Voyages of the Columbia.*
Part III: Howay, *Voyages of the Columbia* and " . . . Voyage of the Hope"; Corning, "Sullivan Dorr . . . " and "Letters of Sullivan Dorr."
Part IV: Paine; Phillips; Cleveland; S. E. Morison.
Part V: Bancroft, *Hist. Calif.* Vol. I; Wagner, "Monterey . . . " and *First Vessel.*
Part VI: Bancroft, *Hist. Calif.* Vol. I.
Part VII: Wagner, "Monterey . . . "; Bancroft, *Hist. Calif.* Vol. I; Ogden, *Calif. Sea Otter.*
Part VIII: Howay, "The Ship Eliza . . . "
Part IX: Cleveland; Paine; Bancroft, *Hist. Calif.* Vol. I; Ogden, *Calif. Sea Otter.*
Part X: Corning, "Letters of Sullivan Dorr . . . "
Part XI: Cleveland; Roy Nichols.
Part XII: Cleveland; Bancroft, *Hist. Calif.* Vol. II; Ogden, *Calif. Sea Otter.*

JOE O'CAIN AND THE RUSSIAN COAST

Part I: Ogden, *Calif. Sea Otter;* Howay, "List of Trading Vessels"; Khlebnikov, *Baranov;* Bancroft, *Hist. Alaska.*
Part II: Ogden, *Calif. Sea Otter;* Chaffin.
Part III: Ogden, *Calif. Sea Otter* and "Russian Sea Otter . . . "; Chaffin; Bancroft, *Hist. Calif.* Vol. II.
Part IV: Ogden, *Calif. Sea Otter;* Bancroft, *Hist. Calif.* Vol. II.
Part V. Bancroft, *Hist. Alaska;* Tikhnenev; Khlebnikov, *Colonial Russian America.*
Part VI: Campbell; Khlebnikov, *Baranov.*

THE LOTUS EATERS

Part I: Phelps; Bancroft, *Hist. Northwest Coast; Niles Weekly Register,* August 12, 1820.
Part II: Phelps; Ogden, *Calif. Sea Otter;* Bancroft, *Hist. Calif.* Vol. II.
Part III: Bancroft, *Hist. Calif.* and *Calif. Pastoral;* Webb; Sanchez; Geiger, *Franciscan Missionaries;* Robinson; Engelhardt, *Mission San Juan Bautista.*

Part IV: Scott; Webb; Robinson; Bancroft, *Hist. Calif.* and *Calif. Pastoral;* Engelhardt, *Mission San Gabriel;* Northrop; Geiger, *Franciscan Missionaries;* Corney; Bealer.
Parts V through VII: Cleveland; Lynch; Dakin.

DANIEL BOONE COUNTRY

Part I: Bakeless; Elliott; Filson.
Part II: Bakeless; Elliott; Peck, *Memoir* and " . . . Daniel Boone"; Flint, . . . *Daniel Boone; Niles Weekly Register,* June 15, 1816 and May 16, 1818.
Part III: Paxton.
Part IV: Morgan, *Jedediah Smith* and *The West of William Ashley;* Carter, "William Ashley"; Schoolcraft; Flint, *Recollections.*
Part V: Morgan, *Jedediah Smith;* Carter, "Jedediah Smith."
Part VI: Morgan, *Jedediah Smith;* Dale; Geiger, *Franciscan Missionaries.*
Part VII: Morgan, *Jedediah Smith;* Dale.
Part VIII: Morgan, *Jedediah Smith;* Dale.
Part IX: Morgan, *Jedediah Smith* and *The West of William Ashley;* Dale; Geiger, *Franciscan Missionaries.* Bancroft, *Hist. Calif.* Vol. III.

THE NEW CALIFORNIANS

Part I: Bancroft, *Hist. Calif.* Vol. III; Batman; Pattie.
Part II: Bancroft, *Hist. Calif.* Vol. III; McKittrick; Tays; Alvarado; Northrop.
Part III. Bancroft, *Hist. Calif.* Vol. III; McKittrick; Tays; Robinson; Nunis.

THE CATTLE-HIDE COAST

Parts I through VI: Dakin; Robinson; Ogden, "Alfred Robinson . . ."; Dana, *Journal* and *Two Years;* Gale; Shapiro.

THE LAST OF THE TRAPPERS

Part I: Camp, *Yount* and "Yount."
Part II: Morgan, *Jedediah Smith;* Dale.

Part III: Morgan, *Jedediah Smith;* Robinson; Ogden, *Calif. Sea Otter;* Camp, *Yount.*
Part IV: Camp, *Yount.*
Part V: Ogden, *Calif. Sea Otter;* Bancroft, *Hist. Calif.* Vol. IV: Atherton; Davis.
Part VI: Bancroft, *Hist. Calif.* Vol. IV: Ogden, *Calif. Sea Otter.*
Part VII: Camp, *Yount* and "Yount."

THE INVASION OF THE HORSETHIEVES

Part I: McKittrick; Tays; Bancroft, *Hist. Calif.* Vol. IV; Dakin.
Part II: McKittirck; Bancroft, *Hist. Calif.* Vol. IV; Robinson; Nunis.
Part III: Bancroft, *Hist. Calif.* Vol. IV; Morris; Farnham.
Part IV: Bancroft, *Hist. Calif.* Vol. IV; Farnham; Robinson.
Part V: Hafen, "Fort Davy Crockett"; Billington.
Part VI: Rockwell; Sonne; Larson; Humphreys; Voelker.
Part VII: Hafen, *Old Spanish Trail;* Beattie; Voelker.

CIVILIZATION

Part I: Bidwell; Wallace, "Antoine Robidoux."
Part II: Bidwell; Stewart; Hunt; Belden.
Part III: Tyler; Stanton; Strauss; Davis; Bancroft, *Hist. Calif.* Vol. IV.
Part IV: Bidwell; Hunt; Belden; Bancroft, *Hist. Calif.* Vol. IV.
Part V: Charles Anderson; Brooke; High; Bancroft, *Hist. Calif.* Vol. IV.

EPILOGUE

Parts I through IV: Dana, *Journal;* Gale; Shapiro.

Bibliography

Alvarado, Juan B. "History of California," translated by Earl R. Hewitt. *Ms.* Bancroft Library, Berkeley, Calif.

Anderson, Bern. *Surveyor of the Sea.* Seattle: University of Washington Press, 1960.

Anderson, Charles. *Journal of a Cruise to the Pacific Ocean, 1842–1844, in the Frigate United States.* Durham, N.C.: Duke University Press, 1937.

Andrews, Clarence. "Voyage of the East Indiaman *Phoenix,*" *Washington Historical Quarterly,* 13 (Jan. 1932): 37.

Atherton, Faxon Dean. *The California Diary of Faxon Dean Atherton, 1836–1839,* edited by Doyce B. Nunis, Jr. San Francisco: California Historical Society, 1964.

Augur, Helen. *Passage to Glory.* New York: Doubleday and Company, 1946.

Bakeless, John. *Daniel Boone.* New York: William Morrow and Company, 1939.

Bancroft, Hubert Howe. *California Pastoral.* San Francisco: History Company, 1888.

————. *History of Alaska.* San Francisco: A. L. Bancroft, 1886.

————. *History of California.* 7 vols. San Francisco: History Company, 1886–1890.

————. *History of the Northwest Coast.* 2 vols. San Francisco: History Company, 1884.

Banks, Sir Joseph. *The Endeavor Journal of Joseph Banks, 1768–1771,* edited by J. C. Beaglehole. Sydney, Australia: Trustees of the Public Library of New South Wales for Angus and Robertson, 1962.

Batman, Richard. *American Ecclesiastes.* San Diego: Harcourt Brace Jovanovich, 1984.

Beaglehole, J. C. *The Journals of Captain James Cook on His Voyages of Discovery.* 3 vols. Cambridge: Hakluyt Society, 1955–67.

————. *The Life of Captain James Cook.* Stanford: Stanford University Press, 1974.

Bealer, Lewis W. "Bouchard in the Islands of the Pacific," *Pacific Historical Review* 4 (Dec. 1935): 328–42.

Beattie, George and Helen P. *Heritage of the Valley.* Oakland, Calif.: Biobooks, 1951.

Belden, Josiah. *Josiah Belden.* Georgetown, Calif.: Talisman Press, 1962.

Bell, Horace. *Reminiscences of a Ranger.* Santa Barbara, Calif.: Wallace Hebberd, 1927.

Bidwell, John. *Echoes of the Past.* Chicago: Lakeside Press, 1928.

Billington, Ray A. *The Far Western Frontier,* 1830–1860. New York: Harper and Row, 1956.

Boswell, James. *Boswell: The Ominous Years, 1774–1776,* edited by Charles Ryskamp and Frederick A. Pottle. New York: McGraw-Hill, 1963.

_________. *Boswell: Laird of Auchinleck, 1778–1782,* edited by Joseph W. Reed and Frederick A. Pottle. New York: McGraw-Hill, 1977.

Boyd, Julian., ed. *The Papers of Thomas Jefferson.* 19 vols. Princeton: Princeton University Press, 1950–1974.

Brooke, George M. Jr. "The Vest Pocket War of Commodore Jones," *Pacific Historical Review,* 31 (August, 1962): 217–233.

Burney, James. *A Chronological History of the North-Eastern Voyages of Discovery.* London: Payne and Foss, 1819.

Camp, Charles. *George Yount and His Chronicles of the West.* Denver: Old West Publishing Company, 1966.

_________. "George Yount," in *Mountain Men and the Fur Trade,* edited by Leroy Hafen. Glendale, Calif.: Arthur H. Clark Company, Vol. 9, 1972: 411–420.

Campbell, Archibald. *A Voyage Round the World from 1806 to 1812.* Honolulu: University of Hawaii Press, 1967.

Carter, Harvey. "Calvin Jones," in *Mountain Men and the Fur Trade,* edited by Leroy Hafen. Glendale, Calif.: Arthur H. Clark Company, Vol. 6, 1968: 207–211.

_________. "Jedediah Smith," in *Mountain Men and the Fur Trade.* Glendale, Calif.: Arthur H. Clark Company, Vol. 7; 1969: 331–348.

_________. "William Ashley," in *Mountain Men and the Fur Trade.* Glendale, Calif.: Arthur H. Clark Company, Vol. 7, 1969: 23–35.

Chaffin, Yule. *Koniag to King Crab.* n.p., 1967.

Cleveland, Richard. *Voyages and Commercial Enterprise of the Sons of New England.* New York: Leavitt and Allen, 1855.

Colnett, James. *The Journal of Captain James Colnett Aboard the Argonaut,* edited by F. W. Howay. Toronto: Champlain Society, 1940.

_________. *Voyage.* London: n.d., 1798.

Cook, Warren L. *Flood Tide of Empire.* New Haven and London: Yale University Press, 1973.

Corney, Peter. *Early Voyages in the North Pacific. 1815–1818.* Fairfield, Wash.: Ye Galleon Press, 1965.

Corning, Howard, ed. "Letters of Sullivan Dorr," *Proceedings,* Massachusetts Historical Society, 67 (October 1941–May 1944): 178–364.

———. "Sullivan Dorr, an Early China Merchant," *Essex Institute Historical Collections,* 78 (April 1942): 158–174.

Cutter, Donald C. *The California Coast.* Norman: University of Oklahoma Press, 1969.

Dakin, Susanna Bryant. *The Lives of William Hartnell.* Stanford: Stanford University Press, 1949.

Dale, Harrison C. *The Ashley-Smith Explorations and the Discovery of a Central Route to the Pacific, 1822–1829.* Glendale, Calif.: Arthur H. Clark Company, 1941.

Dana, Richard Henry. *The Journal of Richard Henry Dana, Jr.,* edited by Robert F. Lucid. 3 vols. Cambridge, Mass.: Belknap Press of Harvard University Press, 1968.

———. *Two Years Before the Mast,* edited by John Haskell Kemble. 2 vols. Los Angeles: Ward Ritchie Press, 1964.

D'Arblay, Fanny [Burney]. *Diary and Letters of Madame D'Arblay,* edited by Charlotte Barrett. 6 vols. London: Macmillan Company, 1904.

Davis, William Heath. *Seventy-Five Years in California.* San Francisco: John Howell Books, 1967.

Dixon, George. *A Voyage Round the World.* London: George Goulding, 1789.

Draper, Lyman. "Draper Collection," *Ms.* Wisconsin State Historical Society, Madison, Wis. [Microfilm, University of California Library, Berkeley, Calif.]

Elliott, Lawrence. *The Long Hunter, a New Life of Daniel Boone.* New York: Reader's Digest Press, 1976.

Engelhardt, Zephyrin. *Mission San Juan Bautista.* Santa Barbara, Calif.: Mission Santa Barbara, 1932.

———. *San Gabriel.* San Gabriel, Calif.: Mission San Gabriel, 1927.

Fages, Pedro. *A Historical, Political, and Natural Description of California,* translated by Herbert I. Priestley. Berkeley: University of California Press, 1937.

Farnham, Thomas Jefferson. *Travels in California.* Oakland, Calif.: Biobooks, 1947.

Filson, John. *The Discovery, Settlement and Present State of Kentucke.* New York: Corinth Company, 1962.

Flint, Timothy. *The Life and Adventures of Daniel Boone.* Cincinnati: U. P. James, 1958.

———. *Recollections of the Last Ten Years,* edited by George R. Brooks. Carbondale: Southern Illinois Press, 1968.

Gale, Robert L. *Richard Henry Dana, Jr.* New York: Twayne Publishers, 1969.

Geiger, Maynard. *Franciscan Missionaries in Hispanic California. 1769–1848.* San Marino, Calif.: Huntington Library, 1969.
_________. *The Life and Times of Fray Junipero Serra.* 2 vols. Washington, D.C.: Academy of American Franciscan History, 1959.
Gentleman's Magazine, 1790.
Godwin, George. *Vancouver, a Life.* New York: D. Appleton and Company, 1931.
Greenberg, Michael. *British Trade and the Opening of China, 1800–1842.* New York and London: Monthly Review Press, 1951.
Hafen, Leroy. "Fort Davy Crockett, Its Fur Men and Visitors," *Colorado Magazine,* 29 (Jan. 1952): 17–33.
_________ and Ann W. Hafen. *The Old Spanish Trail.* Glendale, Calif.: Arthur H. Clark Company, 1954.
Hallet, Robin, ed. *Records of the African Association, 1788–1821.* London: Thomas Nelson and Sons, 1964.
High, James. "Jones at Monterey, 1842," *Journal of the West,* 5 (April 1966): 173–186.
Hill, Beth. *The Remarkable World of Frances Barkley: 1769–1845.* Sidney, British Columbia: Gray's Publishing, 1978.
Howay, F. W. *The Dixon-Meares Controversy.* Toronto: Ryerson Press, 1929.
_________. "A List of Trading Vessels in the Maritime Fur Trade," *Transactions of the Royal Society of Canada,* Third Series, Vol. 24–28 (1930–1934).
_________. "The Ship *Eliza* at Hawaii in 1799." Hawaiian Historical Society, *Forty-Second Annual Report* (1933): 103–113.
_________, ed. *Voyages of the Columbia.* n.p.: Massachusetts Historical Society, 1941.
_________. "The Voyage of the Hope, 1790–1792," *Washington Historical Quarterly,* 9 (January 1920): 3–28.
Humphreys, Alfred G. "Thomas L. (Peg-Leg) Smith," in *Mountain Men and the Fur Trade,* edited by Leroy Hafen. Glendale, Calif.: Arthur H. Clark Company, Vol. 4, 1966: 311–330.
Hunt, Rockwell. *John Bidwell.* Caldwell, Ida.: Caxton Printers, 1942.
Khlebnikov, K. T. *Baranov,* edited by Richard A. Pierce. Kingston, Ontario: Limestone Press, 1973.
_________. *Colonial Russian America, Kyrill T. Khlebnikov's Reports,* translated by Basil Dmytryshyn and E. A. P. Crownhart-Vaughan. Portland: Oregon Historical Society, 1976.
La Perouse, J. F. G. de. *A Voyage Round the World in the Years 1785, 1786, 1787, and 1788.* 2 vols. London: John Stockdale, 1798.
Larson, Gustive O. "Walkara, Ute Chief," in *Mountain Men and the Fur Trade,* edited by Leroy Hafen. Glendale, Calif.: Arthur H. Clark Company, Vol. 2, 1965: 339–350.

Lecompte, Janet. "Jean-Baptiste Chalifoux," in *Mountain Men and the Fur Trade,* edited by Leroy Hafen. Glendale, Calif.: Arthur H. Clark Company, Vol. 7, 1969: 57–74.

Ledyard, John. *John Ledyard's Journal of Captain Cook's Last Voyage,* edited by James K. Munford. Corvallis: Oregon State University Press, 1963.

Lynch, John. *The Spanish American Revolutions, 1808–1826.* London: Weidenfeld and Nicolson, 1973.

McKittrick, Myrtle. *Vallejo, Son of California.* Portland, Oregon: Binfords and Mort, 1944.

Manning, William R. "The Nootka Sound Controversy." American Historical Association, *Annual Report,* 1904. Washington, D.C.: American Historical Society (1905): 279–478.

Meany, Edmond S. "A New Vancouver Journal," *Washington Historical Quarterly* 5 (April 1914): 129–137; (July 1914): 215–224; (October 1914): 300–308; and 6 (January 1915): 50–68.

Meares, John. *Voyages.* London: Logographic Press, 1790.

Menzies, Archibald. "Menzies' California Journal," *California Historical Society Quarterly,* 2 (January 1924): 265–340.

———. *Menzies' Journal of Vancouver's Voyage, April to October, 1792.* Victoria, British Columbia: Archives of British Columbia, 1923.

Morgan, Dale. L. *Jedediah Smith and the Opening of the West.* New York: Bobbs Merrill, 1953.

———. *The West of William Ashley.* Denver: Old West Publishing Company, 1964.

Morison, Samuel Eliot. *The Maritime History of Massachusetts.* Boston and New York: Houghton Mifflin, 1921.

Morris, Albert F. "The Journal of a 'Crazy Man,' " *California Historical Society Quarterly* 15 (June 1936): 103–138 and (Sept. 1936), 224–241.

Morse, Hosea Ballou. *The Chronicles of the East India Company.* 5 vols. Cambridge, Mass.: Harvard University Press, 1929.

Nichols, Roy F. "William Shaler, New England Apostle of Rational Liberty," *New England Quarterly,* 9 (March 1936): 71–96.

Nicol, John. *The Life and Time of John Nicol, Mariner.* New York and Toronto: Farrar and Rinehart, 1936.

Niles Weekly Register, 1816–1820.

Northrop, Marie E. *Spanish-Mexican Families of Early California.* New Orleans: Polyanthon, 1976.

Nunis, Doyce B. Jr. "Isaac Graham," in *Mountain Men and the Fur Trade,* edited by Leroy Hafen. Glendale, Calif.: Arthur H. Clark Company, Vol. 3, 1966: 141–162.

Nuttall, Donald A. "The Goberantes of Spanish Upper California: A

Profile," *California Historical Society Quarterly,* 51 (Fall, 1972): 253–280.

Ogden, Adele. "Alfred Robinson," *California Historical Society Quarterly,* 23 (Sept. 1944): 193–218.

_________. *The California Sea-Otter Trade, 1784–1848.* Berkeley: University of California Press, 1941.

_________. "Russian Sea-Otter and Seal Hunting on the California Coast, 1803–1841," *California Historical Society Quarterly,* 12 (Sept. 1933): 217–239.

Ormsby, Margaret A. *British Columbia: A History.* New York: Macmillan Company, 1959.

Paine, Ralph D. *The Ships and Sailors of Old Salem.* New York: Outing Publishing Company, 1909.

Palou, Francisco. *Historical Memoirs of New California.* 4 vols. Berkeley: University of California Press, 1926.

_________. *Life and Apostolic Labor of the Venerable Father Junipero Serra.* Pasadena, Calif.: George Wharton James, 1913.

Pattie, James O. *The Personal Narrative of James O. Pattie.* Cincinnati: John H. Wood, 1831.

Paxton, John A. *St. Louis Directory.* St. Louis, Mo., 1821.

Peck, John Mason. *Memoir,* edited by Rufus Babcok. Philadelphia: American Baptist Publication Society, 1864.

_________. "Life of Daniel Boone," in Jared Sparks, ed., *The Library of American Biography,* Vol. 23. New Orleans: Charles Little and John Brown, 1848.

Pethick, Derek. *First Approaches to the Northwest Coast.* Vancouver, British Columbia: J. J. Douglas, Ltd., 1976.

Phelps, William D. "Solid Men of Boston in the Northwest," *Ms.* Bancroft Library, University of California, Berkeley, Calif.

Phillips, James D. *Salem and the Indies.* Boston: Houghton Mifflin, 1947.

Portlock, Nathaniel. *A Voyage Round the World.* London: John Stockdale, 1789.

Priestly, Herbert I., ed. "Diary of Pedro Fages," Academy of Pacific Coast History, *Publications,* Vol. 3 (May 1913): 135–233.

Robinson, Alfred. *Life in California.* Oakland, Calif.: Biobooks, 1947.

Rockwell, Wilson. *The Utes.* Denver: Sage Books, 1956.

Sanchez, Nellie Van de Griff. *Spanish Arcadia.* Los Angeles: Powell Publishing Company, 1929.

Schoolcraft, Henry R. *Journal of a Tour into the Interior of Missouri and Arkansas.* London: Sir Richard Phillips and Company, 1921.

Scott, Paul T. "Why Joseph Chaptman Adopted California and Why California Adopted Him," *Historical Society of Southern California Quarterly,* 38 (Sept. 1956): 239–246.

Shapiro, Samuel. *Richard Henry Dana, Jr., 1814–1882.* East Lansing: Michigan State University Press, 1961.
Sonne, Conway B. *The World of Walkara.* San Antonio, Tex.: Naylor Company, 1962.
Sparks, Jared. *The Life of John Ledyard.* Cambridge: Hilliard and Brown, 1828.
Stanton, William. *The Great United States Exploring Expedition of 1838–1842.* Berkeley: University of California Press, 1975.
Stewart, George. *The California Trail.* New York: McGraw-Hill, 1962.
Straus, Ralph. *Lloyd's: A Historical Sketch.* London: Hutchinson and Company, 1937.
Strauss, W. Patrick. "Preparing the Wilkes Expedition: A Study in Disorganization," *Pacific Historical Review,* 28 (August 1959): 221–232.
Tays, George. "Mariano Guadalupe Vallejo and Sonoma—A Biography and a History," *California Historical Society Quarterly,* 16 (June 1937): 99–121; (Sept. 1937): 216–255; (Dec. 1937): 348–372; 17 (March 1938): 50–73; (June 1938): 141–167; (Sept. 1938): 219–242.
Thurman, Michael. *The Naval Department of San Blas.* Glendale, Calif.: Arthur H. Clark Company, 1967.
Tibesar, Antonine. *Writings of Junipero Serra.* 4 vols. Washington, D.C.: Academy of American Franciscan History, 1955.
Tikhmenev, R. A. *A History of the Russian-American Company,* translated and edited by Richard A. Pierce and Alton S. Donnelly. Seattle and London: University of Washington Press, 1978.
Tyler, David B. *The Wilkes Expedition.* Philadelphia: American Philosophical Society, 1978.
Vancouver, George. *A Voyage of Discovery.* 6 vols. London: Stockdale, 1801.
Voelker, Frederic E. "William Sherley (Old Bill) Williams," in *Mountain Men and the Fur Trade,* edited by Leroy Hafen. Glendale, Calif.: Arthur H. Clark Company, Vol. 8, 1971: 365–394.
Wagner, Henry R. *The First American Vessel in California.* Los Angeles: Glen Dawson, 1954.
__________. "Monterey in 1796," *California Historical Society Quarterly,* Vol. I (Oct. 1922): 173–177.
Wallace, William S. "Antoine Robidoux," in *Mountain Men and the Fur Trade,* edited by Leroy Hafen. Glendale, Calif.: Arthur H. Clark Company, Vol 4, 1966: 261–273.
Watrous, Stephen D. *John Ledyard's Journey Through Russia and Siberia.* Madison, Wis.: University of Wisconsin Press, 1966.
Webb, Edith. *Indian Life at the Old Missions.* Los Angeles: Warren A. Lewis, 1952.
Wheatley, Henry B. *London Past and Present.* 3 vols. London: John Murray, 1891.

Index